The Roman Gaze

ARETHUSA BOOKS

Series Editor: Martha A. Malamud

THE ROMAN GAZE

Vision, Power, and the Body

Edited by
David Fredrick

THE JOHNS HOPKINS UNIVERSITY PRESS
Baltimore and London

2002 The Johns Hopkins University Press
All rights reserved. Published 2002
Printed in the United States of America on acid free paper
9 8 7 6 5 4 3 2 1

The Johns Hopkins University Press
2715 North Charles Street
Baltimore, Maryland 21218-4363
www.press.jhu.edu

Library of Congress Cataloging-in-Publication Data

The Roman Gaze : vision, power, and the body / edited by David Fredrick.
    p. cm. — (Arethusa books)
Includes bibliographical references and index.
  ISBN 0-8018-6961-7
  1. Gaze—Psychological aspects. 2. Rome—Civilization I. Fredrick, David,
1959– II. Series.
BF637.C45 R64 2002
937—dc21

2001008644

A catalog record for this book is available from the British Library.

The last printed page of this book is an extension of the copyright page.

For Anita, Erin, and Guthrie

Contents

Contributors

CARLIN BARTON is a professor of history at the University of Massachusetts. She is the author of *Fire in the Bones: The Sentiments of Honor in Ancient Rome* (Berkeley, 2001), *The Sorrows of the Ancient Romans* (Princeton, 1993), and several articles on the gaze, honor, and Roman masculinity. She is currently studying the emotions associated with Roman religious life.

CINDY BENTON received her Ph.D. from the University of Southern California in 1999. She is an assistant professor in classics and women's studies at Cornell College. She is co-editing a book with Trevor Fear, *Center and Periphery in the Roman World*, as a special issue of *Arethusa*. She has published articles and given papers on violence and the gaze in ancient tragedy and on electronic resources for teaching classics.

JOHN R. CLARKE is Annie Laurie Howard Regents Professor of Fine Arts at the University of Texas at Austin. He is the author of *Art in the Lives of Ordinary Romans: Visual Representation and Non-Elite Viewers in Italy, 100 B.C.–A.D. 315* (Berkeley, 2002); *Looking at Lovemaking: Constructions of Sexuality in Roman Art, 100 B.C.–A.D. 250* (Berkeley, 1998), and *The Houses of Roman Italy, 100 B.C.–A.D. 250* (Berkeley, 1991). He has written numerous articles on Roman architecture, wall painting, and mosaics.

ANTHONY CORBEILL is an associate professor of classics at the University of Kansas. He is the author of *Controlling Laughter: Political Humor in the Late Roman Republic* (Princeton, 1996) and articles on Roman poetry, history, and thumbs. He is completing a book on gesture in ancient Rome.

KATHERINE OWEN ELDRED received her Ph.D. from Princeton University in 1997 and spent two years as a Mellon Post-Doctoral Fellow at Northwestern University studying violence and visual pleasure in Lucan and Seneca. She is finishing her J.D. at the University of Chicago Law School, where she holds a

Bradley Foundation Student Fellowship from the John M. Olin Program in Law and Economics. She will spend the 2002–3 term clerking for the Honorable John T. Noonan on the Ninth Circuit Court of Appeals in San Francisco.

DAVID FREDRICK is an associate professor of classics at the University of Arkansas. He has published articles on Roman wall painting, poetry, and dining, and he is working on a book, *Luxurious Bodies: Sensuous Ambiguity in Roman Dining*. He is also the author of "Architecture and Surveillance in Flavian Rome" (forthcoming in *Flavian Rome: Culture, Image, Text*, ed. A. J. Boyle and W. Dominik).

PAMELA GORDON is an associate professor and chair of the classics department at the University of Kansas. She is the author of *Epicurus in Lycia: The Second-Century World of Diogenes of Oenoanda* (Ann Arbor, 1996) and essays on the Epicurean tradition, Ovid, and Sappho.

ZAHRA NEWBY is a lecturer in classics and ancient history at the University of Warwick. Her interests cover the art of the Roman empire and the representation of artworks in Second Sophistic literature. She is the author of "Art and Identity in Asia Minor" (forthcoming in *Provincial Art and Roman Imperialism*, ed. S. Scott and J. Webster) and is working on a book about the representation of Greek athletics in the Roman empire.

ALISON R. SHARROCK is a reader in classics at the University of Manchester. She is the author of *Seduction and Repetition in Ovid's Ars Amatoria 2* (Oxford, 1994), co-editor of *Intratextuality: Greek and Roman Textual Relations* (Oxford, 2000), and co-author of *Fifty Key Classical Authors* (London, 2002), as well as articles on Ovid, Propertius, Roman Comedy, and the representation of women in Latin poetry.

Acknowledgments

I am obliged to Martha Malamud for suggesting the project, to the contributors for their patience and good humor, and to Maura Burnett and Julie McCarthy for seeing *The Roman Gaze* through the press. I am grateful to Stanley Lombardo, Amy Richlin, and Martha Malamud for their inspiration and encouragement over many years, and to my students at Arkansas for their open minds and practical criticism. I would also like to thank the Fulbright College of the University of Arkansas for a generous grant to support preparation of this volume.

The Roman Gaze

Introduction

Invisible Rome

David Fredrick

This entry from Varro's *de Lingua Latina* purports to explain something essential about how the Romans looked at their world and what they thought about the act of looking itself.

> Video a visu, <id a vi>: qui<n>que enim sensuum maximus in oculis: nam cum sensus nullus quod abest mille passus sentire possit, oculorum sensus vis usque pervenit ad stellas. Hinc:
>> Visenda vigilant, vigilium invident.
> Et *Acci*:
>> Cum illud o<c>*u*li<s> violav*i*t <is>, qui in*v*idit
>>> invidendum.
> A quo etiam violavit virginem pro vit<i>avit dicebant; aeque eadem modestia potius cum muliere fuisse quam concubuisse dicebant.[1]

> *I see* from *sight*, that is, from *vis*, "force," since it is the strongest of the five senses. While no other sense is able to perceive something a thousand feet away, the force of the eyes' perception reaches even to the stars. Hence:
>> They watch all night for what must be observed, and hate the vigil.
> Or the verse of Accius:
>> When he [Actaeon] violated that (thing) with his eyes,
>>> who looked upon what must not be seen.
> From which they even say "he violated the virgin" instead of "he ruined her," and, with the same modesty, that someone "was with his wife" rather than that "he lay down beside her."

The derivation of *video* ("I see") from *vis* ("force" or "violence"), though mistaken, may express social truths. In what context, with what methods and assumptions, should we read this passage? How should we approach Roman visual experience as an object of historical inquiry?

From one theoretical perspective, Varro's "strongest of the five senses" illustrates well the connection in Western thought between the phallus, representation, and the eye, which Martin Jay, trumping Derrida by two syllables, dubs phallogocularcentrism.[2] Vision reaches beyond the feebler senses *ad stellas* and so is uniquely suited for the rational investigation of the universe. As a further demonstration of its *vis*, Varro associates visual command of the natural world with the power of the male gaze to violate the female body—not surprisingly, since *vis* sometimes means "sexual violence," "rape." Hence the verse from the tragedian Accius on Actaeon's scopophilic gaze at Diana in her bath. Visual and physical violation are then overlapped in a phrase Varro presents as a euphemism, though *violavit virginem* may not seem like one to us.[3]

Like *cum . . . fuisse* ("to be with") in place of *concubuisse* ("to lie down beside"), *violavit* both suggests and conceals the physicality of sex, the problem of female desire, and, perhaps, the intensity of male pleasure. These are verbal fig leaves that objectify the woman while insulating the male from the body's pollution.[4] It is not surprising, then, that Varro's account is blandly heterosexual, leaving unspoken the penetrability of males by the gaze or the phallus of other males. The "natural" hierarchy of the senses simply corresponds to a "natural" division of the world into male subjects and female objects of *vis*: as male is to female, so intellect is to the body, and so sight is to the other senses.[5] Nonetheless, male vulnerability is present in Actaeon, who is caught looking and then dismembered. Indeed the very fragility of the scopophilic gaze, whether in fantasy or social reality, may explain the attempt to set vision apart from the body as the most powerful, intellectual, and masculine sense.[6]

From a different critical perspective, the use of concepts like scopophilia or phallogocularcentrism will produce a drastic misreading of Varro. We might assert instead that Varro belongs to a visual (sexual, gendered, classed) world utterly unlike the Euro-American present. Since contemporary theory exists to describe contemporary modes of power and representation, it can only result in distortion when used transhistorically, obscuring rather than illuminating the specific attributes of Roman culture. Varro's association of vision with force may thus owe more to ancient theories of extramission than to modern theories of the gaze; for him, the "force of the eyes' perception" may have meant specifically the fine stream of particles traveling from the eye to its object.[7] By the same token, from a Roman standpoint, the most dangerous portion of Diana's anatomy might well have been her eyes. Lurking beneath the surface of *invidit invidendum* is *invidia*, "envy" or "the evil eye," a component of both Actaeon's fascinated, if initially inadvertent, gaze and Diana's enraged reaction. She could transmogrify Actaeon with a splash of water, but even the ordinary human eye, male or female, was felt to have the power to wither with its glare.[8] Finally, since the Romans show little anxiety about images of sex in their dining rooms, reception halls, and bedrooms, Varro's euphemisms may have more to do with protecting the reputations of women associated with elite families than with a fetishistic anxiety about female sexuality per se.[9]

These contrary approaches to Varro's *video* represent opposite sides of the essentialist versus constructionist controversy. On one side are those who argue that basic human institutions (including gender roles and sexual taboos) have their origin in natural selection, produce undeniable physical effects, and persist across time and space (the essentialists). On the other side are those who argue, on the model of language, that even the most elemental human behaviors are products of culture and generally unrelated to selective advantage or environmental pressures (the constructionists). For constructionists, the gender roles and sexual taboos of a given culture are only valid locally and do not have any necessary connection with those of other cultures. Moreover, even the most intense physical consequences of human institutions are always mediated through language so that their meaning does not lie primarily in the pain (or pleasure) that they cause. In its radical form, the constructionist position has questioned the existence in other places and times (for instance, classical antiquity) of notions we take for granted in describing our own social behavior—notions like "gender" and "sexuality."

This controversy has been so intense in classics that Marilyn Skinner has dubbed it "the sexuality wars."[10] It would be more accurate, however, to call it "the Greek sexuality wars," because Rome has been persistently edited out by both sides. According to Foucauldian work, welcomed by constructionist historians in other fields, the ancient world can only lend support to the argument for difference.[11] Rome is like Greece, and together they are examples of traditional Mediterranean cultures before sexuality. Meanwhile, critiques of the origins of "Western" visuality by philosophers from Henri Bergson to Luce Irigaray have concentrated on Greek philosophy while arguing strongly in favor of continuity between Greek ways of seeing and our own; for them, Rome is like Greece, birthplace not only of democracy but also "the metaphysics of presence" and phallogocularcentrism (see Jay 1993.493–542).

Recent publications on Roman sexuality have raised significant questions for both sides.[12] Granted that Roman philosophy is dependent on Greek models, does that mean that the Roman house, urban space, economy, social hierarchy, or political structure were also Greek? If not, how can we claim that their bodies, ways of seeing, or sexualities were the same? How should the Foucauldian penetration model be changed to accommodate Rome? If there are fundamental similarities between Roman ways and our ways of seeing, should this model be retained at all? This volume is intended to explore these questions. The contributions make use of a wide range of theories, fully aware that these theories contain contradictory assumptions about what "the gaze" is and has been historically. Indeed one goal of the collection is to call attention to such contradictions by making Rome, rather than Greece, the test case for the question of difference. The contributors do not agree on the degree of Rome's difference from ourselves or on which theory of the gaze or body is most appropriate for Rome. They do, however, collectively demonstrate that the essentialist versus constructionist debate, by omitting Rome, omits a significant episode in cultural formation.

Western Vision and Rome

The critique of vision as an instrument and symbol of power has been a major theme in twentieth-century philosophy, part of a larger cross-examination of objective knowledge and the unified self.[13] In the 1970s, feminists yoked this philosophical critique with psychoanalysis and began to focus on contemporary media. Gender became a central issue and *the gaze* a frequently used term. Critics like Laura Mulvey, Kaja Silverman, Teresa de Lauretis, and Mary Ann Doane demonstrated that the portrayal of gender in film and television was culturally determined, rather than natural, and politically interested, rather than idle or benign. More recently, this insight has expanded to include sexuality, exploring how geographical and architectural space, together with the print and image industries, help "construct" the normative, heterosexual subject.[14]

As the quotation marks indicate, feminist gaze theory has not unanimously embraced "construction."[15] Pointing to the impossibility of detaching representation from actual behavior, many critics stress the relation between depiction and lived experience. For them, things like poverty, anorexia, or assault cannot be adequately described as constructions or discourses. As Arthur Frank notes at the end of a survey of body theory, "Only bodies suffer" (1991.95). An emphasis on the material and corporeal reality of oppression has thus been linked, through the development of a specifically feminist perspective, with the broader interest of twentieth-century philosophy in Western vision. "Rape," as Amy Richlin puts it, "is rape," a fundamental expression of how power has been represented and experienced across time.[16] Concepts like pornography, the phallus, and the gaze, developed to describe the contemporary sex and gender system, are consequently used as critical models for the past.[17]

This use of transhistorical concepts runs the risk of distorting one culture through the critical lenses of another, and, like other forms of essentialism, it has been strongly contested.[18] Moreover, in making the case for the *longue durée* of Western visuality/sexuality, it has tended to focus on either Greece or the early modern period instead of Rome.[19] The work of Amy Richlin, one of the strongest advocates for the study of Roman sexuality in its own right, illustrates why this is so. She points out that Foucauldian historians of the Greek body have lifted the insights of female scholars on Rome and repackaged them as their own, preserving the originary, privileged status of Greece—and men—within classics. At the same time, she emphasizes the applicability of feminist theories of pornography to Greece and Rome. This compels her to emphasize *both* the shared sameness of Greece, Rome, and the present *and* the differences between Greece and Rome so clearly left out by Foucault. If the most important thing about these three cultures is their common patriarchal structure, how significant are the local differences between Rome and Greece? Had Foucault concluded, like Eva Keuls (for instance), that Greek sexuality was similar to ours in its violent enforcement of phallic superiority and the oppression of women, the absence of Rome, by Richlin's own argument, would amount to the omission of a closely related culture that did much the same thing.[20]

Outside classics, Martin Jay's *Downcast Eyes* (1993) is an excellent illustration of Rome's invisibility in critiques of the Western gaze. Jay provides an overview of ocularcentrism in the West, beginning with ancient Greece. He is careful to recognize differences in the valorization of sight between the Renaissance, the Enlightenment, and the early twentieth century, noting, for instance, a strong tendency in Baroque art to subvert dominant visual structures (1993.46–51). He rejects a simple periodization of visual history into ocularcentric antiquity, antiocular Middle Ages, and ocularcentric Renaissance, finding instead a struggle between a dominant Hellenic ocularcentrism and a subversive Hebraic emphasis on the spoken word. In antiquity, however, he skips from Aristotle to the medieval period, omitting Rome completely. This is consistent with most of the thinkers and artists he discusses—Jacques Derrida, Marcel Duchamp, Georges Bataille, Jacques Lacan, Christian Metz, Luce Irigaray, and Julia Kristeva—who view themselves as reacting against a dominant Western visual tradition, "Cartesian perspectivalism," whose origin was Greek and whose characteristics were definitively shaped in the sixteenth to eighteenth centuries. As Shelby Brown's 1997 survey shows, this pattern is reproduced by the work of feminist art historians using the concept of the gaze: a pronounced concentration on the modern and early modern periods, perhaps a mention of the Greeks, and nothing about Rome.

Yet Rome hardly presents a serene confirmation of the nobility of sight atop a stable social hierarchy. From the Gracchi through Domitian, elite Romans found the clarity of their (proto?) "Cartesian" gaze challenged on all sides: in urban spaces, domestic decoration, theater, oratory, and poetry. As Anthony Corbeill explores in this volume, some of these Romans, notably Julius Caesar, also "played" the Other, the sexually penetrable *cinaedus*. *Cinaedi* challenged the relation of intellect to body, of vision to the other senses, and we would expect them to be excluded from power.[21] Yet, by the late republic, cinaedism (or its pose) could be politically useful. Gender instability is common in the literature and art of this period; does this correspond to an antiocular emphasis on the tactile or haptic qualities of the materials used in representation—the stone, paint, or voice—rather than its content?[22] There are geographies of lower- and upper-class immorality in Rome, spaces where elite standards of discipline and bodily purity are put in doubt (Corbeill 1997, Edwards 1993 and 1997). What becomes of the hierarchy of the senses in these zones, in the amphitheaters, baths, and brothels on the one hand, and the villas, gardens, and dinner parties on the other?

Varro, like Roman philosophers in general, makes an excellent witness for one type of upper-class thinking about vision, but a limited one for Roman visual and corporeal experience as a whole. Nonetheless, largely due to the history of philosophy, Rome has been cast as the uninteresting sequel to Greece. Jay quite accurately represents the tendency of the critique of Western vision in twentieth-century philosophy and art to stress sameness and continuity between now and antiquity, and, even more so, between Greece and Rome. This has left unquestioned the ocularcentrism of the Romans—those other Athenians?

Body History and Rome

The body is both the scandal of social theory and its *aporia*.
—*A. W. Frank, "For a Sociology of the Body"*

Body history emerged from the intersection of feminism and gay activism with structuralist anthropology and linguistics.[23] Structuralism presented the human environment (buildings, landscapes, cosmetics, and food) as languages, artificially constructed codes with synchronic rules but inevitably subject to diachronic change.[24] Thus the most quotidian aspects of culture, precisely those aspects most associated with women (or slaves, children, the poor, and the foreign), became accessible to history.[25] Not interested in marginal people, traditional history appears disinterested in marginal senses like touch, taste, and smell: embarrassed, like Varro, by the body. Shifting the subject of history toward the body promises a welcome change in the hierarchy of sources away from elite texts toward nonelite texts and material evidence (see Kampen 1994).

This promise has been compromised, however, by confusion over just what, besides structure and context, body history is supposed to find. Beyond the ideological grammar of everyday things are physical experiences of pain, hunger, movement, labor, and pleasure. Beyond that, emotions.[26] The word *practice* does not really face up to this distinction, since it still privileges synchronic code over lived experience.[27] For instance, while we may understand the discursive practices embodied in Roman houses, funerary monuments, or marital law, this is not the same as reconstructing the corporeal or emotional content of Roman family life (Dixon 1997, Bradley 1991). As Keith Hopkins observes: "Many Latin epitaphs are touching. But we have to be careful. Grief was expressed on tombstones from a limited stock of conventions. But then feelings always are; the very act of transforming feelings into words automatically channels them along conventional lines. Language is a set of conventions."[28]

Epitaphs are part of a larger set of funerary rituals and behaviors that conjoined feelings with physical movements.[29] The very physicality of these rituals and behaviors, as unavoidable as the tombstone itself, is a thorn in the discursive side of the New History. Obviously, this thorn can be plucked by erasing the distinction between feelings and language, by insisting instead on the conventional, linguistic nature of all perception, movement, and emotion.

The art historian Michael Ann Holly notes (1996.176–77): "It is a commonplace of poststructuralist thought that it is language that sees, not the naked eye" (cf. Scott 1993.399–400). For constructionists, it is language that also touches, hears, and tastes, not the naked senses. It is then a short step to the position that it is language (convention, culture) that feels, despite the apparent profundity and subjectivity of the emotions in question: grief, joy, or erotic desire.[30] Here the noblest sense will have its revenge: if everything from nutritional labels to hatred is a sign in a code, at what point does the body (or emotion) itself cease to be only a code? Joan Scott asserts that it never does: "Experience is a linguistic event (it doesn't happen outside established meanings)."[31] Language then suffers, not bodies. To make this as true for the heat of a branding iron as for frescoes or novels, one must show that a seared forehead acquires its meaning not through pain, but by virtue of not being a purple stripe, an unbent back, or senatorial sandals. This inevitably depends on a shift in the sensory register from touch to sight. This discourse of the body requires reading and subsumes all the senses under a visual metaphor; throughout Scott's essay, "experience" consistently means "visual experience."

Not surprisingly, this has generated enormous controversy among contemporary theorists, since the experience of living bodies is always already there to challenge the textualization of life.[32] As Arthur Frank (1991.65) observes of Jean Baudrillard, "In this stoned Saussurian world there are no referents." On the other hand, essentializing the experience of "being" gay, heterosexual, a woman, a man, or a person of color in terms other than discourse risks perpetuating structures of oppression by treating them as natural or inevitable (Butler 1993). When Frank himself declares, "The only praxis males can conceive of involves 'spilling blood,'" the dangers of gender essentialism are obvious: the past and future praxis of (Greek, Roman, Renaissance, and Euro-American) males is predetermined and relentlessly grim. Yet it would be mistaken to interpret Frank's own praxis in writing his chapter as only more spilled blood.[33]

Why is it so important to understand the distribution of pleasures and pains in the past as something more than discourse or text? After all, there are no living bodies whose condition could be improved. Moreover, it would seem that these past lives are only accessible through textual traces; the corporeal "facts" of their reality are simply beyond us, as is their "real" emotional world. The problem is precisely that past cultures are being used to demonstrate either the essentialist or the discursive foundations of identity, and the assumption that all we have from the past is text is hardly unbiased in this context.[34] It slides easily into the conclusion that all that happened in the past was text, like everything that happens now. Classical Athens is tailor-made for this argument, not just because of its historical distance and therefore necessary difference, but because it was not a large city and never commanded an extensive empire. Its archaeological context is poorly preserved, especially in the domestic sphere.[35] At the same time, Athens' cultural prestige allows it to represent "Greco-Roman antiquity," erasing Rome, a city easily twenty-five times larger (and three times the size of Elizabethan London) and the head of a transcontinental empire, a city whose body history is attested by a far larger material record (cf. Millar 1998.214).

Foucault provides an obvious example of the erasure of Rome by Greece when speaking of "classical antiquity." In his argument, sexuality in the ancient world was generally isomorphic with social role and, consequently, not the source of a private, interior nature or essence hidden from a public, exterior culture. Rather, it was part of an "aesthetics of existence," no more privileged than other forms of self-fashioning like diet or exercise. *Discipline and Punish* (1979) laid the foundation for his view of modern sexuality as the specific creation of social technologies that, beginning roughly in the seventeenth century, increasingly coerced and regulated everyone (schoolchildren, soldiers, factory workers, and the condemned) as individualized cogs of much larger wheels. Similarly pervasive hierarchies of discipline and surveillance simply did not exist earlier, and neither did "sexuality." And so, like the distinction between king and commoner that prevails in his analysis of late medieval punishment, Greek culture is split into a simple, rather than a complex and individualizing, structure: the politically empowered and the not, the penetrators and the penetrated. Citizen men have a morally problematized dietetics, while others do not, and no comprehensive diffusion of sexuality is to be found pervading every nook of Attica, or classical Greece, or the Hellenistic east, or Rome.[36]

Had Foucault situated Rome at the center of his history, the task would have been—and still is—far more difficult. Rome in the first century B.C.E. presents a finely nuanced social hierarchy from elite senators and knights down to the freeborn; "beneath" them, freed slaves of low political status but considerable economic opportunity (many enjoyed economic superiority over freeborn citizens); "beneath" them, cadres of domestic and rural slaves carefully graded in status and function (many slaves enjoyed better living conditions and more responsibilities than free citizens). Rome's enormous army was disciplined and professionalized far beyond the citizen hoplites of Athens, and there were vast apparatuses of urban entertainment. Hence Thomas Gunderson's ability (1996.115) to compare the arena, with its finely graded map of social hierarchy, to the panopticon, despite Foucault's argument that the ancient world had no such structures. While there unquestionably was an elite for whom social and sexual passivity was stigmatized, it is not possible to place many Romans (for example, the average soldier or a relatively successful freedman or woman) unambiguously in the penetrator or penetrated class. Rome did not have a "democratic body" like that of classical Athens.[37] This suggests that many Romans (not just an elite few) sought to constitute themselves as political, ethical, and sexual subjects of a sort. While they may not have essentialized their personal identities around heterosexuality or homosexuality, many did experience corporeal pleasures and pains, including sex, as subjects.[38] It seems very unlikely that the sexual experience of many Romans was unproblematically isomorphic with social position, simply because social position was so often complex, a delicate situational balance between activity and passivity, superiority and inferiority. By the same token, in Rome, the assumption that all is discourse must confront in the archaeological record inequalities in material circumstances that no doubt corresponded to differences in physical comfort or discomfort.[39] The scale is finely graded, and its extremes of pain and pleasure question the usefulness of "discourse" and its synonyms.

Western Vision + Body History + Rome

To sum up, the critique of Western vision represented most prominently by feminist theories of film and pornography is essentialist because it generally recognizes a continuous visual tradition (including antiquity) that it connects with concrete effects on the body. Most body history, on the other hand, is constructionist because it does not accept such a tradition for either visual culture or the body, preferring to see instead a series of discontinuous periods. For any given period, the effects of representation on the body are regarded as textual in nature, deconstructable, negotiable, and not monolithic.

Despite their incompatibilities, the two sides have been wed in early modern and classical studies. It is a troubled union. Andrew Stewart's *Art, Desire, and the Body in Ancient Greece* (1997) is an important and revealing attempt to use the essentialist critique of Western vision together with constructionist body history. His work is important because neither side has concentrated its efforts on Greek material evidence the way

Stewart has, and revealing, due to his attempt to use notions like Western visuality and panoptic surveillance without contradiction.

When outlining his position, Stewart asserts (1997.13, my emphasis): "Fortunately, Martin Jay's exhaustive analysis of the ocularcentric debate makes a full synopsis of it unnecessary, as does *the remoteness of many of its concerns from antiquity* (for example, its complex relations with psychoanalysis; its impact upon film criticism; and the feminist critique that has accompanied and to some extent transformed it)."

Many feminist critics view ocularcentrism as Western, important precisely because it is part of a continuous tradition that is not remote from antiquity.[40] Stewart also claims (1997.14) that Foucault's analysis of the panopticon "ground[s] his ongoing critique of the gaze's role in the construction of the Western will to power" (cf. Meskell 1997.148–51). Stewart refers here to Foucault's use of Bentham's Panopticon (a circular prison whose cells are all open to the gaze of the jailer in the central tower) as a model for the dependence of modern power on pervasive surveillance. Foucault might have agreed with Stewart's use of the word *construction* but not the word *Western*, since his point was to demonstrate the historically specific nature of modern power, vision, and sexuality as distinct from those of the ancient world. With film theory rendered remote from antiquity and the panopticon rendered Western (a reversal of their real positions in terms of history and periodization), the two can be conjoined. Foucault's panoptic gaze becomes "the public eye" through which citizen men police the activities of each other and their inferiors; film theory's complex account of the gaze becomes a "private" eroticized glance.[41]

Attempts to combine the critique of Western vision and body history are familiar in contemporary theory and early modern history; Stewart simply transgresses their *terminus post quem*. For instance, for Victor Burgin, the union between panopticism and ocularcentrism depends precisely on periodization. On the one hand, perspective, "the panoptical-instrumental space of colonialist capitalist modernity," characterizes a visual regime that would emerge only with the Renaissance and be shattered by modernism in the early twentieth century, though it would hardly disappear. Citing Henri Lefebvre, he argues that the concept of the city as body could emerge only within this regime: "Only in the sixteenth century, after the rise of the medieval town (founded on commerce, and no longer agrarian in character), and after the establishment of 'urban systems' . . . did the town emerge as a unified entity—and as a subject."[42] On the other hand, the confusion between inside and outside and perspective space in modernism evokes for Burgin (1996.115, emphasis his): "The imperfect partial development of an image of space latent in all of us: the pre-Oedipal, maternal space: the space, perhaps, that Benjamin and Lacis momentarily refound in Naples. In this space it is not simply that the boundaries are 'porous,' but that the subject itself is *soluble*."

The dialectic between the city as a coherent body/subject in Cartesian perspective (the panoptic gaze) and the "city in pieces" and as soluble subject of (post)modernism (the pre-Oedipal gaze) is thus firmly periodized: the latter could define itself against the former only after the emergence of the city as body metaphor in the early modern period. While pre-Oedipal, maternal space is latent in us all, in Burgin's argument, it cannot have any relation with capitalist, perspectival space until the latter comes into existence around 1400 c.e. Before then, one finds only the precapitalist space of Naples, an image that condenses antiquity and the presexuality Mediterranean together as the land that time forgot.[43]

In a similar vein, Lynn Hunt's collection on pornography (1993b) uses Foucault to back the claim that pornography did not exist before the printing press and an urban reading public made its commodification possible. Several of the essays, however, analyze pornography using psychoanalysis and gaze theory. This necessarily implies that gaze theory can only apply as far back as early modernism, when the senses were eroticized as they had never been before.[44] What then was the abundant sensual apparatus of Rome—amphitheaters, pantomime, saffron showers, villas, wall painting, erotic verse, exotic food, and silk clothes—designed to do? Likewise, M. Bella Mirabella argues (1995.416) for "a new definition of the gaze by showing that Foucault's and Lacan's ideas of the gaze work dialectically to offer insight into the structure of women and dance in the Renaissance and to show how the gaze of desire [cf. Stewart's private glance] leads to the gaze of control" [cf. Stewart's public eye]. Why wouldn't the anxiety created by the gaze of desire call forth the panoptic gaze of control long before early modernism?

The devil is in the date. The arbitrariness of limiting film theory's gaze to the fifteenth century and after because of Foucault's periodization exposes the difficult contradictions any combination of these theories must face. An excellent example here is Abigail Solomon-Gadeau's study of the representation of the male nude in revolutionary France, for which she uses psychoanalytic and feminist theory while also making a comparison with "classical precedents." These precedents are Greek, based entirely on Halperin (1990) and Winkler (1990). Rome is absent, though it would seem to offer abundant parallels to the antithesis Solomon-Gadeau discovers in French painting between the heroic and the eroticized male nude, an antithesis also generated in Rome in the context of political and social revolution. Equally troubling, she does not explore the direct contradiction that her comparison of revolutionary French masculinity and Athenian masculinity presents to the Foucauldian thesis that these two cultures were radically different, so much so that one had a sexuality while the other did not (Solomon-Gadeau 1997.177–225, esp. 212–13).

Body history has accepted that ancient sexuality was "Mediterranean" not because there are no classicists to talk to, but because of the easy handle on antiquity this improbable thesis provides.[45] It becomes possible to use feminist film theory back to early modernism but no further, as if this theory had always embraced constructionist periodizations and metaphors; classical Greece, meanwhile, is acknowledged as the birthplace of Western visuality and yet incongruously maintained to be before sexuality. Rome is the great embarrassment: an immense city before cities, an empire before empires, a network of towns before towns, systematized urban and pictorial space before perspective, a nontraditional economy before capitalism . . . pornography before pornography? sexuality before sexuality? A society of both spectacle and surveillance, much of its art and literature cannot be simply described as ocularcentric. *Monstrum* that it is for both theoretical positions, Rome has become invisible.

Theories of the Gaze

With the differences between the critique of Western vision and body history firmly in mind, it is time to outline "the gaze" in *The Roman Gaze*. The work of Laura Mulvey, Michel Foucault, Michael Baxandall, and Pierre Bourdieu is already familiar to many. Susanne Kappeler's *The Pornography of Representation* (1986) may be less well known, but it is significant because of its insistence on the connection between representation and actual behavior, and because it provides the theoretical model for Richlin's groundbreaking collection, *Pornography and Representation in Greece and Rome* (1992). These theories are far from consistent with one another, and it is important that the differences be stressed if the gaze is not to become a vague catchall.

Laura Mulvey's "Visual Pleasure and Narrative Cinema" remains one of the most influential pieces of contemporary theory. Crucial to its argument is the division of classic cinema into two basic, and contradictory, modes of pleasure. In the first, fetishistic scopophilia, the woman is split into a set of perfect fragments that circle around genital difference but never fully reveal it. Castration is disavowed, and the gaze fixed on a beautiful collection of parts: face, hair, buttocks, legs, and breasts. As Mulvey notes, "One part of a fragmented body destroys the Renaissance space, the illusion of depth demanded by the narrative; it gives flatness, the quality of a cutout or icon rather than verisimilitude to the screen." The second mode, sadistic voyeurism, assumes the woman's castration and directs the plot toward her punishment or forgiveness. Thus it makes the most of the diegesis, of cinema's ability to unfold narrative action in the illusion of three-dimensional space: "Sadism demands a story, depends on making something happen, forcing a change in another person, a battle of will and strength, victory/defeat, all occurring in linear time with a beginning and an end. Fetishistic scopophilia, on the other hand, can exist outside linear time as the erotic instinct is focused on the look alone" (Mulvey 1989.22).

In Mulvey's view, Hollywood cinema gives pleasure to the male viewer by suppressing, rather than exposing, the contradictions between these two looks. Moreover, even the scopophilic look is still active, since it "arises from pleasure in using another person as an object of sexual stimulation through sight," though it need not depend on a controlling narrative.[46] Nevertheless, the ability of the spectator to identify with the look of powerful characters (usually male) within the diegesis can be the basis for a further, more comprehensive fetishism. For Christian Metz, this identification is imbricated with the camera's point of view and refuses to acknowledge that cinema's unparalleled illusion of a substitute world remains, in fact, only an illusion. Thus the viewer, by identifying with the look of the male lead and the gaze of the camera, temporarily acquires an "absolute mastery over the visual domain" (Metz 1982; see Penley 1989.62–63).

Close reading reveals that Mulvey's treatment of the scopophilic look is contradictory. Initially, scopophilia "implies a separation of the erotic identity of the subject from the object on screen," while, at the conclusion of the essay, "the fact of fetishization, concealing as it does castration fear, freezes the look, fixates the spectator, and prevents him from achieving any distance from the image in front of him" (Mulvey 1989.15, 26). This contradiction is the source of one of the major criticisms directed at Mulvey, that she misunderstands and underemphasizes passive pleasure in cinematic viewing. For Gaylyn Studlar, scopophilia is fundamentally masochistic, based on the viewer's desire for pre-Oedipal fusion with the image on the screen, while Carol Clover suggests that horror films persistently urge the viewer to identify with the position of the victim: "I suspect that horror is not as concerned as 'dominant' cinema with disavowing male lack; on the contrary . . . it seems almost to indulge it, to the point of reveling in it."[47] Clover consequently puts forth the notions of the assaultive gaze and the reactive gaze—the explicit masochism of the latter distinguishes it from Mulvey's scopophilic look. It is "the horrified gaze of the victim, or more complexly, one's gaze at surrogates for one's own past victimized self" (Clover 1992.175). Similarly, Kaja Silverman points out that the director Rainer Werner Fassbinder, by emphasizing the disjuncture between the camera's gaze and that of any character within the diegesis, infuses the look with lack. Instead of celebrating the viewer's voyeurism by identifying it with the powerful look of a male lead, Fassbinder exposes it precisely by making his male characters the object rather than the subject of his camera's gaze: "The insistent specularization of the male subject in Fassbinder's cinema functions not only to desubstantialize him but to prevent any possibility of mistaking his penis for the phallus, a dislocation that is at the center of Fassinder's 'aesthetic of pessimism'" (Silverman 1994.283).

Along with the criticism that Mulvey's model fails to recognize the importance of masochistic or pessimistic pleasure, it is, as Constance Penley puts it, a "bachelor machine" (1989.57–92). While it may accurately describe the psychoanalytic condition of the male character or his male viewers, it does little to address the female spectator. This is, in fact, a difficult task. When the male viewer, in a given film or genre, is encouraged to recognize his own lack, this amounts to a transgression of his alignment with the phallus outside the cinema. When the female viewer makes the same identification with powerlessness, it looks like a confirmation of her real distance from the phallus and her closeness to the image as an object to be possessed. If, on the other hand, she identifies with the visual and narrative power of the lead, this can only be a transvestite pleasure, a temporary drag in the clothes of male privilege.[48] Given the sterility of this either-or situation, it is not surprising that some film theorists have emphasized instead the capacity for mobile identification: "It is only the formal positions themselves that are fixed (there are 'masculine' and 'feminine' positions of desire); the subject can and does adopt these positions in relation to a variety of complex scenarios, and in accordance with the mobile patterns of his or her own desire."[49]

At this point, film theory has arrived at a significant crux. Mulvey's point was precisely to show that the representation of women in film had a tangible connection with the coercion of women's bodies and minds in lived experience. If the choices in identification for the female spectator were passive or transvestite, that is because they accurately (if pessimistically) reflected social reality. In the alternative proposed by Penley, desire remains mobile despite the constraints placed upon female —and male—spectators outside and within the theater. Yet there is little reason to think that desire in the cinema is any less constrained and patterned by culture than desire in a restaurant, clothing store, or office. It is difficult to see the play of desire in cinema as free, because cinema remains on a map where political, economic, and erotic choices are not free.

What does this complex body of theory have to offer historians of Rome? Formally, several critics have explored Mulvey's distinction between sadism and fetishism in Roman poetry and visual art. Politically, identification with the passive, feminized position has been associated with social instability in the late republic and early empire and a corresponding interest in the vulnerability of the elite male body.[50] In this volume, Cindy Benton and Katherine Owen Eldred examine the oscillation of the male elite audience between positions using the texts of Seneca's *Troades* and Lucan's *Bellum Civile*. For Benton, the fate of the Trojan women, and the reactions of the Greek heroes to that fate, reflect the interests and anxieties of Seneca's audience. As senators found themselves displaced from the summit of the Roman visual economy and forced, under Nero, both to act onstage and theatricalize their own responses to Nero's performances, they were fascinated with both the assaultive and the reactive gaze. The emotional and physical torment of Hecuba, Andromache, and Polyxena invites masochistic identification, while their gender allows the recuperation of distance and a slide back toward sadistic viewing.

Similarly, Eldred suggests that the suicide of Vulteius in Book 4 of the *Bellum Civile*, staged for the imagined gaze of Caesar, offers a necessarily unstable model of visual pleasure. On the one hand, the reader is invited to share Caesar's sadistic gaze at the mangled bodies of Vulteius and his men, a gaze repeated at the protracted wounding of Scaeva, the slaughter at Pharsalia, and the unveiling of Pompey's embalmed head. On the other, the nature of Caesar's power and gaze is such as to make the world, including Lucan's elite audience, its object. Hence this audience is also compelled to identify masochistically with Caesar's victims. Caesar and the Trojan women thus define complementary poles of one scopic regime in the early empire—that of elite men—in which instability has a political and contextual specificity rather than being simply the expression of the primal fluidity of desire.

From Mulvey and feminist gaze theory we turn to Foucault and the penetration model of ancient sexuality. Pamela Gordon explores the stance of one of this model's most passionate resisting readers, the Roman poet Lucretius. Epicureanism was an easy target in antiquity because its endorsement of true pleasure invited the charge of overindulgence and sexual passivity. Gordon notes that this charge is still made today, though it reflects neither the actual doctrine nor, in all likelihood, the behavior of most Epicureans. It does, however, reflect their rejection of the mastery of others as the goal of elite life. Due to the isomorphism of sexuality and social status stressed by the penetration model, this necessarily amounts to the rejection not just of sexual excess—traditional Roman morality condemns this too—but of the very notion of sex as penetration and possession of the object. Lucretius situates his attack on sexuality at the end of a detailed analysis of vision that suggests that conceiving one's beloved as an object to be possessed will necessarily produce excess because this expectation can never be met. In Epicurean theory, desire is stimulated by the transmission of the image of the beloved to the eye of the beholder as a film of tiny particles, but, unlike these simulacra, the object can never, by the act of sex, be incorporated into one's own body. For Lucretius, the violent cycle of frustration and desire that results is part of a contemporary obsession with display and consumption as a measure of political worth.

While Gordon retains the basics of the penetration model, her analysis shows that it is not well equipped to deal with the phenomenon of "conspicuous consumption" in Roman society. As competition drives the elite into the arms of *luxuria*, it is increasingly difficult to see them as the masters of their own appetites. Conspicuous pleasure penetrates the penetrators. Unlike the penetration model, Lucretius forthrightly attributes pleasure in sex to women, just as he directly condemns the notion that one possesses or masters the desired body by penetrating it sexually.[51] But does his Epicurean disdain for penetrative sex—and political prestige—produce a less objectifying view of women or boys? If not, is his gaze fundamentally different from that of his culture or ours?

According to Foucault, panopticism marks our society apart as one of surveillance, as opposed to the previous ages of spectacle, and panopticism is not to be found before the seventeenth century.[52] Modern power subjects the minutiae of individual lives to an authoritative gaze, while premodern power had exhibited a rebellious few on whose bodies sovereign power was marked in blood. Institutional space was transformed: "In order to be exercised, this power . . . had to be like a faceless gaze that transformed the whole social body into a field of perception: thousands of eyes posted everywhere, mobile attentions ever on the alert, a long, hierarchized network . . ." (Foucault 1979.214). Yet how was Rome's complex social hierarchy enforced visually at the macro level of the forum or the micro level of ordinary baths and houses?

In chapter four, Zahra Newby reexamines the Spada reliefs in the light of the connection between oratory and domestic decoration suggested by Bettina Bergmann and through the habits of viewing presented in the Second Sophistic texts of Lucian and Philostratus. Drawing on Bergmann's argument (1994) that mythological paintings from Pompeii are combined in ways that suggest oratorical figures (contrast, anaphora, and chiasmus), Newby finds that, by the Second Sophistic, this has matured into two distinct rhetorical approaches to viewing: a programmatic gaze that emphasizes lateral connections between pictures and an absorbed gaze that dwells upon the naturalistic quality of individual paintings, frequently of erotic subjects. The Spada reliefs illustrate both, and if, as is likely, they were displayed in an elite villa, they would proclaim their owner's mastery of Greek mythology and rhetorical theory and his high expectations of his guests. At the same time, the fantasy of direct fusion with the image expressed by the absorbed gaze betrays the fact that classical Greek antiquity, by the second century c.e., was a vanished world. While the opposition between the programmatic and the absorbed gaze suggests parallels with the sadistic (or assaultive) and masochistic (or reactive) gazes of film theory, Newby is concerned primarily with developing her viewing assumptions from the pictures and primary texts themselves.

This is even more true for John Clarke, who, in chapter five, investigates the sequence of sexual vignettes from the *apodyterium* of the Suburban baths at Pompeii. These explicit depictions of oral, anal, and group sex might invite the application of contemporary theories of pornography or the gaze, but Clarke emphasizes the need for us to see them, as much as possible, through Roman eyes. Since the Suburban baths were probably used (at different times) by men and women, the eyes in this case belong to both genders. He notes that most of the vignettes express themes of sexual excess or role-reversal (e.g., scene IV, a man performing cunnilingus, or scene VI, a man anally penetrated while penetrating a woman from the rear), and fly in the face of the sexual norms established in literary texts addressed by elite men to their peers. For Clarke, these scenes are intended to make both male and female viewers laugh, thereby dispelling the evil eye, the envy that one exposed oneself to by stripping naked for the luxurious and sensuous pursuit of bathing. Hence these vignettes are not straightforward pornography that degrades for the benefit of a male elite gaze.

The attempt to uncover the social habits and expectations of viewing behind the decorations of Roman villas and baths suggests Michael Baxandall's notion of a "period eye." As Baxandall notes, the period eye that interests him is also a "class eye," specific to those parts of society that patronize painting (1988.38–39):

> We have been moving towards a notion of a Quattrocento cognitive style. By this one would mean the equipment that the fifteenth-century painter's public brought to complex visual stimulations like pictures. One is talking not about all fifteenth-century people, but about those whose response to works of art is important to the artist—the patronizing classes, one might say. In effect this means a rather small proportion of the population: mercantile and professional men, acting as members of confraternities or as individuals, princes and their courtiers, the senior members of religious houses.

Newby's analysis of the Spada reliefs is aimed at the perceptual equipment of a similar "patronizing" class in Roman society: owners of villas with a substantial education in Greek literature, rhetorical theory, and art. Clarke, however, applies a method like Baxandall's to a different kind of content at a different social level. Rather than elite literature or Hellenistic masterpieces, the vignettes of the Suburban baths, Clarke suggests, recall obscene sexual mimes, a favorite form of low-class entertainment. Yet the Suburban baths themselves seem to be "middle," not lower class; they offer amenities not found in the older and more cramped public baths of Pompeii, while still not equaling the level of luxury and convenience provided by bathing facilities in the best individual houses, where depictions of lovemaking are far more refined.

For Baxandall, Newby, and Clarke, pictorial decoration helps to sort space socially and hierarchically. Not only does the viewer gaze at the decoration, but the decoration gazes back, looking for a "class eye" appropriate to itself. While the period eye of the Roman elite may not include the knack for perspective calculations informed by the mercantile algebra of the Renaissance, it nonetheless includes evaluations of skill, cost of materials, thematic appropriateness, and rhetorical complexity in an international environment in which many of the materials and artists are imported.[53] At the same time, as Clarke's analysis of the Suburban baths shows, the elite are hardly the only patrons of art. In baths, houses, bars, and graves, there are many levels of expense and taste. All of these, from a modest freedman's grave to the Suburban baths to the Villa of the Mysteries, include an element of spectacle and self-display. Arguably, they also include an element of "surveillance" in that they are part of a larger system that keeps freedmen out of the curia, knights out of taverns, and slaves out of the bath water.

In chapter six, Anthony Corbeill examines a highly charged arena for the public exhibition and control of elite behavior, the forum. Using Pierre Bourdieu's concept of *habitus*, Corbeill proposes that popular politicians, *populares*, were, in fact, distinguished from their optimate opponents by different ways of walking and gesturing. Cicero repeatedly calls attention to the gait of his adversaries—not as an idle stereotype but because his audience paid close attention to it (as they did to Cicero's own walk) as a reflection of general political orientation, if not attitudes about specific issues or candidates. The optimate *habitus* emphasized restraint in stride, gesture, facial expression, and vocal pitch. The popular *habitus* inverted all of these expectations, producing an orator whose walk was too quick, whose gestures were exaggerated and theatrical, whose voice was pitched too high, and whose facial expressions were too passionate. These differences reflect the orientation of one *habitus* toward the consulate and the authority of the senate, of the other toward the tribunate and the *comitia tributa*. In Cicero's eyes, the latter posture was effeminate. Caesar is the classic example of a *popularis* whose unorthodox (but effective) speaking style was consistent with accusations that he was a *cinaedus* and an adulterer. Rather than dwelling on whether these charges are strictly true or not, Corbeill concludes that they reflect real differences in how orators presented their bodies to the public and in how these differences were understood.

Corbeill uses the concept of *habitus* to emphasize that these ways of walking and talking could not be put on and removed at will but became ingrained and were regarded by the Romans themselves as the natural consequence of the speaker's inner disposition. As Pierre Bourdieu puts it: "Bodily hexis is political mythology realized, *em-bodied*, turned into a permanent disposition, a durable way of standing, speaking, walking, and thereby of feeling and thinking" (1990.69–70, emphasis in original). Corbeill views late republican Rome as primarily a traditional society, and so relies on Bourdieu's *The Logic of Practice* (1990). In this work, Bourdieu uses the Kabyle, a traditional, precapitalist society in North Africa, as his subjects, and discovers essentially two *habitus*, one of men and one of women.[54] There is little movement between them, and social mobility is not an issue.

It would also be possible to approach the late republic from the other direction, using, for example, the complex patterns of space and decoration from Pompeii to support the use of Bourdieu's *Distinction* (1984) as a theoretical model. *Distinction* addresses contemporary French society and discovers an intricate system of *habitus*—bodily dispositions and related tastes in food, clothing, and art—with at least three classes (bourgeois, petit-bourgeois, and working) and numerous class-fractions engaged in a mutual, self-defining struggle. While *habitus* retains an intimate connection with the body, it does change, and social mobility is definitely an issue, as highbrow taste must constantly redefine itself against encroachments from below.[55] With Roman evidence, one might compare the crude sexual depictions found in the slave's quarters in the House of the Vettii with the frank, but clever, humor of the vignettes from the Suburban baths and the atmospheric refinement of boudoir scenes in elite dining rooms and bedrooms. If such distinctions can be shown to be important in Rome, they would suggest that Romans differ from the Kabyle—and presexuality Mediterranean culture—in important respects. To the extent that a complex system of *habitus* implies surveillance, the Romans would also be less a society of spectacle than Foucault would have us believe.

In the seventh chapter, Carlin Barton examines the social behavior of the eye itself, that is, what the Romans thought about the act of looking at other Romans. Drawing upon Max Scheler's notions (1957.67–154) of the restrained gaze that "ensouls" others and the shameless gaze that "desouls" them, Barton collects a wide variety of evidence to show that Romans expected before each other *verecundia oculorum*, "the modesty of eyes." This was especially true of situations like bathing, where retaining honor for one's own naked body demanded that one restrain one's eyes. In this light, the apotropaic laughter evoked by the vignettes in the Suburban baths may help turn aside the "desouling" gaze its patrons might be tempted to fix upon each other. Roman public life demanded a willingness to be on display, to be seen, and therefore to be vulnerable. Before this public gaze, one must retain a sense of shame; moreover, one must also become a witness to oneself, allowing the look one directs at oneself to inhibit and control one's behavior. As a result, "some of the most terrible dramas of Roman life had to do with uninhibited inspection"—precisely the kind of invective gaze Cicero trains upon the walk, gestures, voice, and sexuality of his opponents or, even worse, that an angry emperor trains upon his victims, especially members of his own family and the elite. In the breakdown of reciprocal compunction governing the gaze between social equals, one's own internal gaze could also become desouling: a devouring and relentless surveillance of the self.

In chapter eight, I attempt to refine the either-or logic of the penetration model by constructing a "penetrability map" of Roman space. Beginning with the seating pattern of the amphitheater, I argue that Roman space was characterized by a sliding, rather than binary, scale; the effects of hunger, labor, beatings, and disease were distributed along the same social pyramid that calculated status (and gender) in terms of the best view. Thus the social map of the amphitheater enforces for some the closeness of the body, while suggesting for others its transcendence. For the condemned, the body is made omnipresent through pain, to the exclusion of discursive subjectivity. The gazes of those in the seats, meanwhile, run the gamut from the "aesthetic"—a detached contemplation that allows Martial to ponder his epigrams, Seneca his essays—to a "naive" gaze that is physically absorbed in the spectacle. The Forum of Augustus also maps penetrability: from Augustus, to the elite orators and the *summi viri*, to the caryatids and the conquered barbarians, to the residents of the Subura, screened out by the firewall. The Roman house is also laid out as a social pyramid experienced visually and spatially. The most privileged space for contact with the *dominus* is the dining room, itself a pyramid whose apex is the *locus consularis* in the top left corner. However, these dining rooms are strongly marked zones of crisis and confusion on the map, as the elite body is invaded by an array of pleasures—food, wine, clothing, perfume, poetry, and paintings—that threaten to penetrate it through all of its senses.

The final chapter, by Alison Sharrock, returns to the question of mobile identification and the nature of the Roman gaze. However complex the *habitus*, and whatever the position of Roman society between traditional and modern, spectacle and surveillance, Mediterranean and NATO, does its treatment of gender allow us to bracket it apart from Greece, the early modern period, or now?[56]

As noted above, the chapters of Benton and Eldred reflect the focus of most film theory on the male viewer and the fact that Seneca and Lucan were elite Roman males writing primarily for their peers. Situating limitations like these within a much wider critique of Western representation, the critic Susanne Kappeler questions the ability of psychoanalysis to provide a politically significant account of the gaze. She suggests, instead, that pornography faithfully reproduces the treatment of gender in most "high" art forms and assumes two basic scenarios. In scenario number 1, the male subject performs the action (seducing, raping, and maiming) on a female object, who suffers in response. Scenario number 2 differs only in that the female object experiences pleasure, and so is accorded an illusory subjectivity in response to the male subject's action. But whatever pleasure the object is imagined to experience, and whatever the fluidity of identification by either male or female viewers, "the archeplot has the structure subject-verb-object, and the verb is transitive, always . . . As we have seen, there are two dominant variations in the plot concerning the object-victim. She is either an unwilling, or willing object; victim she remains. She has a 'choice' of attitude to the event, but she has no choice of action in the event. The imperative of the plot is strict: it will happen, whatever her attitude" (Kappeler 1986.104, 105).

For Kappeler, the reason that the transitive nature of the plot does not change between scenarios 1 and 2 lies precisely in the connection of all works of art to a gendered social context. In this context, too, one finds a transitive arrangement of power, patriarchy, that has generally not given women much choice about the position they would like to occupy.

In her chapter, Sharrock develops Kappeler's critique to question the efficacy of the resisting reader when confronted with Greco-Roman representation. Sharrock stresses, as do Benton and Eldred, that Roman works—the Portland vase, elegy, Pompeian wall paintings of Iphigeneia and Pentheus—do fragment the point of view and often encourage identification with both active and passive, sadistic and scopophilic, gazes. Nonetheless, temporary identifications with the passive position do not disrupt the transitive nature of the viewing structure; they are inversions that define the norm, and the norm remains male/active and female/passive. This normative structure of viewing cannot honestly be resisted because it reflects the realities of power in Roman culture.

Noting that Lucian's *Essay on Portraiture* (second century C.E.) repeats the objectification of woman as art object found in earlier Greek and Roman art and literature, Sharrock suggests that such objectification is common to representation in antiquity and still with us today, "perhaps we, too, are caught." On the one hand, then, she questions whether masochistic identification actually reflects elite anxiety about powerlessness or is simply a trick built into the structure and consistently practiced from Euripides (at least) through Lucian. On the other, she also questions whether any periodizing break in this practice can be drawn between Greece and Rome or Rome and now. For that reason, Sharrock's essay closes the collection.

Conclusions

Three significant points emerge from this volume. First, Roman visuality and sexuality resist the imposition of any one interpretive paradigm. The simplicity of the penetration model must contend with the complexity of Roman hierarchies and social spaces, while the notion that Western representation has a fundamentally male-dominated or pornographic structure must consider the vulnerability of many men, of all social levels, in Rome. This liability to physical penetration, painful or pleasurable, finds expression in their art, in their literature, and even in the way they walked, spoke, and ate. Consequently, the discussion of periodization is and should be a difficult one, especially since many of the visual and cultural theories used in this book are comparatively new and have rarely or never been applied to Rome. Second, Rome cannot be collapsed with Greece to support an argument in favor of social constructionism or essentialism. If Greece has been used to illustrate how the cultural poetics of desire differ between antiquity and the present, the spectacular, and everyday, violence of Rome must be respected for its ability to challenge metaphors like "cultural poetics." At the same time, the Roman gaze often does not exhibit the same equation of vision, rationality, and power attributed to that of Greece. Finally, Rome, on the basis of points one and two, must acquire its own place in body history. Making Rome visible is only the first step; it should be followed by interpretive approaches that begin with Rome's distinctive cultural circumstances and institutions. Only then can we begin to answer responsibly the question: "What changed between Greece and Rome, or Rome and now?"

Notes

1. Varro *de Lingua Latina* 6.80, Kent's Loeb edition. Unless otherwise noted, all translations are my own.

2. Jay 1993.494. For ancient and early modern praise of vision, see Baxandall 1988.103–05, Pardo 1993.65–68, Summers 1987.32–41. Varro may have Plato's praise of sight in mind (*Tim.* 47A).

3. *Violavit* suggests the absence of desire on the woman's part—as Lucretia points out, "corpus est tantum violatum, animus insons" ("My body alone has been violated, my mind is innocent," Livy 1.58)—while *vitiavit* implies that she responded to and enjoyed her seduction. On the legal distinction in Rome between *stuprum* (roughly, "illicit sexual contact") and *stuprum per vim* ("forcible rape"), see Gardner 1986.117–25.

4. See Richlin 1992a.18–26 for Latin "four-letter words" and euphemisms.

5. Plato and Aristotle rank the pleasures of the senses from the lowest (touch, closest to the animals) to the highest (vision, closest to the intellect): Summers 1987.54–62.

6. As Irigaray puts it: "More than any other sense, the eye objectifies and masters. It sets at a distance. In our culture the predominance of the look over smell, taste, touch, and hearing has brought about an impoverishment of bodily relations" (cited and translated by Jay 1993.493).

7. "Oculorum sensus vis usque pervenit ad stellas" suggests Euclid's visual rays moving from the eye outward in an expanding pyramid. Other theories current in Varro's time include Epicurus's stream of atoms from the object to the eye (intromission, presented at length in Lucretius's *de Rerum Natura* 4; see Gordon in this volume), Plato's mixture of intromission and extramission, Aristotle's transparent medium, and the Stoic pneuma: Lindberg 1976.1–17.

8. Barton 1993.91–106, J. R. Clarke 1998.130–31, Dickie and Dunbabin 1983.

9. See J. R. Clarke 1998 for depictions of sex in wall painting, jewelry, dishes, and mosaics.

10. See J. R. Clarke 1998.8–12, Demand 1994, Golden and Toohey 1997b, Richlin 1991, 1992a, 1992b, 1993a, 1993b, and 1997a, Skinner 1996 and 1997. Larmour, Miller, and Platter note that essentialist and constructionist are often terms of abuse (1998.28–29), but they also refer to fundamental disagreements about what culture does: Bordo 1993, Butler 1993, Featherstone, Hepworth, and Turner 1991, Poster 1989, Zita 1998.

11. E.g., J. G. Turner 1993.xvi: "A volume of essays like *Before Sexuality* . . . sets the standard to which historians of early modern sexuality should aspire"; cf. Solomon-Godeau 1997.212–13.

12. Clarke 1998, Elsner 1995 and 1996a, Fredrick 1995, Kampen 1996c, Koloski-Ostrow and Lyons 1997, Richlin 1992a and 1992b, Montserrat 1997, Hallett and Skinner 1997.

13. Jay 1993, Jenks 1995, Poster 1989.

14. Visual media: Berger 1972, Bordo 1993, de Lauretis 1984 and 1987, Doane 1987, Jenks 1995, Mulvey 1989, Penley 1989, Silverman 1988b. Geography and architecture: Bell and Valentine 1995 and 1997, Burgin 1996, Colomina 1992, Duncan 1996, Massey 1994, Rendell, Penner, and Borden 2000, E. Wilson 1991.

15. Butler 1993.1–16 suggests "materialization" in place of "construction," but the concepts seem equally discursive. For "construction" and pornography, see Pitchford 1997.

16. Richlin 1992c.173–77; Skinner 1996.120 argues that "rape as trope is infinitely tractable," allowing for female resistance and movement between subject and object positions.

17. Richlin 1992d.xviii: "The Greeks and Romans certainly had their differences from us and from each other, but not so much so that modern paradigms are inapplicable." From the '70s to the '90s, as Shelby Brown notes (1997.17),

"Feminists 'deconstructed' an impressive array of images of naked and sexually vulnerable women in both elite and popular art, documenting over and over again how women were posed, objectified, dehumanized, and idealized as an erotic sight for male pleasure." Her extensive footnote (1997.31 n. 30) conveys the limits of this project: from the twentieth century back to Rubens but nothing before the sixteenth century. In addition, see Bryson 1988, Bryson, Holly, and Moxey 1994, Holly 1996, Pollock 1988.

18. E.g., homosexuality (Boswell 1980 and 1989, Halperin 1990.15–40, Richlin 1993a), patriarchy (Keuls 1985, Richlin 1992d), or "woman" as transhistorical categories (Blok 1987, Pantel 1992b, Rabinowitz 1993a, Richlin 1993b, Scott 1986), or the transhistorical use of psychoanalysis (Caldwell 1989, duBois 1988, 1995, and 1996, Skinner 1993).

19. Cf. S. Brown 1997.20–21: "Another source of the divide between classical archaeology and feminist art history is the latter's focus on the period from the Renaissance to the present."

20. Keuls 1985. Hallett 1993.54 notes that, "The large majority of feminist efforts to challenge historical orthodoxy in regard to the two great 'classical' periods of Greco-Roman antiquity have focused on the Greco- at the expense of the Roman."

21. See Richlin 1993a, concerned mainly with *cinaedi* as a marginalized subgroup rather than "cinaedism" as an aspect of elite political deportment.

22. Fredrick 1997 and 1999, Gamel 1999, Janan 1994, Oliensis 1997, Skinner 1993, Wyke 1989 and 1994a.

23. Frank 1991 and Richlin 1997a; both ask the critical question, "Why bodies now?"

24. Braudel 1981.27 notes "the difficult assembling of a number of *parahistoric* languages—demography, food, costume, lodging, technology, money, towns—which are usually kept separate from each other and which develop in the margin of traditional history" (emphasis in original).

25. See Duby and Perrot 1992, Ferguson, Quilligan, and Vickers 1986, Stallybrass 1986, J. Turner 1993.

26. Cf. Meskell 1997.157: "Archaeology's concern has always been with representativeness, aiming at generalizing practices and behaviors rather than individual responses, the latter being positioned as an insurmountable task."

27. Bourdieu 1990 argues at length that practice is not discourse because it consists of patterns of physical behavior that have goals (often the accumulation of "symbolic capital") but are not, in general, accessible to conscious reflection about their rules or grammar. By contrast, Foucault's *dispositif* and *épistémè* are linguistically ordered, structuralist fields, whether the evidence in question is material or textual. Fowler 1997.92–93: "His 'materiality' is only spoken or written materiality," P. A. Miller 1998, Poster 1989.91: "In the *History of Sexuality* discourse is the only practice," Spivak 1976.lxi–lxii.

28. Hopkins 1983.220; cf. Kampen 1994.133: "What Roman women and

men 'really' felt about reproduction and parenthood is no longer easily accessible to us, and even if we were able to consult some of them, we would still be far from any objective notion of a Roman attitude on the subject."

29. On space, ritual, and movement in Roman tombs, see Hope 1997.

30. Hopkins 1983.221–25 explores disagreements between "cultural relativists" and "ethological humanists" as to whether grief is universal to all human societies or specifically constructed within each.

31. Scott 1993.409. Bordo 1993.291 argues that "the notion of discursive foundationalism as 'cure' suggests that the textualization of the body is itself a privileged theoretical turn immune from cultural suspicion and critique," while Bourdieu 1990 attacks the tendency of structuralism to confuse its synchronic, visual schemata with bodily experience. See Berger and Luckmann 1967 for an early argument in favor of the "social construction of reality." Halperin 1993.426 concludes: "We must . . . be willing to admit that what seem to be our most inward, authentic, and private experiences are actually, in Adrienne Rich's memorable phrase, 'shared, unnecessary, and political.'"

32. Bordo 1993, Butler 1993, Eagleton 1996, Freccero 1990, Pitchford 1997, Zita 1998.184–201.

33. Frank 1991.85–86. His overview of female versus male performance artists on this score is limited: see A. Jones 1994.

34. Scott 1993.408–12. Halperin 1993.417: "Not only does this historical distance permit us to view ancient social and sexual conventions with particular sharpness; it also enables us to bring more clearly into focus the ideological dimension—the purely conventional and arbitrary character—of our own social and sexual experiences." Cf. Halperin, Winkler, and Zeitlin 1990a.6–7.

35. Ancient Greece has an enormous archaeological data base, and sexuality in vase painting has received much attention (e.g., Dover 1978, Frontisi-Ducroux 1996, Keuls 1985, Kilmer 1993, Lissarague 1990 and 1992, Petersen 1997, Shapiro 1992, Stewart 1997, R. F. Sutton 1992). It remains difficult to connect Greek vases with material reality because of the absence of reliable contexts, and a fundamental problem is posed by the poor archaeological record for housing in classical Athens: see Foxhall 1998, Keuls 1985.210–15, Jameson 1990, S. Walker 1983.

36. It is difficult to appreciate the difference Foucault intends between the classical ideal of self-mastery and the care of self in the imperial period. While the discussion of Artemidorus demonstrates the persistence of the penetration model in a "common way of thinking," the treatment of "the wife" concludes that *ta aphrodisia* among the elite are no longer as concerned with penetration as an expression of political mastery as they are with conjugal reciprocity as a means toward a proper relation with oneself. The problematization of the penetration model among the elite thus may have confirmed rather than questioned its valence for the majority of people, estranged alike from conjugal reciprocity and the care of the self.

37. Halperin 1990.102–03: "A new collective image of the citizen body as masculine and assertive, as master of its pleasures, and as perpetually on the superordinate side of a series of hierarchical and roughly congruent distinctions in status: master vs. slave, free vs. unfree, dominant vs. submissive, active vs. passive, insertive vs. receptive, customer vs. prostitute, citizen vs. non-citizen, man vs. woman."

38. For the sense of individual and social worth expressed in the funerary monuments of freedmen and women, see Hopkins 1983.205–17, Joshel 1992a, Koortbojian 1996, Zanker 1988.15–16.

39. See Morales 1996.192–93 for the split between treating the suffering body as material or signifier.

40. Stewart 1997.14 claims: "Lacan's theories have generated spirited and sometimes bitter debate, with feminists in particular attacking his work as a 'phallogocularcentric' (brilliantly paraphrased by Terry Eagleton as 'cocksure'!), patriarchal, voyeur's theory." Eagleton uses "cocksure" to translate phallogocentrism, a neologism coined by Derrida (not feminists) not simply as a critique of Lacan but to suggest the privilege of both phallus and logos in Western philosophy since the Greeks (Spivak 1976.lxvii–lxix). Phallogocularcentrism, in turn, was coined by Jay (not feminists) to indicate the appropriation of Lacan and Derrida by Irigaray and Cixous.

41. The phrase *the public eye* seems to come from Baxandall 1988.109, an elaboration of his chapter title, "The Period Eye," which refers to the cognitive equipment men brought to bear on fifteenth-century Italian painting. Stewart refers (1997.15) to "the reductivist psychoanalytical position that the gaze is omnipresent, monocular, and tyrannical," but later asserts (1997.21): "Greek painting . . . prefers to cater to the scanning eye; indeed I would argue that it tries to reduplicate its parent culture's omnipresent gaze of surveillance."

42. Burgin 1996.142; the quotation is from Lefebvre 1991.271. Lefebvre bases his understanding of Roman cities on Vitruvius—that is, to use Lefebvre's own terms, on one representation of space, rather than spatial practice or representational spaces. However, for an interesting use of Lefebvre as a theoretical model for Roman space, see Laurence 1997.

43. For similar periodic breaks in the history of vision, see Crary 1993, Merchant 1983, Nast and Kobayashi 1996; in the history of food, see Beardsworth and Keil 1997.32–36.

44. Findlen 1993, Frappier-Mazur 1993. For the "eroticization of the senses" in the Renaissance, see specifically Findlen 1993.59–76, Ginzburg 1980, Pardo 1993.

45. The marginalization of classics is suggested by Richlin 1997a and supported by Golden and Toohey 1997b.15 as a primary reason for the acceptance of the thesis of "before sexuality."

46. Mulvey 1989.15. Hence Clover's summary (1992.177) of Mulvey's argument that the male spectator's unease is resolved "either through denial-

driven looking (fetishistic scopophilia) or punishment-driven looking (sadistic voyeurism)." Fredrick 1995 argues that erotic mythological paintings from Pompeii, for specific cultural reasons, highlight rather than suppress the contradictions between scopophilia and voyeurism.

47. Studlar 1988, Clover 1992.181, Creed 1993.

48. See Mulvey 1981 and Doane 1987 for these alternatives.

49. Penley 1989.79–80; she refers to Laplanche and Pontalis's model of fantasy (1968), in which the subject may identify with the subject position, the object position, or the verb. This model is considered (and rejected) by Richlin 1992c as a way of redeeming Ovid's rapes. Burgin 1996.75 argues that the movement between scopophilia and voyeurism on screen may create "perverse space," which he illustrates using Helmut Newton's photograph *Self-portrait with Wife June and Model, Paris, 1981*, also discussed by Sharrock in this volume.

50. For Catullus and elegy, see Fitzgerald 1995, Fredrick 1997 and 1999; Janan 1994 is more specifically Lacanian. For wall painting, see Fredrick 1995, Koloski-Ostrow 1997, Wallace-Hadrill 1996; for Ovid, see Segal 1994; for Seneca, Robin 1993; for Apuleius, N. Slater 1998. Morales 1996 applies Clover's concepts of the assaultive and reactive gazes to Seneca the Elder's *controversia* on Parrhasius.

51. E.g., Walters 1997.31: "Sexual activity is routinely conceptualized in Roman public discourse as penetrative, sexual pleasure (particularly in the male homosexual context) as accruing to the penetrator, and the penetrator-penetrated relationship as 'naturally' involving a more powerful individual wielding power over a less powerful one." Yet *cinaedi* and adulterers were closely associated (Edwards 1993.34–97), and Richlin 1993a gives abundant evidence that Romans attributed pleasure in sex to both women and *cinaedi*.

52. Foucault 1979.216. Hence Winkler 1990.45–70 shows that the surveillance of men's sexual behavior in classical Athens was not panoptic; he notes (60), however, Dionysius of Halicarnassus's observation that the "Romans drew back the curtain on every household even to the bedchamber."

53. See Bergmann 1991, Clarke 1991a.1–77, Wallace-Hadrill 1994.3–37.

54. Stewart 1997 also relies solely on Bourdieu's *The Logic of Practice* in his application of *habitus* to classical Greece. The passage quoted above continues: "The opposition between male and female is realized in posture, in the gestures and movements of the body, in the form of the opposition between the straight and the bent, between firmness, uprightness, and directness . . . and restraint, reserve, and flexibility" (Bourdieu 1990.70). He later remarks (76) that "the rhythm of actions and words" for male Kabyle inscribes on the body "a whole relationship to time, which is experienced as part of the person (like the *gravitas* of Roman senators)." This comparison is intended to express the depth to which *habitus* is impressed on the body, but may also imply that the Kabyle and Rome have similarly traditional systems of *habitus*. My thanks to Anthony Corbeill for this reference.

55. Bourdieu 1984.169–259. Wallace-Hadrill's (1994.148) brief discussion of Bourdieu suggests that Roman society, like French society in Bourdieu's *Distinction*, was minutely differentiated, and that these distinctions were articulated spatially through domestic decoration.

56. Bourdieu himself takes a strong position on this question: "As in every society dominated by male values—and European societies, which assign men to politics, history or war, and women to the hearth, the novel and psychology, are no exception to this—the specifically male relation to the body and sexuality is that of sublimation" (1990.77).

1 Split Vision

The Politics of the Gaze in Seneca's *Troades*

Cindy Benton

The violence associated with the end of the Trojan war provided ancient dramatists excellent opportunities to explore anxieties about the reversal of fortune and fall from power.[1]

In Seneca's *Troades*, the fall of Troy and the experiences of the Trojan women serve as a setting where such anxieties can be displaced and examined. In this chapter, I investigate how the representation of female characters in this play illuminates a crisis in male subjectivity created by the anxiety of the senatorial class over its position in Rome's visual economy and by an attendant concern about corporeal vulnerability among those at the top of the social hierarchy. *Troades* manifests a self-conscious awareness of the pleasures and horrors of viewing violent spectacles occasioned by the destruction of a city and the accompanying reversal of fortune. This play, moreover, specifically centers on women as victims and viewers of the aftermath of war while presenting an intratextual male audience through which we can observe various reactions to these women. It is in this context that I am interested in exploring how the notion of a sadomasochistic dialectic may be useful for understanding the staging of violence and gender in *Troades*.[2]

Carlin Barton argues that "the writers of the Neronian period, in particular, gloried in the violence they abhorred. They not only described but created scenes of violence against victims with whom they could simultaneously identify and sympathize. They were at once both victims and spectators" (1993.25). This observation is especially apt for understanding the dynamics of the gaze within Seneca's *Troades*. As I shall show, there are significant parallels between the Romans' simultaneous pleasure in and horror at violent spectacle and the sadomasochistic dialectic elucidated by film theory.[3]

At, first, film theorists focused on film as an apparatus that encouraged spectators to identify with the omniscient, transcendental gaze of the camera.[4] Subsequently, feminist film theorists argued that mainstream cinematic narratives positioned this gaze as male. Such readings resulted from an emphasis on both the fetishistic and sadistic pleasures derived from viewing the image of the female body on screen.[5] Later, moving away from the paradigm of a sadistic male gaze, several theorists focused on the masochistic dynamics of film in relation to male subjectivity in crisis.[6] Kaja Silverman (1980) uses Freud's observation that dreamers displace their fears and desires onto various surrogate figures to show how female characters can act on behalf of male viewers.[7] In a later article (1988a.35), she notes that Freud infers that "feminine masochism" is a particularly male disorder because the masculine subject is put in a typically feminine position.[8] Tania Modleski takes Silverman's theory a step further and discusses how the male viewer participates in a sadomasochistic dialectic. She shows how the process of displacement enables us to understand how the male viewer simultaneously experiences and denies an identification with victimized female characters: "By acknowledging the importance of denial in the male spectator's response, we can take into account a crucial fact . . . the fact that the male finds it necessary to repress certain 'feminine' aspects of himself, and to project these exclusively onto the woman, who does the suffering for both of them" (Modleski 1988.13). Carol Clover (1992) also uses this notion of a sadomasochistic dialectic to discuss how the mechanism of displacement enables the male viewer simultaneously to experience and deny an identification with the female characters who abound in horror film. She argues that, in addition to the sadistic and voyeuristic pleasures that the sight of a screaming, fleeing, or dying woman on screen might provide a male viewer, the concept of female masochism can show how the male viewer also has an investment in that suffering.

Film theory's recent interest in horror has emerged partly because of the victim-identified nature of the scopic pleasure offered to its audience. The masochistic pleasures provided by horror throw into doubt early theorists' assumptions that the cinematic apparatus is organized around a sadistic, controlling gaze.[9] Clover (1992.172–205) argues that there are two gazes in horror film: a "predatory, assaultive" or "phallic" gaze and the "reactive" or "feminine" gaze. She states: "It [the eye of horror] may penetrate, but it is also penetrated" (1992.191).[10] Thus the theory of a sadomasochistic dialectic indicates that the gaze is more complex, and subject positions more fluid, than was accounted for in the first ten years of film theory. This dialectic explains the oscillation of identification and the greater range of viewers' emotions. It is within this context that I would like to explore how female characters presented in *Troades* may have offered multiple spectatorial positions for the senatorial male gaze. Tragedy, like horror, can be seen as "victim identified."[11] Although male victims certainly abound in Senecan tragedy, I would like to consider what may have been gained by presenting female characters as the primary victims. In other words, what is the male senatorial stake in representing suffering as female in this play?

In Seneca's *Troades*, female suffering dominates the stage. By choosing Hecuba as the first character to appear, Seneca provides the audience an opportunity to experience the atrocities of war through a woman's eyes at the outset of the play.[12] Hecuba emerges and emphasizes the horrors she witnessed during the city's fall. In particular, she recounts having to endure the sight of Priam's gruesome murder ("*vidi execrandum regiae caedis nefas*," 44).[13] After she leads the chorus in lamentation for the deaths of her husband and children, recalling the countless funerals she has seen, the messenger enters and tells of future sufferings that Hecuba will have to endure. During the course of the play, her daughter and grandson will be brutally slaughtered, while she and the surviving women will be divided up as slaves to the men who destroyed their city. Here we see the eye not as a locus of power but as a site of vulnerability, the eye of horror that is wounded by what it sees.[14] As Hecuba is told of Polyxena's fate, she emphasizes the powerless nature of her gaze (963–66):

> dura et infelix age
> elabere anima, denique hoc unum mihi
> remitte funus. inrigat fletus genas
> imberque victo subitus e vultu cadit.

> Come on enduring and unhappy soul,
> slip away and finally relieve me
> from this one death. Tears wet my cheeks,
> and a sudden shower falls from conquered eyes.

The use of *victo vultu* suggests that Hecuba's eyes themselves are captives: hostages to the horrors that come with living in this time of loss. Only death can free them from the sight of yet another child's slaughter.

Hecuba not only emphasizes the Trojan women's position as victims and viewers of the aftermath of war, she also reveals a self-consciousness about their position as paradigmatic spectacles of suffering. In the first lines of the play, Hecuba directs the audience's gaze to herself (1–4):

> Quicumque regno fidit et magna potens
> dominatur aula nec leves metuit deos
> animumque rebus credulum laetis dedit,
> me videat . . .

> Whoever puts his faith in regal power and exercises ultimate
> authority in a great palace, nor fears capricious gods
> and gives his credulous spirit to prosperity,
> let him look on me . . .

As she draws attention to her position as the ultimate example of the changeable nature of fortune, she is conscious of the Greeks' eyes as they survey the ruins of Troy (22–26):

> stat avidus irae victor et lentum Ilium
> metitur oculis ac decem tandem ferus
> ignoscit annis; horret afflictam quoque,
> victamque quamvis videat, haut credit sibi
> potuisse vinci.

> The victor stands eager for violence and measures tenacious Ilium
> with his eyes, and, at last, the savage conqueror forgives the ten years;
> he shudders at her in ruins, and, although he sees her conquered,
> he scarcely believes she could have been defeated.

Similarly, Andromache directs all eyes to herself as she laments what is left of her family (507–08):

> en intuere, turba quae simus super:
> tumulus, puer, captiva.

> Look! See what sort of crowd we are that remains:
> a tomb, a boy, a captive woman.

She, too, is aware of her position as object of the Greek gaze. After she hears the warning that Ulysses is coming to take her son to his death, she knows she will have to put on a convincing act to keep him from detecting her fear. Indeed when Ulysses arrives, he is suspicious that she might be lying when she tells him that the child is already dead. He tells himself *scrutare matrem* (615), directing his gaze, as well as the audience's, to Andromache and looking for any sign that might betray her son's whereabouts. The use of *scrutare* here indicates an investigative, penetrating gaze. Ulysses tries to trap Andromache by outlining the horrors that await her son and then watching her reaction (607–704). As he continues to goad her, both he and the audience watch her become increasingly agitated as she tries to decide which course of action to take.[15] Thus this play not only centers on women as victims and viewers of the aftermath of war, but also presents an internal male audience that responds to these women.

It is precisely this intratextual audience that can give us clues as to the ways the gaze was manifested in the extratextual audience. The parallels between these two audiences is most explicitly drawn in the messenger's description of the site of Polyxena's sacrifice (1123–25):[16]

> adversa cingit campus et clivo levi
> erecta medium vallis includens locum
> crescit theatri more.

> A field encircles the opposite side, and an elevated valley
> rises with a gentle slope, enclosing a space in the middle
> like a theater.

Seneca then goes on to describe the crowd's eagerness to view Polyxena's death, indicating that there is compulsion and pleasure in viewing the horrific (1125–31):

> concursus frequens
> implevit omne litus: hi classis moram
> hac morte solvi rentur, hi stirpem hostium
> gaudent recidi. magna pars vulgi levis
> odit scelus spectatque; nec Troes minus
> suum frequentant funus et pavidi metu
> partem ruentis ultimam Troiae vident.

> The crowded gathering filled the whole shore:
> some think the fleet's delay will be brought to an end by this death,
> some take pleasure in the cutting back of the enemy's stock.
> A great part of the fickle mob hates the crime,
> but watches it anyway. The Trojans no less
> crowd their own funeral and, trembling with fear,
> watch the last part of the fall of Troy.

In this scene, Seneca presents a complex paradigm of spectatorship. By enumerating the different motives of different parts of the crowd, he indicates that the dynamics of the gaze are determined in part by individual reactions and motivations. Although both Greeks and Trojans flock to see Polyxena's death, the nature of the experience is different for each spectator.[17]

While the Greeks described at 1127–28 can be seen as enjoying a sadistic pleasure in the death of the Other, the Trojans experience fear as they rush to view Polyxena's death. The masochistic nature of this compulsion to view such a painful sight is suggested by Andromache as she asks the messenger to recount the events in detail. Here she says that such great sorrows enjoy dwelling on total calamity ("gaudet magnus aerumnas dolor / tractare totas," 1066–67). The simultaneous existence, and intensity, of different types of visual pleasure is made even clearer in the messenger's description of the crowd's reaction to the death of Polyxena herself (1136–44):

> terror attonitos tenet
> utrosque populos. ipsa deiectos gerit
> vultus pudore, sed tamen fulgent genae
> magisque solito splendet extremus decor,
> ut esse Phoebi dulcius lumen solet
> iamiam cadentis, astra cum repetunt vices
> premiturque dubius nocte vicina dies.
> stupet omne vulgus, et fere cuncti magis
> peritura laudant.

> Terror holds both peoples in shock.
> She herself modestly casts down her gaze, yet her cheeks flush,
> and her dying beauty shines more than usual, just as Phoebus's light
> shines sweeter as it sets, when the stars seek again their paths and the
>   wavering daylight
> is closely pursued by neighboring night. The whole crowd is stunned,
> and almost all praise more what is about to perish.

This description suggests the fetishistic and voyeuristic aspects of the audience's gaze.[18] As Polyxena approaches the mound of Achilles, she lowers her eyes and blushes, thus emphasizing her position as object of the gaze. Her beauty transfixes the crowd (*stupet*, 1143) and, for a moment, time seems suspended as the spectators are absorbed in the sight of her radiant cheeks.[19] The viewers' pleasure is heightened precisely because she is about to die ("et fere cuncti magis / peritura laudant," 1143–44). The fetishism only lasts a moment and quickly elides into sadistic voyeurism. This elision, reinforced by "magisque solito splendet extremus decor" and the sunset simile, indicates that the greatest delight for the spectators comes in the instant just before Polyxena's death.

In the *Natural Questions,* there is an interesting parallel that can illuminate the assaultive, sadistic aspect of the gaze directed at Polyxena in *Troades.* In this philosophical treatise, Seneca describes dinner guests who devour the spectacle of a dying mullet. In the midst of castigating the excessive luxury seen at dinner parties, Seneca says that the value of presenting the guests with a dying mullet is not just a matter of ensuring freshness but also of providing a colorful spectacle (*Nat. Quaest.* 3.17.2–18.1):

> Parum videtur recens mullus, nisi qui in convivae manu moritur. Vitreis ollis inclusi afferuntur et observatur morientium color, quem in multas mutationes mors luctante spiritu vertit . . . "Nihil est," inquis, "mullo expirante formosius; ipsa colluctatione animae deficientis rubor primum, deinde pallor suffunditur, squamaeque variantur et in incertas facies inter vitam ac mortem coloris est vagatio."

> A mullet does not seem fresh enough unless it dies in a guest's hand. They are brought out enclosed in glass jars and their color watched as they die. As they strive for breath, death variegates their color . . . "Nothing," you say, "is more beautiful than a dying mullet; in its very death throes, first a red, then a pale tint is spread through it, and its scales become variously tinged, and between life and death there is a changing into indistinguishable shades."

Nothing is more beautiful than a dying mullet, but Polyxena, perhaps, comes close. Like the mullet, which becomes more brilliant as it dies and emits a bright light under its temples ("Vide quomodo exarserit rubor omni acrior minio! . . . Quam lucidum quiddam caeruleumque sub ipso tempore effulsit!" 3.18.5), Polyxena's cheeks flush and her beauty in death is compared to the last rays of the setting sun. Like Seneca's dinner guest, the audience of Polyxena's sacrifice also experiences aesthetic enjoyment in the protracted moment of death. In both cases, the viewer's pleasure is amplified by the spectacular nature of the beauty each object provides just as it is about to die. The aggressive nature of the gaze is evident in the parallels between the diners' eyes and throats ("nec cenae causa occidi sed super cenam, cum multum in deliciis fuit et oculos ante quam gulam pavit!" "It was not killed for the sake of dinner, but over dinner, a source of great delight; it fed the eyes before the palate!" 3.17.3). Here we see the concept of the devouring eye, an active aggressive gaze that delights in consuming violent spectacles. Seneca continues the comparison between watching and eating as he states that the diners are not content to consume only with their teeth, belly, and mouth, but are also gluttonous with their eyes (*oculis quoque gulosi sunt*, 3.18.7).[20] In the sacrifice of Polyxena, the visual appetite of the audience is paralleled by Achilles' mound, which eagerly consumes (*bibit*, 1164) her blood.[21]

While it is clear that there is a sadistic gaze that takes pleasure in the violent spectacle of Polyxena's death, a masochistic gaze is also presented in this scene. When the sword is raised, Polyxena raises her eyes and stares down her killer as she faces the weapon and Pyrrhus head-on (1151–52):

> audax virago non tulit retro gradum;
> conversa ad ictum stat truci vultu ferox.

> The bold heroine did not retreat, but, turning
> toward the blow, she stood courageous, with a fierce gaze.

At this point, Polyxena abandons the modesty that keeps her eyes cast down and exhibits instead the aggressive gaze of a warrior facing death. As this *audax virago* behaves courageously, the soldiers are moved by her bravery and experience a masochistic pleasure (1144–48):[22]

> hos movet formae decus,
> hos mollis aetas, hos vagae rerum vices;
> movet animus omnes fortis et leto obvius.
> Pyrrhum antecedit; omnium mentes tremunt,
> mirantur ac miserantur.

> Her glorious beauty affects some,
> others her tender age, others the fickle turns of fortune;
> but her courage and the manner in which she meets her death
> moves them all. She goes in front of Pyrrhus;
> the minds of all tremble, wonder, and pity simultaneously.

The masochistic nature of the gaze is indicated by the experience of fear (*omnium mentes tremunt*) that accompanies the viewers' pity (*miserantur*) and reveals an identification with the object of the gaze.[23] Thus visual pleasure can oscillate between sadism and masochism within the same viewer.[24] While Polyxena is a young, virginal girl, the heroic nature of the way she faces death allows the soldiers to identify with her and prompts their feelings of pity (1146). On the other hand, her status as a bride about to be sacrificed/married to Achilles' shade reinforces the feminine nature of her position and allows the soldiers to distance themselves from her.

Polyxena is presented as a transgendered figure, as is indicated by the description of her as a *virago*, a word that fuses male and female.[25] According to Clover (1992.42–64), it is just this transgendered nature of the object of the gaze that contributes to the functioning of the sadomasochistic dialectic in horror film. She shows how, through "the politics of displacement," the woman functions as a "congenial double," a vehicle through which the male viewer can "simultaneously experience forbidden desires and disavow them on the grounds that the visible character is, after all, a girl" (1992.18). While Polyxena cannot be read as a "final girl" (the terrorized heroine and sole female survivor of slasher films), nevertheless the transgendered nature of her character allows for a similar sadomasochistic process of identification. The fact that a Senecan character who is killed off before the end of the play can function like Clover's final girl merely points to cultural differences in the way encounters with death are viewed. Polyxena's sort of heroism suggests that the only power one has in a powerless position is to embrace death as one's own choice. The parallels between Polyxena's acceptance of her death, senatorial suicides, and gladiators' simultaneous status as *infames* and heroic figures further reinforces the sadomasochistic elements enabled by her character.[26]

Similarly, Nicole Loraux (1987.59) suggests that it is precisely at the moment of death that a *virgo* becomes a *virago* through her courage in facing the deathblow. In her analysis of virgin sacrifice in Greek and Roman tragedy, Loraux argues that, by taking charge of their own deaths, these female characters display a free will that was traditionally the privilege of a male warrior (1987.42–48). In Seneca's play, the brave manner in which Polyxena faces her death is depicted as masculine in its heroism and thus affords the basis for a male masochistic identification with her. The circumstances of the sacrifice, however, call specifically for a female victim.[27] This need for a female victim, along with the description of voyeuristic pleasure at her death, indicates that there is also a sadistic male gaze operating in this scene. Thus the sacrifice of Polyxena provides the audience (both intra- and extratextual) with a character that it can simultaneously identify with yet distance itself from. If we use this passage as a paradigm for the dynamics of a specific kind of Roman gaze, we can see that the female characters in *Troades*, like those in horror films, may have served as sites for exploring male subjectivity in crisis—in this case senatorial male anxieties centering on issues of class and violence.

First-century Roman audiences were fascinated with violent spectacle.[28] Not surprisingly, the staging of these events, and audiences' responses to them, is a theme throughout Seneca's work.[29] His letters and essays also provide valuable insights into the dynamics of the gaze and the nature of the visual pleasures presented in his plays. Frequently, Seneca can be seen grappling with the issue of scopic desire and visual pleasure, particularly the delight in violent spectacle.[30] For example, he opens *Epistle* 7 with a confession (*confitebor*) to Lucilius of his own weakness: "Nihil vero tam damnosum bonis moribus quam in aliquo spectaculo desidere; tunc enim per voluptatem facilius vitia subrepunt. Quid me existimas dicere? Avarior redeo, ambitiosior, luxuriosior? Immo vero crudelior et inhumanior, quia inter homines fui" ("Truly there is nothing so detrimental to good character than to sit at some spectacle; for then vices sneak up on us more easily through pleasure. What do you think I am saying? I return more greedy, more ambitious, more immoderate? Indeed truly I am more cruel and inhuman because I have been in the midst of human beings," 7.2–3).

The use of *voluptatem* is significant. While *voluptas* in the singular signifies sensual pleasure, the plural is often used of public spectacles.[31] Here Seneca is drawing a parallel between the two, indicating that visual pleasure is an integral part of public spectacle. In *Epistle* 88, he characterizes and classifies the arts, observing, "ludicrae sunt quae ad voluptatem oculorum atque aurium tendunt" ("The arts of amusement are those that strive to give pleasure to the eyes and ears," 88.22). Moreover, it is evident that Seneca considers this sort of enjoyment to be damaging both to an individual's character and to society.[32] In *de Clementia*, addressed to Nero, Seneca is critical of this sort of delight in violence, arguing that it breaks down the social order in its urge to create new ways of torturing and killing (1.25.2):

> Hoc est, quare vel maxime abominanda sit saevitia, quod excedit fines primum solitos, deinde humanos, nova supplicia conquirit, ingenium advocat ut instrumenta excogitet per quae varietur atque extendatur dolor, delectatur malis hominum; tunc illi dirus animi morbus ad insaniam pervenit ultimam, cum crudelitas versa est in voluptatem et iam occidere hominem iuvat.

This is the reason why brutality is the greatest abomination, because it first transgresses all ordinary boundaries and then all human bounds. It seeks out new suppliants, advocates ingenuity in order to invent devices by which suffering may be varied and extended, and delights in the disasters of men; then indeed the terrible disease of such a man's soul has come to the ultimate insanity, when cruelty is changed into pleasure and to kill a human being now is a source of delight.[33]

In this passage, as in *Epistle 7*, it is the pleasure (*voluptas*) in viewing violence that is damaging. Such criticisms of the sadistic dynamics of the gaze, however, are not just a matter of general concern for humanity and the morality of Rome, they also reflect an anxiety about the changing nature of the position of the senatorial class in the visual economy of the imperial period. This, in turn, mirrors a breakdown in the social order that affected the status of the senatorial class itself.

In ancient Rome, it was necessary for men of senatorial status to be in the public eye, and, during the republic, members of this class were at the apex of the Roman visual economy.[34] With the establishment of the empire, however, it became increasingly difficult for them to find their place within this visual economy as the privileged position of the emperor, both subject and object of the gaze, transformed the spectatorial politics of the senate, arena, and theater.[35]

The importance of visual politics during the transition from republic to empire can be seen, for example, in the legislation surrounding the *ludi*. During the republican period, the ability to stage elaborate and expensive *ludi* was itself a visual manifestation of one's wealth and status, but, as the imperial period progressed, this role was usurped by the emperors.[36] Under Augustus, restrictions on the frequency and lavishness of the games given by people other than the emperor were set in place. Nonetheless, elite spectators still held conspicuously privileged positions in the arena. Although Augustus restricted the public visibility of individual senators by limiting their ability to stage *ludi*, he also solidified the visual and social hierarchy within the spaces of the arena and theater. Augustus reinforced the earlier practice of assigning seating according to order by reserving the front row of seats for the senatorial class, separating the soldiers from civilians, and confining women to the back rows (with the exception of the Vestal Virgins who had separate seats). He also strengthened dress codes as another visual marker of social divisions.[37] Catharine Edwards (1997.89) links Augustus's enforcement of seating arrangements to a solidification of the social hierarchy that emphasized his own elevated position. Such measures illustrate the interrelation between the visual economy and the construction of status.[38]

An equally significant dividing line in the hierarchy of the arena was that between the audience and the stage. Under Augustus, a senatorial decree was passed banning senators and *equites* from performing in stage plays and gladiatorial games.[39] Thus senators were in visible positions of honor without being singled out as direct objects of the gaze. An analysis of this division between spectator and performer is important for understanding the politics of spectatorship and Roman attitudes toward the body. Edwards (1994.84) argues that a major difference between elite and *infames* was that the bodies of *infames* were sold and exhibited for the pleasure of the public.[40] She also states that actors, gladiators, and prostitutes were denied the rights of Roman citizenship as *infames* because they exhibited their bodies for financial gain and thus lacked the dignity required of the citizen's body: "And just as actors (along with gladiators and prostitutes) resembled slaves in their lack of control over their own bodies, so they were assimilated to slaves by the law" (1994.84). Acting and gladiatorial combats were ways of objectifying the body, making it a spectacle—like a mullet, or Polyxena—staged for the visual consumption of others.

The seating arrangements, as well as the division between audience and arena, distinguished the elite both from the rest of the crowd and from the *infames* performing in the arena. The prominent seats of the elite made them conspicuous spectators and reflected their social status.[41] Their position in the public gaze, however, was mediated by the social organization of space in the arena. The elite exhibited their bodies, but only as spectators. Thus they could be positive objects of the gaze in a way that the *infames* in the arena could not be.

This ability to retain one's status as a spectator and maintain some control over the way one's body was presented to the public gaze was crucial at a time when there was both a growing visual pleasure in violent spectacle and a change in the fabric of Rome's social hierarchy. Edwards (1997.73–74) notes that one of the privileges of Roman citizenship was protection from corporal punishment;[42] however, during the transition from republic to empire, the immunity of elite bodies from bodily assault and mutilation began to erode. In her discussion of the decapitation of members of the senate during the proscriptions, Amy Richlin states: "By breaking the integrity of the citizen's body, the killers were assimilating that body to others more vulnerable" (1999.196). In a much less immediately violent way, when emperors forced members of the senatorial class to perform in the arena and theater, they also blurred the division between elite and slave bodies.[43] In addition, when a citizen entered the arena or the stage, he became *infamis*, losing his protection from corporal punishment. Thus discourses about emperors' violations of the lines between spectator and spectacle can be seen as symptomatic of the continued concern of the senatorial class about its increasing vulnerability to violence under the principate.

Anxiety about maintaining a visual economy that reinforced elite positions within the social hierarchy surfaces particularly in the criticisms of Neronian rule.[44] Tacitus and Suetonius both present Nero as an emperor who disrupted the visual line between elite and *infames* by forcing the upper classes to appear on stage and in the arena. In the *Annales*, Tacitus criticizes Nero for pressuring Roman elites to "defile themselves" (*polluantur*) with stage performances (14.20). Suetonius adds the criticism that men and women of high rank performed during festivals and that Nero made both senators and *equites* do battle in the arena.[45]

Additionally, Nero is represented as an emperor who destroyed the divisions between spectator and spectacle. It is interesting that he manages to perform both roles as he takes the stage himself.[46] This, as Shadi Bartsch (1994.2–32) demonstrates, reversed the roles of actor and spectator as Nero watched the senators' reactions to his performances. According to Dio's history, senators and others were continuously under Nero's gaze in the theater:[47] ἐτηροῦντο δὲ ἀκριβῶς καὶ τούτων καὶ τῶν ἄλλων ἀεί ποτε καὶ αἱ ἔσοδοι καὶ αἱ ἔξοδοι τά τε σχήματα καὶ τὰ νεύματα καὶ τὰ ἐπιβοήματα, "Constantly, then, the entrances, exits, gestures, signals, and calls of the senators and others were scrutinized precisely" (62.15.2). Suetonius specifically discusses Nero's desire to make the audience perform while he is on stage (*Nero* 20). In this account, Nero was so fascinated with the Alexandrians' rhythmic applause that he hired some of them to teach the *equites* this technique, paying the leaders 400 gold pieces. In addition to making his audiences stage their applause, he further inverted the dynamics between spectators and performers by paying them. Suetonius adds that while Nero was in Greece, no one was allowed to leave the theater during one of his recitals (*Nero* 23, see also Tacitus *Annales* 16.5). This made the audience prisoners and put them in a position similar to that of the *infames* who performed in the arena.

Tacitus contrasts the attitudes of the audiences at the quinquennial contest, who became used to the inverted dynamics of performance, with those from out of town who were outraged and could not keep up with the clapping ("neque aspectum illum tolerare neque labori inhonesto sufficere, cum manibus nesciis fatiscerent," "Neither could they endure that sight nor were they adequate to the degrading task, and their inexperienced hands grew tired," *Annales* 16.5). The newcomers' inability to perform was then punished by soldiers who were stationed along the blocks of seats to enforce compliance. Tacitus also notes that it was just as dangerous to avoid such spectacles as it was to perform incorrectly: "Quippe gravior inerat metus, si spectaculo defuissent, multis palam et pluribus occultis, ut nomina ac vultus, alacritatem tristitiamque coeuntium scrutarentur" ("For the fear was greater if they missed the spectacle, since many openly, and more in secret, noted the names and expressions, the excitement and sadness, of those gathered," *Annales* 16.5). In this depiction, Nero's gaze extends even beyond his own eyes with the use of spies planted both openly and secretly. Tacitus goes on to say that after hearing the spies' reports, Nero instantly punished lower–class people while he waited for a more opportune time to punish elite violators.[48] Thus as the senatorial audience became actors, they also risked exposing themselves to the attendant lack of physical protection more traditional actors experienced.

Throughout the writings of the senatorial class, there is anxiety about being the object of the emperor's gaze and about the difficulty of retiring from the public eye.[49] According to Tacitus, avoiding the emperor's gaze by skipping senate meetings could also arouse suspicion and anger and could be interpreted as a sign of contempt.[50] Seneca himself exemplifies the difficulties of being in the public eye and in the emperor's sights.[51] For example, in *Epistle* 14, Seneca writes about the fine line between avoiding dangerous men in power and provoking them by such avoidance: "Idem facit sapiens; nocituram potentiam vitat, hoc primum cavens, ne vitare videatur. Pars enim securitatis et in hoc est, non ex professo eam petere, quia, quae quis fugit, damnat" ("The wise man does the same [as a pilot avoiding a storm]; he avoids an authority which might harm, taking particular care not to seem to avoid it. For part of safety lies in this, not to seek safety expressly, because what one flees, one condemns," 14.8). In *de Ira*, Seneca characterizes Caligula's gaze itself as a form of torture: "Torserat per omnia, quae in rerum natura tristissima sunt, fidiculis, talaribus, eculeo, igne, vultu suo" ("He had tortured them by means of all the grimmest devices that nature provides—by the string, by the robe, by the rack, by fire, and by his own gaze," 3.19.1). The visual aspect of the degradations senators had to suffer under the emperors is illustrated in a passage of Seneca's *de Beneficiis*. Here Caligula forces a well-respected older senator to kiss his slippers in front of the other senators (2.12.2):

Homo natus in hoc, ut mores liberae civitatis Persica servitute mutaret,
parum iudicavit, si senator, senex, summis usus honoribus in conspectu prin-
cipum supplex sibi eo more iacuisset, quo hostes victi hostibus iacuere; invenit aliquid infra genua, quo libertatem detruderet! Non hoc est rem pub-
licam calcare?

This man, born to change the ways of a free state into Persian slavery, considered it to be of little importance if a senator, an old man, one who had held
the highest offices, threw himself down as a suppliant in sight of the leading
senators, in the same manner in which conquered enemies throw themselves
at the feet of their foes; he discovered a way in which he could push freedom down lower than the knees! Is this not to trample on the republic?

It is not enough to make him kneel, this senator has to kneel in full view
of the other senators. He needs to be *seen* prostrating himself, making
the act all the more shameful. The effect on the senator's status is demonstrated by Seneca's analogy to conquered enemies who must prostrate
themselves. It is also evident that Seneca views this act against an individual as indicative of the general humiliation of the senatorial order.

With this in mind, I would like to examine how the representation
of female characters in *Troades* functions as a site for exploring the social aspects of the gaze and of violent spectacle in the Neronian period.
A change in the social order, or reversal of fortune, is one of the major
themes of *Troades*. If we use the messenger's report of the crowd's reactions to Polyxena's death as a paradigm for the dynamics of the gaze in
a larger sense, we can see how women function in the play as a whole. As
I discussed above, the reactions of the crowd at Polyxena's sacrifice oscillate between sadistic voyeurism and masochistic identification with her
situation and with her vulnerability to fate. In light of our examination
of the social situation in Rome, it can be seen that the intratextual audience of *Troades* reflects a contemporary elite Roman audience that was
predisposed to participate in spectacles of violence, disempowerment,
and survival. I believe it was precisely the opportunity to focus on women
as survivors in an occupied, fallen city that appealed to Seneca. The
women of Troy had lived to see the sack of their homeland and to experience the social discord that followed. Therefore they were chosen as
characters through which the audience could experience the anxieties
brought on by the endurance of violence and the reversal of fortune.

As we saw, the play opens with Hecuba directing the gaze to herself.
She states (4–6):

> non umquam tulit
> documenta fors maiora, quam fragili loco
> starent superbi.
>
> Never did chance give greater proof
> as to how fragile the ground is
> that the proud stand on.

Seneca's departure from Euripides is worth noting.[52] Unlike the ghosts and gods who open Euripides' *Hekabe* and *Trojan Women*, someone living begins Seneca's play, someone who has watched the horror of the reversal of fortune and still has to live through it. It is significant that Hecuba constructs the audience as those who trust in sovereignty and prosperity (1–4). In her, they will see an *exemplum*, a person like themselves who has fallen. On one level, we can see that the audience is constructed as those who are at the top of the social hierarchy, those who put their faith in sovereignty. For them, this play can be read as a cautionary tale.[53]

On another level, the play could also speak to those who might be suffering a change in fortune and can look to the female characters as *exempla* of how to endure such a fate. The women's fall in status from elite to slaves is noted as the lots are being chosen for them (57–62) and as they hear the outcome (974–90). Hecuba emphasizes the upheaval in social rank involved (981–82):

> Quis tam impotens ac durus et iniquae ferus
> sortitor urnae regibus reges dedit?
>
> What reckless, hard, and cruel arbiter
> of the unfair urn has given royalty to kings?

The women's fall in status is emphasized again as Hecuba contrasts her fate with Priam's (145–47):

> liber manes
> vadit ad imos, nec feret umquam
> victa Graium cervice iugum.
>
> Free, he wanders to the shades below,
> nor will he ever bear a Greek yoke
> on a conquered neck.

Throughout the play, it is clear that the fates of the survivors are worse than those of the dead, precisely because the living have to watch the final destruction of the city and experience the horrors of captivity. After the ritual mourning of Priam and Hector, Hecuba states that Priam's death should not be pitied. While she had to stand by and watch his death, he gladly accepted the sword ("quod penitus actum cum recepisset libens," 49).[54] He is happy precisely because he does not have to look upon his captors or be put on display as a war prize (148–56):

> non ille duos videt Atridas
> nec fallacem cernit Ulixem:
> non Argolici praeda triumphi
> subiecta feret colla tropaeis;
> non adsuetas ad sceptra manus
> post terga dabit currusque sequens
> Agamemnonios aurea dextra
> vincula gestans latis fiet
> pompa Mycenis.

> He does not look on the Atridae, nor see deceitful Ulysses.
> He will not, as spoils of Greek triumph, bear trophies on bowed neck,
> hands, accustomed to the scepter, will not be bound behind him,
> nor following Agamemnon's chariot, hands in gold fetters,
> will he become a parade in vast Mycenae.

Hecuba contrasts her position both as spectacle and as spectator with Priam's escape from this fate in death.[55] Although the mention of a triumphal parade is clearly an anachronism, it does draw attention to Roman thought and cultural practice.[56] The idea that death is a better fate than being displayed as part of a triumphal procession can also be seen in the representation of Cleopatra's death in Cassius Dio (51.13.1–2):

> καὶ ἐν ἐπιμελείᾳ αὐτὴν ἐποιεῖτο, ὅπως οἱ τὰ ἐπινίκια ἐπιλαμπρύνῃ. τοῦτό τε οὖν ὑποτοπήσασα, καὶ μυρίων θανάτων χαλεπώτερον αὐτὸ νομίσασα εἶναι, ὄντως τε ἀποθανεῖν ἐπεθύμησε, καὶ πολλὰ μὲν τοῦ Καίσαρος, ὅπως τρόπον τινὰ ἀπόληται, ἐδεῖτο, πολλὰ δὲ καὶ αὐτὴ ἐμηχανᾶτο.

> And he treated her with special care, so she might make a brilliant spectacle at a triumph for him. But, having suspected this and considering this to be worse than a myriad of deaths, she truly longed to die, and not only begged Caesar many times that she might perish by one means or another, but also devised many plans herself.

However, as Hecuba emphasizes, neither subject nor object position is desirable. Being a spectator can also be a painful experience. Dio's depiction of the crowd's reaction to Arsinoë, Cleopatra's younger sister, as she is displayed as a captive in Caesar's celebration of triumph over Ptolemy is of particular interest.[57] According to Dio, the sight of Arsinoë aroused such pity among the Roman spectators that it prompted them to consider their own misfortunes: καὶ ἡ Ἀρσινόη γυνή τε οὖσα καὶ βασιλίς ποτε νομισθεῖσα ἔν τε δεσμοῖς, ὃ μηπώποτε ἔν γε τῇ Ῥώμῃ ἐγεγόνει, ὀφθεῖσα πάμπολυν οἶκτον ἐνέβαλε, κἀκ τούτου ἐπὶ τῇ προφάσει ταύτῃ καὶ τὰ οἰκεῖα πάθη παρωδύραντο, "And Arsinoë, a woman and at one time considered queen, having been seen in chains, something that never had happened in Rome, aroused much pity and, with this as an excuse, they lamented their own misfortunes" (43.19.3–4). This is just the sort of masochistic gaze the Trojan women may have provoked in Seneca's audience. Although watching another's misfortunes might prompt feelings of power and superiority, it could also remind the viewer of his own precarious position in society. Thus the power dynamics of the gaze go beyond a simple subject versus object dichotomy and are dependent on the social position of the viewer.

I have argued that the senatorial class saw the Neronian period as a time in which their status and safety were diminished. These adverse conditions were reflected in a renegotiation of the elite's position in the visual economy of Rome, which was in turn mirrored in Seneca's criticisms of violent spectacle. So too, *Troades* textualizes historical concerns about class and violence. The play focuses on violence suffered in conjunction with a decrease in social status and a loss of authority. While the reversal of fortune is a common theme for tragedy in general (Aristotle *Poetics* 1450a), nevertheless this Senecan play may have had an even stronger resonance for the Roman elite of the time, who could see in the fate of the Trojan women a change in status and a disempowerment that was akin to their own potential experience of imperial violence and humiliation.[58]

In his focus on women as the surviving victims of war, Seneca was able to examine how such victims endure the violence they are forced to suffer, the difficult choices those who survive have to make, and the horrors of those who have to stand by and watch powerlessly.[59] However, while the Trojan women's loss of status and physical security may have resonated with the anxieties of the male senatorial class,[60] the plight of the female characters in *Troades* also reflected a distinctly female position. This allowed male viewers simultaneously to identify with them and to distance themselves from such identification, suggesting that the visual pleasure that the senatorial male may have experienced from viewing this play was derived from both sadistic and masochistic aspects of the gaze.

Notes

I am most grateful to Dave Fredrick for his wealth of insightful comments and for the opportunity to contribute to this volume. I would also like to thank the audience at the University of Texas at Austin, where some of the central ideas of this chapter were presented at a conference on performance in November 1995. Finally, I am indebted to Vincent Farenga, Trevor Fear, Martha Malamud, and Amy Richlin for their critical readings and for many helpful suggestions as this essay evolved. I owe special thanks to Amy for rekindling my interest in horror film and sparking my fascination with Seneca.

1. Fantham 1982.205 and Boyle 1997.91 comment on the fate of Troy as a common paradigm for the fall from power in Roman culture. Rabinowitz 1998.59 and Gregory 1991.86 note that this part of the Trojan myth provided Euripides an opportunity to address the transition from freedom to slavery and the disparity of power in the Greek world. For a discussion of Hecuba as the paradigmatic victim of the reversal of fortune in later antiquity and the Renaissance, see Mossman 1995.210–43.

2. The question of performance has been a perennial problem for discussions of Senecan drama. While we may not be able to come to a consensus on the specifics of presentation, we should consider these plays within the context of the Roman visual culture in which they were written. In fact understanding this visual economy is essential for contextualizing the politics of the gaze in Senecan tragedy. For arguments supporting the proposition that Seneca's plays were composed for the theater, see Bieber 1939.397, B. Walker 1969, Ahl 1986.18–27, D. F. Sutton 1986, Rosenmeyer 1993, and Boyle 1997.9–12. See most recently Harrison 2000, which appeared while this collection was at press. Arguments for recitation and/or reading include Zwierlein 1966, Beare 1955.224–26, and Fantham 1982.34–49. I agree with Ahl 1986.26 and Boyle 1997.11 that the evidence for recitation does not discount the possibility that the plays could also have been performed in their entirety on stage.

3. For a brief overview of film theory, see L. Williams 1995.1–5. Classicists have recently begun to see how film theory may be useful for exploring the politics of representation in ancient culture. On the use of film theory in analyses of classical drama, see Marsh 1992, Zweig 1992, Rabinowitz 1992 and 1993b. 159–62, and Robin 1993. Robin uses film theory to compare the female voice in Seneca's plays to that of mainstream cinema, arguing that it is "the site of hysteria and paranoia" (1993.107). She also compares the male voiceover in Hollywood film to Seneca's choruses of men as "the bearers of reason and clarity" (1993.117) who interpret the hysteria of female characters. On the use of film theory for

analyses of other aspects of Greek and Roman visual culture, see Elsom 1992, Richlin 1992b, Segal 1994, Fitzgerald 1995.140–68, Fredrick 1995 and 1997, Morales 1996, S. Brown 1997, Koloski-Ostrow 1997, Petersen 1997, Stewart 1997.13–14, and Greene 1998.67–92.

    4. See Oudart 1977–78 and Baudry 1974–75. Much of this came from the perception of similarities between the apparatus of the camera and Lacan's discussions at 1978.67–119 of a preexisting, reifying gaze through which subjectivity is defined. For an overview of apparatus theory, see Doane 1991.79–90 and Jay 1993.435–91.

    5. Mulvey 1975.11–18 discusses two ways that mainstream narrative cinema orchestrates a male gaze directed at representations of women, both organized around alleviating anxiety about castration or the potential loss of power and status. Through fetishistic scopophilia, the male viewer gains visual pleasure by fetishizing the female body, disavowing castration, and avoiding his own susceptibility to it. Through sadistic voyeurism, on the other hand, the male viewer's pleasure lies in ascertaining female guilt or lack and asserting control by punishing or forgiving her. Mulvey sees sadistic voyeurism, in particular, as the impetus for the narrative drive in mainstream cinema. See Fredrick 1995 for a lucid summary of Mulvey's two gazes, the contradictions between them, and illustrations from Roman wall painting.

    6. In addition to those mentioned here, see Silverman 1980 and Studlar 1988.

    7. Similarly, Clover 1992.8 notes that characters at variance with each other display a spectrum of potential identifications that appeal to different aspects of the viewer's psyche.

    8. Clover 1992.224 also suggests that feminine masochism explains why male viewers empathize with some female characters in horror film.

    9. Much recent film theory, in fact, questions the notion of a fixed or singular identity. Several feminist film theorists, such as Gledhill 1994, Mayne 1995, and Kaplan 1997, also discuss how spectatorship is determined by both the individual and the cultural history of the viewer as well as the spectatorial relationships constructed by the camera. Gledhill 1994.121, for example, states that "subjects move in and out of different identities constructed by ethnicity, class, gender, sexual orientation and so on. Similarly, cultural products offer a range of often conflicting positions for identification." This departure from apparatus theory, which focused on a viewer's interpellation into an identification with the presumably unifying gaze of the camera, makes recent film theory even more adaptable to other genres of representation. Like film viewers, the dynamics of the gaze for theater spectators is influenced by their cultural and individual identities as well as the space of the theater itself.

    10. Here there are parallels between Clover's analysis of the eye as both a locus of power and a site of vulnerability in horror film and Barton's discussion (1993.91–95) of the same paradoxical nature of the eye as it is perceived in Roman

culture. Morales 1996.200–06 also discusses the dual nature of spectatorship in her analysis of the effect of painted images of violence and pain on Roman viewers. Using Clover's "reactive" and "assaultive" gazes, Morales shows how the viewers of Parrhasius's art are depicted as both victims and consumers of his images.

11. This can be seen in some of the earliest analyses of tragedy. Aristotle, for instance, states that pity and fear are the emotions essential to tragedy. He argues that while pity is aroused by undeserved misfortune, fear is evoked by the sufferings of someone just like ourselves (περὶ τὸν ὅμοιον, *Poetics* 1453a). Commenting on this passage, Butcher 1951.259 n. 1 states: "The fact that fear is inspired by the sufferings of ὁ ὅμοιος indicates that even tragic fear is in the last analysis traced back psychologically to a self-regarding instinct. The awakening of fear as distinct from mere pity depends on the close identification of the hero and ourselves." Another interesting parallel between horror and tragedy is the ritualistic and formulaic nature of each genre. Audiences of both genres know more or less what will happen even before the performance starts. Clover 1992.11, speaking of horror, states: "This is a field in which there is in some sense no original, no real or right text, only variants; a world in which, therefore, the meaning of the individual example lies outside itself."

12. Similarly, the first lines of the chorus emphasize the Trojan Women's long endurance of suffering (67–69):

Non rude vulgus lacrimisque novum
lugere iubes: hoc continuis
egimus annis.

No inexperienced crowd, new to tears, / do you bid to mourn; we have done this / for unceasing years.

Unless otherwise indicated, all translations are my own.

13. Later in the play (409–25), Andromache also emphasizes the horrors she has lived through. She, too, stresses the position of women as viewers of violence as she expresses her fear that she will have to watch the horrible slaughter of her son if she is unable to protect him from Ulysses (651–53):

poteris nefandae deditum mater neci
videre? poteris celsa per fastigia
missum rotari?

Will you, his mother, be able to see him given / over to an unspeakable murder? Will you be able to watch him / sent spinning over the high fortifications?

14. On the eye of horror, see Clover 1992.166–230. She states that "horror privileges eyes because, more crucially than any other kind of cinema, it is about eyes. More particularly, it is about eyes watching horror" (1992.167). She suggests that the emphasis on the introjective gaze can be seen in the proliferation

of images on video boxes that often show a woman's frightened eyes or eyeballs that have been pierced or gouged out.

15. Seneca frequently presents this sort of internal agonizing for the audience's gaze; see, for example, *Medea* 893–977, *Phaedra* 99–128, 177–94, *Agamemnon* 131–44, 192–202, and *Thyestes* 267–86 and 920–69. Tarrant 1985.23 states: "The opportunity to portray human beings under extreme emotional pressure may in fact have been tragedy's strongest attraction for Seneca." Boyle 1997.24–31 discusses the use of asides as an indication that a greater degree of "psychological interiority" is present in Senecan drama than in Attic tragedy. For a discussion of the Roman interest in the moment of internal conflict as a theme for wall painting, see Bergmann 1996.

16. For a discussion of lines 1124–25 and their punctuation, see Fantham 1982.377–78. On the metatheatrical elements in this play, see Boyle 1997.118–22. Ahl 1986.22–23 also notes a parallel between the intra- and extratextual audiences in this scene.

17. Similarly, in an earlier scene, Seneca presents both the sadistic gaze of Ulysses as he tries to provoke Andromache into revealing the hiding place of her son and the more sympathetic gaze of Ulysses' men who are rebuked for being moved by a woman's tears (678–80):

> Cessatis et vos flebilis clamor movet
> furorque cassus feminae? iussa ocius
> peragite.

> Do you do nothing, and does the tearful shout / and useless rage of a woman move you? Carry out your orders / quickly.

Unlike Ulysses, the soldiers are moved by watching Andromache's sufferings and need to be scolded into action. Again we see that the dynamics of the gaze are determined by the nature of the spectator as well as the spectacle.

18. For a discussion of the similarly fetishistic and sadistic nature of the gaze directed at Polyxena in Euripides' *Hekabe*, see Rabinowitz 1993b.59–62.

19. Mulvey 1975.14 and 18 argues that fetishistic scopophilia seems to stop the action and focus solely on the look.

20. This metaphor of the insatiable, devouring eye can also be seen in St. Augustine's reference to a spectator at the games (*Confessions* 6.8). On the concept of a *torvus oculus*, see Barton 1993.90. Morales 1996.206 also cites Seneca's mullet passage as an example of the aggressive, consuming gaze.

21. For an interesting discussion of the equation of women and food and the analogous ways both are consumed at dinner parties in the *Deipnosophistae* of Athenaeus, see Henry 1992.

22. The reaction of Ulysses' soldiers to Andromache at 678–80 also indicates that there is a possibility for men to be moved by viewing the sufferings of a woman (or female character); see n. 17 above.

23. Segal 1993.71 notes: "The female character in fifth-century tragedy often

serves as the field in which the male audience can act out its own emotions of grief, fear, anxiety about the body, or emotional control." The same can be said for the Trojan women in Seneca's play. Such identifications with female figures have also been linked to the social and political alienation of elite males during the transition from republic to empire: see Wyke 1989 and Skinner 1993.

24. For a discussion of the oscillation between masculine and feminine subject positions in Ovid's audiences, see Richlin 1992c.173–78.

25. On the balance between masculine and feminine ideals in Euripides' description of Polyxena, see Mossman 1995.161. The androgynous nature of female characters in Greek tragedy, and the feminine nature of tragic experience in general, is discussed at length by Zeitlin 1985.

26. For a discussion of the arena as a locus for the demonstration of the power to overcome death, see Wiedemann 1992.34–38. On gladiators' *amor mortis* as a paradigm for the senatorial class, see Barton 1993.15–25 and 31–36. For this paradigm in the works of Seneca, see *Epistles* 30.8, 37.1–2, 70.19–27, 80.3, *de Tranquillitate Animi* 11.4–6, *de Constantia Sapientis* 16.2–3, and *de Providentia* 2.8–9.

27. This is clearly indicated by the comparisons between the sacrifice and a wedding at 195–96, 287–90, 361–65, 861–902, and 938–48.

28. On the Romans' fascination with violence, see Hopkins 1983, Coleman 1990, S. Brown 1992, Wiedemann 1992.83–90, Barton 1993, Bartsch 1994.50–60, Gunderson 1996, and Morales 1996.

29. This is particularly true of his tragedies, where violence is not only part of the genre but a reflection of, as well as upon, the visual culture of imperial Rome. In addition to *Troades*, see esp. *Medea* 992–94, 1001 and *Thyestes* 893–95 and 901–07. For discussions of violence in Senecan tragedy, see, for example, Segal 1984, Ahl 1986.22–26, D. F. Sutton 1986.21–25 and 63–67, Robin 1993.106–07, and Boyle 1997.133–37.

30. In addition to the passages discussed here, also see *Epistles* 7.3–5, 95.33 and *de Ira* 2.5, 3.18.3–4. In *Epistle* 69.3–4, Seneca states that the eye is particularly vulnerable to desire and pleasure.

31. This is also noted by Edwards 1997.83; see the list of passages in her note 69.

32. See Tertullian *de Spectaculis* 17 on men being defiled by what is seen through their eyes. For a discussion of the concern about the effect of violent spectacles in Christian writers, see Wiedemann 1992.146–50.

33. Seneca criticizes the use of violent spectacle to stage power throughout his philosophical writings. This is often connected to tyranny; see, for example, *de Brevitate Vitae* 13.6–7 regarding Pompey and *de Ira* 2.5.5 regarding Volesus. The most extreme example of the delight in novel forms of violence was the execution of condemned criminals during dramatic performances. Coleman 1990 indicates that these "fatal charades" occurred primarily during the reigns of Nero and Titus; also see Wiedemann 1992.83–90, Barton 1993.60–65, and Bartsch

1994.50–60. Additionally, Wiedemann 1992.76–77 notes that the state's right to import and execute condemned criminals from the provinces coincided with the development of lavish spectacles during the imperial period.

34. See Hillard 1992.43 and Edwards 1993.150–53.

35. See Talbert 1984.163–74 for a discussion of the diminishing role of the senate during the imperial period.

36. In 57, the year he built the wooden amphitheater, Nero banned gladiatorial contests and all *ludi* in the provinces. One explanation for this is that he did not want any challenge to his popularity as the provider of games. On how putting on games could boost one's status and political career, see Wiedemann 1992.5–7, 13–17 and S. Brown 1992. On the restrictions emperors placed on *editores*, see Wiedemann 1992.8, 43. For an interesting discussion of how the visual politics of the games were reproduced in the mosaics of wealthy homes, see S. Brown 1992.

37. On seating arrangements in the arena, see Suetonius *Augustus* 44, Calpernius Siculus *Eclogue* 7.26–29, Tacitus *Annales* 15.32, Hopkins 1983.17–19, E. Rawson 1987, Zanker 1988.149–51, Wiedemann 1992.20, 26, and 131, and Edwards 1993.111–13. On dress codes, see Suetonius *Augustus* 44 and Wiedemann 1992.131 and 176.

38. Zanker 1988.149–53 also mentions the creation of more rigid class distinctions under Augustus and discusses of the role of the theater in contributing to the consolidation of social order: "Even the architecture of the theater helped to inculcate and make visible the principles of social stratification . . . The network of arched passageways and staircases served not only to insure an easy flow of traffic in and out of the theater, but to separate the audience according to rank. Thus the 'better' sort needed to have no contact at all with the common folk, whose seats were at the very top" (151).

39. Suetonius *Augustus* 43. Barton 1993.25–31, Gunderson 1996, and Edwards 1997.89 argue that there was an elite interest in participation despite these bans. They note that this voluntary debasement was one way of challenging the authority of the emperor. Yet such behavior is represented as an aberration and an illegitimate means of self-promotion that confused the normative social barrier between spectators and performers.

40. On the status of gladiators, see Wiedemann 1992.102–24 and Barton 1993.11–15.

41. Wiedemann's comment on the ideology behind the elliptical shape of the amphitheaters is key: "A circular building implies the equality of all spectators (at least all those seated in each row); an ellipse makes most of the spectators face two specific points on the circumference, thus enabling attention to be drawn to the box of the presiding magistrate" (1992.20). On the importance of being the subject as well as the object of the gaze, see Seneca *Epistle* 94.69–71, Ovid *Ars Amatoria* 1.87–99, and Tertullian *de Spectaculis* 25: "Nemo denique in spectaculo ineundo prius cogitat nisi videri et videre."

42. For further discussion of the freedom from corporal punishment and of impenetrability as a marker of Roman elite masculinity, see Walters 1997.

43. For a discussion of the effect of this on the representation of sexual violence in Roman elegy, see Fredrick 1997.189–90.

44. As scholars such as Rubiés 1994.35–40 have pointed out, the accounts of Nero are filtered down to us through the biased lenses of senatorial writers. While the elite clearly had its own agenda in constructing representations of the emperor, this negative portrayal can itself be viewed as a sign of a strained relationship between Nero and the senatorial class.

45. *Nero* 11–12. See also *Annales* 14.14–15 and Juvenal 8.185–210 on the disgrace of senators performing on the stage and in the arena.

46. Edwards 1994.87–88 notes that, by appearing on stage, the emperor aligned himself with the most degraded members of the community. While this demonstrated his power to turn the social order upside down, Edwards indicates that it also set him up as an obvious negative paradigm of imperial behavior.

47. Thus Nero gave a specifically theatrical expression to the practice of surveillance already present in Tiberius's rule. While Tiberius rarely showed an interest in attending the theater (Suetonius *Tiberius* 47), sending *delatores* instead to various functions to keep an eye on the senators, Nero uses his very public position in the theater to scrutinize them himself. On the presence of *delatores*, see Tacitus *Annales* 6.7, Seneca *de Beneficiis* 3.26–27, Macrobius *Saturnalia* 7.3.2–3, and Pliny's *Epistles* 1.15.4.

48. Bartsch 1994.6–7 notes that recorded violations and punishments are few, suggesting that historians amplified or exaggerated the dangers of poor audience performance. However, as she later notes (1994.30), the senators' privileged seating positions close to the stage only put them within easy eyesight of the emperor once he took the stage. This emphasis on their proximity to the emperor's gaze, along with the prevalence of this trope, indicates that a blur between spectator and spectacle did produce anxiety among the members of the senatorial class. Another way to read the lack of recorded violations is that this group did a good job of playing the part of enthusiastic audience members.

49. On the controlling gaze of emperors, see also Tacitus *Agricola* 45.2 and Epictetus 4.1.145.

50. See *Annales* 14.12, 16.21–22, and 16.27 regarding Nero's anger at senators who missed meetings. On attendance at senate meetings, see Talbert 1984.134–52. Even when the emperor was not physically present at the senate, an attendance record was kept so he would know who was absent (Talbert 1984.284).

51. It is significant that Tacitus (*Annales* 14.52–56) places Seneca's demise within the context of Rome's visual economy, stating that Nero's advisors criticized the conspicuous nature of Seneca's wealth and power. Tacitus also suggests that it was Seneca's awareness that his highly visible position had bred envy among his detractors that prompted his attempt to return some of his estates to

the emperor and to retire from the public eye. This gesture, however, came too late, and Seneca was ultimately forced to commit suicide.

52. For comparisons of *Troades* with Euripides' plays, see Calder 1970, M. Wilson 1983.28–29, and Boyle 1997.89–90.

53. In his debate with Pyrrhus over the sacrifice of Polyxena, Agamemnon himself points out the precariousness of power, particularly when one enforces it by violent means (258–66).

54. Fantham 1982.216 notes that this is the verb used of a gladiator's acceptance of the deathblow.

55. On Hecuba as a potential spectacle, see the chorus's remark at 858–60:

> Quod manet fatum dominusque quis te,
> aut quibus terris, Hecuba, videndam
> ducet?

> What fate and master awaits you, / what lands will he lead you to, Hecuba, / as an object to be displayed?

On death as a better fate than that the surviving women face, see 142–64, 576–77, 969–71, and 1168–77.

56. On the nature of Roman triumphs, see Nicolet 1980.352–56.

57. For a comparison of Octavian's triple triumph to the triumphs of Julius Caesar, see Gurval 1995.19–36.

58. While the line between representation and reality is always problematic, nevertheless it is reasonable to assume that there is some connection between cultural products and their historical contexts.

59. Again Seneca's departure from Euripides' *Hekabe* is significant in that he chooses not to stage Hecuba's vengeance against Polymestor. By omitting any reference to this, Seneca focuses solely on Hecuba as a victim.

60. In *de Beneficiis*, Seneca uses the image of a recently conquered city as indicative of the atmosphere prevalent in his lifetime: "Si tibi vitae nostrae vera imago succurret, videre videberis tibi captae cum maxime civitatis faciem, in qua omisso pudoris rectique respectu vires in concilio sunt velut signo ad permiscenda omnia dato" ("If a true image of our life should appear before you, you would think you were seeing the appearance of a city just now captured, in which consideration for modesty and right had been lost and force is in power, as though the signal had been given for total chaos," 7.27.1).

2

This Ship of Fools

Epic Vision in Lucan's Vulteius Episode

Katherine Owen Eldred

Lucan's scene of supreme sacrifice is the Vulteius episode in Book 4 (402–581). Deceived by a trick and trapped on all sides, the Caesarian Vulteius and his cohort of men choose mutual slaughter rather than surrender to the Pompeians.[1] Vulteius's call to action (478–85) at first reads like a Stoic how-to manual as he dwells on the honor of cutting short their lives and concludes, "non cogitur ullus velle mori," "No man is forced to want to die" (484–85).

Certainly some scholars view this scene as Lucan's illustration of a life well-left; the motives behind Vulteius's actions are worthy of praise in the mind of the poet.[2] At the same time, however, there is recognition that the episode is somehow perverse; not least among the signposts pointing to perversity are Vulteius's own words: *furor est*, "this is madness" (517). Charles Saylor (1990.291 and notes 1–4) explores the twisted nature of Vulteius's *pietas*, his misdirected *virtus*, the spectacle-like quality of the episode, and the parody of the wise man created in Vulteius by his stance toward death. Other interpretations focus largely on the *pietas* of the troop leader, whether misguided or not, and the connection, fatal to Vulteius, between *furor* and *virtus*.[3]

In spite of Lucan's ostensible praise of Vulteius's actions in the epilogue (573–81),[4] this episode leaves us unsettled—not only because it is a vivid illustration of mutual butchery but also because, though Vulteius seems to be conducting his suicide according to the terms of certain philosophical tenets, he and his men recreate, in effect, civil war (558–73):

> pariter sternuntque caduntque
> vulnere letali, nec quemquam dextra fefellit

cum feriat moriente manu. nec volnus adactis
debetur gladiis: percussum est pectore ferrum
et iuguli pressere manum. cum sorte cruenta
fratribus incurrunt fratres natusque parenti,
haud trepidante tamen toto cum pondere dextra
exegere enses. pietas ferientibus una
non repetisse fuit. iam latis viscera lapsa
semianimes traxere foris multumque cruorem
infudere mari. despectam cernere lucem
victoresque suos voltu spectare superbo
et mortem sentire iuvat. iam strage cruenta
conspicitur cumulata ratis, bustisque remittunt
corpora victores, ducibus mirantibus ulli
esse ducem tanti.

Equally they kill and die with deadly wound, and never did right hand fail,
though right hand struck as it died. Nor is wound owed to sword driven deep,
but weapon was struck by breast, and throats attacked hand.
When, by bloody chance, brothers run upon brothers and son upon father,
with hand scarcely trembling, with their entire weight,
they thrust home their swords. Filial devotion for those who strike was not
     to strike
a second time. Now half-dead, they drag their insides falling out to the wide
     gangways
and pour out much blood into the sea. To see the despised light,
to watch their own conquerors with proud eyes, to feel death, pleases them.
Now the raft, piled high with bloody slaughter, stands visible,
and the victors send the corpses to the funeral pyres for burning,
and the leaders wonder that a leader can be worth so much to anyone.[5]

Vulteius appears to urge suicide, but his men kill each other, not
themselves, and so reenact the very civil war they have been fighting with
the Pompeians. It is difficult to reconcile Vulteius's call to *furor* with a
well-reasoned escape from a life too onerous; even more difficult, perhaps, to look positively on Vulteius's civil-war-in-miniature in this poem
filled with anger and despair at the civil wars in which Rome found herself. At the episode's end, we may be forgiven for regarding the Opitergians with some bemusement, even as do the Pompeians.

Indeed this bemusement invites us to wonder *why* Vulteius and his
men rush willingly into death. Such an inquiry seeks to understand the
ideology underlying Vulteius's actions—that Althusserian notion of a set

of imaginary ideals by which an individual constructs his relation to the lived world. What it is about Vulteius's ideals with reference to Caesar and the civil war that convinces him it is better to die than be captured by the Pompeians?[6] In other words, how does Vulteius—or any other character in Lucan's poem—understand the ideological and political framework in which he operates? In what ways are those understandings expressed?

I will argue that an exploration of these questions points toward spectacle as the primary ideal Vulteius uses to construct his relation to the Caesarian world for which he fights. Vulteius's loquacious rationale for self-slaughter begins in the high Stoic vein of defending *libertas* and the equally high epic vein of obtaining *kleos aphthiton*, an undying glory, but descends to a *furor* for death driven by devotion to Caesar and the desire to create a spectacle. The episode, too, tempts the reader toward an ideological reading based on traditional philosophical and epic values, but, in the course of the slaughter, denies those traditional values and substitutes an ideology based instead on spectacle. Thus an inquiry into spectacle, visual pleasure and displeasure, is central to understanding Vulteius's own motivations and the motivations of Lucan's readers, captivated by the sight of the mutual slaughter unfolding before their eyes.

I propose therefore to explore the visual nature of the Vulteius episode, making use of film-theoretical approaches that foreground the element of spectacle in the construction of ideology. Film theory addresses relationships between power and society as expressed in acts of looking and being seen. Key to uncovering these relationships are those issues of visual pleasure and displeasure, identification and lack of identification, experienced by the viewer in the process of reading this poem: again and again we "view" scenes of ruin and destruction carried out before our reading eyes, like Caesar viewing the carnage of the battlefield after Pharsalus (7.786–99). The treatment of visual pleasure in the Vulteius episode, I will argue, demonstrates a pattern of spectacle in the poem, a pattern that tempts the reader to identify with Caesar and share his interest in gruesome sacrifice, but, at the same time, condemns the dictatorial viewpoint and denies the reader any stable identification with any character in the poem.

This process of visual pleasure and shifting identifications depends in part on Lucan's denial of an ideology based on the traditional epic values of *kleos* and sacrifice for the state. The mass suicide of Vulteius and his Opitergian troops illustrates a new social contract elucidated by Lucan's epic: the sacrifice of the many for the one and the corresponding loss of identity and individuality entailed in that excess. Because this new social contract removes the possibility of epic redemption based on traditional ideas of *kleos* and selfless sacrifice for the state, it leaves behind a social identity based only on spectacle.

Lucan's poem denies political closure to his readers by means of its visual strategies. The poet's exploration of Vergil and the traditional metaphors concerning the ship of state further refuses any kind of ideological closure to the Vulteius episode: the reader searches hard for an ideological reason for this slaughter. This sort of ideological refusal, I suggest, is characteristic of the poem as a whole. The major episodes in the epic—the embedded civil war narrative at 2.68–233, Massilia, Scaeva, Erichtho, among others—are presented in strongly visual, spectacular terms and participate in the same visual processes as the Vulteius episode; correspondingly, these episodes lead to the same kind of ideological stalemate. This refusal of closure must affect the reader's identification with any character or position in the epic. In this way, Lucan compels the reader to question her own ideologies when she takes interest or pleasure in contemplating the episode. Vision matters in the *Pharsalia*, and vision is all we have left once the poet denies other avenues of meaning.

The Sight of Caesar

At the heart of this episode lies an explicit concern with sight, vision, the ability to see, and the demand to be seen. Charles Saylor points to the centrality of daylight to Vulteius's project, "a visibility which is argued for, pursued and achieved" (1990.295). The importance of visibility as a structural element of Vulteius's suicide is reflected above all in his name, Vulteius, from *vultus*—he is the "Face-Man."[7] The centurion's deliberate use of spectacular terms indicates the extent to which he relies upon seeing and being seen to promote his own vision of heroic death, and we should note those terms carefully.

The poet's emphasis on the centrality of vision and spectacle to Vulteius's project begins in the setting of the scene itself. The rafts set sail just when light begins to fade into darkness, "quo tempore primas / impedit ad noctem iam lux extrema tenebras" (4.446–47). This half-light proves dark enough to cloak a Pompeian snare, chains hung under the water to catch the sailing rafts, but light enough to allow a battle to be fought—not a long battle (*non longa quidem*), says the poet, because nightfall soon shadows the wavering light (*lucem dubiam*) and brings peace (*pacemque habuere tenebrae*, 472–73). By writing of light and darkness, the empty surface of the sea (*passusque vacare / summa freti*, 449–50), and the chains woven to hang in the middle of the sea, Lucan already makes a point about seeing and obscurity: precisely what the Caesarians *cannot* see, because of the half-light and the smooth surface of the sea, will be their downfall.[8]

In contrast to the underwater Pompeian trick, Vulteius wishes no such obscurity in his actions. Above all, the *dux ratis* seems obsessed with the idea that his death and that of his men will be seen by the surrounding troops. Vulteius urges his men to commit suicide because it will be witnessed by friends and enemies, land and sea (492–95, my emphasis):

> nos in *conspicua* sociis hostique *carina*
> constituere dei; *praebebunt aequora testes,*
> *praebebunt terrae*, summis dabit insula saxis,
> *spectabunt geminae* diverso litore *partes*.

> In plain sight of enemies and friends alike, the gods have placed us
> on this vessel, earth and sea equally bear witness,
> the island will give witnesses from her highest cliffs,
> the twin armies will watch from each shore.

Their vessel is visible; they have witnesses in the sea, the earth, and on the surrounding cliffs; both sides will see their victory. In the words of Werner Rutz: "As Scaeva's highest wish is to die with Caesar as a witness, or at least Pompey, so for Vulteius the fact that both sides can see the fate of his troops is an additional impulse toward death" (1960.466).[9] Vulteius's men will not fall in the blind (or unseeing) cloud of battle,[10] *in caeca bellorum nube* (488), nor be covered by weapons mingled with darkness, "cum permixtas acies sua tela tenebris / involvent" (489–90). This emphasis on the visual continues as the slaughter proceeds. The men have watched the stars in heaven, "sidera caeli / . . . oculis . . . omnes / aspicerent" (521–23) and, when the sun rises, stand waiting for death, *damnata iam luce* ("condemned by the light," 534). When all are dead, the raft is conspicuously loaded with slaughter, "iam strage cruenta / conspicitur cumulata ratis" (570–71).

Thus Vulteius constructs his own death as something to be seen and noted, and claims such a death is more desirable than death in *caeca bella*. Vulteius even addresses Caesar, who is not present, as if he and his men took their lives under the watchful eye of their general: *namque . . . pro te . . . Caesar* (500). For Vulteius, death has become a performance, and spectators are a necessary part of that performance. If death is not seen distinctly, then *virtus* is lost, *perit obruta virtus* (491).[11]

Scholars argue that this emphasis on visibility lends the trappings of a gladiatorial spectacle to Vulteius's actions, some going so far as to suggest that the mass suicide is to be perceived as a *naumachia* (Ahl 1976.118–21, Leigh 1997.259–64). Unquestionably, this episode is "spectacular": modeled upon combat and death in theaters and in the arena. The deliberate construction of death as something to be witnessed and judged by onlookers, and the evocation of Caesar as the one in front of whom and for the sake of whom death occurs, marks it as such. But arguments that only examine the similarities between the Vulteius "spectacle" and the games leave the reader with little to conclude about the nature of her own "looking at" the spectacles in Lucan's poem. Arguments such as Matthew Leigh's, who writes that Vulteius's suicide is largely "the expression of a theatrical aesthetic, the fear of wasting a truly dramatic, magnificently staged ending" (1997.264), amount to claiming that the poet uses spectacle for the sake of spectacle, that Lucan turns to spectacle because he fears wasting it.[12] This does not answer the question of why alluding to the amphitheater would be useful, or even interesting, to Vulteius—or to Lucan. Spectacle cannot be its own explanation. We require a theoretical and critical framework with which to examine the questions of ideology that spectacle both embodies and raises. To answer the question of why Vulteius *needs* an audience—in fact demands an audience—we require a critical theory that sees in Vulteius's desire to be a spectacle something more: an evocation of a "gaze" that bears power.

Shadi Bartsch's recent work on theatrical performance in the age of Nero sets out a starting point for reading the spectacularity of this episode. The interaction between ruler and ruled in the arena underwent radical changes when the emperor himself took to the stage: "In the *Annals* of Tacitus, in Suetonius's *Life of Nero*, and in the epitome of Dio Cassius . . . we find portrayed an emperor in performance who both watches his audience and enlists others to do so for signs of a less than enthusiastic response, and an audience transformed into a gathering of the gagged: actors now themselves, they play the role of happy fans to save their lives in the seats that have become, in essence, the true stage" (Bartsch 1994.3).

Nero's absolute power shows itself not only through his assumption of the actor's role but also through his control of the reactions of the audience, his transformation of spectators into spectacle. Nero is simultaneously before and behind the "camera lens," both director and actor, controlling the spectacle of himself by means of his own spectatorship of the audience that watches him. This "theatrical paradigm" (Bartsch 1994.1) provides a model for understanding Nero's reign.[13]

I would like to take Bartsch's paradigm a step further and develop a program based explicitly on film theory for interpreting the Vulteius episode in Lucan. Such a paradigm will distinguish not only dominant and subordinate positions in the frame of looking (as Bartsch does), but also attempt to uncover the position of the reader and her pleasure, or lack of pleasure, in reading this text of gory slaughter and death.

The aim of film theory is to conceptualize "the look" (also called "the gaze") and the ways people fit into the framework of "looks." This theory ultimately concerns the relation of the subject—both the subject as author and the subject as object—to ideology. In explicit analyses of women in cinema, film theorists implicitly ask questions about images in general: what are the conditions behind the presence of the image in the narrative? How is the image a social vision or how does it become one?[14]

Laura Mulvey's pioneering essay, "Visual Pleasure and Narrative Cinema," argues that viewers find pleasure in traditional narrative cinema because such cinema protects the viewers against the loss of power and status.[15] Such pleasure hangs on the representation of the "woman," for she represents "loss" by means of her physical "lack." The image, Mulvey argues, "of woman as (passive) raw material for the (active) gaze of man" reenacts in representation (cinema) the patriarchal ideology under which it functions, existing only as what she represents for her (male) audience (Mulvey 1975.17). The active male gaze exercises its power through two forms of looking, both rooted in psychoanalysis: fetishistic scopophilia, which turns the woman/female form into an icon, and voyeuristic sadism, which finds guilt in sexual difference (Mulvey 1975.13–14).[16] In the end, "masculinity confers the power of the gaze and control over narrative events, while femininity inevitably consigns the woman to a position as object of desire" (Flitterman-Lewis 1990.5).

But there are fundamental problems with Mulvey's theory. The subject gaze in her filmic setup can only be active/male (maker of meaning) to the object's passive/female (bearer of meaning). This binary opposition precludes the possibility of any female spectatorship, for "the look" is structured so that the spectator identifies always and only with the male protagonist in the narrative, what Mulvey calls the "the 'masculinization' of the spectator position regardless of the actual sex (or possible deviance) of any real-live movie-goer" (Mulvey 1981.12). Furthermore, in this model, the pleasure of the viewer may only come from the masculine position as subject; it is impossible to gain pleasure from an identification with the object position, as pleasure arises from the subject's active gaze. And finally, Mulvey's theory does not make clear why anyone would want to become a spectacle or, in other words, to occupy the "female" position.

Criticism of Mulvey's theory centers around these questions: does the spectator have only two choices, either to identify as female object of desire or to identify as male and dominant? (Kaplan 1983.312). Is there any pleasure in identifying with the object position? Does the gaze "always and inevitably" imply domination over an object? (Clover 1992.206). Some feminist scholars answer these questions by urging "a more nuanced model of spectatorship which emphasizes flexibility, instability and heterogeneity, or one that . . . suggests *multiple positions of identification that shift according to variable scenarios of desire*" (Flitterman-Lewis 1990.6, my emphasis). Teresa de Lauretis posits a process by which the viewer may identify as both subject *and* object; Mary Ann Doane suggests that the female spectator may find pleasure in "a liberating dislocation of the feminine gaze" (Flitterman-Lewis 1990.7).[17] The notion of "multiple positions of identification according to variable scenarios of desire" stems ultimately from the very psychoanalytic framework Mulvey uses for her articulation of the gaze. Amy Richlin's comments on the pantomime bring these criticisms of Mulvey home to the Roman stage, where pleasure may be found in identification with the passive position (1992c.176):

> The connection between Ovid's poetry and the pantomime accords well with the model of fantasy derived from psychoanalytic theory, in which the subject is said to oscillate among the terms of the fantasy . . . Thus, in one of the basic schemas, "a father seduces a daughter," the subject can be in the place of "father," "daughter," or even the verb "seduces" . . . The model exactly describes the performance of the dancer—first one character, then another, with the essential need to enact the interaction between the characters; and not just any characters but, often, the father seducing a daughter (Pelopea) or an equivalent (Leda).

This is a masochistic pleasure, a pleasure based not on the male identification proposed by Mulvey but on a differing aesthetic, one that recognizes the pleasure of the object position. Masochistic pleasure is not based on the fear of castration that Mulvey's theory takes as its center, but instead stems from the maternal influence in the child's prephallic phase. This maternal figure is "powerful in her own right," defined not by means of her lack but rather by the "inseparable plentitude" she provides to the child in the stages of infantile helplessness and symbiosis between mother and child (Studlar 1988.30, 43, 49). The masochist desires pleasure, but finds his pleasure in operations of distancing that recreate the ambivalence the child feels toward the maternal figure of plentitude.

Simply put, in visual theory, masochism is at work in operations of the narrative that delay closure, emphasize suffering, compel repetition, or linger over particular actions. This "masochistic aesthetic" contradicts Mulvey's assertion that pleasure for the viewer can only be achieved through the sadistic, controlling position, arguing instead that pleasure may be found in renouncing domination (Studlar 1988.49). Carol Clover's study of the modern horror film underscores the widespread nature of this masochistic position: in horror, that is, "movies people see *in order to be scared*" (Clover 1992.179, her emphasis), the audience must be made to identify with the victim or the unfolding of the drama will make no sense (Clover 1992.159). For a (more) modern literary example, we might point to Harriet Beecher Stowe's *Uncle Tom's Cabin*, in which the reader is made to identify with Uncle Tom and continues this identification even as Uncle Tom is being whipped to death. The power and pleasure of the masochistic identification may be seen especially in the Gothic novel: for example, the reader's identification with the (painfully) dying Antonia in Matthew Lewis's *The Monk* or with the child Helen in Emily Bronte's *Jane Eyre*.

The desire to provide a spectacle, *to be seen*, then, must be central to the analysis of Vulteius's own ideological beliefs. Vulteius's wish to die in front of Caesar, together with his direct address to Caesar at 4.500, is an indication of Vulteius's desire to be a spectacle *for* Caesar, of his deliberate creation of the suicide as an object of Caesar's look. And he does create that spectacle for *Caesar*, even though it is the Pompeians who watch him. Like Scaeva in Book 6 (138–262, esp. 158–60), Vulteius's "highest" wish is to die with Caesar as his witness (see note 9 above). The Pompeians are mere stand-ins, the audience present rather than the audience targeted.[18]

From Vulteius's own standpoint, his "spectacle" should make his Stoic devotion to *libertas* visible to all. But in the process of creating that spectacle, Vulteius negates his Stoicism with an appeal to *furor* and forces his readers to turn elsewhere for meaning. As Vulteius's speech moves further and further away from the high philosophical and epic ideals with which he starts, the significance of the Pompeians as an audience dwindles; in the end, his death is only for the (absent) eyes of Caesar. Before the eyes of Caesar, Vulteius becomes a theatrical object. His acting-out of devotion to Caesar on the visible stage of the raft—surrounded by an audience perched on rocks much like the filled stands of an arena—places Vulteius and his men in the position of gladiators, actors, and mimes.

Vulteius thus "acts out" his suicide for the sake of Caesar, as a theatrical object, just as the audience of Nero acts out its own interest in and engagement with the acting of their emperor. We may read the episode, then, as an illustration of Vulteius's deliberate objectification of himself in a power matrix, at the head of which is his (absent) commander, Caesar. In this episode, Vulteius constructs himself as an *image*, the object of Caesar's look. If we are to make the comparison between Vulteius's suicide and an arena spectacle, we must also take into account what the comparison implies: the space of the arena is always controlled by the figure of a Caesar. "Caesar" watches what occurs on the sand (which can be sea, cf. Martial *Spectacula* 27[19]) in front of his eyes and controls that scene by his presence and his viewing of the spectacle.[20] I would like to suggest that Vulteius, like "woman" in cinema, is presented to the reader as *what he represents for his audience*, which is Caesar.

With the use of Mulvey's formulation, which argues that the man in power is the "bearer of the look of the spectator" (Mulvey 1975.12), we may read the Vulteius episode as an illustration of power relations between Vulteius, who desires to be seen, and Caesar, who is the "real" spectator/audience in the background of the episode and for whom Vulteius constructs the spectacle. In this reading, Vulteius himself, and Vulteius's men, are of no importance whatsoever. It is only their suicide that counts, or rather, only what that the suicide represents: objectification in the gaze of their commander.[21] Vulteius defines for his mass suicide a specific position as the image-object of Caesar's look—in other words, were it not for the watching eye of Caesar (and the Pompeians), *the "suicide" would have no meaning*.

In Mulvey's view, pleasure comes only from the active gaze, and therefore we, as readers, should identify with Caesar. Studlar claims, to the contrary, that viewers may find masochistic pleasure in occupying the object position, and thus an identification with Vulteius should follow. But the exchange of looks and identification with the dominant or subordinate position is rarely so simple. Other operations in the narrative—poem or cinema—promote a certain restlessness of identificatory positions. For example, we might point back to Bartsch's Nero onstage: the emperor adopts a passive position to mask his imperial controlling gaze and thus constantly oscillates between spectator and spectacle, active and passive positions. Caesar, too, as he feigns sorrow at the death of Pompey (1036–1108), uses that sorrow as a mask through which to judge the reactions of his men.

This varying position of spectator and spectacle is directly relevant to our interpretation of the Vulteius episode. For Lucan seems to invite the reader to look through Caesar's eyes in this scene, to take on the position of Mulvey's masculinized spectator. Other operations in the narrative, however, push the reader away from identifying with this position. Similarly, Lucan's text teases the reader with the possibility of identifying with Vulteius and his men, taking pleasure in the passive position, but those same distancing operations deny stability to a masochistic identification as well.

The acceptance that there can be varying positions of identification in the narrative allows questions to be asked about *where* the reader's pleasure is situated in this gory mess of slaughter. The operations that separate the reader/spectator from any stable identification in the narrative, and insist instead on an instability of visual pleasure, center on the denial of traditional epic redemptive processes. I suggested above that the episode denies the traditional values of sacrifice and epic *kleos* even as it tempts the reader toward an ideology based on those values. The withdrawal of traditional epic purposes from the Vulteius episode, I will argue, underscores and problematizes the spectacle of the Opitergians' deaths. In what follows, I will address the removal of traditional epic redemptive processes (*kleos*, sacrifice, victory) from the Vulteius episode and suggest that the reader is forced to take a position concerning the range of spectatorial possibilities offered by the narrative.

All For One . . .

The image of troopers committing suicide for their commander calls up an image of sacrifice. But Vulteius's is an odd sacrifice indeed, to wage civil war within his own ranks. By examining the Vulteius episode in the context of Vergil's sacrificial scenes and in the context of the Roman custom of *devotio*,[22] I will argue that Lucan arranges it as an *Aeneid*-type sacrifice or as a *devotio*, only to undercut those readings in the course of his scene. Lucan's strategies for undercutting Vulteius's actions concern, on the one hand, the heroic values of *kleos* and individuality and, on the other, political redemption in the ship-of-state metaphor. The poet's narrative processes remove both heroic individuality and the ship-of-state metaphor, pushing the reader toward the acceptance of "spectacle" as the only ideological underpinning of the episode. At the same time, Lucan undercuts any stability of vision in the spectacle and forces his reader to deny any certainty of identification with characters or actions. Ultimately, the failure of Lucan's epic to confirm "epic" values and the instability of vision promoted by the epic will be united in Lucan's vision of civil war.

Vulteius ends his persuasive speech with an appeal to *furor*: "I am altogether driven on by the spurs of coming death: this is madness" (516–17: "totusque futurae / mortis agor stimulis: furor est"). The *furor* of Vulteius's death looks back to *furor* in the *Aeneid*, especially the *furor* of Aeneas that leads to the death of Turnus. Turnus's death has been predicted and Turnus promised notoriety as a sacrificial lamb at 12.234–35 by his sister Juturna in the guise of the warrior Camers (cf. Thompson and Bruère 1970.166 n. 26 and n. 27). Juturna makes use of the verb *devovere* in her acknowledgment of Turnus's self-sacrifice, *se devovet . . . succedet fama* ("He who sacrifices himself . . . prospers by [his] fame," *Aeneid* 12.234–35). Her speech spells out the role that the death of Turnus will play in the establishment of Rome, and Turnus's death is opened to interpretation as the sacrificial death necessary for the (re)imposition of order. L. Thompson and R. T. Bruère see an allusion to Juturna/Camers's speech in Lucan's *devota iuventus* (4.533); Lucan's epilogue speaks of (and is) the fame that succeeds the suicides (1970.166 n. 26). The use of the verb *devovere* strongly suggests we should also read Vulteius's suicide in a sacrificial frame, as a *devotio*.

The best-known *devotio* in the Roman historical corpus is that of the Decii,[23] specifically P. Decius Mus, who devoted himself for the success of the Roman troops in battle against the Latins in 340 B.C.E.[24] In Livy's retelling of the event (*ab Urbe Condita* 8.6.9–14), the same dream appears to both Roman consuls, revealing that, of the two sides, one would lose a general and the other an army, and that if a general would devote himself with the legions of his enemy to the underworld, the army of that general would win. In response to the dream, the consuls together decided that on whichever flank the Roman army began to fail, "inde se consul devoveret pro populo Romano Quiritibusque" ("The consul of that flank should devote himself on behalf of the Roman people and the Quirites," 6.9.13).

Together with this historical *devotio*, literate Romans would point quickly to the sacrifice of Palinurus as a model for Vulteius's watery death. Lucan's allusion to the cove wherein Aeneas and his men find shelter from the storm has already shaded this episode with Vergilian overtones. Further allusions to Dido in the Vulteius episode deepen the impression that Vulteius's actions are to be read against the background of those who sacrifice themselves or are sacrificed for the sake of Aeneas and the one state, Rome.[25]

Neptune demands the sacrifice of Palinurus at *Aeneid* 5.814–15:

> unus erit tantum amissum quem gurgite quaeres;
> unum pro multis dabitur caput.

> There will be only one whom you will miss, lost in the waves,
> one life will be given for many.

The death of this single individual will ensure Aeneas's arrival in Italy and, ultimately, the founding of Rome. Palinurus will die for the sake of his companions and the future of his race, *unus pro multis*. His is a surrogate death, one in place of all, but especially one in place of Aeneas. Palinurus, argues David Quint, is the logical choice for sacrificial victim: the helmsman is expendable once Neptune has agreed to escort the fleet to Italy, and, as the storm at the opening of *Aeneid* 5 has shown, he is an ineffective helmsman in any case (1992.86). The echoes of Odysseus's storm at *Odyssey* 12.403–25, in which another helmsman is lost, indicate that the two episodes should be read together. Odysseus is the sole survivor while all his men are killed; Aeneas's men survive his storm, but lose Palinurus as expiation for the voyage to Italy.[26]

But the *Aeneid* raises disturbing questions about the sacrifice of the one for the many even as it writes this sacrifice into its ideology.[27] How many "ones" will be sacrificed? At what point will "one" really be enough to save the many? Palinurus, as Quint notes, is the fourth to be sacrificed for Rome, after Creusa, Dido, and Anchises.[28] More will come. Even within the terms of "unum pro multis dabitur caput," the line demarcating one from many is unclear. Neptune's answer to Venus's prayer that *all* the Trojans be allowed to cross the sea in safety ("liceat dare tuta per undas / vela tibi," 5.796–97) speaks of the time when he saved *Aeneas* from danger (5.804: *Aeneae mihi cura tui*).

Philip Hardie's recent book reiterates the extensive sacrificial imagery in Lucan first noted by Frederick Ahl and goes on to claim that "of all the first-century epicists Lucan explores most insistently the topic of the sacrifice of the *one* for the *many*" (Hardie 1993.30, my emphasis). Lucan explicitly follows in Vergil's footsteps here. Vulteius's raft is one of three: the other two rafts escape as Vulteius's own is entangled by the Pompeian trick, making the sacrifice motif even more obvious (431, 452–54). But in the Palinurus episode, as noted above, Vergil also toys with the identification of the one (Aeneas) with the many (all the Trojans), a dark undertone to the Girardian picture of one sacrificial victim for the sake of social cohesion in the larger community. In the Vulteius episode, Lucan has reworked these Vergilian undertones and made them explicit. Lucan's reader is no longer vaguely disconcerted by the increasing number of "ones" required by Aeneas's future: the *Pharsalia* delineates in gory Technicolor the necessity of the sacrifice of the many for the one—Caesar. In Lucan, the sacrifice no longer happens for, or can be redeemed by, the collective good, the *res publica* of Rome. In fact in this civil war, sacrifice can only lead to more struggle: as Pompey flees the Pharsalian battlefield, the poet notes that his troops no longer fought for Pompey, but that they fought in the never-ending contest between *libertas* and Caesar (7.692–96). This civil war is eternal and can only generate versions of itself; any "sacrifice" can only lead to another "sacrifice" in an unending cycle.

Vulteius's characterizations of his own actions—his motives for suicide—provide some insight into the theme of Lucanian heroic sacrifice. Glory is Vulteius's primary concern, the lasting *fama* Lucan seems to promise in his epilogue. At 4.479, the Opitergian leader speaks of the glory of death, *gloria leti*, which will not be diminished by committing suicide. The praise of courage, *animi laus* (482), he promises, belongs to those who take their own lives, whether that suicide occurs years or moments before death approaches. He argues that the *virtus* of his men will be recognized (491); they will be a *magnum et memorabile . . . exemplum* (496–97)[29] and monuments to *fides* (*monimenta*, 498). Their death will be unique (*mors unica*), although he wishes the fame of this unique death could be increased (*plus . . . famae*, 509).

It seems Vulteius ingested well his lessons from the *Iliad*: his motives feed into a superstructure of heroic *kleos* in Lucan's epic tradition that calls above all for a named hero who, in the moment of killing or dying, receives in the naming action of poet and poem a fame to last through the centuries. Vulteius offers this kind of glory to his men, a glory that, he says, would only be lost on the battlefield (4.488–91):

> non tamen in caeca bellorum nube cadendum est,
> aut cum permixtas acies sua tela tenebris
> involvent. conferta iacent cum corpora campo,
> in medium mors omnis abit, perit obruta virtus.

> Not for us to fall in the unseeing cloud of battle,
> or when their own weapons cover the confused battlelines with shadows.

When bodies lie densely packed on the field, every death
dissolves into commonality, and dying courage is destroyed.

But battle is not blind in Lucan's tradition. The models of Vergil's
Aeneid and the battlefields of Latium provide a battle narrative directly
contrary to Vulteius's vision. In nine lines from *Aeneid* 10 (388–96), Vergil
names four warriors meeting death at Pallas's hand, gives the ancestry of
two of those warriors, and grants an ancestry as well to the sword Pallas
uses, *Evandrius ensis* (394). Earlier in *Pharsalia*, Lucan's sea battle of Massilia (3.509–762) granted names to the protagonists at the heart of each
individual episode; the deaths of the characters bestowed a Homeric
glory upon killer and killed.[30] Moreover, many of those who are "sacrificed" in the *Aeneid* are remembered by place names: Caieta (7.1–4), Mis-
enus (6.232–35), and Palinurus (6.377–81). Both slaughter and individual
sacrifices on the Vergilian battlefield maintain the epic convention of
death that yields or preserves a name.

This epic convention is soon lost in Lucan. Vulteius and his men
stand on the edge of a new heroic code and conception of *kleos*, one that
denies names to warriors and refutes the idea of *kleos aphthiton*. Of the
1,000 men on the raft (Florus 2.13, see above note 1), only Vulteius receives a name, only Vulteius a voice: he is the single named individual
in the narrative. He has a near epithet: *dux ratis* (466). His status as the
one unique individual is marked by the occurrences of his name: Vulteius
occurs three times (465, 476, 541) and he is called *dux ratis* twice (466,
540). These five instances of naming or identifying are all in the nomi-
native: Vulteius is the only named, human subject in the singular who
governs singular verbs.

Vulteius's death marks the end of even the pretense of the heroic
ideal of individuality in the episode. No one is named, no one speaks.
Collective nouns are used to identify his men: *cunctos* (546), *iuvenes* (557),
fratres (563), *semianimes* (567). Only two are singled out, and the relationship between them is emphasized rather than their identities as individuals: *natusque parenti* (563). In fact the verb governed by the word
natus is neither its own nor singular: it is the plural verb of the previous
clause, *incurrunt*, governed by *fratres*. One right hand and one wound
serve for the whole troop at 448–49; one face looks upon the Pompeian
enemy at 568; there is one feeling of joy for the approach of death at 570.
Even agency is removed from these men. Throats press upon the hand;
the breast offers itself up to be struck (4.560–62):

> nec volnus adactis
> debetur gladiis: percussum est pectore ferrum
> et iuguli pressere manum.

Lucan makes use of two extended similes to describe the actual slaughter at lines 549–66: he compares Vulteius's men to the Dircaean cohort and Medea's "sons of the earth." The comparisons reinforce the anonymity and loss of individuality in the miniature civil war this *cohors* carries out. In Lucan's narrative, the sole purpose of the *Dircaea cohors* and those *terrigenae* springing up by Medea's magic is to kill each other. They have no country, no parents, no offspring, no past or future. Their deaths establish Cadmus's kingdom on the one hand and Jason's right to his on the other. Death in these cases is motivated not by larger ideals of glory or *militiae pietas* (as Vulteius's is meant to be) but by simple blood lust and the desire to rule. These events are called a *dirum omen* for Theban brothers and the *primum nefas* of Medea: the sequels of brother killing brother and mother killing sons are close to mind. The Dircaean cohort and the sons of the earth foreshadow the familial "civil wars" that will be carried out by Medea and Polynices and Eteocles. If the suicides of Vulteius and his men are to be equally symbolic for the coming battle of Pharsalus, then individual glory, *pietas*, and *virtus* are to be entirely absent.

Finally, the *victores*[31] remove the bodies *en masse* for burial (570–72):

> iam strage cruenta
> conspicitur cumulata ratis, bustisque remittunt
> corpora victores.

The Opitergians have become the anonymous *corpora* Vulteius claimed self-slaughter would avoid eighty lines previously. The fame Vulteius promises accrues only to himself, but even that singular fame is lost at the moment of his death. He asks for one of the *iuvenes* to demonstrate his wish to die by killing his leader; many answer his call. Vulteius, the individual, is killed by more than one blow and cannot distinguish the "killing" stroke. His individual self is lost to the *non unus ensis* that transfix him; he dies the death of many.[32] In his turn, he singles out another— an object that remains nameless and voiceless—he kills, not the man who killed him, but the first to strike (546–47): "sed eum cui volnera prima / debebat grato moriens interficit ictu."

Even his own fame is erased at the episode's end: as the leaders wonder that so much could be done for a *dux*, the reader is not told whether the *dux* in question is Vulteius or Caesar.[33] "Ducibus mirantibus ulli /

esse ducem tanti" (572–73), writes the poet: Vulteius—or Caesar—has now become the object of indirect discourse.[34]

Thus Vulteius and his men suffer by their suicide the anonymity their leader would deny; Vulteius promises *fama*, but no one receives a name.[35] Vulteius is the only named "hero," and, upon his death, human individuality disappears from the narrative. What little individuality he claimed is transferred to the weapons, and even then the separate weapons of Vulteius's men shift between one and many (560–62):

> nec volnus adactis
> debetur gladiis: percussum est pectore ferrum
> et iuguli pressere manum.

The fate of Vulteius's men is exactly that which he promised would not occur: the raft has become land, the battlefield on which the whole corps dies a nameless death, and *virtus* belongs only to the epilogue. The singularity of Vulteius's death, the *unica mors* he promises for his men, becomes gruesomely real as the whole of the troop is compressed into one breast, one hand. This sacrifice, which should distinguish the "one" victim and make distinctions within the community based on the kind of violence the victim suffers, only mingles Vulteius and his men into an indistinguishable, bloody mass. The response of the onlookers, a response that Vulteius trusts will be his *fama*, is to fail even to distinguish Vulteius from Caesar. Who is the *dux*?

This Ship of Fools

Thus far I have established a framework of looks within which, Lucan suggests, Vulteius operates. This framework, however, is too unstable to permit the reader any solid identification with Caesar's or Vulteius's point of view because Lucan consistently pushes the reader away from the eye of either man by means of distancing operations that undercut traditional epic redemptive processes. The first of these distancing operations concerned Vulteius's position within a superstructure of heroic *kleos*: Vulteius (and the reader) cannot redeem this spectacle with undying glory.

The Vulteius episode also occurs within the framework of a Greco-Roman allegory: the ship of state. Lucan, however, undercuts the political coherency and stability, often achieved through the sacrifice of a specific individual, suggested by this allegory. The reader gains instead a picture of the Roman state as a perpetually sinking ship, effectively cutting off sacrificial redemption and identification in civil war.

Lucan may have looked back at several renditions of the ship-of-state theme, most notably Vergil's. W. S. Anderson's analysis of this metaphor in Horace proposes a general formula to describe the crises suffered by such "ships": the ship of state is (usually) threatened by a storm, and the ruler of the state is captain or helmsman; the narrator of the metaphor is (usually) either on the ship experiencing the storm or outside the ship commenting on the ship's plight (Anderson 1966.87–88). Palinurus's sacrifice allows Aeneas's ship of state to continue in safety; the closing lines of *Aeneid* 5, in which Aeneas pilots his ship through the sea on the way to Italy, is a famous illustration of this theme.[36]

In these metaphors, the ship of state either survives while death occurs *outside* (e.g., the loss of Orontes at *Aeneid* 1.584–85) or the ship and crew are lost entirely (e.g., *Odyssey* 12.411–25, in which Odysseus's entire crew as well as his helmsman are lost in a storm). On those occasions in which the whole ship goes down, the captain/pilot/head of state may survive, as does Odysseus in the *Odyssey*. In most cases, the threat, or the storm, attacks the ship from the outside, as in *Aeneid* 1 and *Odyssey* 12. In those cases where the threat appears to come from within (e.g., Polybius 6.44, describing the Athenian state as a ship without a captain), the narrator is an observer who is separated from the observed "ship" or state (Anderson 1966.88).

Whether death occurs outside or all go down together in the foundering ship, the killing does not happen on board while the ship is afloat. Palinurus is thrown from the stern and either drowns or is killed by barbarians after washing ashore in an unknown place. Orontes drowns, thrown from his ship. Odysseus's men are killed when their ship sinks; both ship and crew are destroyed.

Vulteius pilots, in J. Henderson's words, a "raft of state" (Henderson 1988.139). His *ratis*, containing a troop of Pompeian soldiers, is the site of a civil war in miniature. I have shown how the sacrifice of Vulteius and his men is a reversal of the sacrifice of Palinurus, but Vulteius shares characteristics with Aeneas as well. Aeneas takes over the forsaken helm at *Aeneid* 5.867–68:

> cum pater amisso fluitantem errare magistro
> sensit, et ipse ratem nocturnis rexit in undis.

> When father [Aeneas] sensed the flowing ship wandering, her helmsman absent,
> even he himself guided the ship [*ratem*] into the nocturnal waves.

Vulteius, too, senses something amiss, and guides his raft, but with his voice (465–66, 475):

> Vulteius tacitas sensit sub gurgite fraudes
> (dux erat ille ratis) . . .
> rexit magnanima Vulteius voce cohortem.

> Vulteius sensed the silent trick beneath the wave
> for he was the leader of the raft . . .
> Great-hearted Vulteius guided his cohort with his voice.[37]

Here again Lucan is rereading and rewriting the *Aeneid:* conflating his captain and helmsman into one. Vulteius is both leader and victim. As both, he tries to experience both fates, but in place of that impossibility—survival and sacrifice—he can only internalize the chaos he creates. Both the usual ship-of-state storm and the sacrifice are part of the Vulteius episode, but the poet has turned these elements inside out. The storm is internal, the sacrifice collective. Vulteius's ship of state, his *ratis* (466), is overwhelmed by the internal *furor* of Vulteius and his men, "totusque futurae mortis agor stimulis: furor est" (516). Here the leader does not survive the storm, on the Odyssean model, nor do the ship and crew, on the Vergilian: on this ship of state, all kill each other. Only Vulteius can commit a sacrifice in which those for whom the sacrifice should have been carried out are themselves sacrificed. His *ratis* remains, piled high with a dead crew, but a ship of state cannot exist without a crew and a pilot to guide it. Vulteius makes a mess of the metaphor and therefore of guiding (*rexit*) the state. He convinces his men that the only way to preserve freedom is to kill themselves; paradoxically, in this act of self-destruction, the "state" is destroyed as well.

Vulteius and the poet create these deaths, this eradication of distinctions, as a sacrifice, a *devotio* for the good of the state. But earlier in Book 3, Caesar has invaded Rome, taken control of the state, and lawlessly compelled the senators to vote at his whim (105–09, my emphasis):

>   non consule sacrae
> fulserunt sedes, non, proxima lege potestas,
> praetor adest, vacuaeque loco cessere curules.
> *omnia Caesar erat*: privatae curia vocis
> testis adest.

>   The sacred seats did not shine
> with their consul, nor was there a praetor present

(the next in rank by law), and the curule chairs, empty,
gave over their stations. *Caesar was everything:* the Curia stood witness
to the voice of a private citizen.

The *dux ratis* has declared that his death and the deaths of his men
will be *pro te, Caesar* (500), not, like that of the Decii, *pro legionibus* or
pro populo Romano Quiritibusque. Caesar has taken their place. Though
Vulteius's ship of state is destroyed, the epic will go on to demonstrate
time and again that where there is Caesar, no ship of state is necessary.

From this analysis, we can distinguish certain characteristics of what
we might call the violence of the Caesarian look, a violence of gaze that
illustrates new social and political contracts under Caesar. The violence
of Caesar's men (or *partes*) does not name; instead it reduces the many to
the one and demands anonymity. Vulteius desires that the deaths of his
men will become an *exemplum* (497), but the *fama* of the episode is confined only to the epilogue, and these *monimenta* receive no further mention in the epic. Vulteius's name is even lacking in Caesar's *Bellum Civile.*[38]

This loss of traditional heroic identity and the subsequent emphasis on "Caesar" as the only identity, which entails the sacrifice of others
on a massive scale, may be seen in other episodes in Lucan's poem, particularly the battle of Pharsalus. With the exception of Crastinus, called
by name as he begins the battle (7.470–75), no soldier in Caesar's army
receives a name at Pharsalus: we hear of Brutus (7.586–96) and Domi-
tius (7.599–616), both followers of Pompey, but on Caesar's side only
Caesar himself has a name. Downplaying the effectiveness of Caesar's
men, the poet writes at 7.474, "cum Caesar tela teneret, / inventa est
prior ulla manus?" ("When Caesar held weapons, / could any hand be
proved superior?"). Starting at 7.557–85, Caesar appears everywhere,
does everything (567, 571, 574–76):

> quacumque vagatur . . .
> nox ingens scelerum est . . .
> ispe manu subicit gladios ac tela ministrat
> adversosque iubet ferro confundere voltus,
> promovet ipse acies . . .
>
> Wherever [on the battlefield] he wandered . . .
> there was present a great night of evils . . .
> he himself brings the swords, supplies the spears
> and orders his men to make unrecognizable the faces of his enemies with iron;
> he himself pushes the battleline forward . . .

Scaeva has read his Lucan: he asks his comrades-in-arms: "cumulo vos desse virorum / non pudet et bustis interque cadavera quaeri?" ("Does it not shame you to be missing from the stack of dead warriors and the funeral pyres, not to be sought among the corpses?" 6.153–54).

Looking at Pompey's Head

In the Vulteius episode, Lucan offers his reader two levels of "seeing": first, a spectacle "to be looked at"—and thought about—along the axis of dominance and submission of imperial spectacles in the arena; and second, a position and identification for the reader that is not so clearly established. The poet insists on a primary *visual* reading of the episode by removing any result from the narrative that would redeem the image of those slaughtered bodies: there is no epic *kleos*, there is no sacrifice for the good of the community, and there is no prospering of the Roman state (there is no Roman state). Instead of Homeric or Vergilian names and everlasting glory, Vulteius and his men receive anonymity and a lack of distinction that becomes corporeal as the raft is heaped high with one gory pile. Their sacrifice, far from endorsing a Decian-Girardian social coherence (though, of course, with all members of the community dead, we have reached the ultimate coherence), destroys all possibility of excising what may be at fault.

Here we may be able to uncover something of Lucan's own ideological stance with regard to Nero's empire. Such an uncovering cannot be much more than a guess, but I would cautiously suggest the following by analogy with Slovaj Zizek's analysis of Laibach, a post-punk group in Slovenia during the disintegration of socialism. According to Zizek, "Laibach staged an aggressive, inconsistent mixture of Stalinism, Nazism and *Blut und Bloden* ideology." Critics originally conceived of Laibach as an "ironic imitation of totalitarian rituals," but became uneasy in the face of the group's self-presentation: "What if [Laibach] really mean it? What if they truly identify with the totalitarian ritual?" (Zizek 1994.71). Zizek's solution to the troublesome picture of Laibach's totalitarian stance is to suggest that Laibach overidentifies with totalitarian ritual and that this *overidentification* cannot in any way support an ideology, since it is not an "ironic imitation," but rather brings to light the obscene underside of the system precisely by identifying with it to its logical—and illogical—extreme (Zizek 1994.71–72). Vulteius's illustration of Lucan's new social contract is perhaps an *overidentification* with the principles advocated by Caesar. It may not be possible to claim that Lucan agrees or disagrees with the imperial system, but, in this episode at least, he highlights the potential effects of an unquestioning and blindly devoted acquiescence.

The overidentification of Vulteius illustrated by his suicide, pushing aside epic redemption through *kleos* or sacrifice, problematizes the Mulvian reading of visual structure by throwing the spectacle, and its interpretation, back on the spectator. Here we turn to the position of the reader. The overidentification of Vulteius with Caesarianism in Lucan's poem brings the reader directly into the issues the poem confronts. In the process of overidentifying with any particular ideological regime, the Opitergians (like Laibach) function not as an *answer* to the questions of "totalitarianism" or "Caesarianism" but as a *question* in themselves: our own uncertainty over how "seriously" to take the episode, where to "place" the philosophy or the politics of the episode in the larger Roman cultural environment, whether or not to "admire" the pseudosuicides of the Opitergians, compels us (in Zizek's words) "to take up our position and decide upon *our* desire" (1994.72).

Those modifications of Laura Mulvey's theory that recognize contradictions between active and passive pleasures become relevant in our search for a position from which to gaze upon this episode. We, as readers, necessarily slip into the object position because Caesar in his grandiosity (*Caesar omnia est*) precludes a simple identification with his gaze. Though we may gain a masochistic pleasure from identifying with Vulteius, the object position also has its dangers: this position—mutilated, "castrated"—can provoke anxiety and considerable "un-pleasure."[39] The object position forces the spectator into a self-encounter against which the subject position protects. If Caesar is "all," and "we" are with Caesar, then "we" are not forced to question where "we" would be if "we" were "all"—and, as Vulteius so vividly demonstrates, "all" becomes insignificant, meaningless, indistinguishable, and so brutally *not* a subject. At issue are those "multiple positions of identification that shift according to variable scenarios of desire" of which Sandy Flitterman-Lewis speaks (1990.6). The position of the spectator is dependent on her desire: not just where she locates her position with reference to the imperial system that the episode seems to promote, but also where she locates her position with reference to the pleasure she finds in a self-encounter, herself as object, and any range of positions in-between.

The Vulteius episode, and the position of the reader that it engages, is paired with other episodes in the epic in which grotesque slaughter is staged for the pleasure of the imperial viewer. The most savage of these are, perhaps, Sulla watching the slaughter in the *Ovilia Romae* (2.207–08) and Caesar gloating over the battlefield after Pharsalus (7.786–94). As Matthew Leigh notes, the scenes are "kingly visions of Sulla and Caesar, two murderers feasting their eyes on the spectacle of Rome's transformation" (1997.292). The episode most often coupled with Vulteius's slaughter is the *aristeia* of Scaeva at 6.138–262 in which Scaeva, too, devotes himself for the sake of Caesar. Tellingly, in Scaeva's devotion, Caesar is also absent; upon his discovery of the battle (communicated to him by the lookout's fire, 6.279), Caesar sweeps through the area without comment. Again the Pompeians are the audience present rather than the audience desired (6.158–60).

But the spectacle of all spectacles in Lucan's poem is that of Pompey's head as it is held up to Caesar at the end of Book 9 (1032–1108). I have already noted the controlling aspect of Caesar's gaze in the exchange of "looks" between himself and his dead rival: Caesar's look is an expression of power. Pompey's head, however, bears its own power in the episode: Caesar is forced to dissemble to the audience of his followers rather than rejoice openly (Ormand 1994.54–55). Both become simultaneously subject and object to the other's gaze.[40] Trapped between the two, the reader as spectator oscillates between subject and object positions, forced to choose where lies her desire.

Where *does* our pleasure lie in the Vulteius episode? In identification with the all-seeing eye of Caesar? With the objectified and mangled bodies—or, perhaps, body—of Vulteius and his men? With the stupefaction of the Pompeians? Or with the constant movement among these positions? I think, as with the spectacle of Pompey's head, it is impossible for the reader as spectator to occupy either the space of the Mulvian subject (Caesar) or the space of the masochistic object (Vulteius and his men) for long. Lucan's epic narrative seduces the reader toward an identification with Caesar, only to push that identification away; the operations that remove epic convention from the episode also forestall a simple identification with Vulteius's position. Thus the reader is lost in a civil war of the pleasures, the desire for identification continually at war with itself. Here, too, we might find the pleasure of civil war: the effort to find identification among equal demands and desires.

This withdrawal of epic redemption functions much more immediately as a descriptive tool for the processes of civil war and its aftermath. The instability of visual pleasure walks hand-in-hand with the inability of this epic to affirm "epic" values because of its political content. Unredeemed sacrifice and a perpetually sinking ship of state doom the reader to circulate among positions in the epic without any firm political closure: the destabilization of "active" and "passive" positions and the constant movement among positions the reader is forced into while reading Lucan's poem reflect back Lucan's own view of civil war as "unredeemed spectacle." And so we turn back again to our own civil wars, searching for a stable identification between competing positions and desires.

I cannot leave Lucan's poem here, in the throes of a spectator's civil war. The interpretation for which I have argued immediately suggests two possibilities. First, since film theory offers some insight into reading this Latin epic, then we should ask the same question of the traditional epic form that feminist scholars ask of traditional narrative cinema. "Woman" in traditional film comes to represent the problems of cinema as a representational form (Penley 1989.46). Is Lucan, by underscoring the importance of spectacle to the operations of his poem, pointing to the problems of epic as a representational form in the age of Nero's imperial Rome? I think the answer must be yes. Ideology in the Vulteius episode, at least, cannot be found among the expected epic values of *kleos*, victory, sacrifice, glory, and fame. There are no "names" to be given to succeeding generations, only Vulteius, whose name represents in itself the centrality of spectacle. I have tried to show that other episodes of spectacular violence in Lucan's poem may be subject to the same operations of vision as the Vulteius episode. It would be necessary to turn back to Rome's epic tradition and explore spectacle in those earlier epics in order to see how drastically Lucan changes the paradigm. Clearly such a task is beyond this scope of this essay, but it seems to this reader that the role of spectacle in ancient epic is unmined and valuable territory.

Second, psychoanalytic models of film theory and Zizek's analysis of the group Laibach offer an interpretation of the poet's role in determining the position of the reader/spectator radically different from that which is traditionally accepted. The question of overidentification represented by Laibach or Vulteius forces the reader/spectator to decide upon the position of her desire—it does not function as an answer, only a question that turns the reader/spectator back upon herself. As such, the episode itself acts as "the reversal that defines the end of the psychoanalytic cure" (Zizek 1994.72), the reversal in which the analysand comes to realize that the analyst has no answers and that all answers lie within the analysand. That is, in the course of the psychoanalysis practiced by Lucan upon the reader, the reader/analysand comes to realize that Lucan/the poem does *not* have "the answer" to "the question" of the reader's desire. At the end of the Vulteius episode, the reader understands that authorization of her desire—authorization for the position in which she places herself with reference to the poem's issues—can only come from within herself, since Lucan, poet and poem, does not offer a firm position from which to view the spectacle. The ignorance of the reader about her desire cannot be reduced to an epistemological issue in which the "truth" of desire lies hidden somewhere in the poem, if only she could find it.[41] The overidentification of Vulteius, and the shifting positions of spectatorship forced upon the reader by the narrative, prove only that Lucan demands answers from his readers and is not the "subject-supposed-to-know," whether his poem is or is not republican, imperialist, pro-Neronian, antidynastic, or anything else.

"Where, reader, do you locate your desire?" is the question Vulteius asks. We cannot be left alone, outside the pleasure of the epic, to regard lightly Lucan's interpretation of events that changed the face of the Roman world. The poet has once again forced us, as readers, to become part of his poem. This demand in the epic, I think, is the reason why even reasonable attempts to "find" the ideology of Lucan the poet or Lucan the Roman conspirator fall somehow flat. Lucan, the analyst, offers no solution to the epistemological problem of where his sympathies lie along the spectrum of republicanism or imperialism. Instead he forces us, his readers and spectators, to ask that question of ourselves and locate our desire.

All theoretical musings aside, the Vulteius episode, at once disturbing and fascinating, does at least offer a new, postimperial formulation of epic narrative. Vulteius's formula of devotion is, perhaps, illustrative of Lucan's future Rome, which the epic foreshadows, when the *res publica* is the emperor—an emperor, moreover, whose title is always "Caesar." Vulteius's death is Lucan's reversal of the sacrifice of Palinurus, the one for the many future Romans: Vulteius and his men sacrifice themselves for the one Caesar—who has become all. Philip Hardie writes: "The body of the empire is indistinguishable from the mortal body of the emperor . . . the one supreme man, the *unus homo* who holds *omnia*" (Hardie 1993.93). Vulteius represents the new hero in the face of the absolutism Lucan's Caesar brings: unnamed, voiceless, *multi pro uno*.

Notes

My gratitude to David Fredrick, Marilyn Skinner, and my anonymous readers for their valuable comments. I give special thanks to John Henderson and S. Georgia Nugent, without whom Vulteius would continue to languish all unknown on his raft.

1. The exact number of men on the raft is unclear. Florus claims there are 1,000 men present (2.13); Lucan calls the band a *cohors* at 4.471, indicating 600 men; Livy (*Periocha* 110) says nothing to indicate number, referring to the Opitergians as *Caesaris auxiliares* (auxiliaries of Caesar).

2. E.g., Thompson and Bruère 1970.164: "For suicide per se (under appropriate circumstances) Lucan as a Stoic has nothing but admiration, and this is not absent from his account of the mutual slaughter [of Vulteius and his men]."

3. Ahl 1986.118–21, esp. his comparison of Vulteius and Scaeva, Thompson and Bruère 1970, Henderson 1988, Saylor 1990, Rutz 1960.

4. On the dubious quality of *fama* in Roman epic, see Hardie 1997.183; on *fama* in *Pharsalia* 7, see Masters 1994.159–63. Up to this point in the epic, the word *fama* has been used to mean something akin to lies, fabrications, or exaggerations: e.g., 1.469–72 on the strength of Caesar's forces. Given this context, I think the reader should be wary of taking *fama* in a positive sense.

5. Unless otherwise noted, all translations are my own.

6. In fact neither side is, strictly speaking, "Roman": the Opitergian Caesarians fight against Cilician Pompeians. Thus to turn their swords on themselves is to wage civil war, as opposed to fighting or being captured by outside forces, not "themselves."

7. Vulteius < Vultus, "Face-Man." Cf. Henderson 1988.139: "In *Vult*eius see the 'face' (*voltus*) of furor, 'Will to Power' (*velle*)."

8. By contrast, the Pompeian Octavius desires to remain unnoticed until his prey ventures forth onto open water (4.433–37).

9. Rutz 1960.466: "Wie Scaevas höchster Wunsch es ist, vor dem Zeugen Caesar oder doch wenigstens ver Pompeius zu fallen, so ist für Vulteius die Tatsache, daß beide Seiten das Schicksal der Besatzung sehen können, ein weiterer Antrieb zum Tode."

10. *Caecus* here is both "unseeing" and "unseen."

11. Cf. Leigh 1997.206–33 on the role of visibility in Lucan's battlefield *exempla*.

12. Leigh 1997 passim argues that, throughout the *Pharsalia*, Lucan takes a traditional *exemplum* to be emulated and turns it into a spectacle to be watched.

13. Cf. Edwards 1994 on Nero's role as actor.

14. For questions and analyses of this more general nature, see de Lauretis 1984.chap. 2.

15. Mulvey 1975. For summaries and critiques of Mulvey in film studies, see Doane 1987 and 1991, Flitterman-Lewis 1990, Kaplan 1983, Penley 1989, Studlar 1988, Silverman 1988b. For uses of visual theory in classics, see Fredrick 1995, Morales 1996, Robin 1993, Segal 1994, Wallace-Hadrill 1996.

16. To continue Mulvey 1975.14: "This sadistic side fits in well with narrative. Sadism depends on a story, depends on making something happen, forcing a change in another person, a battle of will and strength, victory/defeat, all occurring in a linear time with a beginning and an end. Fetishistic scopophilia, on

the other hand, can exist outside linear time as the erotic instinct is focussed on the look alone."

17. de Lauretis 1984, Doane 1991. Work on positionality by Alcoff and Braidotti, among others, supports the notion of shifting positions of identification in cultural media other than film; see Alcoff 1988, Braidotti 1994.

18. Some emphasis must be given to the Pompeian audience, however, as Vulteius's persuasive speech makes use of their presence to convince his men to kill each other. In the speech, he alternates between noting the presence of his enemy (492, 505–12) and addressing Caesar or using Caesar's name (500, 513). When using the presence of the enemy as a persuasive device for his men, Vulteius insists that the enemy will learn Caesar's men cannot be conquered (505: *indomitos*), that the enemy will fear the madness of the Caesarians (505: *timeatque furentes*), and that the enemy will try to make peace, but will realize Caesar's men do not wish for dishonorable life (506–12). In short (to make use of Leigh's structure), Vulteius presents the self-slaughter to the Pompeians *as an exemplum*— for the moral lessons the Pompeians might learn—while he presents the slaughter to *Caesar* as a sacrifice and spectacle (see below).

19. Martial *Spectacula* 27 (24):

> si quis ades longis serus spectator ab oris,
>> cui lux prima sacri muneris ista fuit,
> ne te decipiat ratibus navalis Enyo,
>> et par unda fretis: hic modo terra fuit.
> non credis? specta, dum lassant aequora Martem:
>> parva mora est, dices "hic modo pontus erat."

> If you came here but lately, a spectator from distant shores
>> (today being your first sight of the Sacred Games),
> don't let this naval battle beguile you with its ships,
>> and this water, big as the open wave: yet here recently was the earth.
> You don't believe me? Watch, while these waters exhaust their battle:
>> there is a slight delay, and you will say, "Here recently was a sea."

20. Important work on spectacle in the Roman empire includes Barton 1993, esp. chap. 1, Coleman 1990, Gunderson 1996, Hopkins 1983, esp. chap. 2.

21. The Opitergian slaughter is by no means the only episode in the poem where Caesar's imperial eye is established as the controlling point of view. That Caesar's power lies in his gaze is suggested as early as 1.297–98 as he quells the uproar of his troops with a glance: "utque satis trepidum turba coeunte tumultum / composuit voltu"; Caesar checks the blood lust of his troops at Pharsalus when he sees [*vidit*] enough slaughter (7.728). Before this cease-fire, Magnus has fled, perhaps wishing his death to elude the eyes of Caesar (7.673–75). As Caesar plays his own face-off with the head of Magnus at 9.1032–1108, his long look alternately controls the reactions of his men and himself. Magnus, however, covers his face and sees nothing when he dies (8.613–15). This contest of the strength

of vision between Caesar and Pompey runs throughout the epic and merits further exploration.

22. A Roman general would "devote" himself to the gods, or vow to die in battle, in order to guarantee a victory, especially if the outcome of the battle was in doubt. After reciting a ritual prayer seeking victory for the Romans and destruction of the enemy, the Roman general would plunge into battle and seek his own death.

23. Cicero praises the Decii at *de Fin.* 2.61. The son of P. Decius Mus, also named Decius Mus, devoted himself in the battle of Sentium in 295 B.C.E.; P. Decius Mus's grandson is alleged to have devoted himself in battle against Pyrrhus at Ausculum in 279 B.C.E. Cf. Ennius *Ann.* 208–10; Cic. *Tusc. Disp.* 1.89, *de Fin.* 2.61; *Aen.* 6.824. My thanks to John Kirkpatrick for his footwork.

24. Livy's account preserves Decius's cry to the Pontifex Maximus: "praei verba quibus me pro legionibus devoveam" ("Dictate the words by which I may devote myself on behalf of the legions," 8.9.4). This particular *devotio* holds interest for Vulteius's scene because Livy describes the circumstances of the battle in which Decius devoted himself to be much like a civil war: "curam acuebat quod adversus Latinos bellandum erat, lingua, moribus, armorum genere, institutis ante omnia militaribus, congruentes: milites militibus, centurionibus centuriones, tribuni tribunis compares collegaeque iisdem in praesidiis, saepe iisdem manipulis permixti fuerant" ("Their anxiety was sharpened by the fact that they must fight against the Latins, who were like themselves in language, customs, fashion of arms, and, above all, military institutions; soldiers had mingled with soldiers, centurions with centurions, tribunes with tribunes, as equals and colleagues in the same garrisons and often in the same maniples," 8.6.15).

25. Quint 1992.84: "The death of Palinurus is thus the fourth in a series of deaths—following those of Creusa, Anchises and Dido—that have stripped Aeneas of personal ties and identity."

26. See Quint 1992.88–91 for a full discussion of the parallels.

27. On sacrifice in the *Aeneid* and the questions raised about its efficacy, see Hardie 1993.

28. Quint 1992 leaves several "ones" out, e.g., Polydorus, Laocoön, and the Trojans who die of the plague on Crete in Book 3.

29. He claims they will be *magni* because of their visible suicide; they are not. Magnus, on the other hand, who becomes great though his execution, is unseen—and unseeing (8.610–62).

30. In this context, the Trojan War books of Ovid's *Metamorphoses* (12–13) are especially informative: the one true battle in these books is that between the Lapiths and the Centaurs in the recollection of Nestor, a parody of Homeric battle in which the warriors receive names and detailed descriptions of deathblow and death (12.210–536).

31. This term must be deeply ironic: how can the Pompeians be victors if

the battle was fought among the Caesarians alone? Is it possible that *victores* refers to the other two rafts of Caesarians, which have escaped?

32. Cf. 2.186f., the death of Marius Gratidianus.

33. The Latin does not firmly identify these "wondering leaders" as Pompeian or Caesarian, although the word *victores* provides very nearly solid identification of them as Pompeian: "bustisque remittunt / corpora victores, ducibus mirantibus" ("and the victors send corpses to the funeral pyres, their leaders wondering," 561–62). Because of the word *victores*, we immediately believe the leaders are Pompeian, but given the general indeterminacy of the referents in this passage, I think the meaning is somewhat obscured. That is, I would argue that Lucan does not want his audience to know whether the "wondering leaders" are the Pompeians surrounding the Opitergians or the other Caesarians looking on from safety. This ambiguity matches the anonymity of the rest of the passage and is perhaps another comment on an audience's inability to distinguish between the two sides of a civil war. See above n. 31.

34. Leigh 1997.202 n. 34: "Since Vulteius and his men show such zeal to serve their leader, it is worth wondering whether the *dux* referred to at 4.572–3 is not Vulteius . . . but rather Caesar." The indeterminacy of the referent is precisely the point.

35. On *fama* in the epilogue, see above n. 4.

36. For a discussion of this scene and this theme, see Quint 1992.86–92.

37. For similarities between the cove Aeneas finds at *Aeneid* 1.157–69 and the cliffs to which Vulteius's raft is drawn, see Thompson and Bruère 1970.165–66.

38. Cf. Masters 1992 passim, esp. 13–25, on Lucan's distortion of his sources, especially Caesar. The poet is devastatingly ironic here, dilating the episode and making Vulteius dedicate the suicides to Caesar, secure in the knowledge that Caesar himself never mentions the Opitergian. My thanks to David Fredrick for pointing out the irony to me.

39. See Clover 1992.168–91 and Silverman 1988b.32–41 for analyses of the film *Peeping Tom*, which places the spectator in the object position and provoked great hostility from reviewers at the time of its release. Today it is recognized as "a sustained reflection on the nature of cinematic vision—in the opinion of many the finest metafilm ever made" (Clover 1992.169).

40. On this exchange and the distinct pairing of Pompey's head with Medusa's (9.619–733), see Eldred 1997.chap. 5.

41. See Zizek on Laibach, 1994.72–73.

3

Some Unseen Monster

Rereading Lucretius on Sex

Pamela Gordon

Of all the Greek and Roman philosophical schools, the Garden of Epicurus arguably was, and is, the least respected and most maligned. Although current critiques of Epicureanism cannot approximate the virulence of Cicero or Plutarch (to name the two great champions of anti-Epicurean rhetoric), it is significant that a favorite strategy of ancient anti-Epicurean discourse has survived into current scholarship. To convey the essence of this persistent tactic, I begin by recounting a joke about the Garden that was recorded in Greek during the Roman empire.

> The following pleasantry is told about the philosopher Arcesilaus. When asked why students from various schools can move to the Garden, but no Epicureans ever go over to the other schools, he retorted: "Because men can become eunuchs, but eunuchs never become men." (Diogenes Laertius 4.43)

For Martha Nussbaum, who proffers Arcesilaus's joke as the punch line to a critique of Epicureanism, the eunuch joke is a telling *bon mot* about the analytical shortcomings of the Epicurean method: the eunuch is a metaphor for intellectual castration (Nussbaum 1986.73–74 and 1994.139). Similarly, a recent survey of Epicureanism links Arcesilaus's "revealing witticism" to the secessionist bent of the Garden: the self-inflicted gash cuts the Epicureans off from the life of the Greek polis (Bryant 1996.426).

This chapter tenders the eunuch joke as proem rather than punch line. By beginning with Arcesilaus's retort, I mean to draw attention to its literal content: the gendering of the Epicurean. Here, as when the Stoic Epictetus calls Epicurus a *cinaedologus* (a "preacher of effeminacy" or a "pervert-professor," Diog. Laert. 10.7), the sexual content of the insult is no accident. While untrue on the literal level, these slurs encapsulate a valid (if hostile) evaluation of Epicureanism: in the eyes of the dominant culture, there was something fundamentally unmanly about the Garden. To recognize this figurative emasculation of the Epicurean male is not, however, to concur with recent endorsements of the eunuch joke. What I have in mind instead is a recuperative reading of Epicurean cultural history that acknowledges that the dominant culture claims for the realm of the masculine not only virtue and erudition but also competition and aggression.

My approach offers a new perspective on the Garden in general, but the specific purpose of this essay is to integrate the standard polemic against Epicureanism with Lucretius's Epicurean analysis of sex (*de Rerum Natura* 4.1030–1287). Epicurean theory posits an intimate connection between image and erotic desire, and, for Lucretius, erotic desire is dangerously allied with illusory visual pleasures and the grasping and striving that the Garden rejects. Thus Lucretius's critique occurs for good reason as the finale to his fourth book, a book devoted primarily to visual perception and the problem of illusion. At first glance, Lucretius's position seems an unlikely target for anti-Epicurean rhetoric: the polemic accuses the Epicurean of too great an interest in sexual pleasures, while Lucretius excoriates the pursuit of those same desires. But in my reading, Lucretius's damning analysis of sexual behavior is an Epicurean renunciation of all that sexual intercourse stands for in Roman culture. This means that Lucretius's verdict on sex serves to confirm, rather than to challenge, the dominant culture's suspicions about the deficient virility of the Epicurean male.

Lucretius the *Cinaedologus*

The gender-based polemic against the Garden may be, to some extent, a reaction to the Epicurean assertion that pleasure is the *telos* (the end or purpose of life), for the dominant discourses of both Greece and Rome routinely construe devotion to pleasure as a womanish vice.[1] But pleasure is not the only spark for anti-Epicurean polemic. In fact Cicero and Plutarch (or Seneca, or Athenaeus) would have difficulty reconciling their assertions about the depravity of the Epicureans with their reading of Lucretius.[2] Far from being an advocate of sartorial, culinary, or erotic indulgence, Lucretius urges austerity and describes sexual intercourse (which Epicurus called "natural but unnecessary") not only as unnecessary but as abhorrent. The traditional approach, as I see it, has been to defend the honor of the Garden's detractors by positing a split in

Roman Epicureanism. On one side, there is that small handful of edu-cated, respectable Epicureans: Lucretius and Cicero's friend Atticus, for example. On the other, there is a debased, popular Epicureanism that provides Cicero and Plutarch with their material.

Certainly any philosophical school can attract its share of poor prac-titioners, and there may well have been Roman admirers of Epicurus who styled themselves without sardonic intent as "pigs from the flock of Epi-curus" (cf. Horace *Epistles* 4.16).[3] But I suggest a different approach: rather than assuming the existence of anonymous Roman Epicureans who offended propriety through gross overindulgence in carnal pleas-ures, I seek the offending gesture in extant Epicurean texts.[4] By calling Lucretius a *cinaedologus*, I mean to appropriate the terminology of anti-Epicurean discourse and to reveal Lucretius as a representative target. Here it is crucial to recognize that the most basic tenets of the Garden—a philosophical school that urged its followers to seek pleasure and hap-piness by withdrawing from the turmoil of public life—went against con-ventional notions not only of morality but of virility. In fact it can be difficult to separate those two realms in the Roman imagination.

But before turning to Lucretius and his Roman context, I must pro-vide the reader with a primer on Epicurus's stand on erotic desire. For those unfamiliar with the texts of Epicurus, this primer will also serve as a general introduction to authentic Epicurean pleasures.[5]

Boys and Women, or Fish

In the *Letter to Menoeceus*, Epicurus distinguishes Epicurean pleasures from the sorts of pleasures that hostile outsiders associate with the Garden (131–32):

> When we say that pleasure is the *telos* (the end or purpose of life), we do not mean the pleasures of degenerates and pleasures that consist in carnal indulgence, as some assume (out of ignorance, or because they disagree, or because they misapprehend us), but we mean the absence of pain in the body and the absence of distress in the spirit. For it is neither continuous drink-ing parties, nor the carnal indulgence in boys and women, or fish, and the other offerings of a rich table that produce a pleasant life, but sober rea-soning, and searching out reasons for selection and avoidance, and banish-ing the sorts of received opinions that cause the greatest disturbance of the spirit. The beginning of all these things and the greatest good is prudence (φρόνησις). Thus prudence is even more valuable than philosophy, for all the rest of the virtues spring from prudence, which teaches us that it is not

possible to live pleasantly without living prudently and honorably and justly, nor to live a life of prudence, honor, and justice without living pleasantly. For virtues are naturally part of a pleasant life, and a pleasant life is inseparable from them.

Here it is obvious that Epicurus does not highly value the pleasures of sexual intercourse. His reference to the enjoyment of, or "carnal indulgence" (ἀπόλαυσις) in, "boys and women, or fish" and other expensive foods should be contrasted with the proverbial Epicurean request: "Send me a loaf of bread and a pot of cheese so that I might have a feast."

Since other key texts such as Epicurus's *Symposium* and *On Eros* have not survived, we have to piece together the rest of the early Epicurean stance on desire. A reference in Diogenes Laertius, for example, informs us that Epicurus taught that love is not god-sent (10.118), and thus provides an obvious contrast between Epicurean and Platonic notions (see *Phaedrus* 242d and *Symposium* 206c). Plutarch's *Quaestiones Convivales* (653b–655d) is also an important witness, for there the doctor Zopyrus, "who was well versed in the words of Epicurus," outlines a passage from Epicurus's *Symposium*. The context for Zopyrus's lesson is provided by some ignorant young men who have disparaged Epicurus for engaging his students in a discussion of the right time for intercourse. For an older man to bring up sex in the presence of young men and to discuss whether one should have intercourse before or after dinner seemed to them the extreme of indecency. Zopyrus, however, upbraids his young companions for being careless readers. Epicurus did not propose the problem as though it were a philosophical conundrum and then deliver speeches about it at the dinner table, "but instead, having taken the young men for a morally improving walk after dinner, he was conversing with them and diverting them from their desires, on the ground that it is a business always prone to cause damage[6] but especially for those who engage in it during a bout of drinking and eating" (*Mor.* 653c–d [*Quaest. Conv.* Book 3]). Zopyrus goes on to explain how wine and food exacerbate the symptoms caused by intercourse (and vice versa). His description accords well with Diogenes Laertius's terse report (10.118) that the early Epicureans said that "intercourse is never beneficial, and you are lucky if you receive no harm from it."[7]

Lest this outline of Epicurus's views on eros be misleading, I close by quoting a notorious dictum, one of the few remaining shards of Epicurus's *On the Telos*: "I know not how to imagine the good, apart from the pleasures of taste, sexual pleasures, sound, and form" (Diog. Laert. 10.6).

While this excerpt reminds us that adherence to Epicureanism does not require celibacy, it is important to note that Diogenes Laertius cites it as an example of unfair and deceptive reports on Epicurus.[8] The quotation, which occurs two sentences before Diogenes' complaint that Epictetus calls Epicurus a *cinaedologus*, appears in the lengthy passage on Epicurus-bashers that ends with Diogenes' summation: "But these people are crazy" (10.9).

What is clear from Epicurus's reference to the manly enjoyment of "boys and women, or fish" in the *Letter to Menoeceus* is that Epicurus views sex as a luxury item that is unnecessary at best. Like wine and rich food, it brings more turmoil than pleasure. Thus the person in search of Epicurean ἀταραξία ("inner calm" or "lack of distress") would best abstain. But what happens when this stance on intercourse travels from a Hellenistic Greek context to late republican Rome? My suspicion is that Lucretius's diatribe against the troubles of sex has a sharper edge than any lost texts of Epicurus on the same topic. Despite the perils involved in generalizations about Greek versus Roman culture, I would assert that the symbolic meaning of sexual intercourse is even less savory to the Roman Epicurean than it is to Epicurus.[9] The Roman display of sex as a luxury item, while only part of the problem, serves as a useful starting point.

Recent work on Roman wall painting stresses the nonprivate context of the many depictions of sexual intercourse on the walls of homes and businesses (Myerowitz 1992, Wallace-Hadrill 1994, Riggsby 1997, Clarke 1998). To the untutored modern eye, these scenes seem obviously meant for secluded viewing in the inaccessible reaches of the private home—unless, that is, they were intended to decorate the walls of brothels. But as John Clarke recasts the evidence, "The ancient Romans, rather than consider these images 'pornographic' and hide them away, usually associated them with luxury, pleasure, and high status" (Clarke 1998.4). Thus scenes that appear "intimate" to today's viewers were part of a complex system of competitive ostentation. The main impulse of all elaborate decoration, "erotic" and otherwise, was "not to display wealth but symbolically to affirm status" (Wallace-Hadrill 1994.12; cf. Riggsby 1997.41–42). If we accept this description of the iconography of intercourse, it is not difficult to see how Lucretius's treatment of sex fits into the acerbic critique of political striving that runs through the entire *de Rerum Natura*. The Lucretian *recusatio* of aggressive sex and political striving goes beyond Epicurus's simple rejection of "boys, women, or fish." Clarke views the variety of sexual images preserved by the eruption of Vesuvius as a salutary correction to elite literary sources that por-

tray high-status men as sexual aggressors and boys and women as the objects of their desires (Clarke 1998.2, 85). But I am less optimistic that the
luxury-value of images of sexual encounters can be disentangled from
their use as symbols of power. Can we be so certain that those visual depictions of sexual congress spell "'luxury,' not 'lust'"? (Clarke 1998.161).
The Roman Epicurean might protest that both belong to a nexus of
power and status that brings with it certain ταραχή ("turmoil and dis-
content") and the potential for violence.

   To return to Epicurus's *Letter to Menoeceus*: to some Roman readers, even that text implicates Epicurus as a *cinaedologus*. At the end of his
statement on the *telos* (quoted above), Epicurus asserts: "For virtues are
naturally part of a pleasant life, and a pleasant life is inseparable from
them." To Seneca—who relies for rhetorical effect on the implied ety-
mological link between *vir* ("man") and *virtus* ("virtue")—it is self-evi-
dent that Epicurus's words are contradictory: "Why do you join two
things that are completely different and even opposite? Virtue is something lofty, exalted and regal, unconquered, untiring. Pleasure is something low, slavish, weak, decrepit, whose place and home are the brothels and taverns. Virtue you will find in the temple, in the forum, in the
senate house, defending the city walls, dusty and sunburnt, hands cal-
lused. Pleasure you will find most often seeking out darkness, lurking
around the baths and sweating rooms and places that fear the magistrates;
soft, languid, reeking of wine and perfume, pallid, or else painted and
made up like a corpse" (Seneca *de Vita Beata* 7.3). This gendered characterization of pleasure and virtue is especially relevant here because
Seneca's rejoinder is addressed specifically to the Epicureans and is, in
fact, an intertextual rejoinder to Epicurus's assertion about the insepara-
bility of virtue and pleasure at *Letter to Menoeceus* 132. The broader context of Seneca's retort is a sustained contrast not just between womanish
pleasure and manly virtue, but between the effeminate Garden and the
virile Stoa.[10]

   Seneca would be hard-pressed to find praise for perfumes, baths,
brothels, or taverns in Lucretius's *de Rerum Natura* and other extant Epicurean texts. I wish to show, however, that Lucretius's stand on sex contradicts the particulars but not the spirit of anti-Epicurean rhetoric.

De Rerum Natura 4.1030–1287: The Mechanics of Desire and the Brutality of Sex

   Diverse ancient theories of desire assign a critical role to the
eye, an organ Empedocles describes as the invention of Aphrodite (DK

1.341–42).[11] Empedoclean notions of pores and effluences are fundamental to Epicurean theory, and Lucretius—in his affirmation of a close
connection between eros and the eye—seemingly conforms to a widely
held conviction.[12] The Garden's rejection of the notion of a purposeful
and divinely created world, however, entails a significant reorientation
in regards to traditional Greek wisdom on visual pleasure and desire. As
we shall see, the Epicurean view has little in common with Platonic accounts of the impression of beauty upon the soul of the lover.

Early in his explanation of the mechanics of vision, Lucretius introduces the concept of *simulacra*, "images of things, like membranes
sloughed off from the surface of things, that flit this way and that through
the breezes" (4.34–36). According to Epicurean theory, vision occurs
when these *simulacra* enter the eye of the beholder; thus visual perception is mechanically similar to a rarefied sort of touch. That is, vision results when *simulacra* impinge upon the organ of vision within the eye; the
contact itself is imperceptible (see Asmis 1984.106–07). Thoughts,
dreams, and fantasies are also material in origin, for *simulacra* are so fine
that they can pass through surfaces that appear solid, thus entering not
only the eye but the mind. Having introduced the rudiments of the science of *simulacra*, Lucretius hastens to add that the natural qualities of
images—which can linger in the air long after the source is gone, or can
be distorted or mixed with other images—have given rise to the erro-
neous belief in ghosts and other nighttime terrors (4.33–45). Thus Lucretius plants his warning early on in Book 4: *simulacra* can deceive the
untrained eye.

The most explicit exposition of the role of these images in the Epicurean physics of desire occurs in the opening verses of the discourse
on sex where Lucretius holds that male sexual response is directly
triggered by the airborne *simulacra* of attractive boys and women
(4.1052–56).[13] It is the image that stimulates the production of semen,
causes erections, and sustains a man's interest in a particular love object.
Even boys who ejaculate in their sleep are responding to images of a
lovely face or beautiful skin "from some body or other" (*e corpore quoque*,
1032). As Robert Brown puts it: "Sexual desire is thus reduced to a con-
spiracy of sight and semen" (1987.63). Even the cure for desire entails
strict avoidance of images, for when the beloved is absent, the image can
linger and feed desire (4.1061–63).

One might expect this scientific exposition of arousal via floating
image to be the introduction to a treatise that urges frank acceptance of
conventional sexual behavior. What follows instead is a vehement

polemic against the behavior of lovers that has disquieted readers since antiquity. In Lucretius's disquisition, sexual congress is violent and ugly. Rather than arousing tenderness and affection, the alluring image goads a man to bite, to squeeze, and to scrape the beloved's body in his desperate attempt to acquire what the image promises. Lucretius stresses the lover's delusion: he may as well try to quench his thirst by dreaming of drinking a river (4.1096–1101). Sexual desire may be comparable to thirst, but there is no analogue to fresh water in its consummation. Instead, a profusion of unappealing or outright offensive liquids accentuates the sordidness of sexual intercourse as it is described here: in addition to copious semen (*seminis ingentis fluctus*, 1036), there is an abundance of saliva (1108), sweat that ruins fine clothes (1128), and metaphoric blood (1050–51). Saturation with this sort of sex leads to loss of strength and the destruction of reputation, wealth, and happiness (1121–41). But what is most salient in the Lucretian sex scene is the language of violence, domination, and suffering. The scene is characterized by struggles (1112), nets and shackles (1113, 1147, 1148), biting teeth (1080, 1109), wounds and sores (1048, 1068, 1070, 1120, etc.), and repeated scraping of the beloved's fragile skin (*abradere*, 1103 and 1110). Lucretius makes clear that the pain the lover inflicts is intentional (4.1079–83):

> quod petiere, premunt arte faciuntque dolorem
> corporis, et dentes inlidunt saepe labellis
> osculaque adfligunt, quia non est pura voluptas
> et stimuli subsunt qui instigant laedere id ipsum,
> quodcumque est, rabies unde illaec germina surgunt.

> What they pursue, they squeeze hard and injure physically;
> often they sink their teeth into the lips as they inflict their kisses,
> because the pleasure is not unalloyed and there are secret goads
> that spur them on to hurt the very thing—whatever it is—
> that arouses these germs of madness.[14]

Although recent interpretations of Lucretius's finale to Book 4 have not, to my mind, focused adequately upon Lucretius's pairing of vision and aggression, they have demonstrated persuasively that Lucretius's diatribe against the behavior of lovers is an appropriate and deliberate culmination to his treatment of *simulacra* and illusion. For Lucretius, the erotic has everything to do with the visual because some kinds of "love" are based upon "the mannered, and basically shallow, obsession with external form" (R. Brown 1987.80). Whether a man fools himself into believing that an ugly woman is beautiful, or fools himself into believing that a beautiful woman is a goddess, his love is predicated on illusion and can only end in disillusion and disgust (R. Brown 1987, Nussbaum 1994).

By setting Lucretius's treatment of sex in the context of Epicurean theories of vision, Martha Nussbaum and Robert Brown also take some first steps toward reading Lucretius's polemic as a radical Epicurean critique of the Priapic model of sexuality.[15] Brown, for example, draws attention to the predatory nature of the male lover's appetite: the biting, salivating, scraping lover approaches the woman's body "as if he could make a meal of it" (R. Brown 1987.75). Nussbaum stresses the acting and posturing required even of the beautiful woman, whose lover would flee if he knew that she, too, menstruates (or farts, or undergoes embarrassing medical treatments).[16] As Nussbaum puts it: "Love's fantasies constrain and enclose both men and women, dooming the former to an exhausting alternation between worship and hatred, the other to a frantic effort of concealment and theater, accompanied by an equal hatred of everyday human things" (Nussbaum 1994.182). Brown proposes, furthermore, that Lucretius stresses the doubly offensive acquisitiveness of the male lover by showing how the lover's extravagant gifts (sparkling slippers, luminous emeralds) are meant not simply to please his latest acquisition but to enhance her appearance. In a graphic allusion to the aphrodisiac qualities of an expensive dress, Lucretius presents it rumpled and sweat-soaked, as though the lover has suddenly possessed both dress and wearer (R. Brown 1987.77–78): ("teriturque thalassina vestis / assidue et Veneris sudorem exercita potat," "and rubbed incessantly and abused, the sea-purple dress drinks up the sweat of Venus," 4.1127–28). The role of the visual in this predatory sort of love, and the subtle suggestion of violence here (against both woman and dress), calls for further scrutiny. First, however, I turn to some examples of what I regard as a serious misreading of Lucretius's polemic against the lover. As I hope to make clear, these readings go wrong when they occlude or misname Lucretius's focus upon the violent.

Contextualized Erotics: Sex in the Eyes of a Roman Epicurean

The notoriety of Epicureanism exerts a heavy influence even on "disinterested" scholarship on Lucretius. Few scholars have taken Epicurean social theory seriously enough to seek the historical or philosophical contexts of Lucretius's views on sex.[17] Robert Brown advanced critical discussion simply by remarking: "For a peace-loving Epicurean, the experience of sex is presumably too turbulent and overwhelming to be welcomed without reservation" (R. Brown 1987.67). Although Brown does not explore this particular avenue much further, Martha Nussbaum gives detailed consideration to the Epicurean context of Lucretius's position. Nussbaum's work, however, is ultimately far less appreciative of Epicureanism than is Brown's. For Nussbaum, the problem lies not in the Garden's love of tranquility but in its inadequate understanding of human needs and desires. In Nussbaum's view, Epicureanism promotes a worldview that divests human life of its complexity, mystery, and depth; sex is one of its many casualties. In response to Lucretius's descriptions of the aggression and pain that accompany erotic encounters, Nussbaum writes (1994.190): "Lucretius fails to ask whether there might not be intense excitement and beauty precisely in being needy and vulnerable before a person whom one loves. He fails to ask whether a certain sort of deep sexual excitement might not come precisely from the surrender of control and the acceptance of the intense importance of another separate person for one's entire life." After asserting that the most powerful erotic writers in the Western tradition ("from John Donne through Emily Brontë and beyond") have focused on exposure and receptivity as a source of erotic joy, Nussbaum concludes (1994.191): "Lucretius cannot understand this joy: for, in the end, he is an Epicurean, and as an Epicurean, he cannot permit himself, beyond a certain point, to follow his own advice to 'yield to human life.' Such neediness before the world would be hateful and terrible to the Epicurean."[18]

For some readers, Nussbaum's defense of sex may serve well as a response to Andrea Dworkin's claim that sexual intercourse in the modern West is an act of hate and aggression (Dworkin 1987). I find Nussbaum's elegant peroration inadequate, however, as a response to a voice from the city of the *carnifex* and the arena. While not confident that torture and terror can be safely assigned to "a world not ours" (to quote the title of T. P. Wiseman's chapter [1985] on sex and violence in the late Roman republic), I hear something discordant in the claim that Lucretius overlooks the joys of being "needy and vulnerable." From what vantage point can one lament Lucretius's inability to appreciate the joy of receptivity or the "deep sexual excitement" that comes from "the surrender of control"? A Roman reader might suspect that Nussbaum means to defend the erotic desire of the *cinaedus*, the eunuch, or the slave; for a Roman citizen to embrace such desires might amount to *impudicitia* or *stuprum* (cf. Richlin 1993a).

And yet, although Lucretius does not promote the desire that the dominant discourse attributes to the *cinaedus*, throughout his treatment of "love," he repudiates the mode of desire that the dominant culture reserves for the *vir*. Readers of this volume will be familiar with much recent feminist and Foucauldian work that exposes the way ancient Mediterranean culture schematizes masculine erotic activity as domination.[19] Given the differences in our sources, it is difficult to compare classical or Hellenistic Athens with late republican Rome, but many scholars have argued that the pattern is particularly stark in Rome, where poetry, prose, and the visual arts construe sexual agency as the birthright of elite male citizens and sexual submission as the lot of women, slaves, and low-status men. In Rome, as Ellen Oliensis writes: "Penetration is the prerogative of free men, penetrability the characteristic condition of slaves and women; sexual intercourse is an enactment and reflection of social hierarchy, and, conversely, social subordination always implies the possibility of sexual submission" (1997.154).[20] The competition, violence, and dehumanization implied in such a paradigm leads me to suspect that a Roman Epicurean would indeed find sexual intercourse "hateful and terrible" (to quote again Nussbaum 1994.191).

To return to Robert Brown's dictum on Epicurean reservations about "the experience of sex" (R. Brown 1987.67, quoted at the beginning of this section): my conviction is that recent work has not stressed adequately enough the Roman context of Lucretius's polemic. Martha Nussbaum is right to remark that Lucretius's account "describes lovemaking as one might describe the behavior of an alien tribe engaging in a strange ritual" (1994.173).[21] But the alien tribe is Lucretius's own people, and the word "lovemaking" imports a notion that Lucretius does not find among them. As an Epicurean who views the world—and the human body—as an accident in the atoms and void, Lucretius questions the rightness of social convention; to read his treatment of *amor* as an essay on universal, transcultural, "human" lovemaking is to misread.

Although Lucretius can never strip his poem of all Roman accoutrements, he himself signals the gulf between "the experience of sex" in Roman culture and that experience as it could be (beyond Rome, or in an untroubled Rome) by presenting Venus in the proem to Book 1 in a manner entirely inconsistent with Venus as she emerges in Book 4. In Book 1, Venus ("delight of people and gods," *hominum divumque voluptas*, 1.1) is the life force that quickens "every type of being" (*genus omne animantum*, 1.4). The desire this Venus offers is not only delightful (*lepore . . . cupide*, 1.15–16) but gentle (*blandum . . . amorem*, 1.19), and is capable of bringing peaceful tranquility to mortals generally (1.32) and to Romans specifically (1.40). This "nurturing Venus" (*alma Venus*, 1.2), who is associated with sunlight (1.6 and 1.9), flowers (1.8), springtime (1.10), and the "laughing" seas (1.9), urges birds to populate the trees and wild animals (especially female animals) to cross rivers in search of mates.

In the finale to the fourth book, however, we meet the perverted Venus of Lucretius's reality. Lucretius segues into his diatribe against the "civilized" Roman Venus by means of a reference to people who dream that they are standing by a latrine and so urinate on the bedspread. This leads to a reference to another way to foul the bedclothes (*vestemque cruentent*, 4.1036): wet dreams or "nocturnal emissions" (4.1030–36), which, in turn, lead into an Epicurean explanation of the production, "gathering," and emission of semen. And so begins Lucretius's notorious analysis of sex. It is significant that Lucretius rounds off these opening lines with a sardonic appraisal of sex among his contemporaries: "This is 'Venus' to us" (*Haec Venus est nobis*, 4.1057).[22] Gone is the warm, nurturing Venus of the first proem. Gone, too, is the lover reclining blissfully in her lap; in their place is chilly distress (*frigida cura*, 4.1060).

Much scholarship on Lucretius's two Venuses either pronounces the two passages to be irreconcilable or concludes that the operative contrast is between sex in the world of gods and animals (praised in Book 1) and love-tainted sex in the civilized world (attacked in Book 4).[23] What I propose here is the latter view with a crucial twist: the contrast is between a life-giving Venus who is at once an ideal and a potential and the specific manifestation of Venus that Lucretius, as Epicurean outsider, sees in his own world. Many scholars have recognized the Hellenistic and Roman trappings of the Lucretian lover: the man who waits at the doorstep (while the woman—according to Lucretius's lampoon—is involved in some offensive activity inside) is clearly the *exclusus amator* of the elegiac tradition (Kenney 1968, R. Brown 1987.135); and much of the Lucretian vocabulary for *amor* resembles the vocabulary of Plautus, Catullus, and, later, Ovid.[24] I would emphasize, however, that Lucretius is describing Roman "love" from the vantage point of someone attempting to step outside of his society. By its very clarity, Lucretius's exposition offers a critique not only of the Roman sexual vocabulary, but of the sexual metaphors that pervade Roman discourse.[25]

The contrast between the peaceful, genial Venus of Lucretius's first proem and the Venus of Roman reality comes into even sharper focus when we turn to Virgil's subversion of this passage in *Georgics* 3. In Virgil's "savagely pessimistic" rejoinder (Hardie 1986.159), brute force replaces the joy and innocence of the Lucretian version of the sex life of animals. Under the influence of *amor*, wild boars sharpen their tusks, bulls gore each other, and bears go on killing sprees. As Philip Hardie puts it: "What in Lucretius is a joyful celebration of the miraculous powers of Venus is transposed into an appalled account of the immoderate violence of desire" (1986.160). Virgil's method in the *Georgics* is to import the ugliness and insanity of *amor* (as Lucretius describes it in *de Rerum Natura* 4) into a passage modeled on the Venus proem of *de Rerum Natura* Book 1, thus attributing to animal sexuality vices that Lucretius reserves for men (cf. Hardie 1986.161–64). The few verses in Lucretius that describe the sex lives of animals as troubled reflect Lucretius's sense of the difference between sex as he knows it and sex in some happier— unrealized and yet conceivable—realm. His picture of dogs copulating at the crossroads "stuck in Venus's firm restraints" (4.1203–05) suggests, grotesquely, that even dogs have bad sex in Rome.

The reasons for this distressed state of *amor* are manifold, but the dominant recurring theme is epitomized in the story of Tityus in Book 3 (984–94), which provides a "preview" of the diatribe against erotic passion in Book 4. As Brown demonstrates, *de Rerum Natura* 3 (on the soul and its mortality) and *de Rerum Natura* 4 (on perception and illusion) are closely linked in argument and style: the connections between the books are constantly reinforced through allusions, cross-references, previews, and elaborations (R. Brown 1987.13–19). Brown explains the significance of the story of Tityus thus: "Even the attack on love has its preview in Book Three—in the portrayal of Tityos, the prototypical anguished lover, who receives a longer description than any of the other sufferers in Hades" (R. Brown 1987.15; cf. Nussbaum 1994.178). Brown is right to draw attention to the way the description of Tityus in Book 3 prefigures the treatment of desire in Book 4, but to call Tityus "the prototypical anguished lover" is to conceal the most pertinent mythological "fact" about Tityus. Tityus's *amor* has nothing to do with the vernal, procreative love of the Venus of the first proem. To put it bluntly: Tityus is the prototypical rapist. The crime for which he is condemned to eternal torment in the underworld is his sexual assault upon the goddess Leto.[26] Lucretius's interpretation of Sisyphus (3.999–1002) as a contender for Roman magistracies underscores the parallel between the sexual and the political: the Tityuses and Sisyphuses of real life suffer for their grasping after illusory power.

As an emblem of the contrast between Venus's gentle love (*blandum amorem*, 1.19) and the destructive *amor* of Book 4, Tityus augurs the approach of distress and disquiet. But, for Lucretius, the trouble is not simply a matter of passion as the harbinger of "anguish," "frenzy" (cf. R.

Brown 1987.91–99), or "obsession" (R. Brown 1987.88, Nussbaum 1989 and 1994.140–91). The trouble is not that human beings contaminate sex with love. The problem is the competition, violence, and cruelty inherent in the role of the "lover" as Roman culture constructs him.

Biographer's Revenge: The Sordid Death of Lucretius

In antiquity, a popular story (recorded by St. Jerome) claimed that Lucretius's life ended with a love potion, madness, and suicide. Although the legend still informs some approaches to Lucretius, most scholars now understand it not as history but as interpretation (cf. Nussbaum 1994.173). Thus the legend is itself a commentary on Lucretius's diatribe against passionate sex; a story assembled by readers who could understand Lucretius's apparent aversion to sexual intercourse only as the symptom of a poet's own unhappy love life. The legend also effects an interpretive foreclosure: it is one of many ways that a dominant tradition hampers appreciative readings of the *de Rerum Natura* (cf. R. Brown 1987.70 n. 39).

Tennyson's poem "Lucretius" (1868), however, occupies a middle ground. While it accepts and embroiders Jerome's "historical" account of the death of Lucretius, it also uses the story neither to undermine Lucretius's message nor to deprecate Lucretius's treatment of Venus in Rome. According to Tennyson's poem, Lucretius lived in harmony with the teachings of the Garden (211–18):

> No lewdness, narrowing envy, monkey-spite,
> No madness of ambition, avarice, none:
> No larger feast than under plane or pine
> With neighbours laid along the grass, to take
> Only such cups as left us friendly-warm,
> Affirming each his own philosophy—
> Nothing to mar the sober majesties
> Of settled, sweet, Epicurean life.

Suddenly, however, this happy existence (based, in part, on the proem to *de Rerum Natura* 2), is disrupted by Lucretius's wife. Angry because her husband seems to shun her in favor of his writing, she decides to resort to a love philter. As generally happens in tales of witches' potions, the plan goes astray: the mixture damages the poet's mind and, "tickling the brute brain within the man's" (line 21), gives him dreams and waking fantasies that are not only erotic but threatening. He sees, for example, the breasts of Helen; and jabbing at them from all sides is the nearly murderous sword of Menelaus.[27] Another image that terrifies him is a satyr chasing an Oread (196–200):

> Beastlier than any phantom of his kind
> That ever butted his rough brother-brute
> For lust or lusty blood or provender:
> I hate, abhor, spit, sicken at him; and she
> Loathes him as well;

To the horror of this Lucretius, it suddenly appears that the Oread is about to fling herself upon him, and he finds himself hoping that the satyr will catch her instead. That possibility, and Lucretius's own horrified interest in watching the beast rape the nymph, leads to further revulsion. His fall from the Garden is complete when he realizes that he is becoming too much like Menelaus and the satyr. Although he once lived in Epicurean tranquility, the poison has done its work (219–22):

> But now it seems some unseen monster lays
> His vast and filthy hands upon my will,
> Wrenching it backward into his; and spoils
> My bliss in being;

Thus Tennyson's Lucretius decides that suicide is the only way to escape from his new "beastlike" self (231).

H. A. J. Munro and Richard Jebb, both eminent Victorian classicists, praised Tennyson's "Lucretius" for its accuracy and judged it utterly Lucretian.[28] The poem's popularity has waned, of course, not only with changing tastes but also with decreasing faith in the accuracy of Jerome's historical note. I have quoted Tennyson at length here because his poem is one of the few commentaries on Lucretius's treatment of sex that responds with Lucretian horror to the notion of uncontrolled lust and aggression.[29] The more common reaction is to claim that Lucretius has sex all wrong. Tennyson, however, sees the monster.

Moreover, Tennyson's empathetic reading of Lucretius on sex captures something of Lucretius's interest in the dynamics of the visual. I described above how central vision is to Lucretius's exposition of desire and drew attention to Lucretius's repeated emphasis upon the violence of sex. Here I rephrase my approach: the deeper logic behind Lucretius's placement of the diatribe against erotic passion in Book 4, the book on visual perception, is Lucretius's awareness of a connection between the lover's stare and unacceptable lust. For Tennyson's Lucretius, too, lust has everything to do with the watchers and the watched. Even Helen's

breasts appear suddenly in the dark, glowing like the eyes of some predatory cat ("Then, then, from utter gloom stood out the breasts / The
breasts of Helen," 60–61). Lucretius is spared the sequel to Menelaus's
arrival in this nightmare, for the sensation of being scorched by a fire
shooting out of Helen's breasts awakens him. The visual allure of the
Oread is emphasized: "how the sun delights / To glance and shift about
her slippery sides" (188–89). The satyr follows her, but she has seemingly
caught a glimpse of her other watcher and turns to pursue Lucretius. In
his description of Lucretius's hope that the satyr will stop her, Tennyson
stresses the link between the desire to see the rape in the bushes and the
watchers' own urge toward violence, shared between the satyr and Lucretius: "do I wish / —What?—that the bush were leafless? or to whelm
/ All of them in one massacre?" (206–07). In this neo-Lucretian Physics
of Desire, power and control are constantly on the move, as watchers become the watched, as aggressors and victims trade places. No reciprocity is implied here, only retaliation.

Venus Victrix

The *de Rerum Natura* opens with a hymn to Venus that identifies her immediately both as ancestral goddess of the Romans and as goddess of erotic desire: "Aeneadum genetrix, hominum divumque voluptas" ("Mother of the sons of Aeneas, delight of humans and gods," 1.1).
The import of this proem to an epic that rejects traditional beliefs about
the gods is a vexed question whose resolution I will not attempt.[30] Instead I would simply stress the relevance here of the Epicurean view of
conventional representations of the divine, an attitude encapsulated in a
fragment of the later Epicurean Diogenes of Oenoanda. Rejecting the
notion of an armed goddess, Diogenes proclaims: "We should make statues of the gods genial and smiling, so that we may return the smile, instead of being afraid" (fr. 19, Smith). Lucretius's opening lines may look
"thoroughly ideologically correct" on the surface (cf. Penwill 1994.76),
but Lucretius's vision of the nurturing goddess is, in fact, subversive of
more widely accepted Roman notions of Venus. And in passing judgment
on his contemporaries' disposition toward the acts of Venus (in the finale
to Book 4), Lucretius denounces the immense cultural freight borne by
Venus in the late Roman republic.

Rather than embarking here on a survey of the domains of Venus (a
vast subject that would include references to all genres of the visual and
literary arts), I wish to emphasize one particular manifestation of Venus
in first-century B.C.E. Rome. This is *Venus Victrix* ("Venus Victorious" or

"Venus the Conqueror"), to whom the triumphant Pompey Magnus erected a temple at the top of his monumental theater in the Campus Martius.[31] This temple to Venus (including the theater below it) was dedicated in 55 B.C.E., several months before the traditional (but poorly documented) death of Lucretius. Both the theater itself and the opening spectacles seem to have surpassed all predecessors. Seating 15,000, the theater was the largest yet in Rome, and the *ludi* Pompey presented for the dedication ceremonies included various extravagances such as a *Clytemnestra* that required 600 mules, and a *Trojan Horse* that somehow involved the display of 3,000 wine bowls.

Such opulence is clearly antithetical to the values of the Garden, but even more offensive to Epicurean sensibilities is the fact that these festivities in honor of *Venus Victrix* culminated in five days of wild-beast shows. These games reportedly included the slaughter of 500 lions, and the finale eclipsed all previous shows by featuring a herd of elephants. At this point the spectacle descended further into an unintentional testament to the more horrific aspects of Roman Venus. As Cicero wrote to a friend who was not in Rome at the time, no one could deny that the animal hunts were impressive (*magnificae, nemo negat, ad Fam.* 7.1.3). Although the sources differ on the number of elephants involved in the spectacle (17? 19? 20?), several agree with Cicero's firsthand report that the slaughter of elephants ended up providing the crowd with "great awe but no enjoyment." Without explaining, Cicero tersely reports that "the result was a certain compassion (*misericordia*) and the sense that that huge beast has a fellowship with the human race" (*ad Fam.* 7.1.3–4).

Pliny describes in more detail how a match between elephants and a troupe of Gaetulian hunters at first pleased the spectators: one of the elephants—wounded in the feet and reduced to crawling on its knees against its attackers—managed to snatch their shields with its trunk, "and the shields as they cascaded through the air delighted the spectators, as if they were hurled by skill, not by the wrath of a wild animal." The crowd was also impressed when another elephant died from a single thrust of a javelin that entered its brain through a spot below the eye, and further excitement occurred when the surviving elephants attempted to break through the iron barricades. Ultimately, however, the dying animals despaired and exhibited such humanlike lamentations and entreaties that the weeping crowd sided with the elephants. A later tradition even attributed Pompey's subsequent downfall to the fact that the elephants' plight caused the crowd to rise *en masse* and curse him (Pliny *Naturalis Historia* 8.7). Cicero, who wishes to distinguish himself from the mass of ordinary spectators, makes a brief allusion to both human and animal deaths when he asks his correspondent: "But for a cultured person (*homini polito*), what pleasure could there be when a helpless person (*homo imbecillus*) is mangled by a powerful beast, or when a splendid beast is transfixed with a hunting spear?" Later Seneca would record that Pompey's games were said to have used the elephants to execute people by trampling (*Dialogi* 10.13.6–7).

Although Pompey's games in honor of *Venus Victrix* outdid previous expressions of the power of Venus, this was not the first time Venus was celebrated as a goddess of force and triumph. In fact Pompey seems to have taken Venus as his patron goddess in order to supplant the prior claims of Sulla, who was in turn competing with Marius.[32] Sulla, who reportedly received an omen of his own success against Mithradates via a dream in which he saw *Venus Victrix* leading an army, had recently claimed her as his ally and taken the *agnomen* "Epaphroditus" ("favored by Venus/Aphrodite").[33] The trophy Sulla set up on the battlefield of Chaeronea in 86 B.C.E. was dedicated to Mars, Venus, and Victoria, and the coins Sulla issued in 84/83 depicted Venus and Eros on one side and Sulla's trophies and augural symbols on the obverse (Keaveney 1983. 60–64). Later Caesar, of course, would claim Venus more personally as *Venus Genetrix*. At first glance, the pairing of Venus with triumphant generals may seem an odd juxtaposition. With Sulla's career in mind, one might well ask: what does the goddess of "love" have to do with civil war, land confiscations, proscriptions, the bolstering of the *cursus honorum*, and the generally ruthless employment of violence? Returning to Pompey's games, one wonders how a battle between men and animals captured in Africa could represent an appropriate homage to Venus. One might deflect these questions by claiming that Venus in the *Victrix* mode is simply the divine parent of Rome and that Sulla and Pompey are merely stressing the antiquity and divine authority of Roman power. But if we rephrase the question with the broader implications of the Priapic model in mind and ask what Venus has to do with conquest, we see that her role as conqueror is not necessarily at variance with her role as "lover."

The first proem of Lucretius also associates Venus with the war god, but this *alma* ("gentle, nurturing") Venus is no ally of Mars. Rather than serving as Mars's accomplice, and lending her powers to his pursuits, this Venus calms Mars in her embrace, thus preventing him from wreaking havoc. A war god becalmed is a war god disarmed, and, by opening his epic with Mars lying transfixed in the lap of Venus, Lucretius aligns

Epicureanism not only with *voluptas* ("pleasure, delight") but with the repudiation of violence: a theme that recurs throughout the poem (see
Nussbaum 1994.239–79). Thus even the opening proem implies that the
Garden eschews one of the most basic of Roman notions of what it
means to be male.[34] Renunciation of a similar order is also central to Lucretius's analysis of sex, but there Venus has reemerged in a form befit-
ting her role as patron goddess of invading generals.

Back to the Garden

Lucretius's only reference to women looking at men occurs in
his verses about the behavior that the jealous man attributes to his
woman: "Something bitter wells up and chokes him among the very
flowers . . . because . . . he thinks she is casting her eyes about too much,
or looking at another man, and he sees in her face traces of laughter"
("surgit amari aliquid quod in ipsis floribus angat . . . quod . . . nimium
iactare oculos aliumve tueri / quod putat in voltuque videt vestigia risus,"
4.1134, 1139–40). In fact, although Lucretius argues for the existence of
female arousal and pleasure (4.1192–1200, 5.583–84), he implies that a
woman's arousal stems not from the *simulacra* of any man but from her
own heart or feelings (*ex animo*, 4.1195). Thus in the midst of the scenes
of grabbing, scraping, and wounding, there are glimmers of hope. All
of Lucretius's optimism about sex in the world as he knows it appears in
his description of the woman's comportment. As Brown puts it, Lucretius
describes intercourse in healthy terms only in the verses on female sexual pleasure (1987.65–66): "*She* sighs (1192) while *he* breathes in through
clenched teeth (1109); *she* enfolds her lover (1193) while *he* squeezes
painfully (1079); *she* showers moist kisses (1194) while *he* inflicts painful
bites and exchanges saliva (1080, 1108–09); *she* urges her lover towards
a mutually pleasurable climax (1195–96) while *he* ineffectually scrapes the
other body with his hands or seems intent on driving himself completely
within (1110–12), while his limbs collapse and melt under the force of
pleasure (1114)." In my view, this is precisely where Lucretius's analysis
of sex emerges most clearly as a critique of the Priapic model of male sexuality rather than as a polemic against love or as a judgment against sex
itself.

For Brown, however, the contrast that Lucretius draws is not one
between female gentleness and male predation but between the woman's
"simple instinct" and "straightforward libido" and the man's obsessional
"love" (R. Brown 1987.66). Thus Brown would align the woman's sexuality with that of the happy animals of the Venus proem while the man's

is "corrupted with unnatural expectations" (95). Shifting the focus away from this contrast between "natural" sex and the man's corrupted love, I would emphasize instead a contrast between Lucretius's vision of the possibility for godlike love, gentleness, and tranquility and the grotesque nightmare of sex as he sees it in Roman reality. Here it is important to remember the Garden's total rejection of teleology. For the Epicurean, we all live in a destructible world where many things are good, and some are horrific, but nothing is as it is "supposed to be." Even vision itself is an accident in the atoms and void. As Lucretius warns his readers, it is wrong to imagine that eyes were created for looking (4.824–25). Thus Lucretius's exposition of male desire should be read not as a treatise on a purposeful system but as a description of cold reality. This is not to say that Lucretius construes sexual violence as inevitable. To the contrary: his reference to rape in the early stages of civilization ("violenta viri vis atque impensa libido," 5.964) is followed by references to the "softening" of the human race and the arrival of gentleness and friendship, without which the race would have perished (5.1015–27).

I would align Lucretius's brief glance at female sexuality not just with sex as happy animals know it, but with Lucretius's vision of love (and sex) between gods.[35] The Epicurean's task is always to aim for a godlike existence, but—as Epicurus tells his mother—such an achievement takes time.[36] Although Lucretius could conceive of a nurturing Venus, he apparently could not imagine her arriving at a gathering of Roman Epicureans without disrupting the idyll.[37] Lucretius may valorize the sexual deportment of Roman women (albeit fleetingly), but, in the end, his optimism is limited to a vision of a tranquil and friendly marriage between the Epicurean man and a good but homely woman (4.1278–87; see R. Brown 1987.90 and 126). Despite his efforts to disentangle himself from the constraints of Rome, obvious indicators of a masculine point of view remain. And yet, the concluding words of Lucretius's discourse on sex can also be read as a comment on masculinity and a (apparently ironic) formula for its subversion. The book ends with the homely woman gradually winning the affection of her mate, a slow process, like water dripping on stones. Here Lucretius closes with an obvious reversal of sexual imagery: the *guttae* ("drops") and penetration (*pertundere*) previously attributed to the vocabulary of masculine sexual deportment are now the metaphorical province of the woman (4.1226–27).

Thus Lucretius—through his astringent description of virile perception, pursuit, and penetration, and through his unmanly valorization of female desire—emerges as a *cinaedologus:* the poet of a disruptive discourse that recites with too overt an abhorrence the pervasive formulation of both intercourse and the gaze as domination. A hostile reader of the *de Rerum Natura* may take the "unseen monster" (line 219) of Tennyson's poem as emblematic of Lucretius's personal—and unnatural, or even pathological—fear of sex. New readers of Tennyson may disparage Tennyson's esteem for Lucretius's attitude toward sex as too "Victorian" and "puritanical" (Rudd 1994.114). But my reading recuperates Lucretius's scathing analysis of sex as a social critique that locates the monster not in the private heart of Lucretius but in the horrific specters of Tityus, Venus Victrix, and the paradigmatic Roman *vir*. By recognizing the formative role that the harshest Roman realities played in the making of Lucretius's polemic, my approach finds something both correct and salutary in the dominant culture's complaint that the Garden was teaching men not to be men.

Notes

For their suggestions, I owe thanks to Tony Corbeill, Dave Fredrick, and Kathy Whalen. The American Council of Learned Societies, the Hall Center for the Humanities, and the Graduate Research Fund of the University of Kansas provided generous support. I also wish to thank Harold Washington and Caroline Jewers for another sort of generosity.

    1. On the Greek material, see esp. Carson 1990 (with bibliography). For Rome, see Edwards (1993, esp. 63–97 and 174 n. 1), Joshel 1992b and 1997, Richlin 1993a, and Skinner 1993. Maud Gleason characterizes the Greek view thus: "A man who aims to please—any one, male or female—in his erotic encounters is ipso facto effeminate" (Gleason 1995.65).

    2. I would identify Cicero (see esp. *in Pisonem* and *Tusculanae Disputationes*) and Plutarch (see esp. *de Lat. Viv.* and *Non Posse* [*Mor.* 1086c–1107c]) as the "best" enemies of the Garden. See Gordon 1997a.

    3. Far from betraying any awareness of "Epicurean pigs," Lucretius claims that the Garden lacks adherents because of its austerity: to the outsider it seems *tristior* ("rather sad, austere, or unappealing," 1.944). I take Cicero's remark that Piso, as an Epicurean, comes "from the pigsty, not the school" ("*ex hara producte, non ex schola,*" *in Pis.* 37) as rhetorical *occupatio* to anticipate anyone's objection that Cicero's characterization of the vile Epicurean is unfair.

    Except where noted, all translations are my own.

    4. Cf. Clay 1998, who suggests (in reference to Cicero's ridicule of Epicurean theology) that "Lucretius and not the bad company of Velleius's fellow Epicureans is the object of Cicero's indignation" (178).

    5. See also Diog. Laert. 10.137, who contrasts pleasures of the body with the greater pleasures of the ψυχή, a report consistent with Epicurus *Letter to Men.* 132. See Gosling and Taylor 1982.349–54 and Long 1986.

6. The text delicately refers to intercourse as a thing (*pragma*) that is "precarious toward damage." The Loeb offers the appropriate (if less literal) translation: "Intercourse is always precarious and harmful."

7. Cf. *Sent. Vat.* 51. For interpretation see Brennan's response (1996) to Purinton 1993.

8. Principal Doctrine 8 (which cautions that while "no pleasure is bad," some pleasures are outweighed by the turmoil they bring) suggests a probable context for the quotation from *On the Telos*.

9. If we take Lucretius's contemporary Philodemus as a representative of Greek Epicureanism, his praise (in verse) of sexual pleasures provides an interesting contrast. On Philodemus as an Epicurean poet, see Sider 1997.32–39. Cicero repeatedly stresses Philodemus's Greekness: *Graecus* (*in Pis.* 86, 69, 70), *Graeculus* (70), *Graecus atque advena* ("a Greek and an outsider," 70).

10. Although Seneca partakes of anti-Epicurean rhetoric, he does not completely misrepresent the Garden. In fact his usual method is to follow his polemics with eclectic sermons replete with Epicurean ideas. See Asmis 1989 on the way Seneca first opposes the two philosophies, but then "grafts" (244) Epicurean ideas onto Stoicism.

11. For a survey of Greek theory, see Lindberg 1976.1–17. For non-Epicurean accounts of the role of the eye, see Plato's *Phaedrus* 250d, *Symposium* 206c–207a, and (for a critique of the gaze as described in the *Phaedrus*) Frontisi-Ducroux 1996.

12. For the Epicureans' debt to Leucippus and their debts to and disagreements with Empedocles and Democritus, see Bailey 1947.1180–81.

13. The implied reader (and Epicurean to be) is obviously male; and in keeping with the dominant tradition, descriptions of the physical appearance of women abound in the finale, while the men are comparatively invisible.

14. On "unalloyed" pleasure (*non pura voluptas*) as pleasure unmixed with anxiety or other troubling emotions, see R. Brown 1987.220. On the gender (most likely male) of the subject of the verbs in this passage, see Nussbaum 1990.66–67.

15. On the Priapic model of male sexuality, see Richlin 1992a. C. A. Williams 1999 passim elaborates Richlin's description of the Priapic model.

16. As Nussbaum makes clear, it all depends on how we read *se suffit* in 4.1175 (1994.179–81).

17. For recent attempts, see Fitzgerald 1985 and Graber 1990 in addition to R. Brown 1987 and Nussbaum 1989, 1994, and 1996.

18. In the phrase "yield to human life," Nussbaum is quoting *de Rerum Natura* 4.1191: *humanis concedere rebus*.

19. For introductions to the now copious bibliography, see Skinner 1993 and Richlin 1992a and 1993a. More recent work includes: Larmour, Miller, and Platter 1998, Oliensis 1997, Parker 1997, Walters 1997, and C. A. Williams 1999.

20. Richlin (1993a.538) puts it succinctly: "What defines the *vir* is penetra-

tion." Cf. p. 532: "The highly class-stratified nature of Roman society is an essential component in the construction of Roman sexuality—the two systems can hardly be understood independently."

21. Elsewhere Nussbaum makes an extended plea for the importance of social construction to students of Hellenistic philosophy: Nussbaum 1996.

22. See R. Brown 1987.95, who writes that "the force of the phrase . . . is: 'this is what we have turned into a goddess,' not this is all that I meant by Venus in Book One."

23. Cf. Nussbaum 1994.172 on love as "the sick or bad form of sexual interaction." Although Brown's position is similar to Nussbaum's in that he often describes Lucretius's attack on sex in Book 4 as a polemic against love per se, he comes close to the position I wish to articulate in such statements as: "Lucretius is not condemning all forms of love but only the obsessive type which is based on appearance and false opinion" (R. Brown 1987.88).

24. See R. Brown 1987.140–43, who questions the relevance to Lucretius of Catullus. On sexual violence in Roman elegy, see also Fredrick 1997.

25. For the vocabulary of intercourse and sexual aggression, see esp. Richlin 1992a, Adams 1982, and C. A. Williams 1999.

26. As punishment for the rape or attempted rape of Leto, Tityus is killed by Leto's daughter Artemis and/or her son Apollo. In the underworld, two vultures perpetually tear out his liver. See *Odyssey* 11.576–81 and other sources listed in Gantz 1993.39.

27. Tennyson alludes to the tradition (known from Quintus Smyrnaeus and Euripides' *Andromache* 628–29) that Menelaus wanted to kill Helen when he recovered her in Troy, but faltered when he saw her breasts.

28. See Jebb 1868 and Ricks 1987. For a more recent assessment (largely appreciative), see chap. 4, "Tennyson and Lucretius," in Rudd 1994.

29. On Tennyson's attitudes toward sex, see P. Turner 1976.175–76 and Rudd 1994.114–16. Tennyson's Lucretius compares himself to the rape victim Lucretia, and even describes his own suicide as a "symbolic rape" (Rudd 1994.111).

30. For recent treatments that stress (rightly, I believe) the role of Empedoclean poetics in Lucretius's proem, see Sedley 1998, Jenkyns 1998, and Clay 1998.

31. On this monument to *Venus Victrix*, see Coarelli 1971–72.104, Hanson 1959.1–3 and 43–55, Richardson 1992.411, Schilling 1954.296–97. With Hanson, I view the theater-temple complex as one coherent monument without taking literally Tertullian's report (*de Spect.* 10) that the theater seats were presented as mere steps to Venus's temple at the top of the cavea. As companion pieces to the *Venus Victrix* shrine, Pompey dedicated smaller shrines or *aediculae* to four subsidiary divinities: *Honos* and *Virtus* (the personifications of military valor), *Felicitas* (the personified good fortune of the general), and (possibly) *Victoria* (Victory personified). See Pollini 1996.772. Pollini 1996.773–75 suggests that the cult statue of Venus may have been armed with a sword.

32. Galinksy describes the use of *Venus Victrix* as a sign of the privatization of communal values: "The Roma Victrix of the entire Roman people on a denarius of 119 B.C. changes into the personal goddess of victorious generals from Marius to Caesar, especially the Venus Victrix of Sulla, Pompey, and Caesar" (1996.61).

33. See Plutarch *Sulla* 34.2. For Sulla's dream, see Appian *Bella Civilia* 1.97.

34. Contrast Nussbaum 1994.163, who takes Mars's attitude as an example of an unhealthy "obsession" that makes him neglect "his proper business." Giussani (cited by Bailey 1947.599), suggests that Lucretius is imitating an existing statuary group.

35. On the false notion that the Epicureans were atheists (promulgated by the anti-Epicurean tradition), see Obbink 1989.

36. The text of the Epicurean *Letter to Mother*, which I regard as fictional and idealizing, appears in the second-century C.E. inscription of Diogenes of Oenoanda. See P. Gordon 1996.66–93.

37. For this ideal Epicurean gathering, see *de Rerum Natura* 2.29–33 and Tennyson's homage to it, above.

4

Reading Programs in Greco-Roman Art

Reflections on the Spada Reliefs

Zahra Newby

Introduction and Methodology

In 1620, workmen rebuilding the staircase of the church of Sant' Agnese fuori le Mura in Rome made a striking discovery, recovering eight marble reliefs that had been used facedown as paving stones.[1] Following their subsequent installation in the Palazzo Spada, these reliefs became known as the Spada reliefs (figs. 4.7–4.14).[2] All eight are of Luna marble with similar dimensions, about 1.75 m high and 1.10 m wide, including areas of restoration (S. Lehmann 1989).

These similarities, and the fact that the reliefs were all apparently reused at the same time, lead scholars to see them as part of a coherent group.[3] Indeed it seems likely that the panels were displayed together during antiquity, probably within a residence close to the present site of the church (see Kampen 1979 and the discussion below). Other reliefs of a similar size and style survive from ancient Rome, although it is unlikely that any of these should be associated with the eight Spada reliefs.[4] These can be dated stylistically to the late Hadrianic and early Antonine periods in the second century C.E. They provide us with a unique opportunity to reconstruct a second-century Roman program of decoration and to suggest the viewings and interpretations it may have provoked.[5]

Natalie Kampen has considered the evidence for the architectural display of marble reliefs and suggests that they may have been fitted with clamps and set into shallow niches in walls, such as those in the Baths of Trajan in Rome and Hadrian's Villa at Tivoli (Kampen 1979.597). While no Latin word seems to refer solely to reliefs, she suggests that marble reliefs could have been used like paintings to decorate rooms and porticoes in both public and private spaces (Kampen 1979.595, 598). Indeed Cicero's request to Atticus for "typos . . . quos in tectorio atrioli possim includere" seems to be a definite reference to reliefs that Cicero intends to insert within the walls of his hallway.[6] It seems likely, then, that these reliefs were originally displayed within the domestic context of a suburban villa close to the Via Nomentana, and indeed their subject matter, with its focus on Greek myth, agrees closely with that of domestic wall paintings in Pompeii and Herculaneum.[7]

Cycles of wall paintings provide a close parallel to the programs presented by these marble relief panels, and a look at the different approaches to wall painting may help in our analysis of the Spada reliefs. A number of recent studies continue the work done by Karl Schefold and M. L. Thompson in the 1950s and '60s and investigate the "conceptual and narrative relationships" among mythological images displayed in domestic spaces.[8] Both paintings and reliefs show similar choices of material, and there are stylistic parallels between their representations of landscape, as has been convincingly shown by C. A. Brokaw (1942). In addition, the Spada reliefs show some details treated in very low relief, such as Bellerophon's spear (fig. 4.8), that may originally have been highlighted with paint.[9] It seems reasonable to assume that narrative reliefs and paintings would have prompted similar strategies of viewing.

Richard Brilliant's analysis concentrates on the general themes or contrasts that unify a group of images, such as divine punishment and reward in the Ixion and Theban Rooms in the House of the Vettii.[10] However, Bettina Bergmann suggests a different approach (1994), reconstructing the experience of the ancient viewer as he or she moves through space. While acknowledging that some of the images in the House of the Tragic Poet are linked by one particular theme, the Trojan War, Bergmann also stresses the specific parallels between individual paintings to which their formal composition draws attention. This approach, with its stress on the multiplicity of programs and interpretations encompassed within a single cycle of images, provides a useful tool for investigating the Spada reliefs.

The rhetorical work *ad Herennium* suggests that an orator should associate the different parts of his speech with different areas of the house, so that, by mentally walking through the house, he will be able to recall his speech in the correct order. Bergmann suggests that the same relationship between concrete image and verbalized meaning could also operate within the pictorial programs of Roman houses. Just as the orator mentally starts and stops in particular places or changes his direction in order to give a different slant to his speech, a viewer of the paintings could build up different sets of narratives depending both on the way in which he or she approached the images and on the individual ideas thereby provoked.

Bergmann's approach not only gives us ways to view images, it also suggests that the whole process of viewing within the domestic environment is analogous to the public activity of delivering a speech. The connections that a private viewer perceives between images are constructed in the same way that the orator moves from one part of his speech to the next. The parallel goes both ways. Not only does the orator use his private house to recall his speech, attaching values to the objects that he approaches in his imagination, but the domestic activity of viewing, approaching those objects and forging connections between them, is analogous to public rhetorical activity.

This analogy has profound consequences when we consider the integral link between a man, his status, and his house. A number of recent studies emphasize the social importance of the house for elite rituals.[11] Building on the evidence of Vitruvius, who says that those in the public eye should equip their houses with reception rooms worthy of their dignity and appropriate for the functions required of them, these studies stress the public nature of certain areas within the house.[12] Areas like the atrium were accessible to all and provided the focus for rituals associated with the patron's prestige, such as the morning *salutatio* when he received his clients. The decoration of these areas should thus express the patron's status and culture to those visiting him. Other areas, such as the peristyle or triclinium, were open only to invited guests and often expressed the honor due to such guests by decorative means, such as the expensive colors used to decorate their walls (Wallace-Hadrill 1994.31). Andrew Wallace-Hadrill emphasizes the use of décor to highlight this ambiguity between the private and public. He argues that, in late republican houses in Pompeii, the decoration deliberately alludes to public forms, such as those of the basilica, to exalt the activity taking place within the house to the status of a public act.[13] In the viewing of later wall paintings, at least as suggested by Bergmann, we can see the process of viewing itself as analogous to a public activity, rhetoric, through the shared use of mnemonic techniques.

In the late republic, public oratory still offered the means for social advancement, and private houses fulfilled a crucial role in achieving public prestige.[14] However, with the introduction of the principate, the opportunities for political advancement became more circumscribed, with senatorial authors such as Tacitus suggesting an insecurity about the political use of rhetoric, since to speak openly could lead to imperial disfavor.[15] It is within this context that we find the programs of wall painting discussed by Bergmann, where the public activity of rhetorical speaking is alluded to by the process of viewing, yet internalized within the house. While the house remained a focus for personal prestige, its decoration, which played a key role in expressing that prestige, had changed in accordance with the cultural and political values on which status was seen to rest.

The interaction between public and private in the second century is likely to have changed yet again. This is particularly true when we consider the parallels between public rhetoric and domestic decoration. Catharine Edwards discusses how domestic luxury could be used rhetorically as an analogy to extravagance in other areas, even rhetoric itself.[16] During the first century B.C.E., attacks on the unnatural creation of terraces, moles, and lakes, such as those we find in Horace Odes 2.15, went hand in hand with attacks on the debasement of rhetoric, particularly the flamboyant rhetorical flourishes characteristic of the so-called Asiatic style of rhetoric.[17] Yet later in the first century C.E., we find a growing acceptance of both domestic luxury and rhetorical extravagance—Statius's Silvae and Martial's Epigrams actively celebrate luxurious innovations in elite villa building, especially the manipulation of the natural landscape, and Pliny's descriptions of his own villas also take pride in their luxuriousness and extent.[18]

This acceptance of luxury, in both the decoration and architecture of such villas, is paralleled by a change in attitude toward rhetoric.[19] Although traditional Latin forensic rhetoric continued and was practiced by elite figures such as Pliny himself, interest in a new type of rhetoric also came to the fore: the Greek display oratory whose practitioners are described in Philostratus's Lives of the Sophists. The popularity of this sophistic rhetoric in the west as well as the Greek east of the empire is clearly shown by figures such as the Gallic sophist Favorinus, born in Arles, who chose to pursue a career in Greek rhetoric, and Lucian, who tells us that he had particular success in the west.[20] Chairs of both Latin and Greek rhetoric had been introduced into Rome by Vespasian, and the Greek one was held by a number of the sophists whose lives Philostratus describes. In addition, Philostratus shows that Roman emperors of the second century were keen students of and listeners to the sophists.[21] This type of rhetoric was characterized by its choice of themes from the Greek past, especially those from the fifth and fourth centuries

B.C.E., but also by its theatricality and exuberance. Thus Favorinus apparently manipulated both his eunuch's high voice and his effeminate appearance to stir up the passions of the crowd during his performances.[22] This sort of over-the-top, extravagant public display provides a striking parallel to the increased luxury of architecture and the visual arts within the domestic sphere.

Accompanying these changes in rhetorical and domestic display is a wider change in the culture of the Roman empire: the increased prominence, even idealization, of classical Greek culture. For the Roman elite of the late republic and early empire, Greek culture was confined to the world of leisure, *otium*, and still firmly linked to Rome's conquest of Greece, as in Horace's famous statement "Graecia capta ferum victorem cepit," "Captive Greece enslaved her uncouth conqueror" (*Epistles* 2.1.156). Yet from the later first century, and especially in the passionate philhellenism of the emperor Hadrian, Greek culture came to the fore in a very public way.[23] In part this can be traced to the changing conditions of empire, with the elites of the Greek-speaking eastern provinces gradually taking up Roman citizenship, equestrian and senatorial rank, and even, as in the case of Herodes Atticus in 143 C.E., aspiring to the consulship. In the increasingly cosmopolitan world of the Roman empire, Greek culture became not just an avenue for escape from worldly matters, but also a means for advancement in the political sphere.[24] We might cite the case of Apuleius, a philosopher from North Africa writing in Latin, who seeks in his *Apology* to unite himself with his judge on the basis of their shared knowledge of Greek culture, mocking his accuser's ignorance of the Greek language.[25] *Paideia*, the result of a thorough education in Greek language, literature, history, and thought, had become a badge of culture for the Greco-Roman elite.[26] Changes in the architecture and decoration of elite villas must have been determined, at least partially, by a desire to display this *paideia* and to turn it to the service of Roman *luxuria*.[27]

In my interpretation of the Spada reliefs, I intend to use two texts that are characterized by sophistic rhetoric and that deal, in particular, with the issues of how to interpret and respond to images: the Elder Philostratus's *Imagines*, a text that specifically purports to teach the young how to view paintings, and Lucian's *de Domo*.[28] Both works are later than the Spada reliefs: Lucian dates to the second half of the second century and Philostratus to the early part of the third century C.E.[29] Nonetheless, there are persuasive reasons for using their evidence to guide our viewing of these reliefs. Through their stress on Greek predecessors, either artistic or literary, and their interest in predominantly Greek material, all three works can be seen as characteristic products of the second and third centuries c.e., whose rhetorical and literary activity is commonly referred to by Philostratus's term, the Second Sophistic.[30]

Lucian, Philostratus, and the Spada reliefs all aim toward the same kind of elite Second Sophistic audience. When Lucian differentiates between "educated" and "ordinary" men in their responses to art, he is clearly aligning himself and his audience with the former, οἱ πε-παιδευμένοι.[31] Philostratus says that he was visited by youths wishing to hear μελέται, "rhetorical exercises," a comment that aims at identifying him as a famous sophist and these young men as potential pupils (*Imagines* 1 proem 4). While Lucian's οἶκος may be a public hall specifically designed for rhetorical displays, Philostratus's display is certainly set within a domestic environment, his host's house on the Bay of Naples.[32] Yet this house is also open to the educated youths who importune him. Like the villa in which the Spada reliefs were probably displayed, this space is domestic, yet open to a wider viewing public that includes other members of the educated elite. Such viewers could impose their own strategies of viewing onto the images shown, but the choice of images would reflect back onto the character and status of their host.

Philostratus provides us with a sophisticated and complex account of how a viewer could respond to visual works of art. Whilst a rhetorical agenda may influence much of what he says, including the possibility that the whole scenario, paintings and all, is fictional, Philostratus suggests clear indications of the programs and parallels among the paintings he describes, without ever explicitly naming them. This ability to see through Philostratus's text to a unified group of images led Karl Lehmann to argue for the historical reality of these paintings and the "Villa by the Sea" in which they were exhibited.[33] This particular argument has been widely rejected by scholars (for example, Bryson 1994.255–83), who point out that Lehmann manipulates the evidence, yet he was surely right to identify programs within the images that Philostratus describes. Where we should cease to follow Lehmann is in his assumption that because Philostratus does not group the paintings according to these thematic links, he was unaware of them. Instead, by allowing his readers to perceive links between the images but concentrating, himself, on individual descriptions, Philostratus suggests the coexistence of two different modes of viewing, emphasizing either the links between images or the individual images in isolation.

The viewer of a naturalistic image, here Philostratus, interprets the image by setting it in a context of his own devising: reading in motivations and identifications that seem plausible. In addition to setting the image within his own cultural parameters, however, the viewer also inserts himself into the world of the image, eliding the distinction between real and imagined, as in Philostratus's frequent exhortations to "Look!," his direct addresses to the painted figures, and his professed inability to discern "real" from painted details (Elsner 1995.21–39, esp. 30ff.).

This interaction with the image results in the entering into a fantasy world, one in which direct access to the characters of Greek myth and history is possible. In fact the naturalism of Philostratus's images provokes a response at odds with the desire shown elsewhere to categorize images into thematic programs. Naturalistic, often erotic, compositions entice the viewer into their world, causing him to lose the sense of perspective that is vital to an intellectual discussion of them. It is significant that one feature of this intellectual control is marked by its use of texts. In the description of the image of Scamander, Philostratus specifically urges the boy to look away from the image to the text on which it is based, Homer's *Iliad* (*Imagines* 1.1). This tension between word and image, and the desire to resist the erotic pull of images through the subjugation of them to texts, provides the motivation behind my second text about images, Lucian's *de Domo*.

Lucian's essay as a whole is concerned with the relationship between words and images, the visual and the aural/oral—a theme that pervades Second Sophistic literature.[34] The narrator starts by associating his desire to speak with Alexander's fatal desire to swim in the river Cydnus. The narrator, too, is unable to resist the visual lures that surround him and desires to respond to them with words. He closely associates this reaction with his status as an educated Greek. Whilst ordinary people would simply stare in silence, and barbarians are later characterized as oblivious to beauty, the *pepaideumenos*, the educated man, must reply verbally.[35] The very words with which Lucian expresses this desire, however, λόγῳ ἀμείψασθαι τὴν θέαν, "to equal the sight with words," suggest that his speech is not only a homage to the beauty of the hall, as he suggested previously, but also an attempt to replace or conquer the visual by means of words.[36] The beauty that prompts this reaction is described in sensuous, feminine terms. Like Echo, the hall will repeat and linger on a speaker's words, holding them within its confines. Its beauty is compared to that of a virtuous woman, adorned with modest amounts of gold, and the ceiling described as her face. He then compares his inability to resist this beauty to the peacock's self-display at the start of spring. Lucian makes this a response to the beauty of the season, but the sexual motivation of the bird, to attract a mate, is also implied by his description of it strutting and turning. The captivating effect of the hall's beauty is compared to the effect of the Sirens or a magic wheel (*de Domo* 3, 7–8, 11, 13). The ἐπιθυμία, desire, aroused by such visions is a strongly eroticized one.

At this point, Logos, a second speaker representing the alternative opinion, intervenes. Instead of adding to the beauty of a man's speech, as the narrator had hoped, Logos suggests that beautiful surroundings, in fact, do the opposite, instilling despair in the speaker of ever competing with their visual beauty (*de Domo* 17). This beauty also distracts his audience, so that, instead of an audience to a speech, they become spectators of the visual display.[37] Logos also picks up on the narrator's reference to the Sirens. Whilst the Sirens' song only had the power to delay their audience, the visual beauty of the Gorgons was strong enough to turn their viewers to stone (*de Domo* 19). This contrast between visual and aural stresses the greater power of the visual and, in passing, indicates the impropriety of the narrator comparing the hall's visual effect on him with the aural one achieved by the Siren's song, a mistake that reveals that his ultimate concern is with words rather than with images. Logos brings as a witness to his case the figure of Herodotus, who tells us that the ears are less trustworthy than the eyes in the very words that the historian put into the mouth of the king Candaules when he persuaded his servant Gyges to view his wife's naked beauty (*Histories* 1.10). The fatal consequences of that particular episode would have been well known to Lucian's audience. When considered in the light of the eroticized account of visual beauty that proceeded it, the clear message is of the dangers and temptations of visual beauty, dangers that can be seen elsewhere to lead to the viewer being enmeshed within the illusions of erotic naturalism.

Logos thus seems to warn against the erotic lures of visual beauty. Yet while stressing the impossibility of rivaling those images with words, he proceeds to give an account of the images that have long been attracting his audience's attention, in the hope, he modestly tells us, of at least keeping up with them. This account suggests a number of verbal or intellectual links between the individual images. Through this "bald word painting," Logos manages to achieve precisely what he had said was impossible, exerting the authority of words over images through the intellectual subjugation of images to verbal categories (*de Domo* 21). In contrast to the sophisticated exegeses of individual paintings given by Philostratus, Logos confines his descriptions to brief identifications of subject, subverting his audience's expectations of a series of *ecphraseis* in accordance with his argument that words cannot possibly compete with images. Yet this brevity also deprives the individual images of their visual power to hold the viewer's attention by giving an alternative account that stresses the connections between the images, connections that only emerge when mythological, thematic, and dramatic texts are taken into account.

After considering the suggestions concerning programmatic display that this section of the *de Domo* provides, I shall return to Philostratus's work. In the *Imagines*, the emphasis is on individual images, suggesting both the lures that their naturalism holds over the viewer and Philostratus's attempts to use literary means to subdue them. Their naturalism entails a different type of viewing from that suggested by Lucian's *Logos*. Instead of a programmatic gaze that seeks to tie the images down to words and categories, Philostratus shows himself to be involved with individual paintings and using an erotic and enraptured gaze. The dangers of naturalism are highlighted in the myth of Narcissus, the supreme victim of naturalism, who is unable to distinguish between image and reality.[38] Philostratus reproaches Narcissus for believing that the image in the water is real, yet he himself falls into the same trap by addressing the painted figure in the same way that he addresses his real pupils. The confusion entailed by naturalism is also shown in his discussion of a bee that has been attracted to the image of a flower: it is either a real bee deceived by the painting or a painted bee that almost deceives Philostratus into believing it is real (*Imagines* 1.23.2). Yet alongside this enraptured gaze, which takes Philostratus and his readers and listeners into the painted world, we also find hints of a programmatic gaze, which links images through theme and form. Returning to the Spada reliefs, we will see that they provoke both types of gaze, thus suggesting tensions within the responses to visual art that correspond to second-century attitudes toward the world of Greek culture as a whole.

Programs and Interpretation in Lucian and Philostratus

In chapter 21 of Lucian's *de Domo*, Logos announces that he will "paint a picture in words" of the images that he and his audience see about them. These pictures are said to be worthy of attention since they combine accurate technique with useful and archaic subject matter, a combination that he says is seductive, ἐπαγωγόν, and demands an educated viewer. We might expect to find here detailed exegeses of the individual paintings that would illuminate the responses of an educated man to visual images. In fact, Logos does not give us a Philostratean-style description of the subject and moral import of the different paintings, but instead, resisting the desire to linger over their seductive beauty, his account goes around the room, briefly identifying the subjects of the paintings and allowing the display of the images to be recreated. Because of this, critics have suggested that Lucian follows spatial order regardless of logic and does not point out the connections between the images he describes (Bompaire 1958.713, Thompson 1961.60). Although Lucian does not group the paintings according to their themes, such as the "actions of Perseus" or "paintings depicting Athena," he does actively allow these connections to be made through the words he uses to describe the images. His account is not a catalogue of the types of images displayed but rather a temporal account of how a viewer moving around the room might encounter the paintings and interpret the messages of this particular selection.[39]

The account starts with the viewer entering the room and immediately turning to the right (see fig. 4.1).[40] The first image is of Perseus killing the sea monster and rescuing Andromeda. Here Lucian shows the characteristic concern of the ecphrasist to set the scene in context by stating that soon Perseus will marry the girl and that the incident occurs during his pursuit of the Gorgon.[41] The second painting is "another righteous drama," ἕτερον δρᾶμα . . . δικαιότατον—the slaughter of Aegisthus by Orestes and Pylades (de Domo 23). Logos sees the link between these two pictures to be the depiction of righteous deeds, although this interpretation of the first painting does not emerge until it is examined in relation to the second. He also naturalizes the images for himself by seeking to find literary parallels. The Orestes painting takes its subject from tragedy, "from Euripides or Sophocles, I suppose," whilst the first had combined Argolid myth and Ethiopian romance, μῦθος and πάθος, a combination that would have been familiar from literature in the form of the ancient novels.[42]

Next we find a scene of ἐρωτική . . . παιδιά, "erotic play," in which Apollo watches while Branchus teases his dog by holding up a hare (de Domo 24). A similar scene, without the figure of Apollo, is shown on a relief similar to the Spadas now in the Louvre (Schreiber 1894, no. 22). It can also be seen in the round in a statue group in Boston (Vermeule and Comstock 1988.39, no. 27). These two surviving works suggest that ancient readers of Lucian would themselves have been familiar with this type of scene and able to visualize it. Following this image comes another

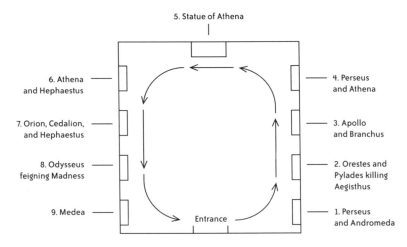

Figure 4.1 Lucian *de Domo*: The placement of the images around the room.

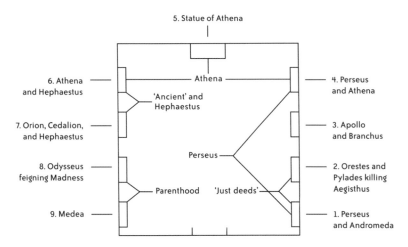

Figure 4.2 Lucian *de Domo:* Connections explicitly indicated by Lucian.

picture of Perseus, ὁ Περσεὺς πάλιν, "Perseus again," in "the adventure before the sea monster," a clear reference back to the first painting (*de Domo* 25). This one shows him cutting off the head of Medusa with the help of Athena, who shields him from Medusa's petrifying gaze. The image relates to the first by dealing with the same hero, engaged in the very action that was alluded to there, "his winged quest against the Gorgons" (de Domo 22). While the first painting (Perseus and Andromeda) seemed initially to have a connection with the second painting (Orestes and Pylades), in that both show a righteous deed, by the time the viewer proceeds to the fourth painting (Perseus and Medusa), it emerges that both the first and fourth paintings show complementary images of the hero Perseus. This connection does not negate the link between the first and second images, but rather shows the role of display that, in separating the two Perseus paintings, allows other connections to emerge. These connections are shown in figure 4.2.

The fact that a single painting can be linked to a number of others is also demonstrated by the next image. This is found on the next wall, above the ἀντιθύρον, that is, in the middle of the back wall opposite the door. It is a shrine of Athena, with the figure of the goddess made of marble and dressed as "a war goddess would appear in peacetime"—a riddle that has the reader searching to find a suitable parallel in his or her visual memory. Lucian does not specifically say that the previous painting and the statue are linked by the figure of Athena, but the repetition of her name allows the reader to make this connection. It is made explicit with the next image, a painting again, γραφὴ πάλιν, that shows "another Athena," ἄλλη ᾿Αθηνᾶ (de Domo 26, 27). These words link it to the previous statue of Athena and, through the mention of painting, to the picture of Perseus and Athena on the opposite wall (fig. 4.2). In the third image, she is shown being chased by Hephaestus, a pursuit that gives rise to Erichthonius's conception.

The next image is described as παλαιά τις ἄλλη γραφή, "another ancient painting" (de Domo 28–29). It shows the blind Orion carrying Cedalion, who leads him to the Sun to heal his blindness. The words that introduce the image suggest that the only connection between this and the previous image is their use of an ancient subject and, possibly, their style. However, the last sentence of the description mentions Hephaestus watching the events from Lemnos. It is almost as though the speaker has not noticed this figure at first, and so has to suggest the general link of ancient subject matter between the two paintings, but then notices the figure of the god who appears in both images. The reader might also draw on his or her own knowledge of mythology and recall that Orion's blindness was a punishment for the rape of his host's daughter, Merope, and that Hephaestus gave him the child Cedalion to restore his sight. When considered next to Hephaestus's unsuccessful pursuit of Athena, we can better understand the god's sympathetic treatment of a fellow seducer.

The following picture shows Odysseus feigning madness to avoid going to Troy, but foiled when Palamedes pretends to be about to kill Telemachus. In the face of this threat, Odysseus "becomes a father," πατὴρ γίγνεται, and gives up the pretense (*de Domo* 30). This reference to Odysseus as father, while not explicitly given as a link, forms a connection with the next painting, the last one, that shows Medea plotting against her children. The reference to τὼ παῖδε, "the two children," picks up on the word "father" in the previous description and thus implicitly contrasts these two representations of parenthood.[43]

In this analysis of Lucian's text, I have moved from the explicit connections that he presents between images, such as "righteous deeds" and the figures of Athena or Perseus, to those to which his choice of words alludes, but which are not openly stated. In fact this appears to be a deliberate movement within the text that seeks to draw the reader into its program of images, and that, through its example, teaches the viewer or reader how to construct unity between individual images. The purported function of this passage is related to Logos's argument that images have the power to distract an audience from listening through the desire to see. The text, which is read by those who do not have direct access to these visual stimuli, achieves this distraction by prompting us to recreate in our imaginations the decoration of the hall and the order in which the images are displayed. Yet the text also subverts the power of images by the key role given to words in creating connections between the images. Their visual power to seduce the viewer is constrained by subjecting them to verbal labels, such as "Athena" or "Perseus." The programmatic gaze, as exemplified by Lucian's representation of it, can thus be seen as an attempt to reduce the seductive power of naturalistic images by resorting to a verbal process.

Because the text teaches us about the connections that can be perceived among images and illustrates the desire of the second-century viewer to construct narratives around paintings, we can expand on those connections given in the text and show the whole web of interrelations that exist. A number of different themes coexist in this same room: the deeds of Perseus; the different manifestations of Athena—as patron goddess, object of worship, and sexually desirable female; differing fates of male seducers; or contrasting models of parenthood, to name only a few. These links are sometimes reinforced by paratactic display, as shown by the three images of Athena that would surround a viewer standing at the far end of the room, perhaps as he or she was offering homage to the shrine of the goddess. Other significant details only become obvious in hindsight, when one reaches the second image in a pair. These links exist within one wall, as with the two images of Perseus, or even across the room. To a viewer standing in the middle of the room, the images of Orestes and Odysseus may seem linked by their contrasting views of events before and after the Trojan War or of protective fathers and avenging (and murderous) sons. This web of connections can best be displayed through diagrams: one for someone progressing around the room as Lucian describes (fig. 4.2), and others for the connections that are implicit, which we can reconstruct for a viewer standing in different areas in the middle of the room (figs. 4.3–4.5).

Sometimes an image may seem at first to have no connection with those that surround it, as in the case of the picture showing Branchus playing with his dog. The peaceful pastoral tone of this image is in contrast to the dramatic and epic events that surround it. Yet it is described as erotic and could be grouped with the images of Perseus and Andromeda and Hephaestus chasing Athena. These three images present us with contrasting views of erotic relations (fig. 4.6): homosexual (Apollo and Branchus) and heterosexual (Perseus and Andromeda or Athena and Hephaestus), and successful and unsuccessful. Within the images, Athena's flight shows that Hephaestus will be unsuccessful, whereas Andromeda's maidenly modesty as she watches Perseus bodes well for him. The situation between Apollo and Branchus is unresolved; Apollo seems content to watch the boy, yet the evidence of another work of art proves the success of Apollo's suit: the statue of Apollo Philesios at the sanctuary of Apollo at Didyma.[44]

Although no one theme is common to all nine of the images that Lucian describes, we can see a number of correspondences that link the pictures into a unified decorative scheme with multiple thematic resonances. The links arise from the characters and events depicted in the images; subject matter and theme rather than formal concerns provide the evidence for unity. However, in interpretations of the Spada reliefs, the evidence for seeing certain of the reliefs as pendants to others is based on clear stylistic and formal parallels in the compositions of the reliefs. Thus since both the Adonis and the Bellerophon reliefs (figs. 4.7 and 4.8) show solitary standing heroes with downcast heads, accompanied only by animal companions, Paul Zanker argues that they should be seen as constituting a balanced pair (1966.766). To these formal devices for linking images, others concerning subject and theme are added, but it is instructive to consider whether there is any ancient evidence for linking images by formal as well as thematic means. Whilst this is not clear in

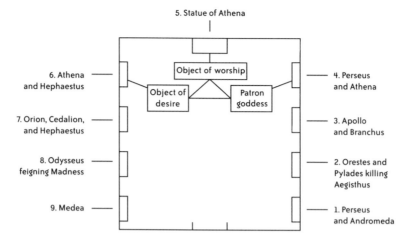

Figure 4.3 Lucian *de Domo:* Views of Athena.

Figure 4.4 Lucian *de Domo:* Before and after the Trojan War.

Lucian's account, we can turn to the greater wealth of images that Philostratus presents us in the *Imagines*.

Identifying cycles or pairs of images in this work is less straightforward than in Lucian's text because while Lucian explicitly sets out to describe the decoration of a whole room, dealing with each image in order,

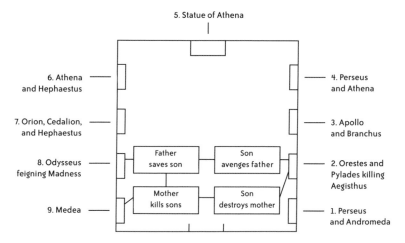

Figure 4.5 Lucian *de Domo:* Parent-child relationships.

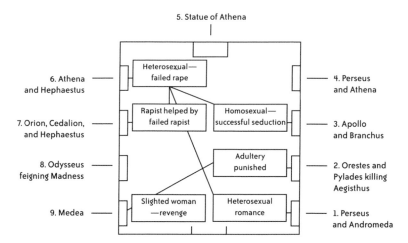

Figure 4.6 Lucian *de Domo:* Erotics.

Philostratus concentrates on describing individual paintings and does not indicate the ways in which they are linked by their display. He does, however, allow us to see certain connections between paintings. From the way in which Philostratus describes some images, it is clear that we are supposed to compare them and their descriptions so that they illuminate one another. Lehmann notes (1941.20) that a group of paintings in Book 1 seem to show parallels of form and composition. These are the two paintings of the boy Olympus and those of Midas and Narcissus (*Imagines* 1.20–23). The first of these presents us with a view of the sleeping Olympus surrounded by adoring satyrs (1.20). This image is repeated in 1.22, where the sleeping figure, himself a satyr caught by Midas, who sits nearby, is surrounded by dancing nymphs. Both scenes occur in a pastoral landscape: there is a cave and spring near Olympus, while the satyr lies next to the pool filled with wine that has caused his drunken sleep. The composition of a sleeping figure lying next to a pool and surrounded by other figures is common to both and demands that we consider them together.

The tone of the first Olympus image is mostly lighthearted and erotic, smiling at the activities of the amorous satyrs, yet the description itself starts with an ominous tone. Philostratus concludes from the cave and springs that this must be Celaenae, but says that Marsyas is not present either because he is watching his sheep or because this is "after the contest," μετὰ τὴν ἔριν (*Imagines* 1.20.1). Philostratus does not dwell on this remark, but it surely makes one think of the musical contest between Marsyas and Apollo after which Marsyas was punished for his arrogance by being flayed alive. Although Philostratus does not refer to it directly, Marsyas's absence from the scene appears ominous and gives a different edge to the innocent sleep of the youth tired out by flute playing.

The atmosphere of the Midas painting is rather more amusing, especially in its description of Midas's long ears and the suggestion that this secret has already been divulged by the reed (*Imagines* 1.22.2). Yet this very mention of the ears also connects the painting to 1.20. Midas was given the ears of an ass by Apollo because of his judgment against Apollo in a music contest, either between Apollo and Pan or, in some versions, that between Apollo and Marsyas.[45] In comparison to the fate of the absent Marsyas, this seems to be a happy escape, but it also reminds the reader of the dangers of angering the gods. Philostratus does not explicitly make this connection between the two paintings, but, by his references to Marsyas and to Midas's ears, he allows the erudite reader to form his own connections between these pieces, already alike in form. The dangers inherent in vying musically with the gods are particularly relevant to Olympus, whose love of playing the flute is emphasized in 1.20 and 1.21, and who appears in myth as Marsyas's beloved pupil (see Pausanias 10.30.2).

The second image of Olympus, 1.21, shows him playing the flute and gazing into a pool of water. Philostratus seems confused by this and addresses the boy, saying that he can describe Olympus's beauty better than the pool can.[46] This image is then mirrored by the painting described in 1.23 that shows Narcissus gazing at his reflection in a pool. Here, too, Philostratus directly addresses the painted figure, urging Narcissus to realize that the image is not real—a play on the lures of mimetic art since Philostratus, too, is being beguiled into addressing a painted image as if it were real, a mistake that he openly admits in his description of the painting Hunters.[47] This preoccupation of youths with their reflections is seen as confusing, in 1.21, and dangerous, in 1.23. The enjoyment of seeing one's own beauty, suggested as the reason for Olympus's gaze, is taken further in the picture of Narcissus, where he understands this beauty not as his own but as another's. Into this reflexive gaze between youth and reflection, the viewer of the picture is an intruder, looking on as a voyeur but also implicated in the dangers of naturalism since our engagement with the painting is parallel to Narcissus's self-deception (Elsner 1996b.253). The power of images to absorb their viewers, luring them into the imaged world, strains against the programmatic gaze that reduces the images to artificial signifiers, denying or subverting their naturalistic power to convince the viewer of their reality. In Philostratus's account, we see both reactions. The danger of absorption into the naturalistic image is shown by Philostratus's direct addresses to Olympus and Narcissus. Yet by linking the images together by means of their formal characteristics, he also suggests a programmatic gaze that reduces them to comments on the power of naturalistic art. The programmatic gaze is his only escape from the seductive naturalism of these erotically charged images.

The erotic gaze, which in the case of Narcissus is a self-reflexive one, recurs elsewhere in the *Imagines*. At the end of the description of the painting Hunters, the victorious youth stands in the pool where he has defeated the boar whilst the other youths stand on the bank and gaze at him, "as if he were a picture."[48] These youths are explicitly described as "lovers," οἱ ἐρασταί (*Imagines* 1.28.8), linking this final scene to the opening of the description where Philostratus suggests that they are actually hunting the beauty of this youth rather than the boar. Philostratus himself is carried away by the naturalism of the painting into directly addressing the hunters, bringing himself into their reality, just as, at the end of the description, the difference between narrator and actors is again elided as his companions look at the youth as if he were a painting. As with Narcissus, we find here an erotic gaze that is closely linked to the act of looking at painted images: the pool "paints," γράφει, Narcissus in 1.23 and, in 1.28, the youth is like a picture, γραφέν. Both, of course, are themselves figured within a painted image. Thus the distinction between the viewers inside and outside the image is compressed, with the result that the external viewer is also implicated in the erotics of the painting.[49]

This discussion of images that Philostratus presents as being similar in composition, the sleeping youth surrounded by other figures, 1.20 and 1.22, or the solitary youth gazing at his own reflection, 1.21 and 1.23, reveals an important fact about the way in which connections and contrasts can be made between paintings. In none of these pairings are there obvious similarities in subject matter. However, by looking at the images together because of their formal parallels, the viewer and reader of Philostratus's text can perceive certain themes that only emerge when two images are seen in the light of each other. In the first pair, this theme is a warning about the dangers of rivaling the gods through the examples of Marsyas and Midas, who both suffered for showing hubris against Apollo. In the second pairing, the theme is one that recurs throughout Philostratus's text: a meditation on the dangers of succumbing to mimetic images and the erotics that unite viewer and viewed in a reciprocated gaze.

In addition to using formal means to indicate links between images, Philostratus also includes more obvious thematic links similar to those found in Lucian. Some of these involve a particular hero, for example, the Heracles cycle (2.20–25), or common subject matter or themes. The suicide of Evadne upon the pyre of her husband Capaneus, described in 2.30, not only relates back to the parallel suicide of Pantheia, who is contrasted with Evadne at 2.9.5, but also forms part of a series of paintings that deal with the outcome of the attack of the Seven against Thebes. Thus, on the Theban side, the self-sacrifice of Menoeceus is the subject of the image in 1.4. The fates of various of the Seven heroes are recounted in a number of paintings: the burial of Polynices by Antigone in 2.29 and of Capaneus in 2.30, and the descent of Amphiaraus into the earth in 1.27, where the description contrasts his fate with that of the other heroes. Of these, Capaneus's destruction by lightning is explicitly mentioned, thus linking the Amphiaraus image with the description of Capaneus's death in 2.30.

Many of these comparisons could not have been made in a real image; the details that Philostratus himself introduces are those that would prompt a viewer of the whole sequence of images. The mention of characters who are not actually central to the main action of a partic-

ular painting sets up the basis for a web of connections when these characters appear in their own scenes later on. By including these comparisons, Philostratus is not only exhibiting his own education, he is also
playing with the parameters he has set himself: whilst pretending to describe only individual paintings, he sets up a whole network of pictorial
programs.

Both the enraptured gaze and the programmatic gaze appear in
Philostratus's account, showing that this coexistence of different types of
gaze does not translate into a simple polarization of viewers looking in
either one way or the other, but that the same viewer could look in a variety of ways simultaneously. Indeed this is evident in Philostratus's description of the painting of Narcissus. Here Philostratus is the absorbed,
enraptured viewer, drawn into the naturalistic world of the image, yet, at
the level of the text, when we see the connections between his descriptions of this and other images, he is also a programmatic viewer, seeing
the individual paintings as illustrations of a theme, a contemplation of
the dangers of naturalism to which, at the level of the individual images,
he himself succumbs.

At first sight, Philostratus and Lucian appear to be treating their images in quite different ways: Philostratus concentrates on contextualizing and interpreting individual images, whilst Lucian describes the interrelations between and the display of a series of images. However, both
reveal awareness of a different way to approach images. Lucian's comments about the seductive and instructive nature of the paintings he describes suggest that these same images could easily have been made the
focus of a discussion like Philostratus's that uses paintings to illustrate
the power of realistic images and often shows the viewer immersed in
their naturalism.[50] In response, Philostratus includes in his descriptions
compositional and comparative details that allow him to imply a nexus
of connections between the images he describes. The tension between
an enraptured and a programmatic gaze can be seen as a motivating force
in both works. This tension is also specifically tied up with the relationship between words and images. If the naturalism of the image is allowed
to take over, images become more powerful than words, as Lucian's *Logos*
suggests. Yet if the images are reduced to words by seeing them solely
as illustrations of the texts that lie behind them, or by subjecting them to
labels that place them within a greater, verbal, program, images can be
stripped of their naturalistic power to entice the viewer and can instead
serve to throw light back on their viewers as a locus for the display of
knowledge and *paideia*. In my discussion of the Spada reliefs, I intend to

examine both their capacity for provoking a programmatic gaze, which sees multiple connections between a series of images, and also their enticement to an enraptured gaze, drawing the viewer into the mythological world of Greek culture.

Rereading the Spada Reliefs

The eight panels of the Spada reliefs present us with a group of mythological scenes and a sophisticated riddle. What exactly are the scenes represented and how should we view them, both separately and in relation to one another? One series of identifications has been accepted by most scholars based on the iconography of the figures and the attributes that they are given.[51] Briefly, the figures on the reliefs have been identified as the Wounded Adonis (fig. 4.7), Bellerophon and Pegasus (fig. 4.8), Amphion and Zethus (fig. 4.9), Odysseus and Diomedes (fig. 4.10), Hypsipyle and the Death of Opheltes (fig. 4.11), Pasiphae and Daedalus (fig. 4.12), and two representations of Paris: with Oenone (fig. 4.13) and with Eros (fig. 4.14). Whilst some of these identifications seem obvious and are familiar from wall painting or scenes on sarcophagi, closer inspection reveals many discrepancies with the usual iconography and may prompt us to consider the interpretation of the individual scenes in more depth.

Recent scholars, most notably Paul Zanker, Natalie Kampen, and Richard Brilliant, tend to divide the reliefs into balanced pairs. After grouping together those reliefs that are similar in form (the two Paris reliefs and those showing Adonis and Bellerophon), Zanker (1966.766–67) then proceeds to divide the rest up according to subject, pairing Diomedes and Odysseus with Amphion and Zethus, as two representations of contrasting personalities, and Pasiphae with Hypsipyle, since both deal with the fates of women. Kampen (1979.587–88) broadly agrees with Zanker's pairs, while also suggesting that other lost reliefs could have extended the series. Brilliant, however, varies the pairings by adding the two similar reliefs from the Museo Capitolino that show Perseus and Andromeda, and Endymion. He then pairs Adonis with Endymion (youthful heroes loved by goddesses) and Bellerophon with Perseus (heroes who fly through the air to kill monsters). He also groups Diomedes and Odysseus with Pasiphae and Daedalus around the theme of destructive impiety, and Hypsipyle and the death of Opheltes with Amphion and Zethus, as both are connected with Thebes and the death of royal children (1984.87ff.).

The fact that these different pairings can all be suggested might prompt us to reject this particular method of interpreting the Spada reliefs. It seems as though, despite formal parallels between some of the reliefs, there are no clear-cut divisions that sort the reliefs into four pairs. Instead, following the lead of Lucian's *de Domo*, we can see that different categories such as impiety, the Trojan War, or contrasting personalities can pair the same relief with a number of others. Thus the Odysseus and Diomedes relief is linked to those of Pasiphae, Paris, or Amphion and Zethus, depending on which category is taken as the decisive one. This capacity for multiple connections between the reliefs makes the scholarly predilection for pairing the Spada reliefs seem somewhat simplistic. A comparison with the programs presented in Lucian and Philostratus and those that Bergmann sees in the House of the Tragic Poet (1994.254–55) also argues against single links between the reliefs and instead suggests that we should look for a complex nexus of themes that bind the Spada reliefs together as a unit.

One might also note that, despite the agreement on identification that one finds in the scholarship, the interpretation of the individual Spada reliefs is not a simple matter. Although iconographical details do allow us to identify the various characters, these figures are often portrayed in an unusual manner; several iconographical models may be mixed to produce a new and individualized mythological representation.[52] The image of the dying Adonis (fig. 4.7) is one example. The story of Adonis is a frequent subject of sarcophagi, where the myth is usually divided up into three scenes: Adonis taking his leave of Aphrodite, his fatal wounding in the hunt, and his return to die in the arms of the goddess.[53] Here, however, we are presented with Adonis alone, accompanied only by his hounds. The image omits the figure of Aphrodite and concentrates solely on the pathos of Adonis's premature death. If the boar's head has been rightly restored, as Zanker thinks, it provides a two-fold allusion for the viewer: to the boar by whose agency Adonis meets his death and to the hunting goddess, Artemis, whose enmity causes the hero's downfall.[54]

The location of the scene is rather obscure and made more so by the false reconstruction of the right side of the panel. The doorway that we see behind the hero would originally have been completed by another pillar along the right side, creating an arch that frames the dying Adonis. Behind this arch, we can see the outline of a tree in low relief, its leaves, in higher relief, protrude over the top. We can compare this arch to the arches that occur on some sarcophagi. Sometimes these represent an indoor setting, but elsewhere, it has been suggested, they represent

Figure 4.7 Dying Adonis,
Palazzo Spada, Rome.

Figure 4.8 Bellerophon,
Palazzo Spada, Rome.

Figure 4.9 Amphion and Hermes (?),
Palazzo Spada, Rome.

Figure 4.10 Diomedes and Odysseus,
Palazzo Spada, Rome.

Figure 4.11 Death of Opheltes,
Palazzo Spada, Rome.

Figure 4.12 Pasiphae and Daedalus,
Palazzo Spada, Rome.

Figure 4.13 Paris and Oenone,
Palazzo Spada, Rome.

Figure 4.14 Paris and Eros,
Palazzo Spada, Rome.

the gate of death.[55] In the Spada relief, the arch as the gateway of death is most appropriate for Adonis, the hero who stands on the very boundary of his mortal life.

The figures of Pegasus and Bellerophon on another relief (fig. 4.8) are easily identified. Pegasus is the only winged horse in Greek mythology, and scenes of Bellerophon watering him occur on some sarcophagi.[56] As Zanker notes, there is an atmosphere of stillness and absorption that prompts the viewer to consider the hero's fate, thrown from this very horse when he attempts to ride up to heaven.[57] The enclosed atmosphere that can be felt in this relief is similar to the effect created by Philostratus's descriptions of the paintings of Olympus and Narcissus, *Imagines* 1.21 and 1.23. There the youths gaze into water, absorbed in their own reflections and untouched by the speaker's words. Here also the hero looks down; the restoration of the head denies us his expression, but the angle suggests that he is looking down toward, and maybe into, the very water that Pegasus drinks. The turn of the body away from the viewer and its downward gaze into the water suggest a reflexive viewing within the picture from which we are excluded.

The absorption of this gaze turns the viewer into voyeur, seeking to penetrate the thoughts of the hero, to intrude into the imaged world. It may provoke us—like Philostratus—to fill this world with words and explanations, which we also often seek in literary texts. This need to supplement images with words, and to fit them into a literary context, is particularly strong in the next relief, usually identified as showing Amphion and Zethus (fig. 4.9), which also shows a reciprocated gaze between the two figures, locking them into an eternal relationship. Whilst A. J. B. Wace admits that this relief could also show Apollo and Hermes, the attributes of hunting dog and lyre have usually led to the figures being identified as the two sons of Antiope, Zethus and Amphion, whose contrasting lifestyles were dramatized in Euripides' *Antiope*.[58]

The unusual poses of the two (the vigorous Zethus is sitting, whilst the brother whom he attacks for wasting his time with music is standing) have been commented on but not fully explained.[59] In Euripides' play, Zethus mocks his brother for his weakness and womanly form, while Amphion replies in his defense that intelligence is more powerful than bodily strength (Euripides *Antiope* fr. 18, Kambitsis). Here Amphion is hardly a weakling, but has a finely tuned physique. In Euripides, Zethus is also supposed to be a farmer; he urges Amphion to take up digging and guarding flocks (Euripides *Antiope* fr. 8). Yet the seated figure here is not shown with a sheep or goat, nor is he dressed for farming. Instead, with his accompanying dog, he looks more like a hunter taking his rest. The positioning of the lyre is also ambiguous. It rests on a pillar next to the seated figure, yet is grasped by the standing figure. In this image, the lyre seems to act as a linking device between the two, hardly appropriate given Zethus's violent rejection of it in myth.

These discrepancies suggest that a different identification of the figures might have been intended. The standing figure, usually named Amphion, is modeled on a statue type of Hermes, as represented in the Belvedere Hermes (see Wace 1910.187). There are a number of changes made, not least the change in the position of the left hand, thus turning the figure into a profile view, yet the original was recognized by modern scholars and probably provoked a similar reaction from at least its more aesthetically educated ancient viewers. They may also have recalled the circumstances surrounding Amphion and his lyre, namely that he was given it as a gift by Hermes, as Philostratus recounts in his description of a painting of Amphion (*Imagines* 1.10). There the musician sits on a mound as he plays wearing a headband and *chlamys*. The word for mound that Philostratus uses here, κολωνός, is rather general, but the overall description sounds similar to the image of the seated figure in our relief. Philostratus also speculates that Hermes gave these gifts to the youth because he was overcome with love for him.

Indeed the image does have certain erotic overtones. A reciprocated gaze unites the two figures. In Philostratus's descriptions, reciprocated gazes are often erotic, as is the case with Narcissus (*Imagines* 1.23). In his description of a painting of Perseus and Andromeda (1.29), the two figures also look at one another: Andromeda "looks at Perseus," τὸν Περσέα βλέπει, and begins to smile at him, while he reclines in the grass "looking toward the maiden," ἐμβλέπων τῇ κόρῃ (1.29.3–4). The gaze that unites the figures on the Spada relief may similarly suggest an erotic relationship, that between Hermes and Amphion. The erotics of the union are also indicated by their positions. Hermes is clearly the *erastes*, the lover, bringing the gift of a lyre to his beloved *eromenos*, Amphion. In response, Amphion's position, with his right arm crooked behind his head, recalls the positions of the sleeping Endymion and Ariadne on sarcophagi. This position was recognized by Hellmut Sichtermann (1992.33) as indicating an "opening-up" of oneself, a readiness for erotic activity. John R. Clarke recognizes the same gesture on a silver cup showing erotic scenes and describes it as an inviting gesture of "erotic repose" (1998.68–70). Here the wakeful Amphion uses the same gesture to indicate his responsiveness to Hermes' approaches. The motif of divine lover and human beloved can also be recognized in the presence of the dog by Amphion's legs who barks in greeting of the god. Similar dogs appear on sarcophagi showing Selene approaching the sleeping Endymion.

The erotics of the image draw in the viewer. As the *erastes* Hermes gazes at his beloved, we gaze at him gazing and at the figure on whom he looks, Amphion, whose body is opened up to the viewer as well as to his divine lover. As we saw in Philostratus's account of the painting Hunters, the viewer outside the image is drawn into and implicated in the erotics of the image. Yet in addition to being a self-contained image that provokes this enraptured gaze, the relief is also linked to several of the other reliefs. The form of Hermes' body is a close reflection of that of Bellerophon. Both stand upright and turn recognizable classical models (the Doryphorus and the Belvedere Hermes) to a profile view. Both also stand with their weight on the front leg with the back one drawn behind and indicated in very low relief. Yet their gazes differentiate them. While Hermes gazes at his beloved, Bellerophon looks down at his own reflection, like Narcissus. He seems more vulnerable than Hermes, and so like Adonis and Amphion, the objects of divine affection, he provokes a voyeuristic gaze, drawing the viewer into his world.

Hermes' gaze links that image to the relief showing Diomedes and Odysseus and the Theft of the Palladium (fig. 4.10). Here, too, the figures stare at one another. However, while the gaze on the Amphion relief may be an erotic one, in the other, it is one of rivalry. Diomedes stands outside the temple clasping the (now lost) Palladium whilst Odysseus emerges from the doorway. As Zanker has commented (1966.762–63), the atmosphere seems to be one of competition: Diomedes already possesses the Palladium and is loath to hand over the glory to Odysseus. This representation is actually in conflict with the account given in Apollodorus that states that Odysseus left Diomedes outside the city, went in alone dressed in rags, and stole the Palladium with the help of Helen.[60] However, Diomedes' role in stealing the Palladium was acknowledged in the second century: Pausanias reports the Argives as saying that they possess the Palladium, a boast he rejects on the grounds that it was taken by Aeneas to Italy (Pausanias 2.23.5).

The relief seems to conflate these different traditions: Diomedes is shown outside the temple while Odysseus is inside, looking crafty as the sources describe him. However, it is Diomedes who actually has the Palladium. This is indicated not only by the position of his hand but also by the fact that here again the artist uses a Greek model, that of the Diomedes attributed to Cresilas.[61] The characterization of the two heroes on this relief is also close to another description given by Philostratus. In *Imagines* 2.7, Philostratus describes a painting showing the mourning of Antilochus by the Greek army. This image includes several of the Greek commanders, whom Philostratus describes. Thus Odysseus, "the Ithacan," is clear from his austerity and vigilance, whilst his "license," ἡ ἐλευθερία marks out Diomedes. The presentation of Diomedes here is clearly that of an arrogant hero, as in the statue by Cresilas. The artist has changed his model slightly to fit into the relief frame, with the effect that Diomedes' left leg (now restored but presumably reflecting the original position) protrudes into the viewer's space. Indeed, his foot is almost stepping out of the frame and into our own world. Whilst the locked gaze of the two heroes suggests they are unaware of our presence, this detail only serves to draw us in.

All four of the preceding reliefs show an upright, well-muscled, naked youth. This youth, in turn, takes on the identities of Bellerophon, Adonis, Diomedes, and Hermes, yet the actual figures, if stripped of their attributes, would look almost identical. Seen as a group, the images reflect more general ideas about the lives and activities of men. A young man may be alone, communing with his horse, or seeking comfort from his dog. He may also be in rivalry with a companion. He can be a hunter, a hero, or a lover. The passivity of some of these figures, and their idealized youthful beauty, also provokes an erotic gaze, setting up a relationship between viewer and image where the viewer's erotic appreciation of the image places him in the role of *erastes*. This erotic lure of the images is closely tied to their naturalism. The viewer of these images sees a figure only slightly under life size, enticingly placed almost within reach. In Pompeian wall paintings, scenes of luxurious foliage or architectural vistas often replaced real views, extending the scope of the house in which they were displayed (see Leach 1988.9ff.). Here the same blurring of the line between reality and representation allows access to a fantasy world peopled by figures of Greek myth who also serve as archetypes of male virtue or beauty.

This visual presentation of different models of manhood can be paralleled in the representation of women in Pompeian wall painting. The composition of many of the paintings in the House of the Tragic Poet draws them together: they show seated, dark-skinned men accompanied by pale standing women. These compositional parallels demand that the paintings be compared, with the result that their implicit messages are revealed. Thus the depiction of both Hera and Briseis in the same modest pose prompts one to compare them, a goddess-bride and a slave. Both

Briseis and Helen are being escorted away, but while Briseis is a prize of war, Helen is the cause of it. Bergmann suggests that "the compositional formula serves as a prod to remember, compare and reason"; the formal parallels between the Spada reliefs serve the same function.[62] This practice of using similarities of composition to draw out a further message from the images is also shown in Philostratus's discussions of the paintings of the sleeping Olympus and the sleeping satyr (1.20 and 1.22) and those of Olympus and Narcissus gazing into pools (1.21 and 1.23).

The other four Spada reliefs introduce women into this male world. Two deal explicitly with the fates of female characters, a feature that led Zanker to see them as a distinct pair. The relief known as Hypsipyle or The Death of Opheltes (fig. 4.11) depicts a child strangled by a snake while two warriors attack it. Behind them, a woman raises her hands in distress. This has been interpreted as the Death of Opheltes, son of the king of Nemea and the nursling of Hypsipyle. When the Seven against Thebes passed through Nemea on their journey to Thebes, Hypsipyle showed them to a well outside the city; whilst Opheltes was left unattended, a snake attacked him. The fallen hydria in the foreground alludes to this trip.[63] Despite the intervention of the heroes, the child died and was renamed Archemorus, a symbol of the fate of the whole expedition. This story was known in antiquity through another Euripidean play, *Hypsipyle*, and is told at length in Statius's *Thebaid*.[64] In its tone, this relief differs significantly from the others. These others are characterized by Frank Müller as avoiding concentrated action and showing a predilection for scenes of tranquility, whereas this scene is full of action.[65] The scene also differs in that we are only asked to identify the occasion, rather than to engage with the characters. There is no sense of a separate world into which we wish to intrude, as was created by the downward gazes of Adonis or Bellerophon. Like the Branchus painting in the hall described by Lucian, the relief presents a contrast of tone; hence, perhaps, its charm lies in its variety. It is also possible that there were other reliefs, now destroyed, that would have extended the range of its meanings.

The relief showing Pasiphae and Daedalus (fig. 4.12) shares many more characteristics with the other Spada reliefs. It represents the inside of Daedalus's workshop, yet this cannot be easily identified as a scene either of the commissioning or the presentation of the wooden cow, both of which are well represented in Pompeian wall painting.[66] Here Daedalus is working on the cow when Pasiphae enters the workshop. It appears to be a chance appearance rather than a scene of presentation. Pasiphae is depicted in a pose commonly shown on Attic grave reliefs, a detail that adds a certain pathos. Daedalus is alone: there are none of the helpful Erotes that appear on sarcophagi and in Philostratus's description of a similar scene (*Imagines* 1.16.3). This adds to the aura of secrecy already created by the fact that the scene is set inside closed doors. The stillness and pathos provoke a deeper realization of the terrible significance of Pasiphae's lust than do the courtly scenes shown in wall paintings.

The last two reliefs feature the hero Paris. Both have been heavily restored, following other images that they seem to replicate.[67] These allowed the upper halves of both reliefs to be recreated; in the lower sections, however, inspiration is drawn from different artistic models. The figure of a river god (fig. 4.13) is similar to sculpture in the round produced at this period, and the lower half of the Paris and Eros relief (fig. 4.14) shows similarities to other pastoral reliefs.[68] In composition, the two reliefs are parallel and form a distinct pair. The seated figures of Paris, each accompanied by another figure, are mirror images. In the Eros scene, there is a clear reference to the temptation of the Phrygian shepherd whose submission to erotic desire had disastrous effects. In the Oenone image, we can see a similar message. The woman looks at Paris and points to the ship that lies below them. The story of Oenone's marriage to Paris and her skills of prophecy is recounted by Apollodorus; she warned Paris of the disasters that would follow from his pursuit of Helen.[69] Her gesture toward the ship seems to suggest this very warning. The positioning of the figures of Eros and Oenone contrasts them; we can also see a contrast in their advice to the hero: to follow the lure of beauty or to stay at home, avoiding its dangers.

The depiction of cows on the Paris and Eros relief links it to the Daedalus and Pasiphae relief. Here again we are prompted to consider the trickery and temptations of naturalistic art. The cow being created by Daedalus seems as real as the "real" cows shown with Paris, hinting at its acceptance by the bull and the resulting birth of the Minotaur. This, in turn, should act as a warning against the naturalistic allure of the other reliefs. Whilst we, like Philostratus, are lured into a relationship with the images of youthful male beauty before us, the Pasiphae relief suggests the dangers of an enraptured gaze that confuses representation with reality.[70] The warning is also appropriate for Paris as a man who succumbed to the lure of beauty—that of the goddess Aphrodite, her verbal description of Helen's beauty, and the image created within Paris's own mind. The power of the imagination to better reality might also be suggested by the fact that, although the Paris and Eros relief seems to be an excerpt from a scene of the Judgment of Paris, the three goddesses are not actually shown, leaving us to imagine them. Paris's proclivity to believe images over reality is proved by his abandonment of Oenone for the described beauty of Helen. For the viewer who remembers Euripides' *Helen*, in which it was not the real Helen but merely a phantom who went to Troy, the message about the power of beautiful images to deceive is made even more acute. Like Philostratus's images of Narcissus and Olympus, the Spada reliefs seem to entice the viewer into their reality on an individual level, but, when considered together, also to suggest the dangers of this sort of absorption.

Conclusion

The division of the two Paris reliefs into different spatial zones provides a clear link between them. It was this feature that led Wace to date them as later than the rest; it also, however, gives landscape a more significant role than in any of the other reliefs.[71] The figure of a river god indicates that the action of the Oenone relief is located near water, whilst the cows show that the Eros scene is set in a pastoral landscape. The Spada reliefs have often been seen as mature examples of landscape relief (e.g., Wace 1910). This analysis sometimes slips into equating landscape with pastoral, as when Brilliant (1984.85–86) compares the spirit of the reliefs to the pastoral novel of Longus. This desire to see all the reliefs as pastoral is especially obvious in the false reconstruction of the Adonis relief with rocky landscape and a tree. However, if we look closely at the reliefs, we can see various types of space: the Pasiphae relief is set indoors, whereas, in the Odysseus and Diomedes relief, we see the action both inside and outside a temple. A similar temple recurs on a smaller scale in the Hypsipyle relief, where the action takes place just outside the city of Nemea. In the reliefs showing Bellerophon, Adonis, and Amphion, the scene is an external one: rocks, trees, and a small shrine appear. It is only in the relief of Paris and Eros that we find a complete pastoral landscape. The other Paris relief also shows a clearly defined landscape. Here it is a marine one with a significant inclusion: on top of a cliff overlooking the sea is a series of structures. These show a remarkable resemblance to the scenes of Roman villas that can be found in wall paintings, such as one in the House of M. Lucretius Fronto in Pompeii (Ling 1991.146ff., plate xiia).

As I noted at the start of this chapter, the find-spot of the reliefs makes it likely that they were originally displayed in a suburban villa. When we look at contemporary descriptions of villas, one aspect of their design that is given particular importance is the ability to manipulate the local landscape and give access to a variety of views. This is especially clear in Pliny the Younger's discussions of his villas, written around the turn of the first to second centuries C.E.[72] In his discussion of his villa in Tuscany, Pliny makes specific mention of the views that can be seen: "From the end of the colonnade projects a dining-room: through its folding doors it looks on to the end of the terrace, the adjacent meadow and the stretch of open country beyond" (*Epistle* 5.6.19, trans. Radice), while, in another letter, he praises the view of the sea from three sides of the triclinium of his Laurentine villa (*Epistle* 2.17.5). A similar variety of landscapes emerges from Statius's description of the villa of Pollius Felix.[73]

Like wall paintings that appear to give access to a real world, the Spada reliefs, too, suggest a variety of views, moving from the internal space of the Pasiphae relief, to civic scenes (Odysseus), sacro-idyllic landscapes (Hermes and Amphion), and pastoral and marine views (the two Paris reliefs), mimicking the variety that Pliny praises in the real views from his villas. The reliefs serve to identify the building in which they were displayed with the sort of elite villas possessed by the Younger Pliny, even to the extent of allowing a sea view that the actual location of the house, to the northeast of Rome, would not permit. Yet there is an extra dimension to this allusion. The world that the viewer of these images looks out onto is both a contemporary one, as is suggested by the presence of a Roman-type villa on the Paris and Oenone relief, and one filled with the characters of Greek myth. In this they show some similarities with Statius's poetry, where mythological figures crop up as spokesmen or simply as inhabitants of the landscapes he describes, blurring, yet again, the boundaries between myth and reality (see Coleman 1999 and Bergmann 1991.55). This is not a case of stepping back into the mythical past, but rather one of bringing that past forward into the Roman present.

This choice of decorative landscapes differs from those we find in republican houses in Campania where, Wallace-Hadrill suggests, second-style wall paintings exalt the position of the *dominus* of the house by their allusions to public architecture (1994.17ff.). Bergmann's link between the viewing of wall paintings and rhetorical techniques such as mnemonics also suggests that the domestic appreciation of art can be seen as parallel to a more public activity. The viewing of a series of images like the Spada reliefs is a rhetorical activity, and indeed, as we see from Lucian and Philostratus, images within domestic spaces could serve as the material for public displays of a new type of oratory: Greek sophistic rhetoric. Images allowed one to reveal one's knowledge of Greek mythology, literature, and art, by explaining, like Philostratus, the texts on which the images are based or by recognizing adaptations of famous works of art, such as the Spada version of Cresilas's Diomedes. Images allowed both the host and his guests to show themselves to be members of the educated classes, Lucian's *pepaideumenoi*, distinguished by their knowledge of Greek culture (*de Domo* 2).

Indeed the Spada reliefs' invocation of Greek myths is directly related to the cultural norms of second-century society. As suggested above, this is characterized by an overwhelming interest in Greek culture, even in the traditionally Latin-speaking west of the empire. We might think of the Gallic eunuch Favorinus, whose sophistic Greek rhetoric had such a powerful effect on his audience; the sophist Aelian, who, despite never leaving Italy, wrote consistently in Greek on Greek themes; or, to take an imperial example, the emperor Marcus Aurelius, who wrote his philosophical *Meditations* in Greek. Even below the highest intellectual level, we see a keen interest in Greek literature and myth expressed by the pupils who come to hear Philostratus in the villa near Naples or, to give a visual parallel, in the sudden emergence around 120–130 C.E. of sarcophagi with Greek mythological themes as the new form of funerary art.[74]

As Lucian's comments about the response of educated men to visual beauty suggest, images provided a central locus for the display of *paideia* by provoking verbal descriptions like those given by both Lucian and Philostratus. These *ecphraseis* often involved an intellectual programmatic gaze, seeing the connections between images and identifying the texts that lie behind. Yet, as we have seen, this programmatic gaze was countered by another way of looking at mimetic art: an enraptured or absorbed gaze in which the naturalism of the image drew the viewer into its world, making him or her forget the boundaries between image and reality. Through the erotic naturalism of individual images and their evocation of a series of views, the Spada reliefs also provoke this type of viewing, suggesting that the figures they show lie in the world just beyond the villa where they were displayed. They hold out the fantasy of direct access to the figures of Greek myth, a fantasy that we also find explored elsewhere.

In the dialogue *Heroicus*, written in the early third century C.E., Philostratus describes a meeting between a Phoenician merchant and a winegrower in the Thracian Chersonese (see G. Anderson 1986.241–57). The winegrower reveals to the merchant that he regularly sees the ghost of the Homeric hero Protesilaus, who resides in the area. A similar meeting with a Homeric hero occurs in Philostratus's *Life of Apollonius of Tyana*, where the sage stops at Achilles' grave to consult with him (4.11f.). This fantasy of direct contact with Greece's mythological and classical past seems to run throughout the culture of the Second Sophistic. It can be seen in the west in the regular reenactments of Greek myth that took place in theatrical mimes and that were also used as a form of capital punishment where a mythological figure who met a particularly grisly end would be played by the condemned criminal.[75] Through their invitation to an absorbed gaze, the Spada reliefs, too, encourage this access, breaking down the barriers between real and imagined worlds.

Through Lucian's and Philostratus's texts about viewing images and the reactions the Spada reliefs themselves provoke, we see that a number of different responses were available to the viewer of naturalistic images. At some times, a viewer was held enraptured by the naturalistic, often erotic, beauty of the images and led into the fantasy world of Greek culture; at others, he might seek to constrain this seductive beauty through an intellectual or thematic approach to the images, seeing them as signifiers of a verbal text or as part of a greater decorative program. These approaches to the images within a domestic house parallel a tension in the wider relationship between members of the Roman elite and the world of Greek culture. While some figures chose to immerse themselves in Greek culture, seeking to relive the values of the past in the present, they, and others, could simultaneously use that culture as a source of prestige, to indicate their membership in an elite club whose badge was *paideia*. The *luxuria* evoked by the promised access to a world of Greek myth and history went hand in hand with the intellectual control of that past for reasons of social prestige. Domestic decoration remained a central arena for statements about the self-identity and prestige of the elite, and the very form those statements took reveals the values and activities wherein status was seen to lie. Throughout, viewing visual images remained an activity with deep political and cultural significance.

Notes

I would like to thank Bettina Bergmann, Jaš Elsner, and Dave Fredrick for their advice and comments on versions of this chapter. I am also grateful to the British Academy Arts and Humanities Research Board for funding my research in Rome.

1. Bartoli 1790.250–51, no. 100, records their discovery during the reconstruction of the great staircase.

2. See Kampen 1979 for the basic bibliography.

3. Early twentieth-century scholars concentrated on the stylistic unities between the reliefs and their use of earlier Greek models: Wace 1910. More recently, attention has been paid to the thematic connections between the panels; see Zanker 1966.766ff., Kampen 1979, and Brilliant 1984.83–89.

4. The two reliefs in the Museo Capitolino in Rome, representing Endymion, and Perseus and Andromeda, are often associated with the Spada reliefs, e.g., Brilliant 1984.87. However, these were found in different locations within Rome and have different dimensions from the Spada reliefs. In my opinion, they are unlikely to belong to the same series. For other similar reliefs, see Schreiber 1894.

5. Schreiber 1894 originally suggested that such reliefs derive from Hellenistic models, however Wickhoff 1900.36–45, 73–80, argued for a Roman date, later placed by Wace 1910.167–69 and Sieveking 1925.23, 29ff., in the Hadrianic period. Wace dates the majority of the reliefs to around 130 c.e., with the two Paris reliefs around 160. See also Brokaw 1942 and Dawson 1944.41–43 for comparisons with Pompeian wall paintings. For the dating of the church in which the reliefs were found, see Krautheimer 1937.14–39 and Deichmann 1946.

6. Brilliant 1984.86, Cicero *ad Att.* 1.10.3.

7. Neudecker 1988.212–13 comments that the area was imperial property by the time Constantina founded the church in the fourth century. Ashby 1906.38–46 notes the remains of three villas in the vicinity. Cemeteries also occupied this area, but the reliefs seem more likely to have come from a domestic context.

8. Schefold 1952, Thompson 1961. The quotation is Thompson 1961.39.

9. Brilliant 1984.83, Zanker 1966.765. No remains of paint can, however, be seen on the reliefs themselves.

10. Brilliant 1984.62–83, esp. 78. See also Fredrick 1995.266–87, 280ff., on eroticized images of submission as an alternative thematic link between paintings. On thematic programs within sculptural collections, see Dwyer 1982.122–28, Neudecker 1988.1–129, and Bartmann 1991.

11. Wallace-Hadrill 1994.1–61 and Clarke 1991a.1–29. See also Laurence and Wallace-Hadrill 1997.

12. Vitruvius *de Architectura* 6.5. See also Cicero *de Officiis* 1.138–39.

13. Wallace-Hadrill 1994.26–29. He also suggests that the change from second- to third-style wall painting can be seen within the context of the political shift from republic to empire.

14. See Edwards 1993.137–72 on houses, status, and the use of their houses by late-republican politicians such as Cicero.

15. See Bartsch 1994.63–125 on Tacitus's *Dialogus* and the perils of rhetoric.

16. Edwards 1993.138. Seneca *Epistle* 100.5–6 defines the simplicity of Fabianus's literary style in opposition to the trappings of luxury houses. Quintilian *Inst.* 7 preface 1–2 suggests that the construction of a rhetorical speech is analogous to building a house or making a statue.

17. See M. L. Clarke 1953.80–84 on Asiatic and Attic styles in Latin oratory. It should be noted that the later praise of Atticism in Greek rhetorical literature referred largely to the use of the Attic dialect and could be quite compatible with Asiatic-style rhetorical flourishes.

18. Edwards 1993.142. See also Bergmann 1991 on how Statius's description of Pollius Felix's villa and contemporary images of villas in wall painting both express the power of the villa owner.

19. See Gleason 1995.103–30 on the changing attitudes toward rhetoric in Greek and Latin authors, which she relates to its changing significance in public life.

20. Philostratus *Lives of the Sophists* 1.8 (489), Lucian *The Double Indictment* 27.

21. See esp. Bowersock 1969.43–58 on this aspect of the Second Sophistic. A number of famous sophists served as imperial tutors.

22. Philostratus *Lives of the Sophists* 1.8 (598). See also Gleason 1995. xxvii–xxix, 17.

23. The philhellenism trend started with Nero and Domitian, but was firmly integrated into the provincial policies of Hadrian. See Toynbee 1934.1–160.

24. On Greek culture as a form of escape, see Bowie 1970.

25. Apuleius *Apologia* 30. See G. Anderson 1993.223–27.

26. For the continuing importance of *paideia* in late antiquity as a force for elite unity, see P. Brown 1992.35–70, esp. 39ff., and K. A. Kaster 1988.ixff., 15–28.

27. Note, for example, the increased importance given to spectacular dining events, including private performances of mimes of Greek myth, associated by Dunbabin with a change in the architecture of the triclinium: Dunbabin 1996, C. P. Jones 1991. See also Bek 1980.165–203 on the changes between the Vitruvian ideal of domestic decoration and the Plinian delight in *utilitas* and *amoenitas*.

28. Philostratus *Imagines* 1 proem 3: "Addresses which we have composed for the young, that by this means they may learn to interpret paintings and to appreciate what is esteemed within them" (trans. Fairbanks).

29. C. P. Jones 1986.8 n. 10, and app. B gives a suggested chronology for Lucian: born between 115 and 125 C.E., with most of his works dating to 160 to 180 C.E. On the complex evidence for dating and attributing the various works of the Philostrati, see G. Anderson 1986, app. I, 291–96. I follow the *Suda* in attributing the first *Imagines* to its "second" Philostratus—to whom it also attributes the biographical works.

30. Philostratus *Lives of the Sophists* 1.481. On the characteristics of the Second Sophistic, see G. Anderson 1993.13–21 and Swain 1996.1–20.

31. Lucian *de Domo* 2. Müller 1994.124 also identifies the audience of the Spada reliefs with that characterized by Lucian.

32. I owe the suggestion that Lucian's work is set within a public hall to Bert Smith.

33. K. Lehmann 1941. "Villa by the Sea" is the term used by Thompson 1961. The debate over the "reality" of the paintings is discussed by Boeder

1996.137–70, esp. 138ff., who argues forcefully against this interpretation and instead suggests that their reality lies in their descriptions and the effect of these descriptions on their readers. She makes similar points with reference to Lucian's *de Domo*.

34. For two examples, see Zeitlin 1990 and N. W. Slater 1998. On Lucian's essay, see Bompaire 1958.713–18 and Mattei 1994.xxxviiiff.

35. Lucian *de Domo* 2, 5. Lucian here clearly associates himself with a Greek identity, despite his own ethnic status as Syrian. See Swain 1996.298–329.

36. *de Domo* 2. The verb ἀμείβω has the sense of "to exchange."

37. *de Domo* 18: ἀντὶ ἀκροατῶν θεαταὶ καθίστανται.

38. Philostratus *Imagines* 1.23. On Philostratus's use of Narcissus to embody the erotics of naturalistic art, see Elsner 1996b.

39. Pausanias uses a similar topos of an individualized periphrasis in his account of the altars at Olympia, which he describes in the order of the Elean's sacrificial ritual: Pausanias 5.14.4, 5.14.10.

40. *de Domo* 22, the first image is introduced by Ἐν δεξιᾷ μὲν οὖν εἰσιόντι, "On the right as you enter."

41. On *ecphrasis*, see James and Webb 1991.4ff. and Bartsch 1989, chap. 1. For the effect of these theories on Philostratus's *Imagines*, see Webb 1992, chaps. 1–3.

42. Generally on the ancient novels, see Hägg 1983 and Reardon 1989.1–16.

43. Thompson 1961.61 n. 120 also suggests that there may be a contrast between Athena as the non-mother, who nevertheless nurtures Erichthonius, and Medea, who is a real mother, but kills her children.

44. Apparently named thus because of his kissing of Branchus, who then became the first prophet of this oracle. See Conon *Narr.* 33.4 and Varro in Schol. Statius *Theb.* 8.198.

45. Ovid *Metamorphoses* 11.157f. has Pan, but Hyginus *Fabulae* 191 says that the contest was with Marsyas; therefore this version was clearly known in the second century.

46. *Imagines* 1.21.1: εἰ δὲ τὸ κάλλος ἀνακρίνεις, τοῦ ὕδατος ἀμέλει, "If you are examining beauty, do not pay heed to the water."

47. *Imagines* 1.28.2. On Philostratus's treatment of Narcissus, see Bann 1989.108–14 and Elsner 1996b.

48. *Imagines* 1.28.8: θεωροῦσιν αὐτὸ οἷον γραφέν.

49. On the viewer and the erotic gaze in wall painting, see Fredrick 1995.

50. On the instructive aspects of Philostratus's work, see Conan 1987 and Beall 1993.

51. The fundamental texts are Helbig 1899, updated as Zanker 1966, and Wace 1910.

52. Wace 1910.184ff. notes the discrepancies with the usual iconography of these subjects.

53. See Koortbojian 1995.23–62. Wace 1910.186 notes that the wound here is in the calf rather than the thigh.

54. Zanker 1966.764. There appear to be original traces of an ear and part of the neck.

55. See Lehmann-Hartleben and Olsen 1942.38–39 on the gateway at the left of an Ariadne sarcophagus in Baltimore.

56. Lochin 1994, nos. 138ff. Many of these may be later than the Spadas.

57. Zanker 1966.765. Bellerophon's attempt on heaven was recounted in Euripides' now fragmentary play, *Bellerophon*.

58. Wace 1910.187 says that this is the "usual name," but identifies them as Amphion and Zethus.

59. E.g., Wace 1910.187 refers to Helbig's comment that Amphion is the more muscular brother.

60. Apollodorus *Bib. Epitome* 5.13. Euripides *Hecuba* 239–40 also implies that Odysseus entered Troy alone and stole the Palladium with the help of Helen.

61. The surviving copies of the Diomedes of Cresilas do not, in fact, hold the Palladium, but, from the evidence of coins, it seems certain that they did originally. See Stewart 1990.68. The same iconography is also reflected in the group from Tiberius's Villa at Sperlonga; see Andreae and Conticello 1974.38–40, 95–103.

62. Bergmann 1994.245. See also Fredrick 1995 on how their poses link together images of different individuals in wall paintings.

63. This is actually restored, along with most of the right side of the relief; the details, however, seem to be correct.

64. Statius *Thebaid* 4.718–5.753. See also Apollodorus *Bibliotheca* 3.6.4. The Nemean games were set up in honor of Opheltes/Archemorus.

65. Müller 1994.123. See also Brilliant 1984.86: "All but The Death of Opheltes . . . exhibit a languorous air of reverie."

66. Zanker 1966.756–57. For the iconography in Pompeii, see Papadopoulos 1994.195. The painting in the Ixion Room of the House of the Vettii is a typical example of a presentation scene.

67. See Zanker 1966.757, 761–62, for full details, though note that S. Lehmann 1989.252 suggests that the Villa Ludovisi relief is almost entirely a Baroque creation.

68. See Stuart-Jones 1912.21 and Vermeule 1981.234, no. 195.

69. Apollodorus *Bibliotheca* 3.12. 6. See also Parthenius *Narrat.* 4 and Ovid *Heroides* 5.

70. A number of different levels of artifice are created by the presence of both the "real" cow and the "constructed" one within the sculpted world of the reliefs.

71. Wace 1910.188ff. If these reliefs were added later, they are clearly identified as part of the same series by the formal similarities of the cows and by the figures of Pasiphae and Oenone, both victims of unrequited love.

72. For the use of this evidence to explain the illusionist architecture and decoration of Campanian houses, see Elsner 1995.76f.

73. Statius *Silvae* 2.2.5of. See Bergmann 1991.

74. Philostratus *Imagines* 1 proem 4; Koch 1993.72ff. See also Müller 1994, app. IV.

75. See Lucian *On the Dance*, Coleman 1990, and, on reenactments of episodes from Greek history, Coleman 1993.

5 Look Who's Laughing at Sex

Men and Women Viewers in the *Apodyterium* of the
Suburban Baths at Pompeii

John R. Clarke

My aim in this chapter is to examine a clear example of visual
representations addressed to both men and women viewers.[1] I attempt
to differentiate between the male and female gaze by trying to understand the viewing contexts for a series of paintings that depict sexual activity. I propose that men's sexual acculturation was different from
women's in the Neronian period when a patron commissioned an artist
to create the paintings in the *apodyterium* of the Suburban baths of Pompeii. By "sexual acculturation," I mean the attitudes toward sexual behaviors and practices that individual Romans acquired because of who
they were: their sex, their class, and their status. Although I also explore
ancient texts—especially those nearly contemporary with the paintings—
for *signs* of sexual acculturation, I privilege the paintings themselves because texts, written by elite men (or by the men working for them), tend
to reveal elite male values. Studying legal texts, medical texts, poetry, or
public political discourse, we get an uneven assortment of information
about sexual acculturation: legal rules and opinions, instructions on the
care of the body, accounts of love-hate relations with the poet's boy-
and/or girl-love, and the attribution of depraved sexual acts to individuals. In the texts, we get the elite men's gaze—or at least a sense of the
ways that such men encoded their sexual gaze in their writings.

It comes as no surprise then that most ancient Romans have no voice
at all in the preserved literature. One will look in vain for the voice of
one woman of any class, whether aristocratic matron or poor slave.[2] The
men put all the words in women's mouths—and attribute to them all the
deeds they are supposed to have done. Similarly, in all of this literature,
no freedman or slave speaks out with anything other than the utterances

constructed by these elite male writers.[3] Where are the voices of the marginal people: the voices of the many foreigners—who ranged from the
red-headed Northern German or Slav to the black-skinned Ethiopian?
The voices of boys and nonelite men who were the elite men's love objects? We hear them speak but only as the male elite wanted them to
speak. None of these ancient people speaks for him- or herself in elite
literature.

What is surprising is how much information lies just beyond Catullus, Ovid, Martial, and Juvenal in anonymous poetry, legal texts, tomb
inscriptions, captions on wall paintings, soldiers' diplomas, and graffiti.
Thanks to new studies of these nonliterary texts, we know more about
the questions about which literature is silent: the condition of women
of different classes, relations between masters and slaves or former slaves,
and Roman attitudes toward everything from commerce to same-sex relationships.[4] Still only rarely does a textual scholar venture to interpret
the much more ample evidence of Roman visual representation.

It is for this reason that I turn to works of art that represent lovemaking to elucidate further what sex meant for the ancient Romans and
to understand how men and women looked at representations of lovemaking, for the visual record is much richer than the textual one. All social classes, and both male and female consumers, viewed works of art
and used artifacts that featured representations of lovemaking. Many
sexual acts and many sexual scenarios that do not appear in the texts find
expression, and often considerable elaboration, in works of art. Such a
wealth of sexual representation results from the conditions surrounding
the patronage, creation, and consumption of imagery. It was the artist's
job to satisfy patrons or consumers who ordered or bought their products. Whether he created fresco paintings for the villa of a rich aristocrat
or crude decorations for the owner of a bordello, the artist had to please
the person who paid him. By extension, he had to create a representation
of lovemaking that appealed to the intended viewers. What is more—
particularly in the case of wall paintings still in place—it is possible to
hypothesize about how female, as opposed to male viewers, responded
to their imagery.

If we want to understand the ancient Romans' gaze, we have to use
responsibly all the information available about each visual representation
of sexual activity to build the fullest possible context. The rules for a
meaningful and fruitful study of Roman sexual imagery are simple. In
every case, with every object, I ask: Who made it? (artist); When did the
artist create it? (date); Who paid for it? (patronage); Who looked at it?

(intended audience); Where did people look at it? (physical context); Under what circumstances did people look at it? (use and purpose of the object); What else does it look like? (iconographical models); What parallels can I find for it within ancient literature?

Notice that the artist, patron, and audience—both men and women—can all find representation here. Asking these and related questions prevents us from the interpretive impossibilities that have characterized the many books on Roman erotic art that have indiscriminately paired ancient texts on sex with visual representations showing people engaged in sexual activity.[5] Furthermore, because these visual representations, unlike the texts, appear at every level of society, their potential for revealing the full range of Roman sexual acculturation is much greater than that of texts studied in isolation.

Whorehouse?

For Luciana Jacobelli, excavator of the Suburban baths, a long-standing tradition posed a problem when she uncovered room 7 of the Suburban baths and discovered eight daring erotic paintings.[6] Traditionally, whenever an archaeologist found a painting of explicit sex, he identified the room—if not the entire building—as a place where sex was for sale. Since most of these paintings, deemed obscene, were cut from their walls and locked up in the Pornographic Cabinet of the Naples Archaeological Museum, it was difficult to study them in relation to their original architectural contexts, with the result that no one questioned that their purpose was to illustrate and advertise prostitution. By 1986, when Jacobelli opened room 7, the number of Pompeian whorehouses and single-room brothels (*cellae meretriciae*) had risen to thirty-four. That made one whorehouse for about every seventy-five adult men in Pompeii—compared to the forty-six listed in the Regionary Catalogues for the entire city of Rome in the fourth century.[7]

Jacobelli bucked the tradition, and with good reason. Reexamining the architectural contexts of all of Pompeii's erotic paintings, she corroborated Andrew Wallace-Hadrill's assertion (1995.53) that there was only one building in Pompeii specifically constructed as a whorehouse: the famous *lupanar* in Regio VII discovered in 1832. Its twenty cramped cubicles on two levels, each outfitted with a masonry couch as well as numerous graffiti, attested to a thriving bordello.

Here the paintings, all featuring male-female couples in various stages of lovemaking, decorate the upper zone of the walls of the ground-floor corridor that gives access to ten cubicles. Despite what the popular guides—and some scholarly works—say, the intent of the paintings was not to illustrate "all the positions available." Close analysis reveals the artist's intention to bring up the tone of the establishment by illustrating *elite* sexual practices and *ideal* lovemaking—a point driven home by the painting of a couple contemplating an erotic picture. The woman is fully clad in a green tunic and stands beside the bed; the man is nude and reclines on the bed as he points toward a painting.[8] Although now much faded, Wolfgang Helbig tells us that the painting was a *pinax*, a painting with shutters, and that its subject was an erotic *symplegma* (Helbig 1868.371, no. 1506). Erotic *pinakes* were a standard feature of many scenes of lovemaking in opulent settings.[9] Visions of beautiful women and handsome men enjoying sex in well-furnished rooms pervade the other paintings in the *lupanar* (despite their relatively crude execution), again pointing to elite representations of fantasy sex—a far cry from the harsh reality of the hasty sex sold in the *lupanar* for two to four asses (the cost of a cup of common wine).

Jacobelli's contention that room 7 of the Suburban baths was an *apodyterium* (dressing room) throughout the building's life rests on firm evidence. The Suburban baths lie just outside Pompeii's walls in a two-story structure located along the steep road that leads from the ancient river port up to the Marine gate. The large bath complex occupies the ground floor; three apartments fill the upper story (fig. 5.1).

Comparison with other baths at Pompeii suggests that the owner of the Suburban baths was an enterprising individual whose establishment offered a number of amenities unavailable in the old-fashioned public facilities at Pompeii (Jacobelli 1995.18–23). Rooms were large and well lighted, and there were many luxury features. There was an elaborate cold-plunge or *natatio* (9) with a mosaic waterfall splashing cold water into it and elaborate paintings on its sides. In addition to the usual heated rooms, bathers could also enjoy the dry heat of the *Laconicum* (10) and even a large, heated swimming pool (2) flanked by richly decorated rooms (1 and 3). The plan also reveals an important fact for our investigation of the relation of erotic representations to the ancient viewer, for the Suburban baths are, unlike all the other baths functioning at Pompeii at the time of the eruption, the only ones not divided into separate sections for men and women.[10] There is only one *apodyterium* in the Suburban baths, marked 7 on the plan. Whether the two sexes bathed there at the same time or at different times, this *apodyterium* had to serve both men and women.[11] This fact is quite important. It means that we can ask

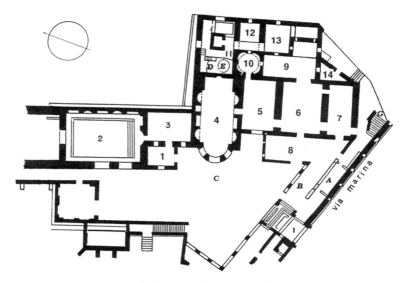

Figure 5.1 Pompeii, Suburban Baths, plan.

a new question about Roman sexual acculturation. Did these scenes have different meanings for the male versus the female viewer?

Aside from the sexual vignettes, the *apodyterium*'s fourth-style decorative scheme follows established practice (fig. 5.2). It differentiates the circulation space from the space where bathers dressed by using different color schemes and different architectural representations.[12] Simple motifs decorate the circulation space, which saw the most traffic since it encompassed three doorways. It has a black middle zone. A tall, thin panel divides the walls at midpoint where the middle zone changes to yellow. Most striking of all is the white-ground decoration of the upper zone, preserved on the right and back walls.[13] Here the artist has represented a deep shelf that supports sixteen numbered boxes. While all that survives of the decoration on the rear wall are the boxes in perspective (numbers IX–XVI), above the boxes on the right wall appear the most audacious ancient erotic paintings found to date.

Jacobelli has convincingly explained the sixteen boxes as two-dimensional representations of the real containers for bathers' clothing that would have rested on wooden shelves directly below (1995.61–64). The numerals appear on white labels in the upper center of each box between the arms of the "x" straps. The sequence starts with number I, at

Figure 5.2 Pompeii, Suburban Baths, *apodyterium* 7, south and east walls (C.E. 62–79).

the right wall's midpoint, and continues to number VIII, located at the corner. The numbered boxes then continue on the rear wall, ending with XVI. By representing the boxes with numbers, the artist also numbered the real containers below where each bather deposited his or her things. As if this were not enough, he added an unforgettable "label" atop each box in the form of an erotic representation.

The most likely date for the original fourth-style decorative program is following the earthquake of 62 C.E. Then some time shortly before the eruption, the owner, perhaps a new, prudish one, paid a painter to cancel out the erotic representations with a simple fourth-style scheme.[14] This overpainting helped preserve the erotic pictures, yet, in some cases, it still adheres, making it difficult to make out details.

Examination of the place of the little sexual vignettes within the whole decorative scheme of room 7 demonstrates how far they are from the *lupanar* in both content and purpose. In the *lupanar*, the decorative scheme depends on the viewer recognizing each erotic representation as a framed picture: the artist has painted them large in relation to the wall, has given them frames, and has isolated them from the plain fourth-style decoration of carpet-bordered panels framing tiny animals on the lower part of the walls. In the baths, in contrast, the viewer has to enter the *apodyterium*, where the wall decoration lacks figural elements and pictures, proceed to the back of the room, find a numbered box sitting on the wooden shelf, undress, and place his or her clothes in that box—all this before realizing that, *above* the box, the artist has painted a trompe l'oeil representation of the shelf and box in perspective and that he has topped that with a tiny erotic vignette. The *lupanar's* cramped circulation space—basically a small corridor—provided no room for a sequence like that of the *apodyterium*: entry, undressing, box-finding, and clothes-depositing.

Central to the mechanisms of comedy are the elements of setup, recognition, and surprise, and these are the very elements that we find in the *apodyterium* of the Suburban baths. If viewing the erotic pictures in the *lupanar*—distributed evenly throughout the space—requires simply standing anywhere and looking, in the *apodyterium*, the visitor only "gets" the erotic vignettes after going through a set series of procedures. These procedures set him or her up for the punch line. And if the imagery of the *lupanar* looks up to high-class models, that of our *apodyterium* looks down to low-class spectacle.

Although most of these images are unique, their aim—to make viewers laugh—is certainly not foreign to Roman sexual representations. Sexual representations in wall painting had a variety of purposes. At one end of the spectrum are the many sophisticated images of lovemaking that emulate the expensive panel paintings that the aristocrats had in their collections, such as those from the cubicula of the Villa under the Farnesina in Rome of about 15 B.C.E. Many homeowners at Pompeii installed similar paintings in their houses as emblems of their refined taste.[15] At the other end of the spectrum are outrageous images of sexual acrobatics like those from the Inn on the Street of Mercury (see Clarke 1998.206–12). Sex shows featured in public entertainments such as the *nudatio mimarum* probably inspired the four paintings found there, and their purpose was to make viewers laugh.[16] The eight little paintings in the Suburban baths, like the paintings from the Inn on the Street of Mercury, had nothing to do with upper-class fantasies. Their purpose was to amuse the viewer with outrageous sexual spectacles, but, in the context of bathing, this laughter takes on an added meaning.

Laughter and the Evil Eye

For the ancient Romans, the baths were a locus of both pleasure and danger. Grudging envy (*invidia*) was apt to rear its ugly head there, where men and women exposed their beautiful bodies to others (Dunbabin 1989). The feared instrument of *invidia* was the evil eye (Dickie and Dunbabin 1983.10–11). Although ancient experts disagreed on exactly how the envious person inflicted harm through the gaze, most believed that particles emanated from the aggressor's eye, invading the envied person's body. These particles could cause sickness or death. How to protect oneself from such disaster at the baths? You could wear amulets, but, in both private and public baths, owners often commissioned artists to incorporate images into the decorative program that were designed to disarm the evil eye (Dunbabin 1989.37–44).

To judge from the surviving evidence, the most efficacious images were those that provoked laughter. Three private bath complexes of the late first century B.C.E. at Pompeii employ images of the ithyphallic *Aethiops* for comic—and apotropaic—effect (Clarke 1996). Their atypical body and skin types, as well as their huge, erect penises, made them perfectly unbecoming, and therefore funny, spectacles. Elsewhere we find the Lucky Hunchback, often equipped with a huge phallus, poised at danger points such as entrances to houses, to dispel the evil eye with laughter (Levi 1941).

Since the *apodyterium* was the first place in the bathing process where the bather, by undressing, exposed his or her beauty to the potentially dangerous gaze of the envious, what better place to counteract the evil eye with laughter? By placing the sexual vignettes of *apodyterium* 7 deep within the room and high up on the walls, the artist made the now naked viewers crane their necks to get the jokes—perhaps making them look a bit foolish in the process. Roman bathers would have welcomed the release of laughter and the protection from *invidia* that it promised.

It is also worth noting that the vignettes of the Suburban baths, unlike the "straight" pictures in the *lupanar*, are highly complex, encouraging repeated viewing. Part of that complexity is their dual address—and double-entendre—to men as opposed to women viewers. In the following sections, I will demonstrate how the artist violated sexual expectations to provoke (apotropaic) laughter, accomplishing his purpose by playing with norms of sexual behavior that differed according to the viewer's gender.

Funny for Whom?

The artist begins the series with a representation that is explicit but fairly common in Roman erotic wall painting (fig. 5.3). The woman, facing the viewer, strikes a relaxed pose as she sits on the man's penis. She plants her feet squarely on the bed to right and left of the man's upper thighs. Although she holds her body upright, the artist has made her position unusually relaxed by having her lean to her right to rest her wrist on her knee while extending her left arm to place her hand on her left knee. (Remains of a thick, green, curving element from the later overpainting cover parts of the woman's left arm, hand, and leg.) The woman's curly hair falls to cover her ears. Overpainting covers the portion of the man's figure to the viewer's extreme left, but enough remains to see that the artist has placed him obliquely on the bed: he reclines, propping himself up with his elbows, so that the viewer looks over his head, back, and shoulders to focus on his erect penis as it enters the woman's vagina. She has removed her pubic hair through depilation, a common practice for women in classical Athens and one that apparently continued in Rome.[17] A few fluid lines near the man's hand and the woman's foot must have indicated the striped bedcovers, otherwise erased by the overpainting.

Closest to this representation among fresco paintings is a panel, probably from Pompeii, now in the Naples Museum (fig. 5.4).[18] It is clearly the work of a more skillful artist than the painter of the Suburban baths: he was better at placing the figures in space and in depicting their interaction. Despite paint losses, it is still possible to see how this artist used light and shadow to give the figures volume. He has also animated the woman; her counterpart in the Suburban baths painting looks quite bland and detached in comparison. In the Naples painting, the woman turns her head sharply to engage the man's gaze even as she pushes up her body to poise her vagina over his waiting penis. The man's pose is also more active than that of the man in the Suburban baths: he sits upright, his torso supported by a big striped cushion. The artist paid attention to details such as the man's floral crown (tied at the back with ribbons) and the woman's hairdo. Yet the major contrast between the Naples picture and that of the Suburban baths—a trait that appears in some of the other scenes there—has to do with relative scale, not details: the artist has underplayed the man's figure both in pose and in size to emphasize the woman. If, in the Naples picture, the man's body matches the woman's in both mass and pictorial valence, it is the woman's pose and body that dominate the painting in the Suburban baths.

Figure 5.3 Male-Female Couple on Bed, Pompeii, Suburban Baths, *apodyterium* 7, scene I (C.E. 62–79).

Figure 5.4 Male-Female Couple on Bed, Pompeii, unknown location (C.E. 62–79). Naples Archaeological Museum, inv. 27686, 38 x 39 cm.

There have been two tendencies in modern interpretations of this sexual position. K. J. Dover notes that it never appears in Greek vase painting, and some scholars wonder whether the popularity of this representation in Roman art might be a sign of the sexual emancipation of the Roman woman (Dover 1978.107). Catherine Johns notes that when the woman is on top, riding the man, she has freedom of sexual expression since, whether facing him or with her back to him, she can move around quite independently: the position requires "her very active co-operation" (Johns 1982.136–37). Others take the opposite tack: Paul Veyne, for instance, sees the *mulier equitans* (woman riding) position as the woman having to do all the work while serving the man who simply lies there (Veyne 1978.53–54). It is difficult to support either of these essentially modern constructions of sexuality from either the visual evidence or the ancient literature. Although both the ancient Greeks and Romans discuss this position in some detail, and although it appears with great frequency in painting and in relief sculpture, nowhere does one get the sense that this position necessarily or intrinsically encoded the woman's domination over the man—or vice versa.[19]

A more fruitful approach is to think of the visual properties of this representation since it, above all, was a way of showing the act of penetration—and the woman's beautiful face, breasts, torso, and legs—to best advantage. Ovid recommends this position for the small woman, but cautions against it for the tall woman.[20] As Molly Myerowitz points out, this and the other seven positions that Ovid specifies address the woman's act of presenting her best features to her lover. The woman, in effect, "composes" herself to look good—a self-conscious act (Myerowitz 1992. 136–37). What is interesting in the Suburban baths image is that the artist has depicted the woman as large not small. In this sense, he has privileged the woman as aesthetic object.

A Roman woman looking at this representation might chuckle, understanding it as a showcase of feminine beauty and power at the expense of the male. For the Roman man who enjoyed sex with women, the artist has constructed a view that shows off the woman's beautiful face, breasts, and torso to her lover—just the effect that Ovid says she will have if she rides the man. The male viewer might also laugh at this representation precisely because it reminds him of Ovid's tongue-in-cheek parody of the sex manuals. But, for both sexes, the comic trope is that of the woman "turning the tables" and dominating. By depicting this position, and by making the woman's figure loom large, the artist gives viewers of both sexes a way of looking at lovemaking that favors different, but comple-

Figure 5.5 Male-Female Couple on Bed, Pompeii, Suburban Baths, *apodyterium* 7, scene II (C.E. 62–79).

mentary, points of view. For both sexes, the artist has assumed the viewer's interest in clearly seeing the penis penetrating the vagina. But it is also a representation that privileges the woman's body over the man's. It is only in this sense that the woman "dominates" the man. She dominates a visual composition that reveals the first-century Romans' avid interest in the beauty of the nude female body in all activities, including making love.

In scene II, the woman reclines on her left side, her upper body resting on a big fringed cushion (fig. 5.5). She supports her head with her left hand, her elbow resting on the cushion, while her right arm curves around her head in a gesture indicating sexual readiness.[21] The man kneels upright on the bed, his right knee between the woman's legs as he grasps her right thigh with his right arm. He turns his head toward the woman. (Unfortunately, the later decoration of this wall covered both the man's torso and the woman's face with a fourth-style carpet border.) Traces of red pigment show the spool ornaments of one of the bed's legs; on the bed itself is a yellow coverlet. There is a green cushion with stripes and fringes at its head and a green sham swagged below the bed frame.

As in scene I, display of the woman's fashionable body seems uppermost in the artist's mind, for this pose turns her graceful torso, thighs, and legs to the viewer. Not only is it a variation of the many representations of male-female intercourse in Arretine ware,[22] it is also the preferred pose for representing a man penetrating a boy, and for similar reasons. Just as the pose permits the artist to show the woman's breasts, in male-male representations, it allows him to feature the boy's genitals. However, comparison with other representations of the woman or boy lying on the left side reveals an ambiguity in scene II. For some reason, the artist, so intent on displaying penetration in scene I, has placed the man's body too squarely behind the middle part of the woman's back to allow him to be in the act of penetrating the woman either anally or vaginally.

It may be that the artist simply miscalculated the man's position or that he wanted to represent approach from the rear but not the act of penetration. The woman's pose, with her right arm raised to frame her head, relays the woman's sexual readiness or, at least, sexual accessibility. As in scene I, the artist has made the woman's body the subject of the picture and the object of the viewer's gaze. If she is available, it is as much to the spectator as to her partner's somewhat clumsy approach.

For the astute female viewer, this depiction of the woman's glamour coupled with the man's seeming ineptitude must have been quite funny. Her eyes would understand the clichés, especially that of the crooked-arm gesture (the gesture of erotic readiness), as well as the awkwardness of the moment pictured. The man looking at this scene would have been equally aware of the clumsiness of the man in the picture—especially since it foregrounded an obvious display of the woman's anatomy to the disadvantage of the man. For viewers of both sexes, the comedy lies in the way that these beautiful lovers bungle their sex demonstration.

Even though scenes I and II feature representations that are well known to us because of their replication in a number of media, the artist has privileged the display of the woman's body in ways that may have elicited different responses from men and women viewers. Scene III takes a different tack by figuring a rarity in the Roman visual record, the act of a woman fellating a man—and that, to be sure, in a unique composition (fig. 5.6). Visual representations of fellatio in Roman art are rare; a few begin to appear in the first century C.E. Both ancient literature and graffiti tell us that fellatio was the province of prostitutes; it was a sexual act that no Roman male of the elite class could request of his wife—and with good reason. The Romans were particularly concerned about the purity and care of the mouth. It was the organ of speech and, above all,

Figure 5.6 A Woman Fellating a Man, Pompeii, Suburban Baths, *apodyterium* 7, scene III (c.e. 62–79).

of public oratory. Social interactions also focused on the clean mouth since it was customary for social equals to kiss when greeting each other. Although we have no oratorical or forensic texts accusing women of having unclean mouths because of their acts of fellatio, such accusations against men do appear. In invective literature, the worst possible insult is to accuse a man of fellating another man, and the worst possible threat against a man is that of forcing him to fellate someone. The word that describes this forced fellatio, *irrumare*, places the fellator in the category of impurity (Krenkel 1980, Richlin 1981). The Romans believed that the unclean mouth (*os impurum*) affected not only the perpetrator of the fellatio, but spread out to infect the whole of society (Corbeill 1996.99–127, Richlin 1992a.26–27). They excluded such impure persons from society by making them outcasts; they suffered the status of infamy, *infamia*, and could not act within the citizen body. This is the same status shared by prostitutes of both sexes, actors, and gladiators. It is logical to extend this Roman belief about the impurity of the male fellator to women; fellatio is an act that any freeborn woman would avoid performing at all costs.[23] Slaves, of course, had little choice in the matter. Even so, the gesture of the man's hand on the woman's head in our painting—about to push her head down on his penis—may encode the woman's expected reluctance to perform fellatio.

It would be a mistake, however, to assume that the threat of *infamia* would have kept men from seeking the pleasure of fellatio as much as it would be incorrect to assume that some women, whether highborn or servile, did not enjoy fellating their partners. They would simply dare not speak of the practice and hope that their partners would keep quiet as well. Martial, writing some thirty years after bathers saw the paintings in the Suburban baths, emphasizes that the *fellatrix* was a low prostitute (11.61). Yet he also satirizes the fact that men competed to have the services of an accomplished one (4.7). He calls attention to the hypocrisy of men wanting to be fellated but not wanting anyone to know about it in 9.4: "Two bits of gold will get you Galla's cunt, and four will get you a lot more. Then why give her ten, Aeschylus? She will give you a blow job for much less. What is this? Hush money."[24] Graffiti from Pompeii, since they are written by ordinary, probably nonelite men, reveal outright enthusiasm for fellatio. They evaluate the relative merits of various *fellatrices*.[25]

If we think of this scene in terms of its intended mixed audience, it seems to send different messages to male and female viewers. The artist has constructed the comic trope of the highborn man enjoying a sexual pleasure that, because of Roman attitudes toward oral purity, was supposed to be somewhat difficult to obtain. He symbolized the man's elite status by clothing him in a tunic and putting a scroll in his left hand. The Roman man looking at this scene would be well aware of the irony in representing an "intellectual" man. The freeborn woman would have found the painting amusing as well but probably for different reasons. She could laugh with impunity at the unfortunate woman—she certainly would have to be a prostitute or a slave—who had to fellate the man in the picture. She would be perfectly content for her husband to pay a woman of the servile ranks to perform this act so as to save herself from the threat of oral impurity.

With scene IV, the artist further explores questions of the pure versus the impure mouth—this time that of a man (fig. 5.7). A naked woman leans back on a bed and spreads her legs to reveal her depilated genitals to the man. The artist has done everything possible to focus the viewer's gaze on the woman's body. He has depicted her nearly frontally, and he has dramatized the woman's act of spreading her legs: she grasps her right leg at the knee to hold it up in the air while resting the other on the edge of the bed.

Figure 5.7 A Man Performing Cunnilingus on a Woman, Pompeii, Suburban Baths, *apodyterium* 7, scene IV (C.E. 62–79).

The man, in contrast, seems insignificant. Not only is he much smaller than the woman, he is crouching down to lick the woman's genitals. He is fully clothed in a white tunic and wears ankle-high shoes. His face is in profile, revealing his turned-up nose and large eyes, gazing, it would seem, up at the woman. The artist has emphasized the man's right hand, resting above the woman's left knee, by making it unusually large and by spreading the fingers.

The scene is unique among preserved wall paintings. When cunnilingus appears on lamps, it is part of a reciprocal act, with the man licking the woman's genitals while the woman responds by sucking the man's penis.[26] Such representations, because they make both partners equal in their sexual activities, contrast markedly with the scene from the Suburban baths. Instead of showing the man the same size as the woman, *on* (not crouching below) the bed, nude, and receiving fellatio in return for his performance of cunnilingus, the artist of the Suburban baths has emphasized the woman—and the pleasure that the man is giving her—while making the man small and subservient. Why?

The answer to this question lies in Roman attitudes toward men who performed cunnilingus. In their thinking, cunnilingus, like fellatio, brought about the disgrace of oral impurity on the person who performed it. In the Roman hierarchy of sexual debasement, the man suspected of performing cunnilingus was even more defiled than a man who was the passive partner in male-to-male sex.[27] In 4.43, Martial first accuses Coracinus of being penetrated by males, then switches his invective to something much worse: he practices cunnilingus on women. "I did not call you, Coracinus, a passive homosexual; I am not so rash or daring, nor one willing to tell lies . . . yet what did I say? This light and insignificant thing—a known fact that you yourself will not deny. I said that you, Coracinus, were a cunt-licker."[28] The artist has made the man in the painting of the Suburban baths nothing more than a *cunnilinctor*: he is all hands, mouth, smaller than the woman, and not even receiving genital stimulation from the woman in return for his act of debasement.

The artist's diminution of the man encodes another Roman belief that is quite foreign to our thinking but essential to understanding the humor of this representation. In the Roman scheme of sexual roles, it was always the man who did the penetrating and the woman who was properly the passive recipient of his penetration. As Holt Parker's careful review of the ancient literature reveals, cunnilingus cast the woman as active and as penetrator. Thus the man in scene IV is a comic figure on not one but two counts.[29]

Over against these constructions of oral impurity and active versus passive that we understand from classical texts, however, we find some evidence that women regularly hired male prostitutes to pleasure them with cunnilingus. Graffiti at Pompeii reveal that male prostitutes were willing to perform cunnilingus on women for a price similar to that which female prostitutes requested for fellatio, between one and three asses.[30] Although it is possible that detractors wrote these graffiti to debase their male enemies by saying that their tongues were for hire, it is equally possible that these graffiti reveal actual sexual practices. If a woman could easily obtain cunnilingus from a male prostitute for little money, the scene in the Suburban baths would have reflected a service that was routinely available to Pompeian women. Even so, the artist's rendering is no straightforward documentation of a routine sexual practice. He has pushed his representation into the realm of parody to make his audience laugh.

It is the artist's very exaggeration of the man's "perversion" that would have made him an extremely comic figure in the eyes of ancient Romans of both sexes. The artist has knowingly played with a deeply ingrained Roman attitude toward a sexual practice to produce sidesplitting comic parody. If the viewer doubled over with laughter—as I am sure many ancient visitors to the Suburban baths did—it was because the artist manipulated the mechanisms of sexual taboo to produce an image of a man so enthusiastic about licking a woman's genitals that he eagerly served her fully clothed—his eyes bugging with excitement—while the object of his enthusiasm, her face expressionless, obliged his perversion. For the male viewer, the fact that the man is clothed and the woman entirely naked—if we exclude her crisscross chain—signaled yet another reversal. In nearly all images of lovemaking, it was the man who was naked and the woman who was clothed—at least to the point of wearing the breastband or *strophium*.[31] His clothed status is inappropriate, just as the woman's nakedness signals that she is a brazen prostitute. The Roman man looking at this picture saw sexual etiquette turned upside down.

A Roman woman looking at scene IV would recognize the same reversals that would have struck the male viewer, with the added thrill, perhaps, of seeing the woman having the upper hand. She is obviously in control of the sexual proceedings: it is the man who crouches and implores. The woman is the object of genital worship—not to mention the artist's focus on her body as the beautiful contrast to the man's ugliness. He depicts her with fine proportions, graceful gestures, and expensive jewelry; the man, in contrast, has no proportions at all: his gestures are comic and his expression desperate.

It is not only the cunnilingus but also the sex and status of the two people pictured that make this scene so funny for Roman viewers of both sexes. That cunnilingus was a practice that was fair game for comic parody is clear not only from this representation but also from scene VII, considered below, where it is a woman who practices it.[32]

Scene V is so abraded and obscured by the remains of the overpainting (here the top of a pavilion) that the sex of the person standing on the left is unclear (fig. 5.8). This figure stands on the floor with its right hand at its side. The head is inclined downward as if to gaze at the genitals of the woman on the bed. She reclines, supporting herself on her left elbow while raising her right leg high up to rest on the standing person's left shoulder. She also inclines her head, but it is rendered in three-quarter view rather than in profile like her partner.

It is lamentable that no amount of scrutiny will yield with certainty the identification of the sex of the standing figure. Jacobelli interprets this standing figure as a man, providing a reconstruction drawing that has the merit of connecting the composition with another wall painting

Figure 5.8 Two Women Copulating, Pompeii, Suburban Baths, *apodyterium* 7, scene V (C.E. 62–79).

Figure 5.9 Scene V.

from Pompeii.[33] Artists frequently used this position in scenes of male-female intercourse. My own reconstruction drawing is more conservative than Jacobelli's and calls into question the sex of the standing figure (fig. 5.9). The standing figure's hair is really dressed in the same manner as that of the figure on the bed: pulled back from the face into a curly mass at the nape of the neck and probably tied with some sort of band.

This figure's body is also distinctly pale; unlike the dark tones used consistently for the men throughout, the color matches that of the reclining woman very closely. In the Suburban baths series, the artist increases the level of perversion/debasement with each successive scene, so that the relatively tame image of male-female intercourse of Jacobelli's reading seems out of place. Much more titillating—and completely without precedent in the visual record—would be a scene of a female-female couple imitating a well-known heterosexual position.

The major difficulty in a "lesbian" reading of the scene is reconstructing what kind of sexual act two women in this position might have been performing. Scene V could of course represent two women stimulating each other by rubbing their clitorises together. It is likely, however, that ancient Roman male viewers would have immediately assumed that the standing woman had a dildo strapped to her genitals. For one thing, the painting replicates a male-female pose where the man raises the woman's leg to increase the degree of penetration. For another, in all the preserved Greek and Roman literary constructions of lesbian lovemaking—all fabricated, of course, by male authors—the lesbian is a phallic woman (P. Gordon 1997b, Hallett 1989).

In sexual intercourse, the phallic woman is literally a woman using a fake phallus so that she is "just like" a man. Seneca the Elder in *Controversiae* 1.2.23, when recounting the story of the man who caught his wife and another woman in bed and killed them both, emphasizes the feelings of the husband, who could only make sense of the scenario by making one of the couple into the penetrator. Seneca has the man say: "But I looked at the man first, to see whether he was natural (ἐγγεγένηται) or artificial (προσέρραπται)." The "artificial man" would be a woman with a dildo strapped on.

Juvenal and Martial construct scenarios focused on the phallic lesbian. These authors make her into a deviant and intractable reversal of the phallic man whom the Romans considered the proper model of sexuality. In Juvenal's sixth satire, he writes of Tullia, a Roman matron, and her lover Maura. Returning from a dinner party, the two women "take turns riding each other." Tullia's husband, the object of the satire, does not realize that a woman has made him a cuckold.[34]

Although there are no extant visual representations of a woman wearing a dildo to penetrate another woman, scenes of *hetairai* fondling dildoes or even sucking on them are fairly common in Greek vase painting (Keuls 1985.82–86, figs. 72–80). Martial, who, as Amy Richlin has pointed out, was fascinated with the mechanics of lesbian sex, fills this gap in the visual record with several descriptions of a lesbian acting "like a man" by using a dildo to penetrate her partner (Richlin 1992a.134). In 7.67, he writes: "Philaenas the *tribas* sodomizes boys, and more savage than her husband's erection, she grinds eleven girls a day," and, in 1.90: "You seemed to me, I confess, to be a Lucretia, but—oh wicked deed— in fact you were, Bassa, the fucker."[35]

Central to both the visual and verbal representations of female-to-female lovemaking is the male construction of the "unnatural" woman. She is unnatural because she has no need of a man to achieve sexual satisfaction. Martial, it seems, was mirroring a widespread anxiety on the part of his class and sex about the independent woman. Changes in laws reflect the aristocratic woman's emancipation during the course of the first century. Marriage law now allowed the woman to divorce easily and to have increasing control over her own property. By the second century, a woman could take her property with her if she divorced her husband. Thus Martial says in 8.12 (trans. Michie in Sullivan and Whigham 1987.291): "Why have I no desire to marry riches? Because, my friend, I want to wear the breeches. Wives should obey their husbands; only then can women share equality with men."[36] His depiction of Philaenis in 7.67 has her not only sodomizing boys and grinding girls but exercising, drinking, and eating like a man.

If one of the mechanisms of comedy is to laugh at the worst-case scenario, scene V as an image of lesbian lovemaking would have provoked mirth even while mirroring anxieties male viewers had about emancipated women pleasuring each other. The female viewer may have found the image amusing specifically because it revealed the very male notion that a woman needs to be penetrated by a phallus to feel sexual pleasure. If the artist has overturned the power of the phallic male as dispenser of sexual pleasures to the passive female in this scene and in the scene of cunnilingus, in scene VI, he further explores this comic mechanism of the (male) world turned upside down by adding the image of the passive male homosexual to the brew.

The artist has depicted a sexual threesome: the man kneeling at the left is anally penetrating the kneeling man in the middle, who, in turn, penetrates the woman who crouches on the bed, her face in the pillow and her buttocks raised (fig. 5.10). The artist has posed the woman carefully, putting her head in profile and crossing her arms beneath her face. Although the torso of the man who has entered her is nearly upright, he leans his lower body back, better to receive the penis of the man kneeling, upright, behind him. His left arm falls behind the woman's buttocks,

Figure 5.10 Threesome of Two Men and a Woman, Pompeii, Suburban Baths, *apodyterium* 7, scene VI (C.E. 62–79).

but the artist has him reaching back with his right arm to clasp the hand of the man behind him. This man has a heavier physique than the man in the middle, and the artist has turned his head so that he looks out at the viewer.

Once again the Suburban baths provide us with a unique visual representation of lovemaking. The most standard component is the woman's pose; Roman artists and artisans freely figure women in this undignified way when they want to show the wild sexual behavior of improper women.[37] Yet the fact that she is being penetrated by a man who is also being penetrated by a man pushes her debasement to the absolute limit. Elite Roman authors heaped scorn upon the *cinaedus*, that is, the adult man who enjoyed being penetrated by other adult men, despite the fact that there are many positive images of sexual intercourse between men and boys in art (Clarke 1993). If we look at Petronius *Satyricon* 126.1–8, for instance, we see the disdain felt by Circe's maid, Chrysis, toward Encolpius, whom she clearly sees as a *cinaedus*. Chrysis also characterizes him as a male prostitute and scorns her own *domina*, Circe, for getting fired up by men like him.[38]

The artist of the Suburban baths is explicit. He is out to show the viewer something that she would not have seen on her Augustan silver cups or Arretine bowls, something as much a sexual spectacle as anything she might have seen in the obscene nude mimes in the theater. Although there is a slight difference in physique between the two men (the man who is doing the penetrating is brawnier than his partner), it would be very hard to make the middle man into a boy. He is the same height, stature, and dark color as the man who penetrates him. This is man-man not man-boy lovemaking. The artist has swept aside the conventions of boy-love that dominate the images of the Augustan period. If the partners often tenderly gaze at each other on Arretine ware, here the positions of all three make it impossible for any of the partners to catch each other's eye. The woman is looking at her crossed arms and the bedcovers, yet her expression is—to judge from the sketchy line—one of pleasure. The man in the middle directs his gaze downward toward the woman's lower back or buttocks. The muscular end man turns to the spectator as if to say, "Look at us, see what we're doing!" His gaze is the link with the spectator, since the other two are fully engaged in their pursuit of pleasure. His gaze also implicates the viewer as voyeur: it reveals that he knows that the viewer is looking at the trio.

In content and perhaps purpose, scene VI parallels Catullus 56, where the poet describes himself penetrating a boy who is penetrating a girl. Not only did Catullus write the poem to offend Cato—and amuse his more worldly friends—he also places himself in the position of the man who looks out at the viewer. In the painting, the man's gaze, like Catullus's address to the reader, could scandalize or amuse the viewer.[39]

Yet while he returns the viewer's gaze, this man also grasps the hand of the man he is anally pleasuring. This gesture increases in significance if we consider that every other option would emphasize the mechanics of lovemaking. If the artist had him grasp his partner around the waist or chest, the viewer would read this as an attempt to increase penetration or contact. Instead he holds his partner's hand: the only tenderness, yet significant, in this otherwise acrobatic display of lovemaking skills.

Although the expected response to scene VI was laughter, it must have provoked different responses from men and women. For the Roman man, the outrageous aspect of the scene was that the penetrated, full-grown man seems to prefer his sensation of being penetrated to his own act of penetrating the woman: the fact that he holds his male partner's hand would have tipped the comic scale in that direction. For the Roman woman looking at this scene, the outrage would have been that a woman—even a prostitute—would allow herself to be penetrated by a man who has lost his phallic status by being penetrated himself.

There is another irony for viewers of both sexes. There are frequent accusations in texts that the man who liked to be penetrated by other men (the *cinaedus*) was also apt to commit adultery with another man's wife (Edwards 1993.83–84). This assumption that the *cinaedus* is capable of all kinds of sexual excess—with both men and women—makes the man in the middle a concrete illustration of a particularly perverse kind of bisexuality. He is perverse for Roman viewers of both sexes precisely because some writers see his effeminacy, part of the life of luxury that moralists railed against, as particularly attractive to women. The representation in the Suburban baths would allow viewers of both sexes to laugh at the very enactment of the fears that moralists expressed. Those unaware of the literary tradition could simply compare their experiences with such men with what they saw depicted on the wall.

The principle that each sex receives its fair share of comic outrage follows through in scene VII (figs. 5.11 and 5.12). A nude man kneels at the left-hand side of a bed and looks out at the viewer while he raises his right hand in the air and penetrates the man kneeling in front of him. The artist has depicted the head of the man being penetrated in three-quarter view; he leans forward as a woman, kneeling on her left knee but with her right leg in the air, crouches on her elbows to fellate him. A second woman, kneeling on the floor, performs cunnilingus on her. (Remains of a green garland from the later painting campaign cover the back of the woman performing fellatio and the knees of the woman performing cunnilingus.)

This scene surpasses the other vignettes in its—to use a Roman term—"impurity." In addition to representing an adult man being penetrated by another man (the impurity is that of the man being penetrated), it shows two forms of oral impurity, putting both the woman who is fellating the man and the woman who is performing cunnilingus on her into the category of those who are utterly depraved. Of course, judgments about the relative debasement of the four would have been the stuff of comic shock—and the occasion for laughter—for the ancient viewer. The man who liked to penetrate other men would have seen his counterpart's waving right arm as a gesture of triumph in attaining pleasure. Artists used this gesture of a man waving his right arm to single out the victorious general in battle reliefs; later they would use it to denote the deceased man's triumph over death on battle sarcophagi (Brilliant

Figure 5.11 Foursome of Two Men and Two Women, Pompeii, Suburban Baths, *apodyterium* 7, scene VII (c.e. 62–79).

Figure 5.12 Scene VII.

1963.184–88). These associations would have only added a comic punch to this representation of sexual triumph. Like the woman being pleasured in scene IV, this male penetrator looks out, addressing the viewer's gaze, and, like the woman, he is the winner in terms of Roman attitudes toward sex, for he has not lost his phallic status like the man he penetrates nor is he performing either cunnilingus or fellatio like the two women in the picture. To the Roman man or woman looking at this scene, his gesture would have indicated a sexual tour de force: achieving maximum pleasure in a foursome without losing status by performing "debased" acts.

Not so with the other three. The man being penetrated and simultaneously fellated has an ambiguous status for the Roman viewer, for although he loses status by being penetrated by a man, he gains a perfectly legitimate phallic pleasure by being fellated. The shame and impurity of fellatio rested entirely on the person who took the penis in his or her mouth, not on the man who inserted his penis into the mouth (this in spite of Martial's mention of "hush money" in 9.4). This is another aspect of the phallic construction of sexuality typical of ancient Roman thinking—what Amy Richlin calls the "socket" mentality: as long as the man does the inserting of his penis into whatever orifice, be it vagina, anus, or mouth of another, he is blameless. The owner of the orifice, the receptive or "passive" partner, is always to blame (Richlin 1993a.536, Parker 1992.56–58).

In scene III, a woman performs fellatio, and, in scene IV, a man performs cunnilingus. What then of the image of a woman performing cunnilingus on her partner? This image is unique in the visual record; there are no representations, not even on Greek ceramics, of this sexual act. In connection with scene IV, I mentioned graffiti advertising the availability of male prostitutes to perform cunnilingus on women. It may also be possible that some women in ancient Pompeii commonly paid *female* prostitutes to provide cunnilingus. If so, the female client of the Suburban baths would have found this aspect of the foursome amusing but not shocking. A woman performing cunnilingus on another woman might have been an act that she was familiar with, perhaps from personal experience. For the woman viewer, scene VII presented a slice of sexual life where the woman actors—both the woman performing cunnilingus and the one fellating a man—were clearly prostitutes. As sex workers, they were simply performing acts that they would be paid to perform. The humor lay in the fact that *both* women were using their mouths to perform "impure" acts in a dual combination of oral debasement; the second woman from the right was unusually outrageous, even in this company, for she was playing the active role in having her genitals licked even while she took the "passive" role in sucking the man's penis. Men who viewed this scene probably constructed the woman performing cunnilingus either as a prostitute or, like Martial, as an entrenched lesbian. In 7.67, Martial represents Philaenis performing cunnilingus: ". . . after all this, when she's filled with lust, she doesn't suck—she thinks this

Figure 5.13 Poet with Hydrocele, Pompeii, Suburban Baths, *apodyterium* 7, scene VIII (C.E. 62–79).

hardly manly—but she eats up girls' middles. May the gods restore your mind to you, Philaenis, if you think cunt-licking is manly." Parker observes that what Philaenis fails to realize is that, from a Roman point of view, cunnilingus puts the *cunnilinctor* in the passive role: by performing it, Philaenis is playing the passive role.[40]

Since scenes I through VII establish a steady crescendo of increasingly comic representations of sexual depravity, one might expect scene VIII to represent five on a bed or an even more acrobatic coupling than scene VII. Instead the artist ends the sequence on the south wall with a single figure (fig. 5.13). A nude man stands in front of a table. The artist has expanded the space between his legs and the man's wide hips because they frame his enormous testicles: they descend nearly to his knees. As if to highlight this conspicuous deformity known as hydrocele, the artist exerted some care to make the man's upper body seem quite normal: his head, crowned with leaves, is in three-quarter view and he wears a pleasant expression as he reads the scroll that he holds in his left hand. At the moment of excavation, traces of writing were visible on the scroll.[41]

The image is clearly a caricature, but of whom? For the ancient

Roman, both the fact that the man is reading from a scroll and that he wears a leafy crown would have meant that he was a literary man, perhaps a poet. Clearly the comic element in the "poet" from the Suburban baths is the contrast between his supposedly high intellectual calling and the fact that the artist has denuded him and afflicted him with a conspicuous deformity of his sexual organs.

If the representation of such a physical affliction for the sake of comedy seems puzzling or even upsetting to the modern viewer, it is because our modern Euro-American culture fosters an attitude of compassion toward people with physical deformities. Not so with the ancient Romans, who thought that it was entirely appropriate to laugh at all kinds of human beings. Sources as diverse as Plutarch and Martial speak of the fact that the wealthy paid especially high prices for slaves who were physically deformed or mentally handicapped.[42] Cicero, in instructing the orator on the mechanisms of humor, points out that people with physical deformities are fair game.[43] Given these social attitudes toward real people, it should come as no surprise that art from both the Hellenistic and Roman periods frequently represented dwarves, hunchbacks, people with enlarged heads, and so on; such use in art of malformations for the sake of comedy is quite common (Garland 1995, Giuliani 1987.701).

Jacobelli's hypothesis that scene VIII might be a caricature of an erotic poet is especially attractive in light of the fact that he reads an open scroll (1995.60). Could our erotic poet be reading from a sex manual? It seems likely, since central to the comic effect of scene VIII is the fact that, of all the men and women represented on the south wall, only the poet is alone and not engaged in any ostensible sex act. If it is a sex manual, he is reading about what the people in the other seven scenes are actually doing. Yet it is better that he is not engaged in sexual activity. The artist achieves his comic effect by encouraging viewers—of both sexes—to imagine what an outrageous figure a man with this deformity would make of himself while engaging in sexual acts.[44]

Many open questions remain in the interpretation of the erotic paintings of the Suburban baths. Because the eight vignettes of the east wall are lost, the preserved paintings constitute only half of the iconographical program. This means that we can only speculate about what meanings the whole would have had. Furthermore, the fact that many of the preserved representations are unique makes it difficult to employ the usual comparative methods of art history. Jacobelli has proposed that the artist had access to a special illustrated manuscript that might have been the treasured possession of the person who commissioned the paintings

(1995.81). From our analysis of the content and context of the paintings that do remain, however, we can draw several conclusions.

We must read the paintings from the Suburban baths in terms of their intended audience. They were not the elite but rather those various strata of Pompeian society that would have used a public bath. They are both men and women, probably bathing at different times of the day.[45] Because the vignettes were meant to be seen and enjoyed by both sexes, they provide an unusual opportunity to hypothesize about the meaning that they would have had for that elusive person, the Roman female viewer. Her presence in this *apodyterium* becomes all the more important in view of the exclusively male constructions of women's sexuality in the extant ancient literature. Here, in a room decorated with many images entirely new within the preserved visual record, we can register the Roman woman's probable understanding of scenes of lovemaking. Although scholars have investigated the female gaze in domestic spaces, this is perhaps the only public space in the ancient world—specifically because its decoration was meant for both sexes—where we can hypothesize a female gaze.[46]

Since these paintings represent the very kinds of sexual activity that the upper classes frowned upon and denied doing—even though the central trope of both Martial and Juvenal is the hypocrisy of this class—they constitute an excellent example of a visual artist giving the lie to literary constructions. As such, the paintings of the Suburban baths underscore a fact that might unsettle textual scholars: visual artists gleefully represented the very sexual acts condemned by most Roman authors. The crescendo in the outrageousness of these activities, from the relatively commonplace male-female intercourse of scene I to the complex foursome of scene VII, is hard to interpret satisfactorily simply because the eight scenes that would have completed the sixteen vignettes have not survived. The single figure of the erotic poet might have been a "pivot" between the first seven and the last eight scenes, poised as he is in all his ridiculousness in the corner. These tiny paintings were more than humorous locker labels; the laughter they evoked protected bathers from the evil eye. They reveal not only the differences between the Romans' sexual acculturation and our own but also how different Roman sexual humor was from ours. Because these paintings fly so outrageously in the face of "proper" sexual acculturation, the only proper response—and this goes for both the male and female viewer—would have been laughter.

Notes

1. This chapter revisits both the Suburban baths and their meaning, first explored in Clarke 1998, color plates 8–16. Except where noted, all translations are my own.

2. One exception is the poet Sulpicia in the poems now listed as Tibullus 4.7–12. Scholars today agree that this poet is a woman rather than a man writing in a woman's persona; see Cantarella 1996.126–31, Hallett 1993.61, 64, Wyke 1994a.

3. A further problem is that of literacy among the people of the nonaristocratic classes. Harris 1989 proposes that only 3% of Romans in the western empire could read and write in this period; authors in Humphrey 1991 provide much more optimistic estimates.

4. See esp. Joshel 1992a and Kampen 1981.

5. Jean Marcadé 1961 and 1962 set the pattern for the ancient erotic picture book. A particularly lamentable recent example of the text/image pastiche is *Eros grec: amour des dieux et des hommes*, exh. cat. Paris, Grand Palais, November 1989–February 1990, and Athens, March–May 1990 (Athens 1989).

6. Valenziano 1988.145 cites the opinions of Antonio Varone, director of the excavations, and Baldassare Conticello, then superintendent of Pompeii, that the paintings advertised additional services that were available to male clients of the baths. Jacobelli 1995.61, 65, 92–97, maintains that neither this part of the establishment nor the upper-story apartments saw use as a *lupanar*.

7. Valentini and Zucchetti 1940.162: "Lupanariae XLVI."

8. Bragantini 1997.528 erroneously states that both the man and woman are on the bed.

9. See especially the representation of a male-female couple making love beneath an erotic *pinax* on a bronze mirror of Flavian date found on the Esquiline: Ferrea 1995, illustrated also in Clarke 1998, fig. 60.

10. Jacobelli 1995.18. Although the Central baths also lacked separate sections for men and women, the building was not in operation at the time of the eruption: Bargellini 1991. By the second century, all baths tend to be designed for use by both men and women.

11. Most scholars believe that men and women bathed at different times of the day in baths without separate sections for the two sexes; for a review of the evidence and the proposal that the sexes bathed simultaneously, see Bowen-Ward 1992.

12. Such differentiation of circulation space from reception space within a single room is common in Romano-Campanian painting: Clarke 1990, Scagliarini 1974–76.

13. The painting of the left (north) wall has not survived. Since there already was a closet set into that wall, it is unlikely that its decoration continued the scheme of the right and rear walls; the excavator did not find holes to support shelves corresponding to those on the opposite wall: Jacobelli 1995.63–64.

14. Jacobelli 1995.80. For an overview of the building's painting program, see Jacobelli 1991.

15. For instance, the House of Caecilius Iucundus (V 1 26): Clarke 1998.153–61.

16. Both Valerius Maximus and Martial repeat the story that Cato, that staunch upholder of old republican values, always left the theater before the *nudatio mimarum* during the Floralia: he didn't want his stern presence to spoil the people's fun: Valerius Maximus 2.10.8, Martial 1 Intro. Valerius Maximus mentions C. Messius as aedile, presumably the aedile of 55, making this Cato Uticensis (the Younger); Martial does not specify the Cato.

17. See Kilmer 1983 for depilation in classical Greece; on depilation in pathic men and boys in the Roman period, see Richlin 1992a.41, 93, 137, 168, 188–89 (anal depilation); vaginal depilation by women, 49, 123 n. 23.

18. Naples Museum, inv. 27686; Jacobelli 1995, fig. 29; Sampaolo 1986.172–73, no. 347.

19. Jacobelli 1995.38–40 underscores the importance, especially in Ovid, of the attainment of *reciprocal* sexual pleasure for both the man and the woman.

20. Ovid *Ars Amatoria* 3.777–78: "parva vehatur equo; quod erat longissima, numquam / Thebaïs Hectoreo nupta resedit equo."

21. For a full account of this gesture of "erotic repose," with current bibliography, see Clarke 1998.68–70.

22. Arretine was a ceramic dinnerware mass-manufactured in the early empire that copied the decorative styles of more expensive bronze and silver plate.

23. Andrew Riggsby points out (personal communication, January 1996), that *infamia* covers several different varieties of civic disqualification and that the jurists never specifically mention fellatio. There are three levels of disqualification (built into the procedural rules for bringing a suit), and those who were *infames* belong to the least restrictive. The middle level of disqualification (i.e., those who can only file suit on their own behalf) includes any man "qui corpore suo muliebria passus est" ("who has suffered his body to be used like that of a woman"); this would probably include *fellatores* and *fellatrices* (Ulpian *Dig.* 3.1.1.6). Women, however, already fall into this class by virtue of their sex (Ulpian *Dig.* 3.1.1.5). The *Lex Iulia* does not seem to address specific sexual acts (Ulpian *Dig.* 23.2.43, Paulus *Dig.* 23.2.44). For a detailed discussion of *infamia* in relation to sexual behavior, see Richlin 1993a.

24. Martial 9.4: "aureolis futui cum possit Galla duobus / et plus quam futui, si totidem addideris: / aureolos a te cur accipit, Aeschyle, denos? / non fellat tanti Galli. quid ergo? tacet."

25. Collected and translated into English by Krenkel 1980.85–87. Some examples: *CIL* 4.2273: *Myrtis ben felas*, "You fellate well, Myrtis"; 2421: *Rufa ita vale, quare bene felas*, "Rufa, may you live long, 'cause you suck so well"; 4185: *Sabina felas non belle faces*, "Sabina, you suck. You do not perform well."

26. See the lamp in the Cyprus Museum, inv. 2759, of a male-female

couple engaging in 69, reproduced in Johns 1982, fig. 116, and Clarke 1998, fig. 93.

27. See Edwards 1993.71 n. 29 (with references to the analyses of Artemidorus's *The Interpretation of Dreams* by Foucault and Price), Richlin 1992a.26–29, Veyne 1978.53 and 1987.204.

28. Martial 4.43: "non dixi, Coracine, te cinaedum: / non sum tam temerarius nec audax / nec mendacia qui loquar libenter . . . quid dixi tamen? hoc leve et pusillum, / quod notum est, quod et ipse non negabis: / dixi te, Coracine, cunnilingum."

29. Parker 1997.51–53. See also C. A. Williams 1992.241–80.

30. *CIL* 4.3999: "Glyco cunnum / lingit a(ssibus) II," "Glyco links cunt for two asses"; *CIL* 4.8940: "Maritimus / cunnu linget a(ssibus) quattuor / virgines am- / mittit," "Maritimus licks cunt for four asses. He accepts virgins." (The writer misspells *lingit* as *linget* and *admittit* as *ammittit*.) See Varone 1994.138, with bibliography.

31. Veyne 1987.203 asserts, without documentation, that only "libertines" made love with completely naked women.

32. An inscription in a second-century mosaic in the Baths of Trinacria at Ostia Antica reads *statio cunnilingorum*. This is a clever reference to the *stationes* or offices arranged around the Forum of the Corporations. Each *statio* represented a commercial enterprise and used inscriptions with formulae such as *statio Sabratensium* with the figure of an elephant, representing ivory traders: Becatti 1961.141, fig. 277; Pavolini 1983.68, 130.

33. Jacobelli 1995.47, fig. 37; Naples Archaeological Museum, inv. 27697; Sampaolo 1986.138, no. 102.

34. Juvenal 6.306–13: "Go now, check it out, with what a sneer Tullia sniffs the air and what the milk-mate of the notorious Maura says—Maura, when she's passing the old altar of Chastity. At night they stop their litters here, they piss here, and fill the statue of the goddess with long squirts, and take turns riding each other, and are moved with the Moon for witness, and from there they go to their homes: you, when light's returned, tread your wife's urine on your way to visit your great friends" (trans. Richlin 1992a.206).

35. Martial 7.67.1–3: "pedicat pueros tribas Philaenis / et tentigine saevior mariti / undenas dolat in die puellas"; 1.90.5–6: "esse videbaris, fateor, Lucretia nobis: / at tu, pro facinus, Bassa, fututor eras."

36. Martial 8.12: "uxorem quare locupletem ducere nolim, / quaeritis? uxori nubere nolo meae. Inferior matrona suo sit, Prisce, marito: / non aliter fiunt femina virque pares."

37. There are three paintings, now in the Naples Museum, that show this position: inv. 27696 and Sampaolo 1986.172–73, no. 348; Sampaolo 1986.170–71, no. 344 (lacking inventory number); inv. 27690 and Sampaolo 1986.172–73, no. 350. Lamps also frequently present the woman in this position: Johns 1982, plates

23, 25, figs. 95, 108, 109, 111, and 114; Kilmer 1993.33, with list of figures on 34; Gualandi-Genito 1986.234 n. 45.

38. "Because you know your own charms, you take on airs and you sell your embraces rather than offering them. Otherwise, what is the point of your hair all curled up by your comb, of your face painted with cosmetics, the soft petulance of your eyes, your carefully composed walk, with little heel-toe steps that never go astray, if you're not selling your beauty like a prostitute? . . . Some women burn for sordid men . . . and my mistress is from this group."

39. I wish to thank David Fredrick for this observation.

40. Martial 7.67.13–17: "post haec omnia cum libidinatur, / non fellat—putat hoc parum virile—, / sed plane medias vorat puellas. / Di mentem tibi dent tuam, Philaeni, / cunnum lingere quae putas virile." See Parker 1992.93.

41. Personal communication from Luciana Jacobelli; the process of removal unfortunately obliterated this writing.

42. Plutarch *Mor.* 520ff., Martial 8.13; see Barton 1993.85–144.

43. Cicero *de Orat.* 2.239; Corbeill 1996.15–46 provides a full discussion of this and related texts.

44. An interesting parallel for the artist suggesting, rather than picturing, the emotions of a protagonist is the painting by Timanthes (Quintilian *Inst.* 2.13.13) in which various sad figures watch the sacrifice of Iphigeneia while the artist veils Agamemnon's face to encourage the viewer to fill in the emotion (*suo quique animo aestimandum*). A painting from the House of the Tragic Poet shows Agamemnon veiling his face, but changes other details (Ling 1991, fig. 139).

45. Jacobelli 1995.94–97 argues that both sexes used the baths simultaneously.

46. Bergmann 1994 and 1996, Fredrick 1995. On the difficulty of hypothesizing the female gaze in contemporary terms, see Doane 1982.

6

Political Movement

Walking and Ideology in Republican Rome

Anthony Corbeill

In a short dialogue by Gregory Bateson entitled "Why do Frenchmen?" there is the following exchange:

DAUGHTER: Daddy, why do Frenchmen wave their arms so much?
FATHER: . . . What does it make you think when a Frenchman waves his arms?
DAUGHTER: I think it looks silly, Daddy. But I don't suppose it looks like that
  to another Frenchman. They cannot all look silly to each other.
  Because if they did, they would stop it, wouldn't they? (1972.9–10)

In his title, Bateson intentionally omits a predicate, since the predicate is always shifting. At the same time, the question mark remains constant: "Why do Frenchmen?" As one reads the dialogue, the missing verbal idea moves from "wave their arms so much" to "act differently from us" (that is, act differently from non-Frenchmen). In part, of course, the French act differently because of various social and cultural factors in France, some of which could be traced historically, but of equal importance—and, I think, more interestingly—they act differently because we perceive them as acting that way. In Bateson's dialogue, a question posed about a third party becomes an opportunity for self-reflection: why do *we* think arm waving is funny? In other words, whenever we ask "why do Frenchmen?"—or "why does anybody?"—we are also asking "why *don't* we?"

In the Roman republic of the first century B.C.E., Cicero publicly voices similar questions concerning segments of his own society. Marcus Tullius Cicero was a prominent speaker and politician born outside of Rome who became established as an important member of the urban elite, first by absorbing and then by perpetuating its most deeply held notions of the role of the citizen in the state. Essential to these notions is the need to restrict access to the elite. In this essay, I shall focus on a particular aspect of Cicero's polemic against his political opponents: his criticism of the way they walk. In so doing, I shall investigate not only "why do Cicero's opponents walk a certain way?" but, more particularly, "what investment does Cicero have in showing that his opponents have a distinctive and distinguishing form of body movement?" Or, to adapt the title of Bateson's essay, "Why do Popular Politicians?"

Philosophy in Action

Recent studies of bodily expression in antiquity have high-lighted the importance the ancients attached to an individual's stride.[1] In the Roman republic as well, different forms of walking were used to maintain political and social boundaries. I am interested especially in why certain forms of movement became standardized and how the meanings of these movements were able to remain stable. This is what I mean by the "ideology" of my title: body movements became systematized in such a way that some forms became perceived as natural and others as unnatural (*contra naturam*). The means available to judge the naturalness of bodily activity arose from the interplay between political posturing, audience expectations, scientific speculation, and the public spaces within which political debate occurred.

"Isn't it true that we consider many people worthy of our contempt when they seem, through a certain kind of movement or posture, to have scorned the law and limit of nature?"[2] This assertion, cast by the Latin particle *nonne* as a question with which the reader is expected to agree, appears near the end of Cicero's moral treatise *On the Limits of Good and Evil*. The context clarifies why Cicero must make this claim: he wishes to demonstrate that the workings of natural justice are discoverable, and, for this to be so, nature must be decipherable in all its manifestations. The code for decipherment includes the marks nature fixes on the movement of its human participants. In the perfection that is Roman nature, the gods both witness and judge the actions of each individual within the community.[3] Fellow citizens have the ability to practice this kind of surveillance as well. We read in Cicero's work *On the Nature of the Gods* that the properly discerning eye can recognize deviance in a human being's movement in the same way that it can judge an art object: the appraisal of color and shape and that of virtue and vice are parallel activities.[4] In republican Rome, the reading of morality becomes an aesthetic practice, and one that can be learned. But like any aesthetic practice, the ability to make moral judgments endows authority only upon those with the time and will to master its intricacies. Moral sensibilities become necessarily the sensibilities of the intellectual elite.

In this chapter, I shall borrow the French sociologist Pierre Bourdieu's notion of bodily *habitus*. Every social and economic group, Bourdieu argues at length, can be characterized by a particular set of external characteristics he calls the *habitus*, as a function of which the political mythology particular to a given group is *"em-bodied*, turned into a permanent disposition, a durable way of standing, speaking, walking, and thereby of feeling and thinking."[5] Simply put, socio-economic origins determine body language. According to Bourdieu's system, the various forms of *habitus* affect and help define one another. In other words, in Cicero's day, the elite-based body of texts—both clearly prescriptive moralizing texts such as *On the Limits of Good and Evil* and public works of oratory, which play a less apparent but no less crucial role in political self-definition—all serve to enforce a particular aristocratic *habitus*. In response to this *habitus*, those persons who have been denied access to the elite create their own particular notions of behavior. From this perspective, bodily movements are not only the product of individual idiosyncrasies, they are an integral part of the way the individual interacts with the social world. All members literally embody the values of their *habitus:* the way you move your mouth or blow your nose or walk all become a function of your past background and present circumstances.[6]

This theory of *habitus* is especially helpful in understanding political competition in the Roman world, for two reasons. First, it can allow access to the beliefs and manners of largely inaccessible members of Roman society: those not belonging to the traditional elite. In fact an analysis of *habitus* may provide more insight than a work explicitly written about bodily etiquette precisely because we are not asking what people think but observing how beliefs have been embodied. *Habitus* expresses not what has been taught in the traditional sense, but what has been experienced: "It is because agents never know completely what they are doing that what they do has more sense than they know" (Bourdieu 1990.69). Second, Bourdieu's theories depend upon, although in a seemingly more objective and politically correct way, the same notions of social constructionism that underlie the passage from Cicero I quoted earlier about certain physical postures scorning the laws of nature. The properly discerning eye, concurs this renowned twentieth-century critic of class structures, *can* judge the social status of a person by bodily movement: by being born into a certain *habitus*, each person becomes natu-

rally inculcated as a representative, and a potential reproducer, of that
habitus.

I do not wish to claim, however, that the Romans continually mon-
itored the way they walked. On the contrary, the very fact that physical
movement is so often unconscious makes it a significant resource for
gaining access to a given person's—or a given set of persons'—thoughts
and beliefs, thoughts and beliefs that might otherwise be inaccessible.
Our movements give us away. In the particular case of Cicero, this hypothesis provides a nice tool of interpretation. We may not, and probably should not, always believe what Cicero says in a political speech about
the nature of justice, but we have much less reason to doubt that his description of how his enemies and allies move, although often exaggerated, does have some relation to actual demeanor. Cicero's audience, after
all, was present as he spoke, and the speaker held its attention with con-
tinual reminders to "look" at the evidence offered as either visible to the
eye or accessible to the imagination. These frequent enjoinders to remain
alert and use the eyes help explain why "Ciceronian oratory was . . .
characterized by its constant allusions to 'things'" (Vasaly 1993.256). Oratory among the Romans, more so than among the Greeks, appealed as
much to the physical senses as to reason and emotion (Pöschl 1975.215,
Bell 1997). In a period when government was enacted most clearly in the
exchange between orator and audience, the visual element of Roman oratory cannot be undervalued. Hence it is going too far to claim that for
"Cicero this sort of dialogue with the crowd was a dangerous innovation
which was all too like the uncontrolled license of Greek democracies"
(Millar 1995.112). While it is true that Cicero was no fan of what he perceived to be democracy, it does not necessarily follow that, as an orator,
he neglected to take into account the power of his audience. It is, instead,
through the very reliance on the concrete and the visible that the possible license of the crowd could be checked. In cases where Cicero offers
up physical movement for public scrutiny, his audience, presumably,
could easily verify the validity of his descriptions. So when Cicero calls
attention to an opponent's body language, I have decided to join his audience in taking notice.

Underlying my investigation is the assumption that Cicero consistently applies his philosophical speculations to political practice. Even the
casual reader of Ciceronian oratory, especially his invective, is struck by
the frequency with which opponents are characterized by descriptions
that emphasize their sheer physicality. Cicero's oratory, I shall claim, attempts to represent in physical terms the dominant political agendas of

his period. Rather than involving simply *ad hominem* attacks, Roman invective against the gait is informed by a complex and yet coherent combination of physiognomics—the study of how physique indicates character—natural philosophy, and political competition. The urban elite, as the dominant force not only in the political sector of Roman society but in the cultural and educational sectors as well, constructed an understanding of nature, a will to truth, by which it could maintain its ascendancy (for the will to truth, see Foucault 1984.114). When the senatorial-based party refers to itself as the *optimates*—that is, as literally "the best people"—they are not simply using transparent rhetoric. They are affirming their self-perceived and self-defined role as those who are by nature best suited to rule.

Body Movement and Political Competition

In assessing the interrelationship between physical movement and political ideology, I shall be focusing both upon those politicians designated in extant texts as "popular" (*populares*) and on other politicians perceived as presenting a threat to urban-based aristocratic politics in Rome. I shall try to explain, insofar as our sources permit, how these politicians walked. By this term *populares*, I do not refer to a political party in the modern sense. Ancient historians now generally agree that these "popular" politicians were not defined by their social or economic status since, like their opposition the *optimates*, those labeled as *populares* came entirely from the Roman senate or senatorial class.[7] As is usual in the ancient world, attempts at political change, even of an apparently populist bent, resulted from divisions within the dominant classes, not from protest from below.[8] In fact these two groups, the *optimates* and the *populares*, were not even defined by specific political programs but by their methods: the *populares*, for example, took advantage of those aspects of the Roman political system that allowed them to bring about change through the people assembled as a whole, such as through public assemblies led by the tribunes of the plebs; the *optimates*, on the contrary, tended to act through the oligarchic senate.[9] The distinction between the groups constantly blurs, however. Even the venue of the speech could affect the self-presentation of the speaker, so that Cicero could, when addressing the people during his consulship, maintain he was a *popularis consul*.[10] One fact remains indisputable: *popularis* was an alluring label for Cicero, who uses it well over one hundred times in his orations to describe at times himself but, more often, his most hated opponents. It is what Cicero's use of this label evoked in the Roman audience that I am interested in.

Perhaps the best that can be said is that the *populares* consisted of individuals who presented themselves as not subscribing to the traditional values of the aristocracy at Rome. This group had frequent success in achieving its goals. In light of these successes, modern historians, most recently Fergus Millar, have used the abundant ancient testimonia describing the interaction between populace and speaker to argue that the republic functioned more as a democracy than has been previously acknowledged.[11] This may be true on what we might call a purely structural or "constitutional" level, but, on an ideological level, things were different. An important feature distinguishes Roman politics from Athenian democracy: republican Rome was dominated by a firmly established oligarchy, one, it has been claimed, that wielded "inherited, unchallenged authority" (North 1990.15–17). But if the people as a whole had the potential to create change, why did elite ideology continue to dominate Roman politics? One fruitful approach to explaining this stability lies in examining the self-conscious exploitation of public display as embodied in funeral processions, triumphs, and art.[12] Yet there simultaneously existed an equally effective way of maintaining ascendancy: in the assumptions and biases that were displayed less prominently by the very fact that they were encoded in the body. Regardless of how we may try to reconstruct actual factions and parties, public texts performed before the public eye constructed popular politicians as a class of persons against whom any clear-thinking Roman must rebel. In other words, the elite as a body created a defense against the power that the Roman people held in theory.[13] I focus on nonverbal forms of representation for, as will become clear, Roman audiences were trained to decipher a speaker's politics without a word being spoken.

Jean-Michel David has recently focused on speaking styles to show what distinguishes the established orator in Rome from the fledgling provincials who are relatively new to big city politics: their accent, pronunciation, sense of humor, and oratorical gestures mark them as incompatible with the urban elite.[14] In turn, their opponents in Rome label with specific vocabulary these perceived threats to the dominant politics: their movements become labeled as "fierce" (*acer*, *vehemens*) and their way of speaking as "rustic" (*rusticus*).[15] The belittling of fierceness and vehemence that we find in Rome has a parallel in fifth-century Athens, especially in the figure of the demagogue Cleon, whose violent movement, public shouting, way of dress, and frenetic stride marked his non-traditional approach to democratic politics.[16] This portrait is echoed in Plutarch's description of Gaius Gracchus, a figure whose innovative physical presence became the prototype for future politicians wishing to associate themselves with his style of antiestablishment politics (Plutarch *T. Gracchus* 2.2, David 1983b). Cicero's own physical descriptions, then, are part of a tradition that takes aim not at specific individuals or specific programs but at any perceived threats to the status quo. Moreover, the structures existing at Rome for the political advancement of young orators only served to validate the accuracy of these labels. To make a name for themselves, fledgling politicians often took on the role of prosecutors in the criminal indictment of established politicians.[17] This common, and even traditional, path to success could understandably lead to unpopularity among the powerful; as a result, rising newcomers ended up being objects of elite invective. In my subsequent remarks, I shall assent to the labels of the elite at Rome and refer to "popular politicians" not as persons representing a definable political platform (or even necessarily a specific individual who has received the label *popularis*) but rather as all those enemies whom the elite attack in their rhetoric for allegedly demagogic behavior.

Movement in Oratory and Philosophy

A young orator at Rome would have heard something like the following at an early stage in his rhetorical training: "Every movement of the soul is endowed by nature with its own corresponding facial expression, voice quality, and gesture" and "gesture is used not merely to emphasize words, but to reveal thought—this includes the movement of the hands, the shoulders, the sides, as well as how one stands and walks."[18] In the early empire, the rhetorician Quintilian was to continue this pedagogical tradition in his own treatise on the education of the orator, where he devotes over fifty pages to the various ways in which the orator should best position his head and fingers. Included in this excursus are numerous references to how the gait conveys thought and intention and how the speaker is justified in reproaching his opponent for the way he walks (*Institutio Oratoria* 11.3.66, 124, 126, 150; 1.2.31, 5.13.39). And yet stride reveals more than simply the presence or lack of refinement. Human beings, argues Cicero in his *On Duties*, are disposed by nature to disapprove morally of ways of sitting and standing that displease the eyes and ears. He includes among the postures especially to be avoided those of the effeminate and the rustic (*de Off.* 1.128–29). A letter by the philosopher Seneca further demonstrates that gait was believed to reveal not only temporary thought but permanent dispositions of character. In attempting to teach his correspondent Lucilius how to distinguish between true and false praise, Seneca draws an analogy from daily life, an analogy that indicates common attempts to standardize body language: "Everything," he writes, "has its own indicator, if you pay attention, and even the smallest details offer an indication of a person's character. An effeminate man (*impudicus*) is revealed by his walk, from [the way] he brings his finger up to his head, and from his eye movement. . . . For those qualities come into the open through signs" (*Epist.* 52.12). The gait is a sign to watch for in oneself and be wary of in others.

This conception of the body and its visible manifestations as a text to be read contributes also to the ambivalent relationship Roman orators had with actors. As is clear from epigraphic and other textual evidence, those actors at Rome who were citizens had limited civic rights since their profession, predicated on public display and the need for profit, marked them as dishonorable.[19] Yet in spite of this lower status, recent studies justly remark on the orator Cicero's emphasis on theatricality, and the ancient rhetorical treatises continually stress how much a political speaker can gain from observing an actor.[20] In fact Cicero and Demosthenes, the two ancient orators best known for their impeccable delivery, were both reputed to have trained with the best actors of their day. But these same treatises also include a caveat: imitate actors, but only up to a point.[21] What is signified by that point has been the topic of much recent discussion. Most obviously, the respectable orator could sacrifice his reputation from too close an association with the dishonorable character of the actor's profession. Too close a resemblance to acting could also endanger the masculine status of the speaker.[22] More importantly, the association will have implications for the speaker's relation to truth. Treatises repeatedly stress the importance of an orator's speech being a reflection of true feelings.[23] Hence the orator should cease from imitating the actor at the point at which the body stops imitating the movements of the soul and begins to display emotions that are no longer actually being felt internally. When Cicero finds himself in the potentially difficult position of speaking in defense of the comic actor Quintus Roscius, he steps over himself in justification: "I swear to god! I speak with confidence: Roscius has in him more trustworthiness than artful skill, more truth than training. The Roman people judge him a better man than actor—his talent makes him as worthy of the stage as his restraint makes him worthy of the senate house."[24] In Roscius's case, we are encouraged to believe that humanity overshadows histrionics. Only through such an appeal can Cicero convince the jury of Roscius's believability.

The careful distinction between actor and orator also explains the force behind a cryptic joke of Cicero. An opposing speaker had given a particularly serene performance in court, although he was referring to a time when Cicero's client had attempted to poison him. Cicero rebuked his opponent with the sarcastic question: "If you weren't faking it, would you be *acting* like that?" The pun on "acting" works in Latin as it does in English; in both languages, the verb (*agere*, "to act") describes the natural actions of the body as well as its self-conscious performance.[25] In this case, the speaker's bodily movement did not accurately reflect his expected internal anguish. The tirade did not simply involve an attempt at winning over the jury with humor. Cicero recalls later how this remark helped dilute the believability of the charge of poisoning; the audience accepted the orator's contention that the body should not lie (*Brut.* 278). In his treatise *On the Orator*, Cicero has the great orator Antonius give the following praise to Lucius Crassus: "You are in the habit of representing such strength of spirit, such force, such grief, by using your eyes, expression, gesture—even with a single finger . . . that you seem not only to ignite the judge but to catch fire yourself."[26] And yet Crassus was known for his calm demeanor when speaking; his vehemence was projected in his language and in the slight bodily indications noted by Antonius.[27] Not present was the physical excess that marked the actor. Crassus could convey emotions without appearing emotional and perform convincing actions without acting.

Another ancient source explicitly remarks on how the bodies of the actor and orator have a different relationship to the truth-content of their words. An actor's movements, we read, could be so unreal that, if you were to remove all his gestures, the beauty of the poet's words will still be felt.[28] This certainly does not hold true for the political speaker, for whom gesture and idea must cohere. Marcus Scaurus, for example, receives praise from Cicero for possessing such natural authority as an orator "that you'd think he wasn't pleading a case, but rendering testimony" (*Brut.* 111). It comes as little surprise that the Romans were fond of repeating a story about Demosthenes, the finest orator of Athens; when asked what he thought were the three most important aspects of public speaking, Demosthenes replied: "Delivery, delivery, delivery."[29]

Movement in Daily Life

This attention to fine points of movement was not confined to those trained in rhetoric and philosophy. As early as the third century B.C.E., the family of Claudia pointed out in her epitaph not merely her skills as a conversationalist, but how her walk was appropriate to her station in life ("sermone lepido, tum autem incessu commodo," *CE* 52.7). The audience of Roman comedies was also expected to recognize correlations between movement and character: members of the dominant class move slowly upon the stage, whereas slaves, attendants, and workers were marked by stereotypically swift movements (Quintilian *Inst.* 11.3.112). Further proof that the different codes for walking were widespread is found in the fact that they invited mockery. In the *Poenulus*, some pretentious legal advisors are made to justify their calmness by proclaiming that a moderate gait marks a freeborn person, whereas to run about in a hurry bespeaks the slave.[30] In fact the "running slave" appears so often in Roman comedy as to render the expression almost tautological.[31] The literary tradition also depicts the gods as conscious of the ways human beings move. In Vergil's *Aeneid*, Cupid's impersonation of the young Ascanius involves mimicking his gait, whereas Iris's disguise as Beroe is penetrated in part because the goddess fails to walk appropriately.[32] Indeed when hymns request the appearance of a deity, Greeks and Romans commonly pay special attention to the gait the divinity should adopt during its epiphany before the person praying (Fraenkel 1957.204 n. 4).

No less importantly, the type of walk adopted could also convey an individual's sexuality. Among Ovid's instructions in his *Art of Love* are details on the carriage that a woman should adopt to best attract a man (*Ars Amatoria* 3.298–310). In this area, a particularly telling anecdote comes from Petronius's romance, the *Satyricon*. The maid Chrysis remarks at one point to the hero Encolpius: "I don't know how to predict the future from bird signs, and I don't usually bother with the zodiac, and yet I infer character from the face (*ex vultibus*), and when I see somebody walking, I know what they're thinking" (*Satyricon* 126.3). This Petronius passage, I should note, depicts the maid discussing the walk that characterizes a male prostitute. This is not an irrelevant coincidence. It's not a big step to move from the walk of the effeminate male to that of the popular politician of the late republic. In fact I will argue that it is the same step.

Incessus in Cicero

The word most commonly used in invective texts to describe a person's walk is *incessus*. (The corresponding verbal form *incedo*, on the contrary, occurs only twice in Cicero outside of quotations.) The word alone appears to be colorless, meaning simply "travel by foot," and it can designate any type of gait, from a slow stride to speedy determination (Köstermann 1933, Horsfall 1971). However, like the maid in Petronius or the watchful Seneca, the spectator of Roman oratory would have had no trouble discerning the reasons why a public speaker such as Cicero would choose to call attention to his opponent's gait. A passage from his speech on behalf of Sestius exhibits Cicero's two principal uses of this practice. Amid vicious invective against two of his favorite enemies, Piso and Gabinius, Cicero exclaims to the jury: "By the immortal gods! If you're not ready yet to recall the crimes and wounds with which Piso and Gabinius have branded the state, then consider in your minds their expression (*vultus*) and their walk (*incessus*)" ("quorum, per deos immortales! si nondum scelera vulneraque inusta rei publicae vultis recordari, vultum atque incessum animis intuemini," *pro Sestio* 7.17).

As I shall demonstrate below, Cicero refers here to two distinct types of stride: in the case of Piso, to an affected, stately gait; in the case of Gabinius, to an effeminate stroll. These two types correspond to the dichotomy between walks offered by extant texts on physiognomy, those scientific texts that are predicated on the notion that the universe is rational, consistent, and decipherable.[33] On the one hand, writers describe the feigned gait (*incessus affectatus*) by which individuals try to suppress their true nature; and, on the other, the natural walk (*naturalis*), which a spectator can use to read character. Piso's walk, in fact, is too impressive: "How monstrous was his walk, how aggressive, how frightening to behold!"[34] His gait exceeded the moderation of the normal magistrate, cultivating instead a showy appearance worthy of the excesses of the trendy shopping districts of Capua, where his arrival is likened to a *pompa*, a formal procession.[35] Since he does not have the gentle inclination of the head that the physiognomists ascribe to the *magnanimus*, he betrays himself by being too serious, too *gravis*.[36] Cicero advises in *On the Limits of Good and Evil* against affecting a walk that is too pompous, and the physiognomic treatises declare this practice to be especially dangerous, warning that those who feign a dignified walk are "easily uncovered as their true nature conquers them and leaves them naked."[37]

The tribune Rullus also adopted a deceptive appearance but of the opposite type to Piso's. Cicero claims that one of the credentials that allowed Rullus to represent the land bill of 63 was his ability to project an exceptionally aggressive persona with a new countenance, voice, and walk. Cicero suggests that Rullus adopted these three elements of deportment to convey bodily the power of the office of tribune.[38] These attacks by Cicero would seem to provide rare instances in which seeming is not being, since his invective normally depends upon the ability to read morality from a person's appearance. And sure enough, Cicero spends the bulk of his invective speeches against Piso and Rullus exposing their hypocrisy and demonstrating that they are not what they seem. As a result, in both cases, Cicero is careful to stress that the appearances of his opponents are far from natural. In fact the word *truculentus*, commonly used to denote the behavior of beasts or of men who act like beasts, occurs only twice in Cicero's speeches—to describe the physical deportment of Rullus and Piso. Like the actor whose extreme showiness the student orator is warned to avoid, these men adopt walks that go over the top. Their motions are calculated to deceive the people. By appealing to gait, Cicero can prove this assertion through visual cues. In the case of Rullus, he recalls the tribune's different appearance in the past; Piso is exposed by his overly solemn eyebrows and the revelation that he has assumed a false name.[39]

The exposure of Rullus and Piso depended upon showing the audience how to penetrate and read through appearances. More commonly, the relationship between internal character and its external manifestation is more direct: Cicero claims that a walk directly reveals a depraved character. The popular politician in particular seemed to have his own distinct gait. In a digression on the sensitivity of Roman crowds to contemporary political issues, Cicero discusses the fame of Saturninus and the Gracchi, three popular tribunes from Roman history (the word Cicero uses to describe them is *populares*). The men were always greeted wildly in public assemblies. The people, Cicero tells us, loved these men's name, speech, face . . . and walk (*pro Sestio* 105). Cicero calls attention to similar features of the Antonii brothers in his *Thirteenth Philippic*: their mouths, faces, breath, look, and manner of walking all indicate, in Cicero's words, that "if they have a place in this city, there will be no room for the city itself" (13.4). The walk again intrudes with teasing concision—its connotations presumably clear to Cicero's audience. A section of *On Duties* in which Cicero warns his son Marcus against an excessively quick walk permits us to reconstruct something of those connotations (*de Off.* 1.131). Still, precision is wanting. Cicero the orator seems unwilling to describe the walk in detail, yet the context shows that he probably did not have the need. Even when not immediately visible as Cicero delivered his attack, the opponents he describes are well-known public figures. The repeated emphasis on gait indicates that his audience must have recognized something behind his references.

Cinaedi and Elite Politicians

May those who love us, love us.
And those that don't love us, may God turn their hearts.
And if He doesn't turn their hearts, may He turn their ankles,
So we'll know them by their limping.—*Gaelic blessing*

The modern reader of republican texts that mention bodily movement needs to go further than the words that have come down to us. It is possible, I believe, to recover from our extant texts the connotations of the popular walk by carefully considering what type of invective is applied toward whom and by accepting Bourdieu's contention that the body languages of different social and political classes are in a constant state of mutual determination: if the dominant class behaves in one way, it does so in a negative feedback relationship with nondominant groups. I begin from the abuse leveled against three men in particular, three men closely allied to what were usually recognized as "popular" causes: Sextus Titius, Publius Clodius, and Aulus Gabinius. Gabinius, as I have already mentioned, was notorious for his effeminacy, and, on one occasion, Cicero calls him a "female dancer" (*saltatrix*, *in Pis.* 18). Similarly, Clodius's impersonation of a woman during the Bona Dea scandal gave rise to accusations of his being a "Greek female lyre player" (*psaltria*) who could step and lift his body with grace (*in Clod.* 22). Titius, a tribune of the plebs, was so gentle in his bodily movements that a dance, the "Titius," was named in his honor (*Brut.* 225). Similar charges were levied against the great orator Hortensius, who would not seem to belong in this company.[40] Perhaps it is relevant that the one attested attack on him occurred when he was defending an alleged ally of the Catilinarians, a particularly notorious group of *populares* who were thought to dance naked at predawn banquets (for the connotations, see Corbeill 1996.138–39).

All this emphasis on dancing becomes suspicious in light of one of Quintilian's guarded remarks regarding the education of the public speaker. The teacher is justified by precedent, he says, in allowing potential orators to study under instructors of bodily movement, who will teach proper positioning of the arms and hands, as well as the appropriate ways to stand and walk. During boyhood, however, the instruction must be of only limited duration, and, once the boy reaches adolescence, it should be stopped altogether.[41] To show that he has given this matter sufficient consideration, Quintilian justifies the teaching of dance by pointing out its significance in such venerable areas as Platonic philosophy, Spartan military training, and archaic Roman religious practice. The reason for Quintilian's uneasiness about dance instruction becomes clear from a complaint of Scipio Aemilianus uttered over two hundred years earlier: young Romans "are learning to sing, something our ancestors wanted to be considered disgraceful to the freeborn; they go, I say, to dancing school, freeborn girls and boys among the *cinaedi.*"[42] Scipio plays here with the Greek loan word *cinaedus*. As is commonly known, this word, a frequent term for referring to a dancer in early Latin, denoted in Greek culture the sexually penetrated male in a homoerotic relationship. By this point it should come as little surprise to learn that numerous texts, both political and nonpolitical, attest that the *cinaedus* revealed himself by his walk.[43] As was the case with studying under an actor, Quintilian seems to fear that students may learn too much.

Turning to how the writers on physiognomy describe the *cinaedus*, one discovers striking correspondences between the movements of the sexually submissive male and the popular politician of the republic. What seems to emerge is that *cinaedi* divide into two types: those who try too hard to hide their natures and those whose "true" movements are observable. Among the former strides Rullus, distinguishing himself among his tribunician colleagues: he steps very slowly with a feigned aggressiveness. The latter group encompasses our dancing politicians: their arms and fingers gesticulate in a manner overly exuberant for a person moving at a leisurely pace, and both the neck and the sides of the torso sway gently from side to side.[44]

The elite politician—or the politician who wishes to appear allied with the elite—can also be described as he walks before his colleagues. Extant texts prescribe for the aristocrat a way of walking in direct contradistinction to the type I have been reconstructing for the *popularis*. A full gait, according to the second-century C.E. physiognomist Polemon, exhibits loyalty, efficacy, a noble mind, and the absence of anger.[45] Cicero requires the same type of stride for the proper orator without alluding to physiognomic principles. He also adds features that directly oppose the physiognomist's vision of the *cinaedus*: keep the neck and fingers still and the trunk straight, bending it only as a man does; the right arm should remain close to the body, extended solely in times of impassioned delivery.

In other words, "let nothing be superfluous" (*nihil ut supersit*).[46] As for speed, these empiricists advise the elite politician to be slow—*bradus* in Greek, *gravis*, not surprisingly, in Latin—but not too slow, for that marks a lack of effectiveness.[47] It was tricky to maintain the appropriate balance; hence Cicero's admiration of Crassus's ability to effect the difficult combination of being both dignified and elegant (*Brut.* 158; see, too, *Brut.* 143). Criticism could also arise if the speaker was overly erect in the upper body—this overcompensation appears to be what betrayed the hypocrite Piso and what was later to constitute part of Augustus's criticism of the way Tiberius carried himself.[48] Instead, the neck should lean slightly forward in a sign of determination while the shoulders gently move. In short, remarks the pseudo-Aristotelian treatise on physiognomics, the dignified man walks like that "most male of animals," the lion.[49]

This reconstruction of the elite walk recalls one of the emperor Augustus's cryptic mottoes: "Hurry up . . . slowly."[50] That the emperor was conscious of the public recognition of proper modes of walking is clear from a letter he wrote to Livia in which he worries about the walk of the young Claudius.[51] In fact the motto "Hurry up . . . slowly" may find concrete exposition in the famous statue of Augustus from Prima Porta. One art historian has argued in detail that the position of the feet in the Polykleitan antecedent of this sculpture depicts a man commencing "very slow gait activity" (Tobin 1995.52–64). The ready determination of Augustus's pose finds its inspiration not only in artistic precedents but in an elite ideology of the body.

Types of walk provide a model for how ideology permeated Roman society at all levels. Moralizing texts of Cicero's day such as those I quoted in my opening remarks assert that nature desires internal character to be manifested externally. To judge a human being's character on the basis of physical movement is not a practice that went unexamined. Rather, this mode of observation, upon which the entire study of physiognomy is based, depends upon an understanding of what is essential—and not constructed—about being a human being. By simple observation, we recognize that proper care of the body undoubtedly affects clarity of thought and so, it follows, the soul must conversely affect the body. Beginning from this premise, a close empirical observation of nature, "science," combined with speculation on the origin of the world and its inhabitants, "philosophy," becomes a powerful *political* tool, a way of separating us from them, a way of proving, from objective, external signs, who is naturally born to lead and who, misled, is simply dancing his way through politics.

Enforcement

But an important question remains: if there really did exist some kind of political etiquette of bodily aesthetics, and if it really were so all-pervasive as I claim, then why would anyone even bother to try to violate it? In other words, if there was some transitive equation between being a popular politician, an effeminate male, and a social deviant, then what prevents someone like Gabinius from simply moving a little more quickly and holding his head still? I would like to suggest three possible answers: they entail (1) access to education, (2) the topography of political debate, and (3) willful self-definition on the part of the popular politicians themselves.

Education

I have already mentioned Jean-Michel David's research on "popular eloquence" (*eloquentia popularis*), that is, the speaking style of political newcomers, people who may have been important in their native communities, but who, upon arrival in the big city, became marked by their non-Roman style of pronunciation, use of vocabulary, and even sense of humor (David 1980 and, esp., 1983a). I would add that these newcomers also probably had styles of deportment that distinguished them from their counterparts in the urban elite. Numerous examples survive, as we have seen, of the ways in which rhetorical treatises from ancient Rome instruct their pupils in proper body language. Other ancient references make it clear that this kind of physical training would have been clarified and reinforced through constant practice before a teacher (Seneca *Epist.* 94.5, 8). In fact the *Rhetorica ad Herennium*, an anonymous rhetorical treatise from the early first century B.C.E. containing the kind of instruction that Cicero and his elite contemporaries would have received, apologizes for even trying to discuss delivery in a written form: "The rest," the author writes, "we'll leave for practice drills."[52] The meaning of the visible becomes, in effect, invisible to the reading audience.

So it seems likely that, in the late republic, the means for learning proper gesture rested with those who had access to an urban education. Furthermore, "proper" walks would be inaccessible not only to the sub-elite but also to leading provincials, whose political influence would have been hindered by their visibly rustic mannerisms. For urban education entailed at this period an intimate association with members of the elite, an education recently characterized as "wordless replication of the elite *habitus*."[53] What is more, rhetorical training during this period would

have been almost entirely in Greek, not Latin, thereby further restricting the class of students who could learn at these schools.[54] When Latin
teaching was eventually introduced, it gained immediate popularity, as
students flocked to lessons.[55] In fact in the early first century, rhetori-
cians in Rome who tried, for the first time, to establish schools for instructing potential orators in Latin were censured in an edict from the
censors on the grounds that, to quote the actual document, "Our ancestors have decided what they wanted their children to learn and what
schools they should attend."[56] Cicero puts in the mouth of Crassus, one
of the censors responsible for this edict, the additional opinion: "These
new teachers could teach nothing—except daring" (*de Orat.* 3.94). Is this
a distinctly Roman appeal to tradition?[57] Or do we have here a means
of maintaining the ascendancy of the elite, who, of course, are the true
descendants of "our ancestors?" It is an intriguing coincidence that L.
Plotius Gallus, one of the rhetors at whom this edict seems to have been
aimed, wrote in Latin a work on gesture—perhaps the first such work
entrusted to writing (Quintilian *Inst.* 11.3.143). Here, as elsewhere, we
are hampered from making further conclusions by the fact that direct
references to the edict are confined to elite sources. A Greek philosopher, however, writing on rhetoric at about the same period and probably in Italy, gives clear voice to what I believe the censors couched in
their traditional language. Philodemus writes: "Instruction in delivery
is a product of recent foolishness. . . . The writers on rhetoric are in fact
making clear a basic truth that is hidden by politicians, namely that they
are designing their delivery to appear dignified and noble and, most of
all, to mislead their audience."[58]

Topography

Archaeological studies of the past two decades seem to indicate
that beginning around 290 B.C.E. the *comitium* at Rome consisted of a circle approximately forty meters in external diameter, situated between the
speaker's platform at the republican rostra and the senate house, the
Curia Hostilia.[59] According to this reconstruction, the people assembled
as a whole in the third century would have been sandwiched in an open-
air space between the speaker and the senate house. It is little wonder
that literary sources regard it as a popular move when, in 145 B.C.E., the
tribune Gaius Licinius Crassus transferred popular legislation from this
limited area to the more spacious forum (Cicero *de Amicitia* 96, Varro *Res
Rusticae* 1.9). In a similar but likely separate move, Gaius Gracchus first
began the practice of addressing from the rostra the people assembled in

the forum—and not in the *comitium*. The tribune who, as noted earlier, fashioned a public *habitus* that became identifiable with his popular intentions, also refashioned spatial relations in the forum through a move Plutarch hails as another step toward "democracy" (δημοκρατία).[60] Plutarch's enthusiasm about the change in venue entices us to agree with recent claims that the Roman republic functioned more as a popular democracy than is normally recognized.[61] In support of this position, Millar has appositely observed that the *comitium* has much greater importance in the archeological and literary record than the meeting places of the senate. And it is in open spaces like the *comitium* and elsewhere in the Roman Forum, as opposed to within the roofed and walled curia, where the majority of the texts I examine were played out (Millar 1998, esp. 141). But what had the two tribunes Crassus and Gracchus achieved other than providing a larger area for popular assemblies, which could number several hundred people in the *comitium* but approximately six thousand in the open forum? (The estimates are from Thommen 1995.364.) The dynamic between speaker and audience has not changed, and, in fact, I will argue that the new orientation, resulting in a larger and more dispersed group of auditors, serves only to increase the distinction between senatorial-based and popular-based political appeals. Cicero himself points to one feature of the new dynamic. The arrangement by which the crowd faces the speaker, framed by the senate house, creates a situation in which "the curia watches over and presses upon the speaker's platform, as an avenger of rashness and a regulator of civic duty."[62] Visually, the senatorial element of the government looms larger than ever before.

Archaeologists believe the *comitium* in Rome to have been circular in part by comparison with other extant *comitia* in Italy and Sicily. I am not here concerned so much with their reasoning—although the identification of these provincial structures is not entirely certain—as with a singular and obvious way in which the meeting places outside the capital seem *not* to be parallel.[63] Simply put, outside of Rome, no traces of a rostrum survive, and there are no clear indications that a raised speaker's platform parallel to the type found in Rome ever existed.[64] Moreover, it seems likely that, as in Greek places of assembly such as the Pnyx in Athens, elsewhere in Italy the speaker spoke *up* to the citizens assembled around him. Marcel Detienne has neatly demonstrated how this arrangement, with the speaker at the center (ἐς μέσον), provides a physical analog to the value Greek society placed on democracy and equality of speech (Detienne 1965, with a focus on archaic Greece). Contrast then the situation in Rome, where the magistrate literally looks *down* upon (*despicere*) his listeners.[65] In both civil and criminal proceedings, the presiding magistrate sits on a raised platform at a higher level than the participants in the case and the crowd of listeners (Greenidge 1901.133–34, 458–59). A similar relationship governs the magistrate addressing the people, a situation that presupposes an unequal position between speaker and addressees.[66] While retaining the Greek architectural form, the Romans invert the relation between speaker and citizen.[67] In so doing, the physical relationship mirrors the relationship of political status (A. Bell 1997.2). The symbolic value of this relationship was recognized by Cicero and, in fact, the level at which one stood while addressing the people at a public assembly could depend on one's political rank at the moment. Cicero implies it was not normal for a nonmagistrate to speak from the rostra during an assembly (and one could do so only at the invitation of the presiding magistrate) and that those officeholders who had not called the assembly spoke from steps lower than the speaker's platform proper.[68] This hierarchy of speaking height literalizes the notion of rank, which is normally rendered by the Latin word *gradus* ("step"). The contrast between Greek and Roman modes of civic communication is especially interesting since, inside the senate house, there would have persisted the Greek-style relationship of speaker below, with the audience of peers ranged above on benches (*subsellia*) (*LTUR* 1.333, E. Tortorici).

Yet the simple physical relationship between political speaker and listening populace does not tell a complete story. We still need to look at the question: "why do popular politicians?" I return to the motifs that recur in Cicero's attack on opponents he designates as popular politicians, where he employs a rhetoric centering on peculiarities of the body and of physical movement. It is no coincidence that these are the very attributes that would be visible on the rostra to the *populus* gathered in the forum. The orator associates the tribune Vatinius's foul political program with an equally foul external appearance (e.g., *in Vat.* 4, 10). In his speech *On Behalf of Sestius*, Cicero mocks the walk of Aulus Gabinius, the Gracchi, and Saturninus, distinguishing their gait from that of a serious politician (*pro Sest.* 105: Gracchi, Saturninus; *pro Sest.* 17: Gabinius). Even the amount of control the speaker had over his mouth had political connotations (Richlin 1992a.99, Corbeill 1996.99–127). The popular ideology, it is clear, has become literally embodied in its proponents. It is surely no accident that the elite virtues of *gravitas* and *constantia* stand in direct opposition to the swaying walk and gaping mouth of Cicero's popular politicians. In the section of *On Duties* where Cicero is purportedly instructing his son on the proper carriage of the body, he warns against an excessively quick walk, since it prompts "quick breathing, a changed facial expression, a misshapen mouth—these features," he continues, "make perfectly clear a lack of *constantia*."[69] The equation of physical with moral stability also informs the historiographic tradition. Pro-Gracchan sources show Tiberius Gracchus firm and silent in the face of death, whereas hostile writers depict him during the same period scurrying all around the city.[70] Those who saw him as an unrestrained speaker, of course, could not imagine him facing death in any other manner.

Artistic representations support this contrast between elite self-mastery and popular excitability. Richard Brilliant has posited for Roman art what he calls an "appendage aesthetic": rather than being interested in using anatomical details of the trunk to render meaning to the viewer, Roman artists concentrated on attributes that are attached to the torso, especially the head, arms, and dress. This appendage aesthetic presumably finds its origin in Roman daily experience. The gestures of public figures as rendered in art rely on "the developed sensitivity for gesticulate address" possessed by those familiar with daily oratory (Brilliant 1963.10, 26–37). I have already suggested how such a reliance may have affected the stance of Augustus's statue from Prima Porta. The walk functions in a way analogous to the folds of the toga in sculpture—just as the literal and metaphorical *gravitas* of the garment "dematerializes the body" and makes the once living model into a political icon, so, too, that gait impresses most that draws the least attention to itself.[71] In a recent study of Roman portrait busts, Luca Giuliani has suggested that the Romans tried to convey political signs in portraiture as well—the elite, for example, wished their marble not only to bear a physical likeness, but also to express sternness and steadfastness (*gravitas, constantia*), two key concepts underlying the ideological program of the conservative *optimates* (Giuliani 1986.214, 322 n. 44). At the same time, it is apparent that Roman sculptors of the elite tended to avoid sculptural techniques popular in Hellenistic times that represented movement, enthusiasm, and excited breathing (Giuliani 1986.239–45, with 215). Giuliani even conjectures that depictions of Pompey strike us as strange because Magnus is, characteristically, trying to have it both ways: he is *popularis* from the eyebrows up, as embodied especially in the evocation of Alexander the Great's hairstyle, but stern optimate from the eyes down.[72] Unlike Brilliant, however, Giuliani balks at suggesting whether these artistic practices had a direct correlation with the real physical appearance and real political activities of the persons so represented.

The invective texts already cited from Cicero allow us to glimpse this elusive physical reality. It is not only the way we move but the space within which we move that shapes personal ideology. Elite politicians, speaking within the confines of the curia, easily maintain *constantia*, self-mastery. Cicero remarks from the rostra that consuls regularly considered it a "legal condition" (*lege et condicione*) to avoid addressing the *populus* assembled as a whole (*de Lege Agraria* 2.6). He, of course, exaggerates motive, but the people must have been able to judge the accuracy of his primary claim. Men of consular rank should not grandstand. When speaking from the rostra, a concern for restraint dominates: the rhetorical tradition stresses repeatedly how the serious orator moves slowly, avoiding excessive gesticulation (Graf 1992.46–47). The same reserve applies to the magistrate. In a passage from his *Florida*, Apuleius remarks that the more important a person is, the more he should expect general scrutiny for his speech and demeanor. As an example of this predicament, Apuleius contrasts the outward restraint of a proconsul, speaking quietly and infrequently from a seated position, with the public crier who stands, walks, and shouts contentiously. "Being low class provides plenty of excuses, having status plenty of difficulties."[73]

Vocabulary is also a function of public demeanor. It is a common phenomenon in Latin for words denoting ethical and aesthetic concepts to derive from concrete and tangible notions in the external world: *rectus* means physically "straight" as well as morally "upright," behavior that is *perversus* has "turned away" from a posited straight course, and so on (Corbeill 1996.34). The same tendency toward the concrete prevails both in political terminology—the "magistrate" (*magistratus*) has "more" (*magis*)—and in public behavior—the "heaviness" (*gravitas*) and "coherence" (*constantia*) of the admirable citizen (Paulus *Festi* 126 M, Wagenvoort 1947.104–27). In a world of embodied political ethics such as this, it is natural to assume that sensitivity to bodily movement is at least subliminally active in daily interaction and that any disruption of physical reality could provoke a disruption in politics. Such concerns are still felt in the twentieth century: "During the debate on restoring the House of Commons after the war, Churchill feared that departure from the intimate spatial pattern of the House, where opponents face each other across a narrow aisle, would seriously alter the patterns of government" (E. Hall 1966.106–07). "We shape our buildings," Churchill remarked famously, "and afterwards our buildings shape us."

The popular politician, especially the tribune of the plebs, reached his constituency while speaking in the open spaces of the forum and in other wide-open areas such as the Circus Flaminius.[74] Even speeches in important political trials would have had an audience that extended beyond the judges to the corona of interested citizens (Millar 1998.91). A reference in a speech of Cicero, where he describes "a packed forum and the temples filled to the brim," gives us an idea of how difficult it would have been for a speaker to make himself heard at these gatherings.[75] To reach the people gathered in such open spaces, exaggerated movement, expansive gesticulation, and open, shouting, mouths were essential. In fact recent studies of the role of charisma in mass persuasion suggest that sheer physical presence can compensate for not being heard; being audible, in other words, is not a necessary precondition to being persuasive (Atkinson 1984.88). In Rome, we are told, one popular tribune captivated the people not through his persuasive ability but through, in Cicero's words, his "public appearance, his gestures, and even through his very clothing" (*Brut.* 224). *Species, motus, amictus*—these qualities may, in fact, have been the only aspects of the speaker much of his audience was able to perceive. Representations of the emperor addressing the people show "an arrangement of the *populus* according to the status of its members" (Torelli 1992.90–91). There is no reason to think republican gatherings offered an appreciably different scenario; a parallel is offered by the hierarchical seating arrangements at Roman public festivals where senators sat close to the action with those of lesser rank ascending behind in descending order of status. It then becomes even less surprising to read an imperial writer remark about how the "unwashed crowd" of the empire takes special pleasure in the speaker who claps, stamps his feet, and strikes his chest (Quintilian *Inst.* 2.12.10). Appeals to the masses create a nearly inescapable double bind: the politician becomes his demeanor, the demeanor denotes his politics.

The popular politician excited not just aesthetic revulsion. In Roman society, where aesthetic and moral evaluations intertwine, his very appearance was represented as inimical to truth-telling. In one of Cicero's direct confrontations with a tribune of the people in 63, he spitefully remarks that, unlike the tribunes, he himself owes his popularity—the word he uses ironically is *popularis*—to "truth, not display" (*veritate, non ostentatione*).[76] The subdued appearance of the consul Cicero provides direct access to truth. In his philosophical works, Cicero also warns against the extremes of showy *ostentatio*, since it involves the altering of an individual's facial expressions, walk, and clothing, precisely those features of his appearance that Cicero accuses Rullus of manipulating upon taking office as tribune: "He planned to have another expression, another voice, another walk; with more worn clothing . . ."[77] Display (*ostentatio*) also comes under criticism in Cicero's prose treatises as being insufficient for securing an individual's *gloria* and as inappropriate for a senator speaking in the curia (*de Off.* 2.43, *de Orat.* 2.333). As an example of excessive display being ineffective, Cicero offers the two famous tribunes, Tiberius and Gaius Gracchus. The constant contrast between *ostentatio* and *veritas* brings us back to Roman notions of acting, where gestures of the stage are contrasted with those of the orator, a contrast represented as being between *demonstratio* and *significatio*, between artful mimicry and the natural expression of the emotions (Cicero *de Orat.* 3.220). Hence the elite politician could point to the mere physical presence of a popular opponent to demonstrate the visible violation of the elite virtues of *gravitas* and *constantia*, virtues not only endorsed in literary, rhetorical, and philosophical texts, but delineated in contemporary portraiture.

One final consideration needs to be confronted. If a popular and a senatorial speaker are both speaking in a public assembly, experience and common sense might seem to dictate that the elite speaker would use more ostentatious gestures in this setting than when speaking in more confined quarters. An observable fact argues against such an hypothesis. Cicero's references to walking and movement occur in all types of speeches: in juried trials, in the senate, as well as before the people. This indicates that each audience would be attuned to the same contrasts in carriage regardless of the venue. Furthermore, recent studies of the role of gesture in communication show that, when attention is drawn to excessive gesturing, the audience does indeed notice. Not only that, but drawing attention to gesture induces the hearer to find the speaker *less* persuasive because, in a sense, the body and not the emotions is perceived as doing the speaking (Rimé and Schiaratura 1991.272–76). Elite ideology succeeds in part by intruding the gestures of opponents on the listeners' attention. When not distracted by gesture, as in the case of constructed elite *gravitas*, attention focused on words, on truth. *Veritas, non ostentatio*.

The Self-Made *Popularis,* or "Sulla Made Me a Homosexual"

My third point considers the possibility that some popular politicians, by embracing the *habitus* that formed in response to their elite rivals, consciously advertised to the populace their political stance.[78] As has been recently argued, "the popular will of the Roman people found expression in the context, and only in the context, of divisions within the oligarchy" (North 1990.18). The adoption of a popular persona, then, together with a popular agenda, provided a member of the elite with the opportunity to promote his own projects. The display of battle wounds, for example, seems to have been a component of popular rhetoric used by prominent politicians to contest elite claims to privilege of birth (Leigh 1995, esp. 202–07). I use as my own test case Julius Caesar, who, during his lifetime, was subjected to accusations of being an androgyne, a catamite, and a wearer of effeminate clothing. Rather than rejecting, as every ancient historian does, the truth-content behind these charges, I would like to consider instead what these accusations may reveal about political competition and self-representation.

Charges of wearing nonmasculine dress appear frequently in the late republic in connection with two major political figures: Julius Caesar and Publius Clodius.[79] References to Clodius's activities occur only in connection with his violation of the rites of the *Bona Dea* in 62 B.C.E., a religious celebration normally restricted to Roman matrons. On this occasion, Clodius's alleged adoption of female dress did not represent the adoption of an effeminate lifestyle, in spite of Cicero's frequent claims to the contrary. Instead, the clothing simply provided Clodius a means for escaping detection, for covering up what he was not (Cicero *in Clod.* 22, Geffcken 1973.82). Caesar's choice of dress, on the other hand, seems to represent a move not toward deception but toward political self-advertisement.

When captured by pirates in the 70s B.C.E., Julius Caesar was careful to continue wearing in their presence the toga, the typical mark of Roman citizenship, perhaps as a sign to his captors of his claims to sexual inviolability (Velleius Paterculus 2.41.3, Bell 1997.15 n. 102). If we can trust our sources, Caesar had already displayed an awareness of the symbolic power of dress while a young man in Rome where, however, the image he wished to project was quite different. During the rule of Sulla, a clear opponent of popular politics, the dictator warned his political allies to beware of the young man Caesar, whose style of wrapping the toga denoted an effeminate character.[80] Clothes, in this case, literally unmake the man. The threat that Sulla envisions from Caesar's dressing up is not immediately clear, and one is quick to dismiss the attendant claim that Caesar's peculiar apparel almost drove Sulla to kill him (Dio 43.43.4). Yet Suetonius, too, mentions Sulla's desire to eliminate the young Caesar: something, "either divine inspiration or personal inference," told him that the boy had "a lot of Mariuses in him" and that Caesar's rise to power would signal the end of the optimate party.[81] Jokes told by Cicero, furthermore, suggest that Julius Caesar's appearance had some connection with his eventual victory in the Roman civil war. As Cicero says, "I never would have thought that a man who scratches his head with one finger and has such exquisitely arranged hair could have ever overthrown the Roman state."[82] Cicero's alleged failure to read Caesar correctly represents his own wry commentary on the political codes of external appearance. The figure of the effeminately adorned male represents, I suggest, a recognized but contested social construction that Caesar has adopted for a specific reason: to align himself with modes of behavior contrary to those of the dominant political class. Behavior contrary, that is, not only to the Sullas but also to the Ciceros, who had advanced their own careers by adopting the elite model.

I have already mentioned Pierre Bourdieu's theory of bodily *habitus*, whereby the different segments in a given society express values through specific forms of dress, language, and gesture. According to Bourdieu's theory, the various forms of *habitus* affect and help define one another. One of Bourdieu's contemporary examples provides a parallel to what I am suggesting about Julius Caesar. Bourdieu claims that members of the dominant social class in twentieth-century France have acquired effeminate characteristics that stand in contradistinction with the values of the working classes. The style of the elite, Bourdieu writes (1991.88), "is seen as a repudiation of the virile values." In the creation and maintenance of the values of the working classes, then, two isolable vectors are at work: one that labels from above, and one that labels from within.[83] Applying these notions of *habitus* to the case of Julius Caesar, one can observe that the optimate class, through its public invective, has identified certain forms of behavior, speech, and action as contrary to its own *habitus* and has, as a further corollary, defined these characteristics as being contrary to the proper Roman way of life (Bourdieu 1990.62, 1984.170–72). It is not surprising that, in the creation of this dichotomy, divisions arose along lines of gender: since the elite adopted masculine-coded walk and dress, the popular politicians became aligned with feminine traits.[84] The popular politicians were forced into their own particular *habitus* both through the power of the aristocratic ideology and through their own willingness to comply with the rhetoric of that ideology.

To return to Caesar's case. In addition to sporting a form of dress readily identifiable as feminine, Caesar flouted other traditional categories of sexual behavior. All these maneuvers should be attributed to the same identity, but it is a political, not a sexual, identity. In a public oration, the elder Curio referred to Caesar as "a man for all women, and a woman for all men." Marcus Bibulus, Caesar's colleague in the consulship of 59 B.C.E., published official edicts in which Caesar's alleged sexual involvement with the Asian king Nicomedes yielded for him the nickname "the queen of Bithynia"; this affair also produced for Caesar the descriptive epithet "innermost support of the royal bed" (Suetonius *Iul.* 52.3, 49). The sources do not preserve Caesar's immediate reactions to this abuse, but if he had followed both the rhetorical handbooks and contemporary oratorical practice, he would have immediately denied these allegations with a quick and witty joke. One-upmanship was a skill to be pursued and mastered.[85] Another anecdote finds Caesar exposed to a similar type of abuse. His response on this occasion would have surprised his teachers of rhetoric. According to the historian Suetonius, after Caesar was granted the proconsulship of Transalpine Gaul, he boasted in a crowded senate house that he would force all his opponents to fellate him. "Whereupon," Suetonius continues, "somebody said abusively, 'That would be hard to do to a woman!' Caesar replied, in an allusive manner, 'In Syria, Semiramis had been a queen, too, and the Amazons once possessed a great portion of Asia'" (Suetonius *Iul.* 22.2). This refusal to deny the implications of an opponent's abuse is rare for rhetorical invective.[86] The fact that the charge here is effeminacy makes Caesar's retort all the more peculiar since, despite the numerous charges of effeminacy one finds in Roman texts, "no Roman author ever calls himself effeminate in surviving Latin literature" (Edwards 1993.66). By embracing the charges, Caesar focuses attention upon them in order to expose them to ridicule. In so doing, he positions himself in opposition to the dominant standards of appearance that this type of humorous abuse is designed to enforce. Other quips of the future dictator reveal a desire to align himself in opposition to the normally acceptable representations of political conduct. As general, Caesar excused the extravagance permitted his victorious soldiers by saying: "My soldiers can fight well even while wearing perfume."[87] It is not necessary to assume that the Romans fighting in Gaul actually did use the local eau de cologne. It is the political fact standing behind this playful fiction that Caesar is attempting to isolate.

Julius Caesar's public persona constituted an obvious target for humorous abuse.[88] Even if this invective only came into being as a postmortem assault in the aftermath of his assassination (although the anecdote from Suetonius is likely to be historical), it is still necessary to explain why this particular kind of invective developed. I present as one possibility that this polemic arose from the deliberate misrepresentation on the part of the elite of the ways in which popular politicians appealed directly to the assembled people—through self-consciously untraditional dress, gestures, and speaking styles. In the case of Julius Caesar, the three most common areas about which abuse circulated all promote a potentially ambiguous sexuality. The opportunities that these features provided for the invective of his opponents could have been neither a secret nor a surprise to Caesar himself. We recall Quintilian's judgment: if Caesar had had the time to devote to study, his oratorical skills would have rivaled those of Cicero himself (*Inst.* 10.1.114). The likeliest explanation, then, for Caesar's willingness to expose himself to ridicule lies in the representational tension that continually existed between senatorial and popular politics.[89] By not avoiding behavior specifically marked in his society as feminine, Caesar could be perceived as transgressing normal modes of male, aristocratic behavior. In violating the accepted relationship between appearance and reality, Caesar fashioned himself as a proponent of political change.

Conclusion

The spectacle-oriented aspects of Roman culture have received much attention in recent scholarship. In the area of politics, however, to recognize spectacle simply means to recognize the existence of an audience, not necessarily to conclude that that audience constitutes a healthy democracy.[90] We can read about what the Romans saw, but it is much more difficult to determine how they were taught to see. It is likely, however, that the awareness of a diverse audience will increase the performative aspects of those political speakers who wish to direct their appeals primarily to that audience. This is precisely the situation Cicero must exploit in his attempt to safeguard the interests of the elite.

So as we stand back from the rostra, one hundred or even one thousand heads back, struggling to hear the speaker, who are we to believe, the calm and composed Cicero, his right arm elegantly harmonizing with his rhetorical points, or the excited, shouting popular politicians? "Why do popular politicians?" I have two answers, one Cicero's and one mine. The popular politician moves about so much because he is trying to reach me, cramped as I am in a space arranged almost by accident and not designed for a proper political assembly—although purportedly an auditor, I am simultaneously aware of my own physical needs. Cicero's answer to the same question? The overt physicality of the popular speaker betrays his disconnectedness from *gravitas* and *constantia*, from stability and composure, from truth and reason.

I do not intend to offer a necessarily negative critique of the elite ideology that dominates our sources for ancient Rome. Roman society was able to justify some of its most deeply felt religious and social values by pointing out that such values stem from a proper understanding of nature. My primary aim in this essay has been to narrate how the Romans removed one specific form of bodily movement (the way we walk) from what we would consider the realm of learned behavior. The Romans categorized these movements differently, as "natural" (nature has encoded in human beings that a certain kind of politician should walk a certain way). The Romans ordered the apparent arbitrariness of their own society by deifying nature and then by making its contemplation the greatest activity a human being can have (Seneca *Dial.* 12.8.4). With this model lost, aporia results. During the political uncertainty and shifting alliances that followed Julius Caesar's assassination on the Ides of March, Cicero learns, while in his villa at Tusculum, that a group of discharged soldiers is beginning to stir up trouble in Rome. Cicero writes his friend Atticus to say that the potential for violence prevents him from returning to the capital, the site of his life's greatest glories. "Besides," he writes, "among people of *that sort*, what kind of expression should I have and how," he concludes, "how should I walk?"[91]

Notes

This chapter finds its impetus in the incredulous but polite reactions registered against shorter versions by Amy Richlin, Nathan Rosenstein, Robert Gurval, Jerise Fogel, and Robert Morstein-Marx; fuller versions benefited from the suggestions of the Beer and Politics Seminar at the University of Kansas and the keen eye of David Fredrick. Research and writing were generously supported by grants from the National Endowment for the Humanities / American Academy in Rome and, at the University of Kansas, by the General Research Fund and the Hall Center for the Humanities.

1. Bremmer 1992, Gleason 1995.60–64; Church fathers: Adkin 1983.

2. Cicero *de Fin.* 5.47: "nonne odio multos dignos putamus, qui quodam motu aut statu videntur naturae legem et modum contempsisse?" Unless otherwise noted, all translations are my own.

3. Cicero *de Legibus* 2.16. Perfection of nature: e.g., Cicero *de Orat.* 3.178–79; nature as guide: Cicero *de Amicitia* 19, *de Senec.* 2.5.

4. Cicero *de Nat. Deorum* 2.145: "oculi in his artibus quarum iudicium est oculorum, in pictis, fictis, caelatisque formis, in corporum etiam motione atque gestu multa cernunt subtilius, colorum etiam et figurarum venustatem atque ordinem et, ut ita dicam, decentiam oculi iudicant, atque etiam alia maiora; nam et virtutes et vitia cognoscunt." See, too, *de Off.* 1.128, *de Amicitia* 88. On modern links between aesthetics, ethics, and *habitus*, see Bourdieu 1984, esp. 44–50.

5. Bourdieu 1990.69–70. Bourdieu 1984.170–75, passim, applies *habitus* to class structures in contemporary France.

6. Bourdieu 1990.68 allows the possibility of changing one's *habitus* only "by a slow process of co-option and initiation which is equivalent to a second birth." Jenkins 1992.76–84 critiques Bourdieu's imprecision on this matter.

7. Taylor 1949.13 and n. 52. Meier 1965.572–83 can name only one *eques* who is called a *popularis* (L. Gellius Poplicola, at Cicero *pro Sestio* 110).

8. MacMullen 1966, esp. 242–43. Millar 1998 offers a model in which popular protest plays a more active role.

9. Taylor 1949.12; Gruen 1974, e.g., 27–28; Seager 1972. Perelli 1982.5–21 offers a concise overview of scholarly debate on the issue.

10. *De Lege Agraria* 2.7–9; see, too, *pro Rab. Perd.* 11. I follow Perelli's thesis that *popularis* was meaningful as a label for a particular person at a particular time: an ambitious politician who advances his views by appealing to the voting potential of the disempowered citizenry (1982.5–21); compare North 1990.18–19, Vasaly 1993.74, A. Bell 1997.3.

11. Millar 1984, 1986, 1995, and 1998. Among the many responses to Millar, see Jehne 1995, Pina Polo 1996, and their bibliographies.

12. For the role of display in promoting dominant values, see Gruen 1996 and the perceptive analysis of spectacle in Polybius by A. Bell 1997.3–5.

13. Gruen 1991, esp. 252–54, discusses the importance of inquiring into the elite's "stimulus to unity rather than the mechanism of [its] fragmentation."

14. David 1980 and 1983a. See, too, Ramage 1961 (primarily a collection of evidence).

15. *Acer* and *vehemens*: *Brut.* 130, 136, 186; *pro Cluentio* 140. *Rusticus*: Ramage 1961.483–86. This behavior is to be distinguished from the use of *amplificatio*: *Rhet. Her.* 2.48–49; Cicero *de Invent.* 1.100–05, *pro S. Rosc.* 12; David 1979.153–62.

16. [Arist.] *Ath. Pol.* 28.3, with Rhodes 1981.351–54; Plutarch *Nicias* 8.3.

17. David 1979 traces the political risks and rewards of this practice; see, too, David 1992.497–589.

18. See, for example, Cicero *de Orat.* 3.216: "omnis . . . motus animi suum quendam a natura habet vultum et sonum et gestum" (for the triad of expression, voice, and gesture, consult *Thesaurus Linguae Latinae* 6.2.1970.42–1971.45 (I. Kapp and G. Meyer); *Brut.* 141 (Antonius's opinion); Valerius Max. 8.10.1–2 (Hortensius); Seneca *Epist.* 114.22.

19. Julian *Dig.* 3.2.1, citing the praetor's edict (further, Ulpian *Dig.* 3.2.2.5); Gardner 1993.138–49; Edwards 1993.123–26, 1997.

20. See the bibliography in Axer 1989, esp. 299–303, who offers a salutary refinement of previous views.

21. A very select list: *Rhet. Her.* 3.26; Cicero *de Orat.* 3.220, *Brut.* 203; Seneca *Contr.* 3 praef. 3; Quintilian *Inst.* 1.11.3, 11.3.184; Martianus Capella 5.543.

22. Gleason 1995.105–07, 114–16; Richlin 1997b.99–108; Edwards 1997, esp. 79–81.

23. Select examples: Philodemus *Rhet.* 1.195, Sudhaus; Cicero *de Orat.* 3.220, *Brut.* 87–88, *de Divin.* 1.80; Quintilian *Inst.* 4.2.127; Gleason 1995.117 on Quintilian *Inst.* 1.11.9; Narducci 1997.77–96. Actors cannot blush: Seneca *Epist.* 11.7; contrast Quintilian *Inst.* 6.2.36.

24. Cicero *pro Q. Rosc.* 17. Cicero *de Orat.* 1.132 preserves Roscius's own comments on propriety.

25. *Brut.* 278: "tu istuc, M. Calidi, nisi fingeres, sic ageres?" (Valerius Max. 8.10.3). Gotoff 1986.128 discusses a similar contrast in *On Behalf of Caelius*. See, too, Cicero *pro S. Rosc.* 82, with Gotoff 1993.307–08.

26. Cicero *de Orat.* 2.188. The "single finger" seems to be the index (Quintilian *Inst.* 11.3.94).

27. Cicero *Brut.* 158: "non multa iactatio corporis, non inclinatio vocis, nulla inambulatio, non crebra supplosio pedis."

28. Cicero *pro Sestio* 121: "cum iam omisso gestu verbis poetae et studio actoris et exspectationi nostrae plauderetur."

29. Philodemus *Rhet.* 1.196, Sudhaus; Cicero *Brut.* 142, *de Orat.* 3.213; Valerius Max. 8.10.ext. 1; Quintilian *Inst.* 11.3.6; Plutarch *Demosthenes* 8.

30. Plautus *Poenulus* 522–23: "liberos homines per urbem modico magis par est gradu / ire; servile esse duco festinantem currere." See, too, Turpilius *Com.* 102.

31. See esp. Terence *Heaut.* 37, Lindsay 1900.294–95.

32. Vergil *Aeneid* 1.690, 6.646–49. Apuleius *Met.* 10.32 describes the walk of "Venus."

33. Gleason 1995.29–37 provides a review of the physiognomical writings.

34. Cicero *pro Sest.* 19: "quam taeter incedebat, quam truculentus, quam terribilis aspectu."

35. Cicero *in Pis.* 24: "fuit pompa, fuit species, fuit incessus saltem Seplasia dignus et Capua." For criticism of walking as if in a *pompa*, see Cicero *de Off.* 1.131.

36. Anon. *Physiogn.* 76; see, too, Horace *Serm.* 2.3.310–11: "corpore maiorem rides Turbonis in armis / spiritum et incessum."

37. *de Fin.* 2.77, Anon. *Physiogn.* 74, Gleason 1995.76–81.

38. *de Leg. Agr.* 2.13: "truculentius se gerebat quam ceteri. iam designatus alio voltu, alio vocis sono, alio incessu esse meditabatur, vestitu obsoletiore, corpore inculto et horrido, capillatior quam ante barbaque maiore, ut oculis et aspectu denuntiare omnibus vim tribuniciam et minitari rei publicae videretur."

39. Rullus: *de Leg. Agr.* 2.13. Piso: *in Pis.* 1 fr. 8; see further Corbeill 1996.169–73.

40. Gellius 1.5.2–3 (*ORF* 92.xvi offers historical testimonia). For Hortensius's histrionic delivery, see Cicero *Brut.* 303, Valerius Max. 8.10.2.

41. Quintilian *Inst.* 1.11.15–19, who particularizes the instruction as a type of dance: "neque enim gestum oratoris componi ad similitudinem saltationis volo"; cf. 1.12.14.

42. Macrobius *Sat.* 3.14.7 = *ORF* 21.30.

43. Walk of *cinaedi* or effeminate males: Varro *Men.* 301 (with *CIL* 4.1825 and Cèbe 1987.1324–1325), Seneca *Contr.* 2.1.6, Phaedrus 5.1.12–18, Seneca *Epist.* 114.3, Petronius *Satyricon* 119, l. 25, Juvenal 2.17, Quintilian *Inst.* 5.9.14, Carm. *ad Senat.* 13, Housman on Manil. 4.519. Compare Zeno, *Stoicorum Veterum Fragmenta* 1.82, Cicero *de Off.* 1.129. On the *cinaedus* in general, see Richlin 1993a and Parker 1997.

44. [Arist.] *Physiogn.* 808a.14–15: καὶ βαδίσεις διτταί, ἡ μὲν περινεύοντος, ἡ δὲ κρατοῦντος τὴν ὀσφύν; Anon. *Physiogn.* 74 ("et collum et vocem plerumque submittunt et pedes manusque relaxant . . . plerumque etiam oscitantes detecti sunt"), 98, and 115 (numerous details); Polemon 50 ("latera moventem articulosque agitantem"). Herter 1958.4.635–36 offers evidence from other kinds of texts.

45. Polemon 50; compare Ovid's Tragoedia (*Amores* 3.1.11). For Greek precedents, see Bremmer 1992.16–20.

46. Cicero *Orat.* 59; see, too, *de Orat.* 3.220, Seneca *Epist.* 40.14, 66.5. Efron 1972.22 discusses how researchers of the Third Reich reached quite different conclusions about their Mediterranean neighbors, whose "mental energies are all turned rather outwards, in the Nordic inwards . . . Mediterranean ferment stands opposed to Nordic restraint" (citing H. Günther, *Rassenkunde des deutschen Volkes* [Munich 1925]).

47. Anon. *Physiogn.* 100, with André ad loc.; Clement of Alexandria *Paed.* 3.11.73. *Gravitas* as a moral and political designation: Achard 1981.392–99, Hellegouarc'h 1972.279–94, Wagenvoort 1947.104–19, who speculates over the word's semantic evolution.

48. Anon. *Physiogn.* 75, compare Cicero *de Off.* 1.131. Tiberius: Suetonius *Tib.* 68.3, Tacitus *Annales* 1.10.7.

49. [Arist.] *Physiogn.* 809b.15–35 (summarized in Polemon 50). Winkes 1973.902–05 considers whether Roman artists attempted to express leonine characteristics in portraiture.

50. Suetonius *Aug.* 25.4 (σπεῦδε βραδέως), Gellius 10.11.5.

51. Suetonius *Claud.* 4.5. Pliny praises Trajan's stride for matching the vigor of his soul (*Panegyr.* 83.7).

52. *Rhet. Her.* 3.27. See also 3.19: "No one has written carefully on delivery"; he either does not know or respect the work of L. Plotius Gallus (Quintilian *Inst.* 11.3.143). Quintilian seems to have been the first writer to describe oratorical gesture in any detail (Cousin 1935.1.626–27).

53. Gleason 1995.xxv, who further conjectures that the proliferation of written handbooks during the second century C.E. corresponds to a broadening of education that allowed greater permeation into the cultural elite (which can no longer be identified with the political elite); see further 162–68.

54. Cicero *Brut.* 310, cf. Quintilian *Inst.* 1.1.12.

55. Cicero apud Seneca *Rhet.* 26.1; E. Rawson 1985.146–47 discusses teaching resources available in Latin.

56. Suetonius *Rhet.* 25.2: "maiores nostri quae liberos suos discere et quos in ludos itare vellent instituerunt," 26.1; Cicero *de Orat.* 3.93–94; Gellius 15.11.2; Tacitus *Dial.* 35.1. For bibliography, see Gruen 1990.179–91, Kaster 1995.273–75, 292–94, Pina Polo 1996.65–93.

57. Gruen 1990.179–91 examines the paradox of Greek training becoming an integral part of Roman tradition. See further Corbeill 2001.

58. Philodemus *Rhet.* 1.200–01, Sudhaus; my translation borrows from Hubbell 1919–20.301.

59. Coarelli 1992.1.148–51 contains the fullest account; see also Krause 1976. Pina Polo 1995.213 asserts without argument that "it is, in fact, unlikely that the Comitium was a circular enclosure with steps" (cf. Pina Polo 1996.24 n. 70).

60. Plutarch *C. Gracch.* 5.3; I follow Coarelli 1992.2.157–58 in distinguishing between the actions of Crassus and Gracchus, *contra* Taylor 1966.23–25.

61. Millar 1984, 1986, 1995, 1998, Thommen 1995.363.

62. Cicero *pro Flacco* 57: "speculatur atque obsidet rostra vindex temeritatis et moderatrix offici curia." The passage offers a strikingly visual illustration of the principle enunciated at Cicero *de Leg.* 2.30.

63. Krause 1976.53–61 evaluates the evidence for *comitia* outside of Rome.

64. F. Brown et al. 1993.27–28 considers the possibility that the speaker at Cosa spoke from a raised position.

65. Pina Polo 1996.23–25. See Cicero *de Haruspicum Responsis* 33 for the pun ("tollam altius tectum, non ut ego te despiciam").

66. Gellius 18.7.7, where Gellius claims that one of the three meanings of *contio* is the platform to which the speaker ascends.

67. Krause 1976, following the suggestions of Sjöqvist 1951.405–11, details Greek influence on Rome's circular *comitium*. Coarelli 1992.1.146–51 follows Krause, but differs on the date when the circular *comitium* was introduced in Rome.

68. Botsford 1909.149, on the basis of Cicero *ad Att.* 2.24.3, *in Vat.* 24. Pina Polo 1995.34–38, 178–82 notes that of the *privati* known to have addressed *contiones*, two-thirds consisted of former consuls (34).

69. *de Off.* 1.131: "anhelitus moventur, vultus mutantur, ora torquentur; ex quibus magna significatio fit non adesse constantiam." At Cicero *de Orat.* 1.184, an arrogant orator, ignorant of the laws, wanders with a crowd in the forum *prompto ore ac vultu*.

70. Sordi 1978.306–07, 318. Compare how the sources depict Cicero's calm acceptance of death (Livy apud Seneca *Suas.* 6.17, Plutarch *Cicero* 48).

71. On the limited gesticulation of togate statues, see Brilliant 1963.69.

72. Giuliani 1986.97–100, citing Cicero *ad Fam.* 8.13 for comparison.

73. Apuleius *Flor.* 9.1–12 (9.8: "tantum habet vilitas excusationis, dignitas difficultatis").

74. Cicero *ad Att.* 1.14.1–2, *Red. in Sen.* 17, *pro Sest.* 33; Livy 27.21.1; Taylor 1966.20–21; Thommen 1995.367.

75. Cicero *pro Lege Man.* 44 (the occasion is the voting on the *lex Gabinia*); see, too, *in Catil.* 4.14, Tacitus *Dial.* 39.5.

76. Cicero *de Leg. Agr.* 1.23; see, too, 2.15: "consul re non oratione popularis," where *oratio* presumably refers to "way of speaking" (*OLD* 1) as opposed to simply "words," which would have been expressed by the common *re non verbo* (or similar: *OLD* s.v. *res* 6b). A similar distinction occurs at *Brut.* 116 ("simplex in agendo veritas, non molesta"), where again a comparison is made with acting.

77. Cicero *de Fin.* 2.77, *de Leg. Agr.* 2.13.

78. This section offers a new perspective on passages discussed in Corbeill 1996.194–97 and is inspired, in part, by Kennedy 1992.39, who discusses Maecenas's effeminacy in similar terms.

79. Other examples of this charge from the republic include Gellius 6.12.4–5 (P. Sulpicius Galus); Cicero *in Verr.* 4.103, 5.31, 5.86 (Verres); *in Catil.* 2.22 (Catiline and his followers); cf. Varro *Men.* 313. Manfredini 1985.257–71 surveys the stigma of cross-dressing from late republican invective to the Codex of Theodosius.

80. Suetonius *Iul.* 45.3, Macrobius *Sat.* 2.3.9. Clothing reveals effeminacy: Horace *Serm.* 1.2.25; Seneca *Nat. Quaes.* 7.31, *Epist.* 114.21; Martial 1.96. Sulla's stance has startling resonance with Nazi propagandists who claimed that bodily *habitus* determines choice of dress (Efron 1972.26 n. 7).

81. Suetonius *Iul.* 1.3: "satis constat Sullam . . . proclamasse, sive divinitus sive aliqua coniectura . . . <Caesarem> quandoque optimatium partibus . . . exitio futurum; nam Caesari multos Marios inesse."

82. Plutarch *Caes.* 4.9; see, too, Macrobius *Sat.* 2.3.9, Dio 43.43.5. Corbeill 1996.164–65 discusses the head-scratching gesture. The disjuncture between effeminate appearance and masculine reality resembles Phaedrus's story of the *cinaedus* soldier who quite unexpectedly turns out to be a great warrior (Phaedr. app. 8). Gleason 1995.134 relates the story to Phaedrus's freedman status, speculating that "some males might deliberately opt out of the competition that governed public interaction among 'real' men."

83. Hacking 1986.234 and, for a general discussion of societies as self-regulating systems, Bateson 1972.88–106 ("Morale and National Character").

84. Bourdieu 1990.70–79 speculates on the origin of dividing gait along gender lines (for details, see 271–83).

85. See, e.g., Quintilian *Inst.* 6.3.72–74, Cicero *de Orat.* 2.54.220.

86. Corbeill 1996.196 n. 38. Dio 43.20.4 describes Caesar after the civil war as pained by the charges concerning Nicomedes, which, Suetonius contends, was the only challenge to his *pudicitia* (*Iul.* 49.1). This behavior contrasts markedly with that at the senate meeting a decade earlier.

87. Suetonius *Iul.* 67.1. It is interesting that the sole surviving fragment of Caesar's poetry mentions people anointing themselves with scent: *corpusque suavi telino unguimus* (Isid. *Etym.* 4.12.7).

88. I have not found a source that attacked him for effeminate gestures; on

the contrary, Cicero describes his oratorical style as "voce motu forma etiam magnificam et generosam quodam modo" (whatever *quodam modo* means: *Brut.* 261. See, too, Suetonius *Iul.* 55).

89. Compare the similar findings of Gleason 1995.161–62, who believes that effeminate speakers in the second century C.E. adopted their personae since "there was something manly, after all, about taking risks—even the risk of being called effeminate. Then there may also have been a temptation to appropriate characteristics of 'the other' as a way of gaining power from outside the traditionally acceptable sources." She declines, however, to speculate why "this more androgynous style of self-presentation was so effective with audiences."

90. See Jehne 1995.7–8 and, in more detail, Flaig 1995, who argues that the popular assemblies acted not as a body making decisions, but as one marking consensus (*Konsensorgan* as opposed to *Entscheidungsorgan*).

91. Cicero *ad Att.* 15.5.3: "quis porro noster itus, reditus, vultus, incessus inter istos?"

7

Being in the Eyes

Shame and Sight in Ancient Rome

Carlin Barton

> Shame exists wherever there is a *mysterium*.
> —*Friedrich Nietzsche*, Human, All Too Human

In my gym, there is an unwritten law: although the temptation is great, no woman ever stares or looks directly at the body of another woman. No woman comments on the body of another either to compliment or disparage her. Dressed, we eagerly examine and remark on each other's clothing, but we glance at one another's naked bodies through a foggy haze. The "secrets" of any woman who enters the dressing room are safe. Every woman knows that her own honor, her sense of bodily integrity, is a product of this inhibition. This shame, this shyness, this *pudor*, is a gift that the women in my gym give to one another. In the words of the anthropologist Unni Wikan (1984.641): "The person's own honour, in the sense of value both in [her or his] own and other's eyes . . . requires that she or he honour others." The result of this covenant we make with our eyes is a feeling of security, camaraderie, and freedom.[1] A woman who undresses behind a door deprives herself of this gift of Being.

The philosopher Max Scheler (1957.67–154) speaks eloquently of the *Beseelung*, the animation, the "ensouling" of others that we accomplish through the inhibition in our eyes, and the *Entseelung*, the "desouling," the depriving others of their spirit, effected by a shameless gaze. We humans have the capacity to veil another's nakedness with our own reverence; we can dress another in an aura of chastity or untouchableness. As Scheler points out, one of the rewards for our own shame, for treating other persons and things with awe, for restraining the desire to look, to invade with the eyes, is that we find ourselves in a world with depth, in a world

216

where the visible surface, the "facade" (*facies*) or "mask" (*persona*) expresses rather than hides an infinite profundity. "It is reverence that first allows us to glimpse into the deep well of worth in the world, whereas shamelessness must ever content itself with a world whose value is 'skin deep.'"[2]

That the Romans, with their communal baths and latrines, had comparable (if differently nuanced) visual temptations and inhibitions is suggested by the *apotropaia* on the walls of the baths that attracted and diverted the leering eye,[3] by Seneca's and Martial's singling out for scathing ridicule those who, like Hostius Quadra, Cotta, Maternus, or Philomusus, went to the baths to look,[4] by the traditional sanctions against fathers bathing with sons and sons-in-law,[5] and by Petronius's hilarious scene where the patrons of the bathhouse surround and devour with their eyes the irresistibly well-endowed Ascyltos.[6] Some things simply should not be looked at. Some things ought to evoke what Seneca calls *oculorum verecundia*, the restraint, the modesty of one's gaze (*Naturales Quaestiones* 1.16.4).[7] Catullus remarks of the vicious extravagance of Mamurra: "Who is able to watch this? Who can endure it—except the shameless, the voracious, and the gambler?" (29.1–2).[8] "Wanton Rome, will you look at this and bear it?" he asks (29.5).[9] Seneca's Hippolytus, having seen his stepmother Phaedra and heard her shameful confession of love, reprimands the sun for enduring the sight (*Phaedra* 677–78). Worse still, in the eyes of Seneca, was the salacious Hostius Quadra performing his lewd acts before a mirror. "Not content to suffer unheard of and unthinkable acts, he summoned his own eyes to witness his own degradation" (*Naturales Quaestiones* 1.16.4).[10]

Contrast the gaze of Hostius Quadra with that of the empress Livia. On encountering some naked men who were, in consequence, to be put to death, Livia saved their lives by saying: "To a woman with self-control, such men were indistinguishable from statues" (Dio 58.2.4).[11] Or contrast the shameless gaze of Hostius Quadra with that of the Roman soldiers who, in Livy's moving depiction, forgot their own miserable plight and averted their eyes from the ritual humiliation of their officers at the Caudine Forks *velut ab nefando spectaculo* (9.5.13–14).[12]

Shame and honor were not antithetical emotions for the ancient Romans.[13] To have a sense of honor was to have a sense of shame, of *pudor* or *verecundia*, a shyness, an ability, a willingness to be awed or intimidated by others.[14] The Romans lived in a sort of "zero-sum" universe; by withdrawing one's gaze before another person or a god, one augmented, one increased the portion of that person or god. It was one of the essential acts of cult, of cultivation, that allowed human beings to have gods at all—indeed to have anyone or anything that mattered. "*Cultus* and *verecundia* are synonyms for *honos*," Friedrich Klose remarks.[15] The dazzling and secret face of god that inhibits the worshiper's gaze *is* the shame, the veiled head and lowered eyes, of the reverent (see Wagenvoort 1956). Conversely, *pietas* could be wounded by a glance: *vultu saepe laeditur pietas* (Cicero *pro Roscio Amerino* 37).

Reverentia, observantia, in ancient Rome, might be an inhibition of the eyes or it might be, conversely, an "observing," an accepting or affirming look. Cicero speaks of "*observantia* by which we revere and cultivate those whom we recognize as preceding us in age or wisdom or honor or in any form of worthiness" (*de Inventione* 2.66).[16] In Livy's extended account of the humiliation of the Roman army at the Caudine Forks, the Capuan allies with their *voltus benigni*, their healing, embracing, annealing looks, try to reanimate the dispirited Roman soldiers, arisen from the defile like zombies from a crypt. Livy sharply contrasts the way the Capuans looked at the Romans with the way the victorious Samnites, with their scornful *voltus superbi*, regarded the Roman soldiers bowing under the yoke and running the Samnites' gauntlet of blows and derision (9.6.8, 5.8).[17]

The *verenda* were those parts of a Roman's body to be regarded with awe or reverence, the *pudenda* were those parts to be protected by inhibiting shame. The genitals were the "shameful" parts of the body *only* when the veils of shame were torn away (which violation could be accomplished simply by staring at them or speaking of them). As the social psychologist Kurt Riezler points out, "*Pudenda* and *veneranda* imply each other. Behind every *pudendum* is hidden a *venerandum*."[18] The Romans were conscious of the paradox of the sacred: it was shame that made the holy. The person with a sense of shame was acutely aware of the potential for the most sacred parts of him- or herself to become, with a glance, the most "shameful" parts.

This paradox helps to explain the development in much modern anthropological thought of a gender split between a man's "honor" and a woman's "shame." With reference to the Kabyle society of Algeria, Pierre Bourdieu explains: "A man should never be asked about his wife or sister: this is because woman is one of those shameful things (the Arabs say *lamra'ara*, 'woman is a shame') that one never mentions without apologizing and adding 'saving your respect,' and also because woman is for man the sacred thing above all others, as is shown by the phrase customarily used in pledging an oath: 'May my wife be taboo to me' . . . or 'may my house be taboo' ('if I fail to do such-and-such')."[19] Compare the statement ascribed to the Elder Cato: "The man who struck his wife or child laid violent hands on the holiest of things" (Plutarch *Cato Maior* 20.1).[20] Romulus, according to the same author, legislated a series of prohibitions against violating the eyes, ears, and space of women in order to honor them (εἰς τιμήν).[21] By not uttering any indecent word in their hearing, by not appearing naked in their sight, and by giving them the right of way in the street, men could insure themselves against the shame with which women threatened them. They could, by their inhibitions, make the *pudenda* the *veneranda* (*Romulus* 20.3).[22] In light of this paradox, one might consider Cicero's comments on the apologetic expression *praefari honorem* (= *dicere honorem*) that polite Romans used to excuse mention of *de Aurelia aliquid aut Lollia* (*ad Familiares* 9.22.4) and the frequent use of the respect-saving phrase *honoris causa* used by Cicero when naming a women whom he does not intend to shame by mentioning.[23] And so it is important to remember that if women were somewhat less visible than men in ancient Rome it was, at least in part (as in Heian Japan or Moslem Algeria), *honoris causa*. If Roman literature appears misogynist it is due, at least in part, to the fact that to speak of a woman at all in public was to offend her—and her menfolk. The "overlooking" of a woman did not necessarily, as in our culture, imply insult or inattention; it might be just the reverse.

As I pointed out in an earlier work, the *pudenda/veneranda* shared with the eyes the paradox of being both extremely vulnerable and extremely aggressive (Barton 1993.95–98). The eyes and the genitals were therefore often used by the Romans as homologies for one another (*testis/testis*). They were the parts of the body that most profoundly exemplified the paradox of socialization; if they were respected one could endure being in the sight of others, if not, being visible was unendurable. The veiling of both the eyes and the genitals signaled one's commitment to the shared system of inhibitions, to the collective social lie, the pious falsehood by which the Romans hid from one another (just as we do) the fact of their nothingness and death.

And as one could endow or deprive others of spirit by the manner in which one regarded them in ancient Rome, so one could "ensoul" or "desoul" oneself by the way in which one watched oneself. "Cato [the Censor]," Plutarch tells us, "thought it especially necessary for every man to feel shame before himself (ἑαυτὸν αἰδεῖσθαι), since no man is ever separated from himself" (*Regum et Imperatorum Apophthegmata*, Cato 9 [*Moralia* 198F]).[24] How did one respect oneself?—by caring for, by cultivating oneself, by revering one's own *facies* and *persona*, by observing

oneself from a distance as if one were the audience of one's own performance. Just as men and women fought the *Entseelung* of the death
camps of World War II by maintaining their posture, by sewing on their
buttons, and by washing themselves with filthy water, so the Romans did
not suffer themselves to be contemptible in their own eyes like Seneca's
poster child of humiliation, the excrement-smeared Telesphorus of
Rhodes, mutilated, caged, and suffering himself to be put on display.[25]

Visibility

> I am a man among men; I stroll about with my head uncovered.
> —*Trimalchio in Petronius's* Satyricon

Being, for a Roman, was being seen.[26] Cicero regretted serving in Cili-
cia because it meant acting in squalid obscurity far from the limelight
of Rome (*ad Familiares* 2.12.2). He wanted to be, in Horace's scornful
words (*Epistulae* 1.16.57), "the good man whom the forum and every
tribunal sees."[27] The stance of honor in Roman art was, as Richard Brilliant has pointed out, the full frontal posture with arm extended. A man
made himself as conspicuous, as tender a target as possible, in order to feel
the immediacy of his being.[28] It was as if the Roman said, "Here
I am, come and get me. I am not hiding; go ahead and look . . . if you dare."

No less than her husband, the *casta matrona*, sheltered by the walls
of her house, had to be prepared to be seen at any moment. Being visible
was the great test of a Roman woman's honor (Livy's *certamen muliebre*).
To his comrades intending to test their wives by returning unexpectedly
from the front, Livy's Collatinus declares: "Let every man regard as the
surest test (*spectatissimum sit*) what meets his eyes when the woman's
husband enters unexpectedly."[29] Terence's Syrus and Dromo, the slaves
of Chremes and his son Clitiphon, arrive suddenly at the home of
Antiphila, the young woman loved by Clitiphon, with a test in mind.
They barge in with the intention of surprising Antiphila. "That's where
one could find out . . . what way she's been spending her life in your
absence—I mean by breaking in on her unawares. Why, this way we had
the means of reckoning her everyday life and it's that that best tells what
a person's *ingenium* is" (*Heautontimorumenos* 274–84, trans. Sargeaunt).[30]
When Plautus's Alcmena is shocked to discover on her doorstep the
husband who had only just left her, her first assumption is that Amphi-
tryon has devised a trial for her. "Why has he returned so soon after saying he had to rush off? Is he deliberately trying me? (*Amphitruo*
660–62).[31]

If Being, for the ancient Romans, was being seen, being seen was a basic existential risk. The person with a sense of honor, with a sense of shame, accepted the danger of being visible. His or her Being needed to be tested, "proved" (*probatus, spectatus, expertus, argutus*) to exist. When Simo discovers that his son has frequented the house of the prostitute Chrysis, but that he has not slept with her, he declares: "I consider him to be sufficiently 'seen' (*spectatum satis*) and a great example of self-control" (Terence *Andria* 91–92, cf. 93–95). Proven men were *spectati viri* (Plautus *Mercator* 319). Cicero's brave Caecilia was a *spectatissima femina* (*pro Sexto Roscio* 50.147). Tacitus's Octavia was a woman of *probitas spectata* (*Annales* 13.12.2).[32]

The *spectator* was, for the Romans, an inspector, judge, and connoisseur.[33] Terence presents his comedy, the *Heautontimorumenos*, as a case being tried in court, with the actor as the orator and the *spectatores* as judges (Prologus). Plautus's goddess is judge and mistress (*spectatrix atque era, Mercator* 842).[34] One can compare the Latin notion of the *arbiter: arbitrari* meant to hear, behold, observe, or see, as well as to think, and the *arbiter* was a judge as well as a spectator.[35]

Willingness to Be Witnessed

Roman honor was a willingness to be exposed and so, to use a phrase of Sandor Feldman, "a readiness to be ashamed."[36] The person with a sense of shame demonstrated his or her willingness to be shamed by calling upon witnesses to his or her words or acts. Cicero calls on the judge Aquilius and his counselors to attend to and commit to memory the limitations and boundaries to which he (Cicero) has committed himself in his defense of Quinctius (*pro Quinctio* 10.35–36). Livy's Horatius Cocles, when the enemy Etruscans had taken the Janiculum and the Roman soldiers were fleeing in terror and confusion, "stood his ground and called upon the *fides* of gods and men as witnesses" (Livy 2.10.3).[37] Calling upon gods and men as spectators—or judges, for they were inseparable notions in the Roman mind—of an oath or an action was a Roman's way of saying: "Go ahead; put me in the spotlight. My words and my actions will stand the test of your scrutiny." The presence of witnesses made one's every move into a test.[38]

Amy Richlin points out (1995.185–213, 1992a.176–77) that the Romans frequently made the distinction between "the undisguised looks of respectable women and the deceptively dressed-up appearance of prostitutes." Wearing *obvious* makeup (like getting undressed in the bathroom of the gym) proclaimed one's unwillingness to be ashamed, to be naked to others' eyes. Hiding behind painted-on blush proclaimed not one's blushing modesty but one's brazen shamelessness. And so, ironically, it was a challenge and an invitation to violation. Martial punishes Saufeia for not being willing to bathe with him by the brutal publication of the bodily faults that he imagines Saufeia is trying to hide from his eyes (3.72).

Keeping a Sharp Eye on Oneself

Plautus's tutor Lydus scolds his student Pistoclerus (absent amusing himself in the house of the courtesan Bacchis) for having had no shame before the eyes of his old tutor—or before himself ("neque mei neque te tui intus puditumst factis quae facis," *Bacchides* 379). The honorable person scrutinized and judged himself or herself even when others did not. The honorable person inhibited himself or herself even when he or she could not be seen. Plautus's slave Palinurus, tutor of his young master Phaedromus, advises the latter to live and love as if always in the eyes of others. Playing on the two meanings of *testis*, the slave Palinurus warns his young master to be careful in loving: "If you're wise, you'll so give your love that it won't be to your disgrace if the people should come to know what it is you love; take care you do not become *intestabilis*" ("ne id quod ames populus si sciat, tibi sit probro. / semper curato ne sis intestabilis," *Curculio* 29–30). "Love," Palinurus advises, "but with your 'witnesses' present" ("quod amas amato testibus praesentibus," 31).

Each man, to use a phrase of Juvenal, has his own witness in his breast (*suum . . . in pectore testem*, *Saturae* 13.198). "With himself as his own judge, no guilty man is absolved—even if he has won his cause by the favor of a corrupt praetor" (*Saturae* 13.2–4).[39] There could be, Cicero explained, no excuse for that Gyges of the story who took advantage of his magic ring to make himself invisible in order that he might act shamelessly (*de Officiis* 3.19.78). The good man or woman, he suggests, was someone with whom you could play "odds and evens" in the dark (3.19.77). He or she was visible even in the densest fog or deepest night.

To this end, the Roman incorporated others into himself or herself as witnesses and ideals. "I tell my son to look into the lives of all others as if into a mirror and to take from others a model for himself" (Terence *Adelphi* 415–16).[40] Seneca advises Lucilius to chose a venerable man of outstanding qualities and to keep him ever before his mind's eye as an inhibitor (*Epistulae* 11.8–10):

> We should have high regard for a particular good man and keep him ever before our eyes so that we might live as if he were always watching and judg-

ing us. . . . Most sins would disappear if there were a witness of the man about to sin. The will (*animus*) should have someone to fear, by whose authority even one's most guarded secret would be still more carefully hidden.[41] He is a happy man who is able to amend the faults of another, not only when he is present, but when he is merely thought of! And he is a happy man who can so fear another that, at just the thought of this other, he can compose and regulate himself. Who can so venerate another will soon be worthy of veneration. So pick a Cato. And if he seems a bit too rigid to you, pick a man of gentler spirits—a Laelius. Chose one whose life and speech and soul-baring face please you. Always present him to yourself as custodian or *exemplum*.[42]

Roman honor, then, was a way of self-regarding as well as other-regarding. Honor required self-splitting; one needed to be, at all times, both the watched and the watcher. For the Roman, there could be, finally, no integrated psychic whole, no stable notion of self. If a Roman had a sense of "integrity" it was one built, paradoxically, on the dividing of the self.[43] Cicero speaks of the self-control needed to resist shameful reactions to pain: "I'm not exactly sure how to say it, but it is as if we were two people: one who commanded and one who obeyed."[44] The Roman with a sense of shame was subject and object, master and servant. Master "Horace" was also his oh-so-critical and knowing slave "Davus" (*Sermones* 2.7). Ovid's young Medea, torn between her passion for Jason and her obligations to her father, "spoke to herself and before her mind's eye stood Righteousness, Piety, and Shame" ("dixit, et ante oculos rectum pietasque pudorque / constiterant," *Metamorphoses* 7.72–73).

Visual Assassination

Even Nero averted his eyes and did not deign to watch the outrages that he ordered. The worst of our torments under Domitian was to see him with his eyes fixed upon us—with our every sigh being registered against us.—*Tacitus* Agricola

There was never a guarantee that one's own or another's eyes would not "desoul" one. Toxic shaming occurred any time, any instant, when one sensed that there was no inhibition in the eyes of others, when the eyes of others would violate and consume.[45] Cicero gloats over his enemy Piso (Cicero *in Pisonem* 41.99): "Your blood, Piso, I have never sought. . . . But I wanted, rather, to see you abject, scorned, despised by your fellows, despaired of and abandoned even by yourself, a creature peering nervously about and quaking at every whisper, without trust in itself, without a voice, liberty, or authority, without even the semblance of being a consul, a shivering, trembling, fawning wretch—this have I desired to see. . . . And so I have seen."[46]

Some of the most terrible dramas of Roman life had to do with uninhibited inspection. Tacitus's Germanicus, bitter with anguish, felt that he was being forced to die under the gloating eyes of his enemy Piso (*Annales* 2.70). Ovid's rejected lover moans: "I have kept vigil, lying like a slave before the closed doors of your house. I have seen your wearied lover come forth from those doors. . . . yet this is an easier thing to endure than being seen by him—oh may shame like that befall my enemies!" (Ovid *Amores* 3.11a.12–15).[47] Livy's Roman soldiers were sent under the yoke, "and what was almost heavier to bear, before the eyes of the enemy" (9.6.3).[48] Suetonius's Caligula had the wives of his dinner guests pass before his couch while he leisurely and closely assessed them—like a merchant inspecting the goods—stretching out his hand to raise the chin of any woman who kept her gaze lowered from shame (36.2).[49] In this way the women were visually violated twice over: firstly, by Caligula's uninhibited inspection of their bodies and, secondly, by having to look at him while he examined them. (Their husbands were, meanwhile, compelled to watch this "dress rehearsal" of the emperor's physical violation of their wives.) Pliny the Younger gleefully asserts: "Nothing was so popular, nothing so fitting for our times as the opportunity we enjoyed of looking down at the informers at our feet, their heads forced back and faces upturned to meet our gaze" (*Panegyricus* 34.3).[50] Staring a person directly in the eye was the consummate form of insult because it obliged the offended one to witness his or her own visual violation. To force another to watch you watching them with soul-withering contempt was a form of violence—of vivisection—as penetrating, as mutilating, as any that one human being could inflict upon another.

We are accustomed to think of men as the active penetrators and women as the passive receptors,[51] but, in ancient Rome (as with all cultures that felt the fear of the evil eye), women could violate with as much damage to the spirit as men.[52] Cynthia, Propertius tells us, first took the miserable poet captive with her eyes, and love of Cynthia compelled him to bow his head and lower his haughty gaze (1.1).[53] Apuleius's Pamphile is able, with her riveting gaze, to invade the spirit of young men and snare them in the unbreakable bonds of boundless love (*Metamorphoses* 2.5).[54] Horace's Canidia looks at the youth she will bury alive with a gaze like "that of a stepmother—or like a hunter at a animal brought to bay."[55]

The uninhibited gaze pressed hard on the imagination of the ancient Romans. In a scene meant to send shivers up the spine of any parent,

Ovid's Procne thrusts a knife in the side of her child with a gaze un-flinching (*nec vultum vertit, Metamorphoses* 7.642).[56] Plutarch describes the Roman people watching the eyes of the elder Brutus watching the public whipping and execution of his own sons. The spectators gaze at his face in wonder and horror: "In either case, his [Brutus's] act was not a trivial one nor a human one, but either that of a god or a beast" (*Publicola* 6.3–4). The spies of Tacitus's Tiberius reported to the senate every beating administered, every moan emitted, every humiliation suffered by Tiberius's grandson Drusus while the latter was starving to death in his prison cell in the Palatine dungeon. The senators were amazed and ter-rified that Tiberius would expose his grandson's humiliations to them "just as if the walls had been removed" (*ut tamquam dimotis parietibus*). "This," Tacitus declares, "seemed the supreme cruelty" (*quo non aliud atrocius visum*), "that agents had stood by Drusus all these years noting every look on his face and every groan he emitted, taking note of even the words he uttered under his breath (*occultum etiam murmur*); that a grandfather could have heard, read, and published these observations seemed incredible" (*Annales* 6.24).[57]

The uninhibited gaze did more than violate, it cannibalized. The malicious Vitellius "feasted his eyes" on the spectacle of his enemy's death (Tacitus *Historia* 3.39).[58] Just so, Encolpius fed his on the sight of his rival being beaten (*Satyricon* 96). According to Cicero, the seafaring Syracu-sans "longed to feast their eyes and satisfy their souls" with the torture and execution of Verres' captured pirate (*in Verrem* 2.5.26.65).[59]

The gaze without compunction signaled the loss of trust, the end of the collusion between the seer and the seen, the breakdown of a com-mon bond and of the security and camaraderie created by the mutual in-hibition of the eyes. The uninhibited gaze made every Thou an It, some-thing one could consume, something one could destroy with impunity and without regret.

The Razor-Sharp Eye

Happy are you, Hester, that wear your scarlet letter openly upon your bosom! Mine burns in secret.—*Nathaniel Hawthorne*, The Scarlet Letter

One could turn this desouling eye on oneself. Juvenal reminds his audi-ence that just because one may have committed a transgression unde-tected, one did not thereby escape one's inner eye (*Saturae* 13.192–98): "But why should you suppose that they escape punishment whose minds are ever kept in terror by the consciousness of evil deeds that lash them with unheard blows, their own souls ever shaking over them the unseen whip of torture? It is a grievous punishment, more cruel by far than any devised by the stern Caedicus or by Rhadamanthus, to carry in one's breast, by night and day, one's own accusing witness."[60]

Apart from being the inhibitor, *pudor* was the guilt, the anguish of the person who could not bear the trial of either one's own or another's eyes. *Conscientia* was the "guilty secret" that made one sweat to look another in the eye—those informers, those betrayers of the soul. ("As the face is the image of the spirit, so the eyes are the informers," Cicero *Orator* 18.60).[61] For the person with a sense of shame, *conscientia* was a sort of appalling super self-consciousness resulting from the unwillingness, the impossibility of Being while being seen.[62] "O silent torment, *animi conscientia*" (Publilius Syrus 490). "He is crucified by *conscientia*, tormented by *pudor*" (Calpurnius Flaccus *Declamationes* 49). "Nothing is more miserable than an *animus conscius* such as the one possessing me" (Plautus *Mostellaria* 544–45).[63] Ovid's poor Byblis, driven wild by her unspeakable desire for her brother, dreams of transgression and blushes even in her sleep (*Metamorphoses* 9.468–71).[64] The nurse admonishes Phaedra: even if heaven should keep her incestuous secret, "what of the ever-present penalty, the soul's conscious dread, and the spirit filled with crime and fearful of itself?" (Seneca *Phaedra* 162).[65] *Conscientia* was the guilty knowledge of their enormities ("stuprorum sibi incestarumque noctium conscii") that stopped the candidates for office from daring to show themselves either to god or man (Pliny *Panegyricus* 63.7–8).

When one turned on oneself or another the basilisk stare, one's face, one's expressive *persona* stiffened and ossified. It became *only* a mask or facade. When the fear of exposure became so great that one could not afford a slip—one could not afford to be naked—the splitting of the self necessary for voluntary self-control became a laceration. Self-control became unbearable when there was no indulgence in others' eyes for the loss of it. As Seneca says, "It is a torture to be constantly watching oneself and to fear being caught in other than one's usual role" (*de Tranquillitate* 17.1).[66] Horace describes the misery of trying to present an appearance, a face that one cannot live up to and that, one feels, others can see through (*Epistulae* 1.18.21–36). While Sejanus, commander of the Praetorian Guard, acted as vicar for Tiberius sojourning on Capri, "There was a crush and rivalry around his door, not only from fear of not being seen by him, but from fear of being among the last. For every word and sign was closely watched, especially those of the leading men" (Dio

58.5.2). Having just executed a man on a trifling charge, the emperor Caligula invited the dead man's father, the knight Pastor, to celebrate with him. He set a guard to scrutinize the latter's every reaction. The cruelest torture inflicted on Pastor was the smile carved on the bereaved father's face by the fatal edge of the emperor's gaze (*de Ira* 2.33.3–5).[67]

One could strip oneself naked, pry into one's own deepest secrets. One could "desoul" oneself. Shame could be unbearably aggravated by identifying one's inner eye with a higher authority who watched one with unsleeping eyes. Like Job before the God who had conquered Leviathan, or Apuleius's Lucius before the all-powerful Isis, the Roman could be ashamed of his or her unlimited inadequacies before his or her limitless desires and aspirations.[68] The emperor Marcus Aurelius, in the solitude of his tent on the Danube, turns a desouling eye on himself, watching and criticizing himself relentlessly, like a bug under glass, as unforgiving of himself as Dostoyevsky's Underground Man. The supremely powerful emperor—and wretchedly impotent mortal—describes the soul of an evil man: "A black, feminine heart, the heart of a wild beast of the field, that of a child, lazy and unreliable, stupid and deceitful, the heart of a tyrant" (4.28). "Whose soul," he asks, "inhabits me at the moment? Is it a little child's, a youngster's, a woman's, a tyrant's, that of a beast of burden or a wild animal?" (5.11). Marcus's internalized critic is more severe than any Cato. As a result, the self-splitting, the shared, blurred social identity that ideally molded and formed the personality was experienced as a loss of identity, an unsightly chaos of the self.

Conclusions

The tension for the person of honor in ancient Rome had ever been the need to display him- or herself to others and, simultaneously, to preserve an inviolate and protected sphere, the source and power of one's will, one's *animus*. It was impossible to do this by oneself; one depended on and was at the mercy of the gaze of others. In the risky oscillation of exhibition and inhibition, one created and was created through the gaze. We are liable to think of the Romans as without introspection. But no one apprised of the Roman exacerbated sensitivity to the gaze could imagine the Romans as existing in a comfortable and "primitive" unself-consciousness. They were more like Dostoyevsky's Underground Man than his Zverkov, more like Nietzsche himself than his Blond Beast. The Romans were aware of themselves as fragile, naked creatures, clothed only in the majesty of mutual and self-regard. Both they and their social world could be animated or shattered with a look.

Notes

The material in this chapter is derived from Barton 2001, an extended meditation on Roman honor and its relationship to the body. Unless otherwise noted, all translations are my own.

This chapter is dedicated to Gayla.

1. Wikan explains (1984.641) that consciousness of the reciprocity of honor encourages the women of Oman to overlook faults and reincorporate the transgressors of their own stringent social code.

2. "[So] . . . lässt auch die Ehrfurcht erst die Werttiefe der Welt erblicken, wogegen der Ehrfurchtslose sich immer nur mit der Flächendimension ihrer Werte begnügen muss" (1957.101; cf. 87).

3. See esp. Dunbabin 1989.18, 33–46, Barton 1993, pt. 2, J. R. Clarke 1996.184–98.

4. Seneca *Naturales Quaestiones* 1.16, Martial 1.96, 1.23, 11.63.

5. "According to our own customs, grown sons do not bathe with their fathers, nor sons-in-law with their fathers-in-law" ("Nostro quidem more cum parentibus puberes filii, cum soceris generi non lavantur," Cicero *de Officiis* 1.35.129). Cicero describes this inhibition as *verecundia*. Cf. Plutarch *Cato Maior* 20.

6. Petronius *Satyricon* 92. For a discussion of the voracious eye, the eye without shame, its channeling and obstruction, see Barton 1993, pt. 2.

7. Anthropologists such as Jean Briggs, Richard Lee, and Nurit Bird, who study band societies where there is little privacy and where humans are subject to constant mutual surveillance, have often remarked on the respectful "civil inattention" members of such societies afford one another. See Redfield 1968.32, P. Wilson 1988.27.

8. "Quis hoc potest videre, quis potest pati / nisi impudicus et vorax et aleo."

9. "Cinaede Romule, haec videbis et feres?" Horace imagines the insolent hooves of barbarian steeds trampling the ashes of the Romans and—*nefas videre*—scattering their bones (*Epodi* 16.11–14).

10. "Ille, quasi parum esset inaudita et incognita pati, oculos suos ad illa advocavit."

11. For Roman anxiety with regard to exposing themselves nude to one another, see Ennius (at Cicero *Tusculanae Disputationes* 4.33.70: "Disgrace originates in baring one's body to one's fellow citizens" ("flagiti principium est nudare inter cives corpora"). An edict of Romulus, according to Plutarch, designed to honor (εἰς τιμήν) Roman women, forbade men to appear naked before women or be subject to prosecution before the judges of homicide (*Romulus* 22.3). For the difference between Greek and Roman attitudes toward nudity, see Bonfante 1989.563.

12. "Suae quisque condicionis oblitus ab illa deformatione tantae maiestatis velut ab nefando spectaculo averteret oculos."

13. I will use the rubric "Romans" advisedly in this chapter—and with more

than a little trepidation. I do not intend the word "Romans" to essentialize, totalize, or idealize but rather to embrace as many related human associations as I can. There are times when I can and will explicitly narrow my generalizations to a particular gender, class, or individual, but when used without qualification, the word "Romans" is meant to cross and blur those boundaries. In general, the sense of shame of the poor moved in delicate counterpoint to that of the aristocrats, the shame of the women with that of the men, sometimes mirroring, sometimes complementing, sometimes appearing as alternatives, sometimes as opposites, sometimes as mockeries—but always in relation. A certain sense of what shame was served as the ground bass to an intricate dance in time filled with syncopations, improvisations, strange fugue-like movements, miscues, and mistakes.

14. Scheler's *Verschüchterheit* (1957.88). "Shyness," as the derivation of the word in several languages indicates, is closely related to fear. See Darwin 1965.330. According to the *Oxford English Dictionary*, "shy" derives from the Teutonic root *skeuhw-, "to fear, to terrify."

15. Klose 1933.122–23; cf. 24, 83. One's *dignitas* was one's claim to this cultivation. "*Dignitas* is the possession of an authority (or office) meriting respect, honor, and reverence" ("dignitas est alicuius honesta et cultu et honore et verecundia digna auctoritas," Cicero *de Inventione* 2.166).

16. "Observantiam, per quam aetate aut sapientia aut honore aut aliqua dignitate antecedentes veremur et colimus." For the benevolent, kindly gaze, see also Seneca *de Clementia* 1.19.8.

17. In Tim Robbin's 1996 film, *Dead Man Walking*, Sister Helen Prejean is determined to counteract the "desouling" looks of many of the witnesses of the execution with her own "ensouling" look. She bids the doomed man, in the seconds before his death, to keep his eyes fixed on her own. Her look admits, accepts, respects—dissolving the distance and the distinctions between the seen and the unseen. For this sort of melting look passing between lovers, see Plutarch *Quaestiones Conviviales* 5.7 [*Mor.* 681a–b].

18. Riezler 1942–43.464. The genitals were the *sanctissima pars corporis* (Cicero *post Reditum in Senatu* 5.11), the *viscus sacrum* (CIL 1.2.2520.33), *pars tegenda* (*Priapea* 1.7, Ovid *Metamorphoses* 13.479–80), *velanda* (Pliny *Epistulae* 6.24.3), *secreta* (Ammianus Marcellinus 28.1.28, Isidore *Etymologiae* 11.1.102, Lindsay); Adams 1982.56.

19. Bourdieu 1979.124–25. For Anton Blok, "Women [are] the most precious and vulnerable part of the patrimony of men" (1981.434).

20. τοῖς ἁγιωτάτοις . . . ἱεροῖς προσφέρειν τὰς χεῖρας.

21. Cf. Valerius Maximus 2.1.5, Festus-Paulus p. 142, Lindsay. For the inviolability and privileges of *matronae*, see Richlin 1997c.346–50.

22. As William Robertson Smith long ago pointed out, persons and things sanctified or tabooed could easily become objects of anxiety and disgust—the line between "unclean" and "tabooed" was always a delicate one (1914.162, 447–50).

23. Cicero is not embarrassed, for instance, to name the dishonorable

women who were involved sexually with Verres, but he declines to mention the Roman matrons (*in Verrem* 5.13.34).

24. Compare Nietzsche 1990.215, no. 287: "The Noble Soul has reverence for itself" ("Die vornehme Seele hat Ehrfurcht vor sich"). In the words of Leon Wurmser (1981.48; cf. 51), "I feel shame before myself" ("Ich schäme mich vor mir selbst").

25. Telesphorus: *de Ira* 3.17.3–4, *Epistulae* 70.6–7. See the stories of Steinlauf and Alfred L. in Primo Levi's spare and moving *Survival in Auschwitz*: "So we must certainly wash our faces without soap in dirty water and dry ourselves on our jackets. We must polish our shoes, not because the regulation states it, but for dignity and propriety. We must walk erect, without dragging our feet, not in homage to Prussian discipline but to remain alive, not to begin to die" (1961.36; cf. 35, 85–86). Compare the words of Billy A., inmate of an American high-security prison: "The way I keep my self-respect is by keeping my body clean" (quoted by Gilligan 1997.100).

26. To veil the head in Rome was to participate in a complex dialectic. Voluntarily covering one's head was a sign of a sense of shame. The Romans, for instance, were expected to veil their heads before the gods. "Who is this man who dares to greet Aesculapius with an uncovered head?" ("Quis hic est qui operto capite Aesculapiam / salutat?" Plautus *Curculio* 389). The involuntary covering of another's head was a brutal humiliation. The community might deny personhood to those they shamed by covering or wrapping the head, the focus of one's social being: "Go lictor, tie his hands, cover his head, hang him from the Tree of Misfortune" ("I, lictor, conliga manus . . . caput obnubito, arbori infelici suspendito," Cicero *pro Rabirio Perduellionis Reo* 4.13). For killing his sister, Horatius Tergeminus was compelled to "go under the yoke," to pass, with head covered, beneath the yoke, the *tigillum sororium*—a shaming that was simultaneously an expiation and resocialization. "Go ahead, lictor, tie those hands that but a little while ago secured *imperium* for the Roman people. Go ahead, cover the head of the liberator of this city; hang him from the Tree of Misfortune" ("I, lictor, colliga manus, quae paulo ante armatae imperium populo Romano pepererunt. I, caput obnube liberatoris urbis huius; arbore infelici suspende," Livy 1.26.11). The law ordered the head of the person who had murdered his parent to be wrapped ("legem iubere caput eius obnubere qui parentem necavisset, quo est obvolvere," Paulus ex Festus, Müller, p. 170). For a beautiful and highly nuanced description of the politics of veiling in a modern Bedouin community, see Lila Abu-Lughod 1986.

27. "Vir bonus, omne forum quem spectat, et omne tribunal."

28. Brilliant 1963. For the full frontal position as the "sincere" position, see Spiegel and Machotka 1974. The honorable man of Kabylia was, according to Pierre Bourdieu, "the man who faces, outfaces, stands up to others, looks them in the eye" (1977.15). For the ability to keep one's head raised distinguishing humans from other animals see, for example, Cicero *de Legibus* 1.9.26, Ovid *Metamorphoses* 1.82–86; cf. Sallust *Catilina* 1.1, 2.8.

29. "Id cuique spectatissimum sit quod necopinato viri adventu occurrerit oculis," Livy 1.57.7.

30. "Quo studio vitam suam te absente exegerit, / ubi de inprovisost interventum mulieri. / nam ea res dedit tum existumandi copiam / cottidianae vitae consuetudinem, / quae quoiusque ingenium ut sit declarat maxume."

31. "Nam quid ille revortitur, / qui dudum properare sese aibat? an ille me temptat sciens." See also the scene in the *Bacchides* that begins at lines 829–31.

32. The fidelity of Claudius's freedman Pallas was *spectatissima* (Pliny *Epistulae* 8.6.13). "And people especially admire the man who is not moved by the desire for money. If a man has proven himself in this direction, they consider him to have been tried by fire" ("qui pecunia non movetur . . . hunc igni spectatum arbitrantur," Cicero *de Officiis* 2.11.38). "Our hearts are strong in battle and our spirits and our youthful vigor tried in action" ("sunt nobis fortia bello / pectora, sunt animi et rebus spectata iuventus," Vergil *Aeneid* 8.150–51). "I thought you had sufficiently tested me and my abilities by now" ("me quidem iam satis tibi spectatam censebam esse et meos mores," Plautus *Persa* 171). "Tuam probatam mi et spectatam maxume adulescentia" (Lucilius apud Nonius 3.703, Lindsay); "homo in rebus iudicandis spectatus et cognitus" (Cicero *in Verrem* 1.10.29); "homines . . . spectati et probati" (*de Oratore* 1.27.124); "fidem . . . spectatam iam et diu cognitam" (*Divinatio in Caecilium* 4.11, cf. Ovid *Epistulae ex Ponto* 2.7.82); "spectata ac nobilitata virtus" (Cicero *pro Flacco* 63); "spectata multis magnisque rebus singularis integritas" (*Philippicae* 3.10.26); "ni virtus fidesque vostra spectata mihi forent" (Sallust *Catilina* 20.2); "spectatae deinde integritatis viro" (Livy 26.49.16); "spectata est per mala nostra fides" (Ovid *Epistulae ex Ponto* 2.7.82); "Tiberium . . . spectatum bello" (Tacitus *Annales* 1.4.3).

33. It should be stressed that, for the Romans, seeing was the privileged source of knowledge. In the words of Plautus, "Look and then you'll know" (*em specta, tum scies, Bacchides* 123). "Those who see, they know distinctly" (*qui vident, plane sciunt, Truculentus* 490). "They believe because they see" (*credunt quod vident, Asinaria* 202). "If you could see, you'd agree" (*rem quom videas, censeas,* Terence *Heautontimorumenos* 1023). For the spectator as active and judging, see Kellum (forthcoming) mss. 13, 15. For the privileging of sight, see Miles 1995.9–12.

34. "None of the generals . . . was a keener observer and judge of bravery" ("neminem omnium imperatorum . . . acriorem virtutis spectatorem ac iudicem fuisse," Livy 42.34.7). "You know what a refined judge of beauty I am" ("quom ipsum me noris quam elegans formarum spectator siem" (Terence *Eunuchus* 566). "Ut fulvum spectatur in ignibus aurum" (Ovid *Tristia* 1.5.25).

35. See Plautus *Amphitruo* Prologus 15, *Captivi* 220, *Mercator* 1005, *Miles Gloriosus* 1137. The *testis*, witness, was also a judge. When one called on the gods or other men as "witnesses" one also called on them as "judges." See, for example, Tacitus *Annales* 3.16.

36. Feldman 1962.371. When Cicero wants to assure Appius Claudius that he is committed to acting honorably and doing everything possible to assist him,

he says: "If I leave anything undone, I shall confess to having committed a crime and having covered myself with disgrace" ("si quid a me praetermissum erit, commissum facinus et admissum dedecus confitebor," *ad Familiares* 3.10.2 [May 50 B.C.E.]). Wikan's female informers in Omani Sohar labeled the emotion that kept them from doing dishonorable acts *yistiḥi*. "It could be, in some contexts, translated as having the power to be shamed by one's acts" (1984.647, 650 n. 19). Among the Japanese of the early twentieth century, according to Ruth Benedict, a willingness to be shamed formed part of the complex Japanese notion of honor: "A borrower may pledge his *giri* [duty] to his name when he asks for a loan; a generation ago it was common to phrase it that 'I agree to be publicly laughed at if I fail to repay this sum.' If he failed, he was not literally made a laughingstock; there were no public pillories in Japan. But when the New Year came around, the date on which debts must be paid off, the insolvent debtor might commit suicide to 'clear his name.' New Year's Eve still has its crop of suicides who have taken this means to redeem their reputations" (1946.151).

37. "[Horatius] reprehensans singulos, obsistens obtestansque deum et hominum fidem testabatur nequiquam deserto praesidio eos fugere" ("[Horatius] laying hold of them one by one, standing in their way, and appealing to the faith of gods and men, declared that their flight would avail them nothing if they deserted their posts"). In Plautus's *Mercator* 625–27, Charinus accuses Eutychus of faithlessness (and, by implication, shamelessness) for calling upon the gods as witnesses when the gods are clearly absent (i.e., having abandoned his cause). For the *fetiales* calling upon divine witnesses, see Livy 1.32.7.

38. Beryl Rawson remarks on the intimate proximity of slaves and masters and the former's vulnerability to the gaze of the latter (1991.21–22). Rawson refers to the evidence given by J. J. Hecht that masters were sensitive to being closely observed by their servants and that this imposed on the masters "an onerous constraint" (Hecht 1956). However satirical, the intimate knowledge of his master's follies expressed by Horace's Davus on the Saturnalia (*Sermones* 2.7) and the Roman masters' cruel fear of the servants who knew too much and had "looked upon them naked" in Lucian's *de Mercede* 41 (compare the slaves of Cicero's Clodia: *multarum rerum consciis servis* [*pro Caelio* 29.68]) lead me to believe that the Romans experienced the eyes of their slaves quite differently from those of their mullets and lapdogs.

39. "Se / iudice nemo nocens absolvitur, improba quamvis / gratia fallaci praetoris vicerit urna." Cf. 192–95, Seneca *Phaedra* 159–64.

40. "inspicere tamquam in speculum in vitas omnium / iubeo atque ex aliis sumere exemplum sibi." "It is the part of a young man to show reverence to his elders and to elect for himself the best and most highly approved of them in order that he might advance by their counsel and authority" ("Est igitur adulescentis maiores natu vereri exque iis deligere optimos and probatissimos quorum consilio atque auctoritate nitatur," Cicero *de Officiis* 1.34.122).

41. This is a very interesting sentence. Although its meaning is not alto-

gether clear to me, it suggests that the inner authority would also be your friend, your ally in maintaining your secrets; it would not expose and "desoul" you.

42. "Aliquis vir bonus nobis diligendus est ac semper ante oculos habendus, ut sic tamquam illo spectante vivamus et omnia tamquam illo vidente faciamus. . . . Magna pars peccatorum tollitur, si peccaturis testis adsistit. Aliquem habeat animus, quem vereatur, cuius auctoritate etiam secretum suum sanctius faciat. O felicem illum, qui non praesens tantum, sed etiam cogitatus emendat! O felicem, qui sic aliquem vereri potest, ut ad memoriam quoque eius se componat atque ordinet! Qui sic aliquem vereri potest, cito erit verendus. Elige itaque Catonem. Si hic tibi videtur nimis rigidus, elige remissioris animi virum Laelium. Elige eum, cuius tibi placuit et vita et oratio et ipse animum ante se ferens vultus; illum tibi semper ostende vel custodem vel exemplum." Here you have the internalized "ego ideal" of psychologists such as Melanie Klein or Helen Lewis rather than the hostile "superego" of Freud.

43. The self is always an unstable construct as, in all cultures, the self is construed interpersonally, but for the particular instability of the notion of the self in societies without a highly developed concept of the individual as an independent psychic and moral whole, see Dodds 1951.34, 53, and passim, Kluckhohn 1960.395–96, Morisaki and Gudykunst 1994.60, 62–63. Florence Dupont remarks (1992.11) on the Roman man: "The gaze of others lay in wait for him wherever he went, and whatever he did he would be aware of others sitting in judgement over him. Romans were never alone; there was always a witness to a man's good or wicked actions, even if it were only a neighbour strolling across a terrace, a servant gossiping at the fountain or his wife confiding in her aunt."

44. "Quamquam hoc nescio quo modo dicitur, quasi duo simus, ut alter imperet, alter pareat," Cicero *Tusculanae Disputationes* 2.20.47.

45. Perhaps the most vicious—and effective—modern examples of "Entseelung" through the gaze I have ever read are Jonathan Swift's "Celia shits" poems from the 1730s, especially "The Lady's Dressing Room."

46. "Numquam ego sanguinem expetivi tuum . . . sed abiectum, contemptum, despectum a ceteris, a te ipso desperatum et relictum, circumspectantem omnia, quidquid increpuisset pertimescentem, diffidentem tuis rebus, sine voce, sine libertate, sine auctoritate, sine ulla specie consulari, horrentem, trementem, adulantem omnis videre te volui: vidi."

47. lines 14–15: "hoc tamen est levius, quam quod sum visus ab illo / eveniat nostris hostibus ille pudor!"

48. "Ita traducti sub iugum et quod paene gravius erat per hostium oculos."

49. "Praeter pedes suos transeuntis diligenter ac lente mercantium more considerabat, etiam faciem manu adlevans, si quae pudore submitterent."

50. Radice translation, slightly modified. "nihil tamen gratius, nihil saeculo dignius, quam quod contigit desuper intueri delatorum supina ora retortasque cervices." To "despise" was to "look down upon" (*despicere*).

51. Foucault 1986.24: "Penetration . . . the manly act par excellence." Cf. Walters 1997.29–43.

52. Consider those monsters of *invidia* Ovid's Aglauros (*Metamorphoses* 2.637ff.) and the sisters of Apuleius's Psyche (*Metamorphoses* 4.28–6.24, esp. 5.8–27). If men were to maintain authority over women (or master over slave, adult over child), they had to train the latter to keep their eyes lowered. Just as a woman could insult or challenge a man by looking at him, so she could challenge or insult him by exposing other parts of her body. See chap. six of Barton 2001.

53. "Cynthia prima suis miserum me cepit ocellis /. . . tum mihi constantis deiecit lumina fastus / et caput impositis pressit amor pedibus."

54. "Nam simul quemque conspexerit speciosae formae iuvenem . . . in eum et oculum et animum detorquet. Serit blanditias, invadit spiritum, amoris profundi pedicis aeternis alligat."

55. "Quid ut noverca me intueris aut uti / petita ferro belua?" (*Epodi* 5.9–10).

56. Contrast the averted eyes of the daughters of Pelias wielding their knives on the body of their father (*Metamorphoses* 7.340–42). At least, Tacitus asserts, Nero (unlike Domitian) had the decency to turn his eyes away from the crimes he authorized; he had at least that much shame (*Agricola* 45.5).

57. I owe this citation to David Fredrick. Suetonius's Caligula did not hesitate to watch fathers watching the executions of their sons (*Gaius* 5.168). The brutality of the adolescent general Octavian was expressed, for Suetonius, in his ability both to order and to observe coolly the execution of a father and son (*Augustus* 60).

58. "Se . . . pavisse oculos spectata inimici morte iactavit"; cf. *Historia* 3.44. For more on the consuming eye, see Barton 1993.90. For the benumbing consequence—for the onlooker—of this uninhibited gaze, see Barton 1993. 91–95, 98.

59. "Cum eius cruciatu atque supplicio pascere oculos animumque exsaturare vellent." For the joy of seeing the defeated enemy humiliated and in chains, see 2.5.26.65–66.

60. "Cur tamen hos tu / evasisse putes, quos diri conscia facti / mens habet attonitos et surdo verbere caedit / occultum quatiente animo tortore flagellum? / poena autem vehemens ac multo saevior illis / quas et Caedicius gravis invenit et Rhadamanthus, / nocte dieque suum gestare in pectore testem." Compare Cicero: "It is their own evil deed, their own terror that torments them more than anything else; each of them is harassed and driven to madness by his own crime; his own evil thoughts and *conscientia animi* terrify him" ("Sua quemque fraus et suus terror maxime vexat, suum quemque scelus agitat amentiaque adficit, suae malae cogitationes conscientiaeque animi terrent," *pro Roscio Amerino* 24.67). Tormented by *conscientia*, the son acquitted of his father's murder but burning in his soul is driven to confess (Pseudo-Quintilian *Declamationes Minores* 314.15–17). "Even in the absence of law, *conscientia* punishes" ("Etiam sine lege poena est conscientia," Publilius Syrus 683, Friedrich).

61. "Nam ut imago est animi vultus, sic indices oculi." *Conscientia* made one timid and untrusting (Cicero *in Verrem* 2.5.29.74).

62. For *conscientia* as "guilt," see, for example, Cicero *in Verrem* 2.5.59.155; Pseudo-Quintilian *Declamationes Maiores* 1.10, 10.16, Hakanson; Juvenal *Saturae* 13.192–95.

63. "Nihil est miserius quam animus hominis conscius, / sicut me habet." "Nothing is more miserable than when what we have done causes us shame" ("Nil est miserius quam ubi pudet quod feceris," Publilius Syrus 432, Friedrich).

64. "Spes tamen obscenas animo demittere non est / ausa suo vigilans; placida resoluta quiete / saepe videt quod amat: visa est quoque iungere fratri / corpus et erubuit quamvis sopita iacebat." Compare the *conscius amor* that burns the silent Phaedra in Ovid's *Heroides* 4.52.

65. "Quid poena praesens, conscius mentis pavor / animusque culpa plenus et semet timens?" Cf. 159–64. The emperor Tiberius wrote to the senate in 32 C.E.: "If I know what I should write to you, *patres conscripti*, or in what manner I should write or what I should not write at all at this time, may the gods destroy me more effectively than I feel myself perishing daily." Tacitus remarks: "His crimes and wickedness had rebounded to torment him. How truly the wisest of men used to assert that the souls of despots, if revealed, would show the wounds and mutilations—weals left on the spirit, like lashmarks on a body by cruelty, lust, and malevolence. Neither Tiberius's autocracy nor his isolation could save him from confessing the internal torments that were his retribution" ("'quid scribam vobis, patres conscripti, aut quo modo scribam aut quid omnino non scribam hoc tempore, di me deaeque peius perdant quam perire me cotidie sentio, si scio.' Adeo facinora atque flagitia sua ipsi quoque in supplicium verterant. Neque frustra praestantissimus sapientiae firmare solitus est, si recludantur tyrannorum mentes, posse aspici laniatus et ictus quando ut corpora verberibus, ita saevitia, libidine, malis consultis animus dilaceretur. Quippe Tiberium non fortuna, non solitudines protegebant, quin tormenta pectoris suasque ipse poenas fateretur," Tacitus *Annales* 6.12.1 [= 6.6.1]). I owe this citation to David Fredrick.

66. "Torquet enim adsidua observatio sui et deprendi aliter ac solet metuit . . . non . . . iucunda vita aut secura et semper sub persona viventium."

67. Cf. Suetonius *Gaius* 27. Frederick Douglass tells of the crippling effects of constant surveillance on the life of the slave (1845.56–73).

68. Compare Scheler's formulation: "One is ashamed, finally, before oneself and the God within oneself" (1957.69). Jacques Salvan formulates one of the consequences of Kierkegaard's God not being an object but an alter ego, a Thou, an absolute subject: "Before God, one can only feel guilty of standing, finite and contingent, before the Infinite. Our finitude is our metaphysical sin and we experience it in various kinds of anguish" (1962.xviii). In Sartre's super self-conscious Existential philosophy, one's consciousness is split from one's being. One sees oneself as both the center of the universe and as a shamefully contingent being (Salvan 1962.xiii).

8

Mapping Penetrability in Late Republican and Early Imperial Rome

David Fredrick

Bodies and Space

Any analysis which pretends to be able to encompass every vector of power runs the risk of a certain epistemological imperialism which consists in the presupposition that any given writer might fully stand for and explain the complexities of contemporary power.—*Judith Butler,* Bodies that Matter

Roman cultural historians would do well to keep Judith Butler's caution in mind. As Stephen Dyson observes (1993.205): "Classical archaeologists provide access to several of the most complex cultural systems the world has ever seen." Given the amount and difficulty of the evidence, most cultural historians concentrate on one or two vectors of power (e.g., gender, class, sexuality) at a time, a sensible approach reinforced by the traditional separation between disciplines. Yet power in Rome, like contemporary power, clearly depends on more than one vector.[1] Consequently, analyses of one or several vectors must finally tell us something about the relations between them or lose much of their explanatory force. Though it resists a totalizing account, power nonetheless consists of a sum greater than its parts.

This chapter proposes a synoptic analysis of Roman space, tying together several vectors of power under the rubric of "penetration." It will examine theaters, the Augustan Forum, and the elite house, outlining the common pattern that they collectively impart to the Roman experience of space and the gaze. It does not aim at a complete discussion of these forms or their associated institutions (entertainment, politics, public cult, and the family). Simply put, Roman space reflects and encodes degrees of immersion in the body that vary with social class and gender. It sorts people according to their carnal needs and wants—and their ability to meet them.

In making this argument, I employ a much broader notion of penetration than that found in the Foucauldian model of ancient sexuality. According to this model, sex equals penetration and is seamlessly imbedded in power relations.[2] One might therefore expect a generalized account of power in antiquity as penetration, yet penetration continues to be defined in strictly sexual terms as the insertion of one person's penis into the orifices of another's body. Viewed instead as the concerted action of economics, politics, gender, and sexuality, "penetration" provides a model we can use to question the view of Roman power as pure discourse, as well as the claim that Roman sexuality is utterly different from our own. This essay is thus a step towards the broader notion the Foucauldian model implies (but has so far resisted), and is intended to recuperate the term "penetration" for a less constructionist view of Rome.

As Jonathan Walters puts it (1997.39): "Sexual penetration and beating, those two forms of corporeal assault, are in Roman terms structurally equivalent." Moreover, he notes that, for the elite Roman male, freedom from penetration applies not just to the actual surface of the body but to its social surface as well. The impetus for this essay is the simple observation that sexual penetration and beating are far from the only forms of corporeal assault. The social contours around the elite body addressed by Walters are primarily legal, but freedom from penetration by beating, sexual assault, or sexual propositioning can be correlated with key issues in archaeology and the understanding of space: the establishment of personal boundaries, access to privacy, the means to meet physical needs, and the ability to control the flow of information in one's environment (Sanders 1990.46–51, Bell and Valentine 1995). Movement down the social scale corresponds to an increasing liability to sexual and violent penetration (inevitably, an increasing liability to pain), together with diminished control over one's own space and an increasing level of psychological stress.

In this essay then, "penetration" is defined most fundamentally as the encroachment of one's body upon one's social self. We can regard a wide variety of grating, piquant, agonizing, delightful, or otherwise unignorable physical sensations as penetrating: the pungency of saffron, the spectacle of bears devouring a still-living man, the humiliation of forced oral copulation, the seductive rhythm of an Asiatic-style oration, the pain of a severe beating, starvation. There are several reasons for using the single term "penetration" to embrace this apparently disparate set. First, the Romans themselves link them together. Those who can satisfy their most elaborate wants are but a step away, in moral discourse, from those unable to satisfy their most basic needs. Consequently, those subject to extreme and degrading kinds of pain are also viewed as unable to resist extreme and degrading forms of pleasure, or, conversely, those unable to resist intense pleasure are often deemed fit for the punishments of slaves, though they rarely suffer them in fact (Edwards 1993.173–206). Second, corporeal pleasures and pains are not distributed randomly through Roman space. They have a geography that can often be correlated with the physical features—doors, stairs, walls, podia, tribunals—that appear on our maps. Third, the distribution of pains and pleasures impinges upon a basic psychological fact: the ability of the body in pain or pleasure to cripple one's ability to think, to exist as a discursive subject. "Intense pain . . . destroys a person's self and world, a destruction experienced spatially as either the contraction of the universe down to the immediate vicinity of the body or as the body swelling to fill the entire universe. Intense pain is also language-destroying: as the content of one's world disintegrates; as the self disintegrates, so that which would express and project the self is robbed of its source and its subject" (Scarry 1985.35).

This vulnerable self is the true locus of penetrability, not the bare employment of one's anus, vagina, or mouth in copulation. In general, the closer one is to the body in the form of overwhelming sensation, the more penetrable one is.

Space offers a particularly fruitful approach to the analysis of power because it has both local and general implications, discursive and material aspects. Resist it though I may, the pseudocolonial ranch house I live in shapes my own behavior minutely, while exemplifying a much larger set of shared assumptions and actual patterns of behavior centered on the home. The sequence of rooms (foyer, front living room, dining room, family room, hallway, bedrooms), in its very existence and predictable arrangement, is part of the constitution of my "self" in terms of gender, sexuality, economic status, and ethnicity. Whatever I make of my rooms, their power to construct "me" is partly resident in their architectural forms. I perform "myself" as a subject around, through, and against the terms provided by this space.[3]

Moreover, certain physical sensations—caresses, blows, smells, and tastes—seem to revolve around the home. There would simply be something out of place about whipping egg whites, making love, or chasing children around under the suspended tile ceiling of my humanities building. The home is the place for these bodily activities, the office is not. Even as a simplistic truism, this very split betrays much (though certainly not everything) about the shape of contemporary power. Not the least is the implication that to be in "time" (the world of reason, work, change) is to be out of "body," temporarily above its pleasures, needs, and pains. The split between work and home is often the basis for mapping gender in contemporary culture, a process that is more complex than simply labeling one space masculine and another feminine.[4] The split has different configurations depending on one's location in a given society, while the recent collection by David Bell and Gill Valentine emphasizes the sexing as well as the gendering of space: masculine or feminine, but not queer in either case.[5]

Queer sexuality lacks expression in traditional architecture, producing a constant, physical sense of not fitting in—even in the private space of the home. This is clearly related to verbal and physical attacks on lesbians, gays, and bisexuals: architectural and spatial unease is overlaid with violence and fear as corporeally rather than simply discursively experienced. The invasion via the messages of place comes long before the invasion by blows and lingers long after. The same point can be made about women's fear of violent attack in urban settings (Koskela 1997, with bibliography). Elizabeth Wilson suggests (1991) that much of the criticism of modern cities, where women frequently work and queer communities are visible, is driven by the perception that the spatial separation of masculine from feminine and gay from straight has eroded, leading to sex and gender chaos. In simple terms, this could be expressed as the irruption of the body where it ought not to be.

In several important respects, the mapping of gender and sexuality in contemporary culture may provide a better model for Rome than the penetration model derived from classical Greece. According to the latter, Greek space is binary: the feminine *gynaeceum* is enclosed by the masculine part of the house and the masculine public space of the city; the city is surrounded by orderly ploughed fields, themselves encircled by a wild and mountainous exterior where the boundaries of civilized behavior are tested temporarily but ultimately confirmed ("the terrain of the hunter").[6] Consequently, the "men's club" of the classical polis can easily appear monolithic; there seems to be but one male citizen body, "what Pierre Bourdieu would call the Athenian *habitus*, the set of durable dispositions that generated and organized the practice of masculinity in Attica" (Stewart 1997.63). Sexual roles reflect this binary division of space and *habitus*: "'Active' and 'passive' sexual roles are . . . necessarily isomorphic with superordinate and subordinate social status; hence, an adult, male citizen of Athens can have legitimate sexual relations only with statutory minors (his inferiors not in age but in social and political status)."[7]

By contrast, Pompeian *insulae* illustrate the enormous, but quite complex and varied, disparity in space that defines lived experience in Roman society. Most *insulae* are dominated by several large houses whose finely decorated interiors probably sheltered between two and ten family members and at least twenty slaves. Crowded in between and around the large *domus* are more modest houses and many small shops, poorer in decoration and light, more cramped, poorer in water. As Andrew Wallace-Hadrill notes, "If the classical Greek evidence points to democratic societies with *oikoi* (households) of regular and predictable size, Pompeii and Herculaneum surely suggest a society with very unequal distribution, whether of wealth or of family or household size."[8] It is impossible to attribute a single *habitus* to Pompeii's male citizens. They clearly do not all go to the same places, do the same things, eat the same food, or wear the same clothes. They do not have the same "citizen" gaze, since they do not look from the same places at the same things. If, as Doreen Massey puts it, "the spatial is social relations stretched out," and if, as the penetration model would have it, Roman sexuality is isomorphic with Roman social relations, then Roman sexuality and *habitus* should be as finely graded as space in a Pompeian *insula*.[9]

First-century Rome itself rivaled the modern city in the size, density, and diversity of its population. The dismay of modern commentators in the face of urban disorder can easily be paralleled in the complaints of Roman writers about the *urbs* that so often overwhelmed and horrified them. The number of starving people willing to riot over the grain supply likely exceeded the entire population of Pericles' Attica.[10] This puts issues of personal space, wealth, health, and gender—in short, the body—in a far different context. Crushing poverty rubbed shoulders with extraordinary luxury. Both were characterized in Roman literature by reversals of gender and sexual roles, and both became standard features of the Roman concept of Rome.[11] They were also localized in space: connected with certain areas of the city and, surprisingly, the home. All of this points to the need to map Roman penetrability using a generalized definition and a variable scale to fit Rome's dynamic but highly structured urbanism—in short, a theory of penetration as a general modality of power (the ability to inflict another's body on him- or herself) that receives a specific inflection in sex. The sexually penetrated body in Roman culture has already been penetrated by other means (Catullus 59):

> Bononiensis Rufa Rufulum fellat,
> uxor Meneni, saepe quam in sepulcretis
> vidistis ipso rapere de rogo cenam,
> cum devolutum ex igne prosequens panem
> ab semiraso tunderetur ustore.

> Rufa from Bologna, the wife of Menenius, sucks
> Rufulus. You've often seen her in the graveyards
> snatching a "feast" from the funeral pyre, when she
> chased after a loaf rolling down from the fire,
> she was beaten by the half-shaven corpse-burner.[12]

In this Catullan vignette, Rufa starves, submits to oral sex, and is beaten. Her penetrability through sex and violence is not distinct from her hunger; what she must "eat" sexually is part of the same complex cultural system that denies her food. There is clearly distance between those writing and reading this poem and the woman it depicts, between those at the highest level of discourse and those overwhelmed by the body practically to the point of death. In the graded pyramid of Roman society, Rufa is very close to the bottom and Catullus very close to the top. This pyramid is dispersed across the Roman city (Rome itself and towns like Pompeii) through a series of architectural forms that represent real barriers. Rufa cannot run into Cicero's house and take the mullet from his table, and even the corpse-burner in the graveyard beats her for stealing a crust of bread.

Well-to-do freedmen, meanwhile, call attention to the importance of social mobility. Slaves of all kinds were often freed, becoming citizens; many freedmen were assisted in their trade by their former owners, now their patrons. If and when they became prosperous, their tastes in housing, clothing, food, and art emulated, to a certain extent, the tastes of the elite. This is a complicated issue. Read as attempts to ape elite style, freedmen's houses in Pompeii provide good examples of genuinely bad taste, a bad taste consistent with the clumsy excess associated with freedmen in literary satire.[13] In their funerary inscriptions, moreover, freedmen often proclaim their occupations (usually manual labor or trade) and broadcast material success obtained through hard work.[14] Sandra Joshel notes that this is an important aspect of their transitional status. They identify themselves through the kinds of labor that elite writers denigrate because, from the perspective of the landed elite, labor for money contaminates the self with a quasi-servile relation to the body. From the standpoint of the prosperous freedmen, however, work is what made them successful and distinguishes them from slaves and the free poor.[15] The body of the successful freedman was thus situated somewhere between the absolute dependence and lack of physical integrity of the slave and the ideal of independence and impenetrability of the established elite.

What are we to make of the sexuality of this group? On the one hand, freedmen clearly remain penetrable, subject to sexual advances and even physical assault by their former owners, as well as to the demands of their occupations.[16] On the other, they just as clearly possess the means to be penetrators in their own right. They own slaves, sometimes in substantial numbers, whom they may beat, starve, or violate sexually. Many can afford luxuries on a scale approaching that of the elite. Satire asserts that this only leads them to resubmerge themselves, through gluttony and greed, in their own bodies. Without agreeing that wealthy freedmen were naturally boors, we should wonder if their attitude toward food, clothing, art, and sexuality was, like their attitude toward work, different from that of the elite. We might then begin to view their aesthetic "mistakes" positively. Trimalchio's numerous "blunders" may be the result of a deliberate strategy of evoking and then breaking elite rules of decoration and deportment because he views his own body, and theirs, differently.[17]

In other words, the sexuality of freedmen, like their aesthetic tastes, may not be based on a clean social and psychological transformation from penetrated to penetrator. They may have a collective sense of themselves as "in between" and a shared *habitus* distinct, like their houses and funerary monuments, from that of the free poor or the established elite. A third gender, "boy," has been suggested for classical antiquity, a designation that gives formal recognition to the role of the adolescent male as penetrable, despite his anatomical gender.[18] Perhaps a third—or fourth—gender should be proposed for successful Roman freedmen, based on the ambiguities of their political and economic position rather than an ambiguity of age. This would simply recognize that, just as successful freedmen do not clearly belong to one side or the other of most social binaries (free versus slave, rich versus poor, noble versus humble), their sexuality is similarly unpolarized. They are somewhat penetrable, by a mixture of choice and force, in a number of areas having to do with physical desires and needs (food, sex, violence, sensual pleasure), as opposed to slaves, who are necessarily, forcefully penetrable in all of these areas, and the elite, who are penetrable in them only by choice or by the compulsion of a flawed inner character.

Theater

Roman theaters and amphitheaters take the pyramid of Roman social relations and stand it on its head, with the base corresponding to the highest tier of seats, and its apex to the lowest tier and the imperial box, both closest to the circle of the arena itself or the stage. "It was therefore decreed by the senate that whenever a public spectacle was put on anywhere, the first rank of seats should be left vacant for senators, while, at Rome, Augustus forbade the ambassadors of free and allied states to sit in the orchestra when he found out that some of them were freedmen. He divided soldiers from ordinary citizens, gave a separate set of seats to plebeian married men, and a wedge of seats to boys, right next to their tutors. He forbade anyone who lacked a citizen's toga to sit in the middle tier, and he did not allow women, who before had sat everywhere, to watch even the gladiators from anywhere but the upper seats."[19]

As Gunderson notes, "With each subdivision and distinction, the arena's seating produces a more careful and comprehensive map of Roman society."[20] He also points out that this map is disproportionate: a large percentage of the total number of *nobiles* (knights and senators) are provided a seat, while a quite small percentage of poorer Romans and women are able to attend. The result is a kind of spatial ruse. While women and the poor occupy what seem to be the largest ring of seats, they are crowded into them in relation to their total numbers; similarly, knights and senators occupy the smaller seating rings closest to the bottom, but, in fact, much more space is available to them in relation to their numbers. Not only is the space closer to the sand privileged in terms of its view, but there is, in social terms, considerably more of it.[21] As one moves up through the stands, the social contours of the body shrink. On the arena sand itself, these contours contract absolutely.

The point is not simply that the condemned die. The progression of a typical day, from animal hunts to executions to gladiatorial combat, places an increasing premium on the intensity and sophistication of the victims' reaction to fear, pain, and death. First, the more dangerous and socially complex animals (lions, leopards, bears) hunt down those that lack the quasi-human ability to hunt. Next, the predators themselves are killed by superior human hunters. Finally, the first act is repeated with human subjects in the place of antelope and ostrich.[22] When the flesh is opened by the animals' teeth, spatial relations that are so crucial to human life in an ordered environment are simply obliterated, and the victims' ability to have a world constructed by discourse is visibly destroyed. A criminal cast in the role of the famous bandit Laureolus is nailed to a cross and mauled by a bear; our source observes, "His lacerated limbs were yet alive, pieces dripping with blood, and in his whole body there was nowhere a body."[23] In an apparent accident, a dancer playing the role of Icarus makes his first attempt at flight, either leaping aloft or hoisted up by a crane. He misses the net, or his rope snaps, and he plunges to his death, spattering the emperor Nero in his front-row seat.[24]

Intentional or not, the death of this actor illustrates well the thematics of body and space in mythological executions. When he begins his flight as Icarus, the actor floats through a magically expanded world, free of spatial constraints. At the moment he falls, his body reasserts itself as a weight that obliterates this artificial world and puts only itself in its place. It is then broken open, staining the spectator who, by his very proximity, commands the most expansive social space. The radical diminution of the victim's world from magical freedom to nothing but pain provides the *punctum* for another of Martial's epigrams (*Spectacula* 8): "Torn limb from limb by a Lucanian bear, Daedalus, how you wish you had your wings right now."

The space of the sand is not simply constructed as Other, non-Roman and uncivilized. It is crowded with civilized artifice: moving cliffs, trap doors, sacred groves, saffron mountains, and familiar stories, some from Roman history. All of this is part of the instrumentation of torture. The victims are bludgeoned with mythology, often in "childish" or burlesqued forms, so that it is not only the bear that dismembers them but the mythological setting itself, as if contemporary torturers were to use Mother Goose for their *mise en scène*.

> Whatever they say Mt. Rhodope—Orpheus's theater—admired,
>   the sand, Caesar, has exhibited for you.
> Crags crept along and marvelous forests ran about—
>   people think the Hesperides' grove was just like that.
> Mixed in with the domestic herd was every kind of wild beast,
>   and birds hovered in flocks above the bard.
> But he himself lay there, dismembered by a bear (that philistine):
>   this thing alone happened contrary to the tale.[25]

As the spectators "read" this myth, they can delight in a shared code, a marvelous, and marvelously intelligible, world. "Orpheus," meanwhile, cannot read, think, or speak coherently at all. His body has become an engulfing, hideously involuntary presence.

Different types of contemporary torture—in fact incomprehensible forms of suffering—have grotesquely familiar names: "the Motorola," "the plane ride," "the birthday party." In the Roman games, the dismemberment of a human being becomes "the Prometheus," a woman's sexual mutilation becomes "the Pasiphae," the immolation of a man "the irritating shirt."[26] Meanwhile, mythology also represents the most privileged type of education and social refinement. In his temporary flight, "Icarus" enacts what every child knows, but also what the *boni* know best. Arrayed as tyrant, demigod, or Orpheus, the victim briefly becomes an aristocrat manqué, rising, impossibly, a step above the knights and senators in the closest rows.

As the victims' world collapses, the spectators' world expands, but not to the same extent or in the same way. In mapping status and gender so carefully, the arena maps penetrability, not only by sexuality and violence, but by host of other experiences: hunger, fatigue, disease, and pleasure.[27] Those most penetrable by the first two are also, in general, more liable to the latter. The arena invites visceral reactions, and our sources (elite men) expect these to be distributed hierarchically: those in the highest, most distant seats are condemned for their simpleminded absorption. "But some are no different than little children; often, when they see criminals at the spectacles wrapped in golden tunics and purple cloaks, doing Pyrrhic dances, they are agog and gaze at them in wonder as if they were blessed—until they are witnessed punctured, whipped, and going up in flames from those garlands and elaborate costumes."[28]

At the beginning of his seventh letter, Seneca declares what one ought to avoid most: *turbam*, "the crowd." He illustrates its ability to corrupt by citing his own experience at the games. "Nothing is as damaging to good morals as sitting around at some spectacle. Easily then through pleasure the vices creep in" (*Epistulae* 7.3). The midday mob demands that condemned criminals slaughter each other without the benefit of skill or defensive armor. They cry out, "Kill him, whip him, burn him!" with a ferocity that shakes the elite philosopher to his core.[29] As he admits, he finds it very difficult not to succumb to their intense passions. They "read" the arena not only with their eyes but with their bodies, as each blow to the condemned becomes a source of overwhelming pleasure. Augustine's Alypius is seduced by the roar of the crowd into opening his eyes, and the sight reduces him to practically all body. He is over-come, wounded, riveted, mad, intoxicated: "He found delight in the mur-derous contest and was inebriated by bloodthirsty pleasure" (Augustine *Conf.* 7.13, trans. Chadwick).

This is clearly a class-based view of the potential for extreme, over-whelming pleasure at the sight of the victims' pain, a pleasure that comes from the upper seats and moves down (cf. Edwards 1997.83–85). If, through the spectacle, the poor escape awareness of their own physical misery, it is replaced by a pleasure whose intensity rivets them to their bodies just the same. Meanwhile, the elite man is—or would like to be—free, like Seneca, to have an internal discussion with himself about the propriety of all this, or, like Julius Caesar, to answer his correspondence, or, like Martial, to jot down witty observations. "The naive exhibition-ism of 'conspicuous consumption,' which seeks distinction in the crude display of ill-mastered luxury, is nothing compared to the unique capac-ity of the pure gaze, a quasi-creative power which sets the aesthete apart from the common herd by a radical difference which seems to be in-scribed 'in persons'" (Bourdieu 1984.31).

Though the torture and killing of human beings was uncommon on the dramatic stage, the spatial and visual cone of the theater was funda-mentally similar to that of the arena. Again knights and senators were seated in the lowest rows with the best view of the performance; on stage were the actors.[30] Often they were highly skilled performers but nonetheless slaves or *infames*, barred from participation in military, legal, and political life. They remained subject to corporal punishment even if they were Roman citizens, and they were customarily regarded as pros-titutes, sexually penetrable whether male or female. The actor sold his or her body, and, for this reason, no matter how sensational or extrava-gant the role played, he or she was always subject to the body.[31] Conse-quently, though they might not be eaten or incinerated onstage, their po-sition was structurally similar to that of the victims in fatal charades: they attract awe and admiration, but they perform, ultimately, under physi-cal compulsion.

As Catharine Edwards points out, the intense pleasure of watching theatrical performances was of a piece with that of the games. Both were considered sensual and low rather than intellectual and noble, and, in this regard, both were linked with taverns, gambling, and prostitution. She observes (1997.84): "These were the pleasures of those whose base na-tures prevented them from enjoying the refined pleasures of the mind—or so it was conveniently believed by the educated elite." Yet the "base

natures" of the poor were more than the empty constructions of aristocratic discourse. They were created by Roman urban space precisely as
it is mapped out in theater seating. What shrank the world of those in
the back was, in part, the effect of the physical abuse most of them received by virtue of where they lived and what they did. What kept them
from the "pleasures of the mind" was not just an impalpable aristocratic
prejudice but the cumulative ability of power to make their bodies ever-
present to them.

Forum

The theater does not offer a single, monolithic "Roman" gaze,
nor an absolute opposition between the penetrable and the impenetrable. Instead, the effect of looking is given a hierarchical structure as the
self/body mix is mapped across the seats, from bottom to top, as a range
between proper discipline and intoxicated delight. This structure offers
useful comparisons with two other kinds of space, the Forum of Augustus and the Roman house.

The Forum of Augustus (fig. 8.1) was vowed in 42 B.C.E. and finally
dedicated forty years later.[32] It commemorated, initially, the victory of
Octavian over Caesar's assassins and, later, the return of the standards
taken by the Parthians from Crassus. Architecturally, it reproduces much
that is found in the earlier Julian Forum: a rectangular space enclosed by
porticoes on three sides with a temple building centered at the far end.
These features reflect religious requirements: a rectangular *templum* on
the ground, corresponding to the *templum* inscribed in the sky by the
augur, and an *aedes*, a temple building in the center rear, to provide a platform for augury and an altar for sacrifice.[33] The Forum of Augustus also
contains some striking new features, but these complement rather than
obscure its relation to the fundamental Roman pattern of open areas enclosed by temples and porticoes. It synthesizes the architecture that had
always framed elite life, and it does much to announce and enforce the
triumph of the elite man over his own body and his power over the bodies of others. Yet by its very existence, and the order it imposes on its inherited visual repertoire, the Augustan Forum intimates new and lasting
holes in the social contours of the elite.

The Forum of Augustus extends its space laterally through the addition of hemicycles on the northwest and southeast side. Each hemicy-
cle provides an expanded niche within which sculptures are centrally
placed: on the north, the family group of Aeneas, on the south, Romulus with the spoils of Akron. Together the two hemicycles look emphat-

Figure 8.1 Model of the Forum of Augustus.

ically toward the Temple of Mars Ultor, with a statue of Augustus centrally placed on its porch. The figures of Aeneas and Romulus cap the
second innovation in the Augustan Forum, the statues of the *summi viri*
("greatest men") located in niches along the rear walls of the north and
south porticoes. The *summi viri* in the north portico were drawn from
the family of the *Iulii*; those in the south represented the great families
of the republic. Each had a caption below giving his name, his offices,
and his achievements on behalf of the state. The *summi viri*, in turn, were
complemented by a third innovation, the addition of a row of caryatids
at the attic level of the porticoes, centered, like the *summi viri* in their
niches, between the columns below. In between the caryatids were marble shields depicting, alternately, Zeus Ammon and a Gaul with a torque.

Augustus relocated to his Forum the rituals of the removal of the
bulla, an apotropaic phallic amulet that protected freeborn elite children,
and the donning of the *toga virilis*. He also moved to the Temple of Mars
senate meetings concerned with the declaration of war and the awarding
of triumphs. From this temple, generals would now depart to their new
provinces, and those who triumphed would dedicate their scepter and
crown there. Their statues in bronze, erected in the Forum, would complement the rows of triumphant *viri* from the past standing in both porticoes.

It seems difficult to imagine a more complete realization of the space
of the "impenetrable" penetrators, and Barbara Kellum has recently ar-

gued that the plan of the Augustan Forum is intentionally phallic (1996 and 1997.165–73). While her evidence that its "two bulging *exedrae* and projecting forecourt" were meant to evoke an erect penis is circumstantial, the connection of the Augustan Forum with the male body seems beyond dispute. As a piece of anthropocentric architecture, it is not alone. Amy Richlin suggests that the Romans may have conceptualized the Roman Forum itself in terms of the human body, with the Capitolium and curia as its head, the cloaca maxima as its guts, and the Regia and Shrine of the Vestals as its reproductive organs. This notion coincides with Emily Gowers's analysis of metaphors for the entire city of Rome as a human body.[34]

More questionable is Kellum's use of the Foucauldian model of sexuality for Augustan society. Kellum assembles a wide variety of evidence to make the point that the Romans, since they connected power closely with sexuality, were not surprised by sexual references in political contexts, including the Augustan Forum, and they appreciated political references in their sexual humor. She concludes (1997.181): "The usefulness of gender as a category of analysis is in the potential it holds for questioning the fixity of binary absolutes, whether it is the supposed opposition between male and female, between official and private, between 'high' and 'low' art, or between the ribald and the serious."

Absent from this list are the terms "penetrator" and "penetrated," and, indeed, Kellum maintains that the binary opposition of sexual roles defines "the nature of the phallus as a signifier in the Roman sphere."[35] While other binary absolutes have been destabilized, Rome's population remains split between these two positions. Also retained is the notion that penetrability ("receiving") is primarily a question of sexual role-playing. Hence her conclusion that "the clever allusion, the simultaneous concealing and revealing of art, the familiarity with figured speech were not simply the adversarial strategies of beleaguered writers, but the cultural strategies of the entire population, emperor and freedperson alike" (Kellum 1997.181). In this attractive picture, all Romans are equally in discourse despite lying on opposite sides of the penetrator versus penetrated divide. Some are well-fed and housed (Catullus), and others unhoused and starving (Rufa), but all are equally clever cultural strategists. I would argue to the contrary that penetration, to the extent that it forced the penetrated to be aware of their bodies, made it difficult if not impossible for a substantial number of Romans to play the game of concealing and revealing very well. The Forum of Augustus is, in part, a monument to this fact.

As Kellum points out (1997.168), its anthropocentric shape incorporates rectilinear and circular forms, thus expressing both a linear and circular conception of time. It confers upon the *summi viri* a transcendence of the body and death, inscribing the social contours of the elite self in stone. The "best men," according to their own fictions, had denied themselves quotidian physical pleasures in pursuit of "history," and they had won it, seemingly forever.[36] In linear terms, this "forever" stretches from Aeneas to Romulus through the *summi viri* to Augustus; walking down the porticoes, one seems to measure history's length. At the same time, Roman history turns around upon itself. Aeneas anticipates Augustus, who completes the destiny for Roman rule unrolled in the *Aeneid*. Hence Aeneas is represented, in his niche, carrying his father Anchises on his shoulders and leading his son Iulus by the hand.[37] A circular conception of history is harder to appreciate kinesthetically, that is, through the medium of one's body as it moves through space, because it asks the walking viewer to accept that, by returning to the same place, he has returned to the same time. To put it another way, a circular conception of history is beyond the physical grasp of someone moving around the periphery of the Forum, whose body can occupy only a single point at any given time. The Forum of Augustus thus invites one to stroll through Roman history from *vir* to *vir*, while realizing that its beginning and ending are ideologically equivalent, to recognize the paradox of *imperium sine fine* with one's body.

Obviously, not everyone has equivalent access to this kind of space/time. Creusa, Iulus's mother, is notably missing from Aeneas's sculptural group, and the rear end of the Augustan Forum is sealed off from the Subura, a residential slum, by a firewall one hundred feet high. Not only did the poorest Romans typically not enter the Augustan Forum physically, they could not even see it (Zanker 1988.155–56). And vice versa. As much as they complain about the intense emotions of the crowd in the theater, here the *viri* seem immune. Thus the inappropriate irruption of the body was all the more evident when the emperor Claudius, "most eager for food and wine at whatever place and time," while presiding over cases in the Forum, was struck (*ictus*) by the smell of a feast being prepared for the Salii in the Temple of Mars. He abandoned his tribunal and reclined with the priests, stripping their banquet of whatever sacred pretext it possessed.[38] True or not, the vignette illustrates the distance elite men were supposed to maintain from their appetites, the self-disciplined *habitus* to which the Augustan Forum is a shrine. This *habitus* depends on the systematic denial of basic needs to many slaves and the poor, whose self-control in the face of food and drink is consequently neither expected nor even possible.

In this respect, the immense wall at the back becomes, like the lowest bank of seats in the arena, a spatial ruse. While it screens out the poor residential quarter of the Subura, and in its twists and turns seems to respect the rights of smaller property owners, it actually encloses that space symbolically and marks its shrinkage conceptually in comparison to the enormous open space consumed by the Forum—much the way the acts of the *summi viri* enclose the lives of humbler Romans. At the same time, caryatids—smaller, anonymous, less significant bodies—hold up the attic roof. The female body does not provide the proportions for space; it does not represent, like the male body, a principle of order, a challenging juxtaposition of linear and circular time through which the body itself might be transcended. Rather, it is controlled and enclosed within—or as— space itself. Thus the caryatids define the penetrable bodies upon which the weight of the Augustan Forum rests. Even less visible, Rome's enemies have apparently been swallowed altogether, leaving in their place shields that stand for the conquered peoples of east and west. In the very fabrics used to construct the Forum, the enclosed world is represented.[39] Rome's empire was acquired through physical agony, through the reduction of millions of selves to bodies, first in war and then through their absorption into Roman social and economic space.[40] However, neither the caryatids nor barbarians are absolutely excluded, any more than the Subura is by the immense rear wall. Just as in the arena, world-destroying pain must be visibly present for this architectural form to create its meaning.

As in the building, so, too, in the body.[41] John Stambaugh has summarized (1988.214–16) the enduring formal qualities of the Roman temple: axiality, frontality, elevation. These qualities are comparable to the self-presentation of the elite male body as it is idealized in oratorical training and framed in dress by the toga (Cicero *de Oratore* 18.59): "The first-class orator will use gestures, but never to excess, his posture will be erect and elevated . . . There should be no unmanly softness in the neck, and the fingers should not make delicate gestures or move in time with the rhythm. He will instead regulate himself with his entire torso by the vigorous and manly modulation of his upper body."

Like a professional business suit, the toga imposes a sobering *habitus* on its wearer, restricting gait, emphasizing frontal presentation, and limiting the movement of the arms. Augustus eventually required that the aediles forbid anyone from appearing in Rome's fora "if not in a toga, with arms properly arranged" (*nisi positis lacertis togatum*, Suetonius *Aug.*

40).[42] If enforced, this must have slowed the pace of things considerably—an effect not unrelated to Augustus's architectural program. Maud Gleason's analysis (1995.55–130) of the medical and dietary aspects of the orator's training is important here: by regular practice of the proper style of declamation, the orator "aerated his flesh," drawing in air through his pores so as to dry his body and emphasize its virile qualities. Similarly, certain foods were to be eaten or avoided because they desiccated the body or made it too moist. The outward performance must be manly in order to represent truthfully the ordered interior.

As Claudius's impromptu feast demonstrates, transcending the body is no easy thing. The expanded social contours of the elite man, the measure of a conquered world, expose him to an equally expansive and dangerous realm of pleasure. One of the most common charges in oratory is that one's opponent conceals just such a secret world within and so corrupts the public spaces he seeks to occupy (Edwards 1993, Corbeill 1997). As Anthony Corbeill describes in his chapter in this volume, some popular politicians (*populares*) may have shaped their deportment precisely in order to invite such charges. They rejected the measured gestures, walk, and rhetoric of "the best" in favor of a rapid, effeminate walk, excessive and mannered gestures, and an extravagant style. As a result, they were frequently branded *cinaedi* by their opponents. It is tempting to speculate that the egregious physical display of these politicians connected with their target audience precisely because the latter were so close to the body themselves. At the same time, the ability of the mob to control the Roman Forum in the late republic could produce the nightmare image of the elite politician, in this case Cicero's brother, literally submerged in lower-class bodies (Cicero *pro Sestio* 76): "Nevertheless he submitted to the unspeakable violence of those foul thugs, and, although he had come to plead for the safety of his brother, beaten from the rostrum, he lay down in the Comitium and covered himself with the bodies of slaves and freedmen; he preserved his life by escaping under the cover of night rather than with laws and justice."

The Augustan Forum gives a clear message that such clashes between optimates and popular politicians are a thing of the past.[43] Nonetheless, the subordination of Roman history to the Julian family in the Augustan Forum points to the existence of a new kind of coercion in public life. As impenetrable as the *summi viri* appear in their statues, the proscriptions, especially the beheading of Cicero, had shown that the physical integrity of the elite was now threatened from above.[44] Augustus's very ability to create such a vast, monumentally organized space in the crowded heart of the city underscores their penetrability. Whose phallus, after all, is being planted in the center of Rome? If, as Kellum argues (1997.177–78), the Forum of Augustus "penetrates" the Julian Forum below it, reversing the sexual relation alleged between Caesar and the youthful Octavian, the *summi viri* must ultimately find themselves at the bottom of the chain, playing the receiving role to the Julian gens. Behind the explicit differences between the *summi viri* and the caryatids is an implicit, terrorizing equation.

Domus

Cicero uses a handy geography to map out, across urban space, Antony's internal corruption: the arena sand, the brothel, and the stage (*Philippicae* 2). Thus he hints at something the orator tries consistently to exclude from himself: an interior space liable to penetration, a space of darkness and corruption seen as feminine, slavish, or bestial.[45] Yet, as Richlin notes (1996), "the excluded subject is there even if it is not supposed to be," a remark that might be rephrased in this context: "the excluded body is there even if it is not supposed to be." Antony's occupation of Pompey's house is described in polarized terms of decency and license; the *domus* becomes at one stroke a brothel. In ordinary practice, the space of the house was more finely distributed between these extremes. A spatial and visual cone, corresponding to relative degrees of status and therefore penetrability, was clearly established. From the *fauces*, one gazed across the atrium, open to all visitors, to the *tablinum*, an elevated platform where the owner of the house received clients, to the peristyle garden, where guests could normally come only by invitation. Invisible to the disinterested gaze were the quarters of the slaves, the most penetrable (fig. 8.2). As Andrew Wallace-Hadrill has shown (1994.38–61), the articulation of space in the house corresponds to the progression of social status from slaves to freedmen to clients to *amici* (friends of elite standing) to *familiares*, close friends and the owner's family.

The *domus* was one of the most important Roman institutions through which goods and services were delivered. While it is difficult to calculate precisely what percentage of Rome's, or Pompeii's, population lived in which kind of house, there is little doubt that a substantial fraction in the late republic and early empire received their food, shelter, and clothing in the spatial context of the elite house (Wallace-Hadrill 1994.91–117). A gender-based distribution of space and goods in the house is not clear from the evidence, but a distribution based on social rank is beyond doubt. As light, decoration, and visibility decreased with

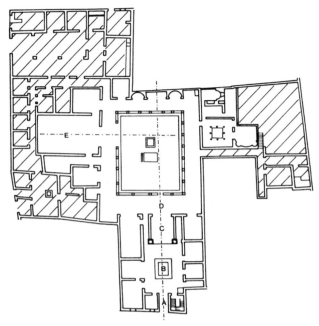

Figure 8.2 Plan of the House of Menander from Pompeii, with the service areas shaded.

decreasing status and access to the *dominus*, so, too, the quality of food, clothing, and hygiene. It is very difficult to trace inequalities of this kind through the archaeological record and so establish firmly the degree and distribution of hunger, exhaustion, or exposure in the "typical" elite house. Nonetheless, the literary evidence gives a consistent picture of domestic slaves as hungry, dirty, and beatable, especially those occupied with menial tasks: unskilled food preparation, cleaning, stoking fires, and hauling (Foss 1995.7–8).

One of the most privileged spaces in the house, the dining room, paradoxically subjected the hierarchy of bodies and food distribution to considerable stress. Here the ambivalence of elite Romans about bodily pleasure conflicted with the need to display and consume luxury goods. Expanded social contours, which in moral discourse were expected to correspond with a self-discipline that minimized the body's hold on the self, demanded here direct contact with the pleasures of the flesh. These threatened to swell the physical body, deepening its hold on the self.[46] At the same time, despite the contempt for food as a literary subject and the condemnation of its pleasures in philosophy, eating was not a minor social activity, and the dining room was not a peripheral space.[47] It was one of the most important focal points for patronage and indispensable to the expression of elite status (Wallace-Hadrill 1994.143–74). Moreover, eating, and especially cooking, were intimately associated with the household cult of the Lares, centered on the hearth (Foss 1997). This guaranteed that the elaborate dining habits of the late republic and early empire could not help but be measured against the past, a past enshrined in domestic rituals associated with food.[48] Finally, the same visual/spatial principle at work in theaters and fora, the graded pyramid of status, continues to apply at the microlevel in the triclinium. The host and most distinguished guest were positioned in the top left corner, the *locus consularis*, with the other guests and family members arranged in a descending order from this apex. The *locus consularis* often commanded the best view out of the dining room to the statues, paintings, and fountains in the garden, and its privileged spatial position was matched by concern about similar inequalities in the distribution of food and wine.[49]

Cicero assures us that the pleasures of dining should be primarily mental: "I am not thinking of the physical pleasure, but of community, of life and habit, and of mental recreation, of which conversation is the most effective agent; and conversation is most agreeable at dinner parties" (*ad Familiares* 9.23.3, trans. Shackleton Bailey). The rest of the literary record, and the decoration of the triclinia themselves, indicates that they often were not. What emerges instead is a picture of pleasure threatening to penetrate the diner through every available route (Edwards 1993.173–206). Given the combined impact of the paintings, gardens, statues, clothing, attractive slaves, perfume, food, and entertainment, it is not surprising that one of the most common charges in oratory is that one's opponent had been corrupted by the atmosphere of the triclinium into allowing himself to be penetrated sexually.[50] The truth of this allegation with respect to any particular individual is beside the point. It describes a truth about the setting and the space as the Romans saw it.

The representation of food in contemporary culture is often strongly erotic. As David Bell and Gill Valentine point out (1997.54–56), such images depend on the use of the mouth as a locus of pleasure in its activities (chewing, sucking, licking, biting), as well as its confusion with other orifices. They suggest a label for the genre, "gastroporn." This is a provocative but perhaps not inappropriate description of the elite Roman triclinium, with its overlap of gastronomic, sexual, and visual pleasures

Figure 8.3 Selene and Endymion, from the House of the Ara
Maxima, Pompeii.

and its fascination with pleasure and pain as bodily invasions of the self.
The Romans frequently had depictions of copulation on their cups and
dishes.[51] In wall painting, attractive female bodies are commonly exhibited as objects of the gaze, as are attractive males (see fig. 8.3). Narcissus is the most common subject in Pompeii, and paintings that depict
rape are nearly as common.[52]

From the fetishizing and sadistic modes of visual pleasure in these
paintings, diners could shift their gaze—and, perhaps, their hands—to
the bodies of the slaves serving them. "Did a slave drop a cup?—then box
his ears. Steal sweetmeats off the platter he was passing?—then inflict a
blow. Did he pinch two napkins?—then scald him with burning iron. Is
he slow with the hot water?—then give him 300 lashes."[53]

These punishments are not occasional and unnecessary disruptions
of an otherwise humane evening. The sexual display, hunger, and pain of
the slaves are required to set off the pleasures of the diners. Yet that "gastropornographic" pleasure is itself a problem. The dinner party demands
consumption, and, indeed, it seems to have aimed at—and nonetheless
feared and denied—an intensity of pleasure to rival the excruciating misery that often defined the bottom of the Roman social scale.

Figure 8.4 Pan and Hermaphroditus, from the House of the
Dioscuri, Pompeii.

This may help explain a curious feature of the paintings in Roman
dining rooms. Unlike narrative cinema in Laura Mulvey's well-known
analysis (1975), the contradictions between scopophilia and voyeurism
are not resolved in these paintings but accentuated. The viewer is invited
to identify, alternately, with both penetrating and penetrated positions;
indeed, the closer these are brought together (see fig. 8.4), the more
closely these paintings reflect the fact that elite status, which otherwise
demands distance between self and body, here demands that the self be
invited into the body, if only so it can resist. Pan approaches what he
takes to be a sleeping maenad, but when he attempts to rape "her," "she"
awakes with an erection and takes hold of his arm, inviting him into the
different, perhaps more absorbing, role of the penetrated.[54] Pan throws
up his hand—a neat visual rhyme with Hermaphroditus's erection—and
turns away. This is not the only reaction possible. In a painting in the
House of the Vettii, Silenus gazes down at Hermaphroditus's face and
lap, apparently in admiration and anticipation.

In collapsing the distinction between penetrator and penetrated, the
paintings of Endymion and Hermaphroditus point to the possibility of
cross-gender identification in the gaze and rape paintings. They also
elide the distinction between pleasure and pain as equivalent invasions

of the body. In this capacity, the paintings confirm the combined, gastropornographic effect of the tactile and visual pleasures concentrated in the dining room.[55] The ability to display the extensive paraphernalia of Roman dining demonstrates the expanded social contours of the host; at the same time, the closeness of the body, in the taste of the food or the pain of the slaves, in the eagerness of Hermaphroditus or Daphne's terror, in the music of poetic verse or in the couple depicted copulating on one's cup, is precisely what measures the interior virtue of the *vir* who can resist. Or vice versa: the ideal of resistance, no doubt often failed, measures the intensity of pleasure.

Conclusion

There is a fundamental "scopic regime" for Rome in the late republican and early imperial periods, a spatial and visual cone or pyramid terminating in an area—the senators' seats, the orators' platform, the triclinia of elite houses—where most people simply cannot go. Whether one walks into a house, a theater, or one of the fora, this is the bedrock of physical and spatial experience: at the apex, "impenetrable" penetrators, elite men; at the base, the most penetrable: the least important slaves and the poor free of either gender. The farther one is from the apex, the closer one is to the body as a source of irritation and pain, and so the more precarious is one's hold on discourse, on subjectivity as the ability to assert oneself outside the limit of one's body. Toward the top of the apex, one is close to entering pure time where all one does is a kind of history: simultaneously an expression of one's present influence over events near and far and (connecting past to future) one's ability to be a model for others' behavior. As Pierre Bourdieu puts it (1984.177): "The same economy of means is found in body language: here, too, agitation and haste, grimaces and gesticulation are opposed to slowness . . . to the restraint and impassivity which signify elevation. Even the field of primary tastes is organized according to the fundamental opposition, with the antithesis between quantity and quality, belly and palate, matter and manners, substance and form."

Between the bottom of the pyramid and the top there are many gradations and areas of confusion rather than a simple division between "penetrator" and "penetrated." Moreover, one's place in the pyramid is not primarily a question of sexual role but of the degree to which the body penetrates the self in a multitude of ways. The definition of the *vir* can thus be restated more simply as freedom from or transcendence of the body, penetrated as it is by a host of pleasures and pains. This freedom was conspicuously tested, and also demonstrated, in the dining room, where the need to express one's status through an elaborate apparatus of pleasure conflicted with the inevitable tendency of the body in pleasure to penetrate the self.

How different is all this? It seems that relative distance from the body remains an important indicator of social status today. "But what remains the constant element throughout historical variation is the *construction* of body as something apart from the true self . . . and as undermining the best efforts of that self. That which is not-body is the highest, the best, the noblest, the closest to God; that which is body is the albatross, the heavy drag on self-realization" (Bordo 1993.5, original italics).

This element remains constant partly because the body's ability to be a drag on the self is, in the most extreme instances, beyond construction. Intense pain and intense pleasure are not simply what a culture makes of them. The complex act of forcing people to live close to their bodies by denying them food, shelter, or medical care, by restricting or compelling their labor, by restricting their access to knowledge, by terrorizing them through physical or sexual assault, remains central to how the spaces of contemporary power—be they houses, cities, or transnational economies—are organized. Sexual penetrability was not disembedded from the social, political, and economic exercise of power in ancient Rome. The premise that sexuality is disembedded from it now is quite doubtful. Today, as in Rome, certain types of sexual behavior—not necessarily the same types—are stigmatized as part of a larger cultural contempt for the body and exaltation of the mind/self. But if the split between mind and body is important to both Roman and contemporary power, then neither the sexualities nor the notions of penetration involved can be utterly estranged. Further, the enforcement of this split as a function of status, across everyday spaces and lives, cannot be accurately described as discourse since the ability to be in discourse is part of what each culture rations.

Notes

Versions of the argument in this chapter were presented at the State University of New York at Buffalo in April 1997, at the University of Arkansas in October 1999, and at the Annual Meeting of the American Philological Association in December 1999. I am grateful to the anonymous readers for their comments and to Amy Richlin and Martha Malamud for their encouragement.

1. Cf. Kampen 1996a.14: "Gender, thus, speaks constantly in the languages of age, status, ethnicity, and they in the language of gender: it exists only and always in relation to other social categories."

2. Foucault 1985.46–47, Habinek 1997, Halperin, Winkler, and Zeitlin 1990a, Larmour, Miller, and Platter 1998, Richlin 1991 and 1997a, Skinner 1996 and 1997, Walters 1997.

3. Sanders 1990.46: "For example, suppose a person is invited to someone's house for the first time. Even though the visitor had no prior knowledge of the details of the furniture style, wall colors, or floor covering, the newcomer could immediately recognize the public spaces, because the spatial cues . . . fit general expectations. The private areas could also be recognized, and the newcomer could probably determine the general layout of the house, such as the relationship between the kitchen and dining room or between the living room and bedrooms." Cf. Pearson and Richards 1994.1–37.

4. Duncan 1996, Massey 1994 and 1996, Valentine 1997, E. Wilson 1991.

5. Bell and Valentine 1995, Massey and McDowell 1994.

6. E.g., Carson 1990, Detienne 1977 and 1979, Vernant 1980, Vidal-Naquet 1986. Lissarague 1992.194–97 and Pantel 1992a.470–71 challenge this view; for the difficulty of supporting it through archaeology, see Jameson 1990.

7. Halperin 1990.30; cf. Foucault 1985.82–83, Skinner 1997.3–4. Richlin 1991.173 notes that Skinner articulated the essentials of this picture at 1979.142, considerably in advance of Foucault.

8. Wallace-Hadrill 1994.75; see 65–117 for housing patterns in Pompeii, the difficulty of establishing its total population, and the question of density at the various levels of housing.

9. Massey 1994.2; cf. Douglas 1972.513: "The organization of thought and of social relations is imprinted on the landscape."

10. Stambaugh 1988.90 notes: "If we assume a population of about a million, we must conclude that Rome in the early principate was one of the most densely populated cities the world has ever known." Cf. Garnsey 1988.244; for dismay about this in Roman literature, see Edwards 1996. Using the figures given by Jameson 1990.94, the total urban population of Greece in the classical period was less than twice that of the city of Rome in the Augustan period. For food riots in Rome, see Garnsey 1988.198–243; for the role of hunger in the modern food system, see Beardsworth and Keil 1997.32–47, Bell and Valentine 1997.189–207. Bennett 1987 describes the modern system as a "Hunger Machine," as was the Roman economy for many.

11. Jongman 1988.207–329 argues, using Pompeii as an example, that urbanism in Roman Italy did not produce a revolution in economic structure (such as that attributed to the early modern city) because of the persistence of traditional structures of social inequality.

12. Except where noted, all translations are my own.

13. Clarke 1991a.23: "After the middle of the first century of our era, a great number of city houses were remodeled to imitate villas, but in miniature. This phenomenon . . . often resulted in packing in a great number of disparate and uncoordinated villa features into modest spaces." Cf. Wallace-Hadrill 1994.169–74.

14. Treggiari 1969.91–142 divides "successful" freedmen into two basic categories: "learned professions and fine arts" (doctors, teachers of rhetoric, philosophers, actors) and tradesmen (merchants, potters, jewelry makers). The latter group dominates funerary inscriptions and was numerically far greater.

15. Joshel 1992a.167: "Occupational title names the freedman's means of establishing a normal order in his family and social life. Professional or commercial success enabled the freedman to reduce the disabling aspects of his past and to provide a basis for his children's integration into society as insiders."

16. Joshel 1992a.33–34; Seneca *Controversiae* 4 praef. 10: "Losing one's virtue is a crime in the freeborn, a necessity in a slave, a duty for the freedman" (trans. Joshel).

17. Clarke 1991a.234 compares the style of the Vettii with Trimalchio, noting: "If the overdone display that results bewilders and amuses us today, we are receiving messages that these up-from-under freedmen wished their guests to receive." Cf. Bourdieu's analysis (1984.177–97) of the differences in diet and presentation between the working class and professionals.

18. Richlin 1997a.30–31 suggests that Greece and Rome had "three gender roles: man, woman, and boy. Each of these genders has an appropriate role, either insertive or receptive."

19. Suetonius *Aug.* 44. On the distribution of seating in theaters, see Gunderson 1996.123–26, Hopkins 1983.17–18, E. Rawson 1987, Zanker 1988.149.

20. Gunderson 1996.125; cf. Stambaugh 1988.236: "The amphitheater thus provided a model of the social world of the city."

21. Cf. Gunderson 1996.130. This principle extended to the entrances and exits. Zanker 1988.151 observes: "The 'better' sort needed to have no contact at all with the common folk, whose seats were at the very top, just as in the opera houses of the nineteenth-century bourgeoisie."

22. See Coleman 1990.55 and S. Brown 1992 for the progression of events in the arena, often reflected in the composition of domestic mosaics.

23. Martial *Lib. Spect.* 7.5–6: "vivebant laceri membris stillantibus artus / inque omni nusquam corpore corpus erat." See Coleman 1990 for discussion of these "fatal charades."

24. Suetonius *Nero* 12. Coleman 1990.69 suggests: "Since the performance was a *pyrrhicha*, we should probably envisage an acrobatic leap rather than propulsion by a *ballista* or the like, and we should assume that 'Icarus' was not meant to die in his 'accident.'"

25. Martial *Lib. Spect.* 21; see Coleman 1990.62 n. 163 for discussion of the text.

26. Scarry 1985.44. The *tunica molesta* was a garment soaked in pitch and wrapped around the victims, who might be affixed to a piece of wood ("the axlemen"), buried in sand, or allowed to run through the arena (Tertullian *Apol.* 50.1). Christians accused by Nero of setting the fire that destroyed much of Rome were burned at dusk as torches (Tacitus *Ann.* 15.44).

27. As Scarry remarks (1985.39): "It is only when the body is comfortable,

when it has ceased to be an obsessive object of perception and concern, that consciousness develops other objects, that for any individual the external world . . .
comes into being and begins to grow."

28. Plutarch *Mor.* 554b. Cf. Horace *Epistulae* 2.1.185–86: "Amid the poetry,
they demand either a bear or some gladiators; the little plebs delights in these
things." Gunderson 1996.113–15 notes that elite writers condemn excessive delight in the games.

29. Seneca *Ep. Mor.* 7.5: *occide, verbera, ure.* At 7.3 he notes: "I return more
greedy, more ambitious, more intent on luxury, rather even more cruel and more
inhumane, precisely because I have been among human beings."

30. It is not clear that the segregation of seating in the theater in general was
as rigorous as it was during gladiatorial spectacles.

31. Edwards 1997; it does not follow, however, that actors, especially successful ones, necessarily looked upon themselves as simply penetrated. The freedman Tiberius Claudius Tiberinus declares: "Once I gave pleasure to the people,
and I was marked by their favor; now I am a bit of ash wept over on the pyre.
Who has not seen elegant dinner parties, with smiling faces, that went on all
night charmed by me and my best passages?" See Koortbojian 1996.226–28 for
text and discussion.

32. Primary sources: Suetonius *Aug.* 29.1–2, 31.5, 56.2; *Claud.* 33.1; Dio
55.10.1–8; Ovid *Fasti* 5.545–98; Macrobius *Sat.* 1.6.7–9, 2.4.9; Pliny *Naturales
Historia* 22.13, 35.6–7, 36.102. For discussion and bibliography, see Kellum 1996
and 1997, Kockel 1995, Packer 1997.309–11, Richardson 1992.160–62, Zanker
1988.192–95.

33. Stambaugh 1978. Many of these features were retained in subsequent
imperial fora; Packer 1997.327: "The architecture of each forum reinforced the
general impression of unity. The ubiquitous Corinthian order linked all of the
buildings visually. The dominant temples were raised on podia. Frontally ori-
ented, axially symmetrical shrines with nearly identical plans, almost all of the
temples . . . were of or faced with white marble."

34. Richlin 1996, Gowers 1993.12–15 and 1995. Richlin notes that the activities and people located in the Roman Forum were mostly male, but given the presence of the Shrine of the Vestals, she maps the Forum onto a two-gendered body.

35. Kellum 1997.173; cf. 171: "In sexual, military, and judicial encounters,
it was not the genitalia that mattered, but the role that one played."

36. As Cicero puts it (*pro Sestio* 138): "My speech is entirely concerned with
virtue, not sloth, with dignity, not with pleasure, with those who judge themselves
born for their country and their citizens, for praise and for glory, rather than
sleep, dinner parties, and delight."

37. This circularity is expressed in detail: Iulus wears a Phrygian cap and
shoes and carries a hunting stick, while Aeneas is dressed in Roman armor and
wears patrician sandals (Zanker 1988.202).

38. Suetonius *Claud.* 33.1. He goes on to report that Claudius never left the

table until he was gorged and drunk (*distentus ac madens*); he then went to sleep with his mouth hanging open and a feather down his throat to induce vomiting.

39. Cf. Kellum 1997.167–68 for the overlap of sexual and military conquest represented by the caryatids and the shields.

40. See Garnsey 1988.244–68 for the often negative effect of Roman government on provincial food supplies.

41. Suetonius *Aug.* 29.1 states that the Augustan Forum was built "for the sake of the multitude of men and court cases, which seemed to require a third forum when two were not enough"; the anecdote about Claudius supports this. Richardson 1992 questions the practice of oratory in the Augustan Forum because Dio does not mention it, but Dio is listing the functions of the Temple of Mars Ultor specifically, not those of the wider Forum. See Kellum 1997 for the inscriptional evidence.

42. Stone 1994.17: "The width of a developed imperial toga of the first century A.D. was fifteen to eighteen feet . . . and it was consequently impossible to don the garment without aid. Its tendency to slip from its draping made it unsuitable for any physical endeavor. It is therefore not surprising that the imperial toga was avoided by all other than those who devoted their lives to public service."

43. By focusing elite masculinity on his Forum, Augustus diminished the importance of the Roman Forum, which belonged to the Roman people and had an inherent connection with the optimate-popular conflict; see Purcell 1995, Millar 1998.13–48.

44. Richlin 1999.195: "But decapitation really effected a change in *caput* for the decapitated themselves, whose bodies were treated like those of the less-than-citizen, the tainted."

45. Wallace-Hadrill 1995 analyzes the seclusion of brothels from more respectable housing in Pompeii; D. Hall 1998.53–63 synthesizes literary and artistic representations of lower-class prostitution under the rubric, "the cunt of the city."

46. Gowers 1993.13: "Like the state that had exceeded its proper boundaries, the body that had gone to seed was not thought to be effective as a political or military machine . . . An over-indulged stomach was thought to disturb the equilibrium of a body where desires ought to be ruled by the head."

47. Gowers 1993.25 notes conflicting Roman opinions about dining as "the heart of Roman communal life" or "obviously peripheral."

48. Gowers 1993.16: "Rome presented two different images simultaneously: an image of ritual purity—the frugal sacrifices, the hallowed agricultural surnames of its leading men, the primeval festivals; and an image of adulterated or contaminated confusion—the smoky cookshops, the profusion of foreign delicacies, the debauched dining clubs."

49. On the seating arrangements, see Bek 1983, Dunbabin 1991, Foss 1995; for anxiety over equality and hierarchy in the distribution of food, see D'Arms 1990.

50. On performance at dinner parties, see Gamel 1999, C. P. Jones 1991, Starr 1991. On the charge of sexual passivity, see Corbeill 1997, Booth 1991.

51. See J. R. Clarke 1998.108–18 for discussion and illustrations of Arretine ware: ceramic plates and bowls of the Augustan and Julio-Claudian periods that imitated the erotic imagery found on more expensive dinnerware for the elite.

52. On fetishism and sadism in Roman wall paintings, see Fredrick 1995, Koloski-Ostrow 1997, Wallace-Hadrill 1996.

53. D'Arms 1991.75. D'Arms 1991.175 also notes the example of a slave accused of stealing a silver plate at a public feast given by Caligula: his hands were cut off and tied around his neck, and he was forced to circulate among the diners with a placard that described his crime.

54. Fredrick 1995.281: "Hermaphroditus' erection produces a reversal in the role of Pan, from active penetrator to potential penetratee, both physically and visually."

55. Henry 1992.256–57 discusses Athenaeus's anecdote (13.605f.4–10) about Cleisophus the Selymbrian, who fell in love with a statue of Venus on Samos. Unable to consummate his passion because the marble was cold and inflexible, he set out a piece of meat and copulated with that. While Cleisophus was a Hellenistic Greek, the anecdote illustrates well the fusion of visual, gustatory, and tactile pleasure in Roman dining.

9

Looking at Looking

Can You Resist a Reading?

Alison R. Sharrock

The act of viewing requires a viewer. This tautology, stated here simplistically, is central to my thesis but hardly unclear. What is not so clear is that the "viewer" is not just me standing in front of a painting or holding a book but a whole history of other readers, and also—this will be the focus of the present essay—a multiplicity of perspectives that may or may not constitute a "viewer" and that contribute to constituting "me."[1] One such perspective is that of the internal viewer (or reader), viewers who are straightforwardly visible to other viewers.

Many works of art contain more or less visible internal viewers. There are the internal audiences of plays within plays (Blänsdorf 1982); there are eavesdroppers and others in New Comedy, for example, who act as metaphors for the audience, as, in some measure, does the chorus in tragedy; there are internal audiences also in narrative poems, and very complex examples in Ovid's *Metamorphoses*; there is the addressee in satire and, even more explicitly, in didactic poetry. One of the most useful examples of the interface between art and literature is the "boy" to whom the ancient art critics Philostratus and Callistratus address their instructions on the correct way to read art. In the visual arts, there are internal spectators who are explicitly part of the work of art, directing the gaze of the external viewer onto some other part of the work.[2] In ancient art, there is, for example, the painting in the House of Gavius Rufus (Pompeii VII 2, 16), where Theseus, triumphant over the Minotaur, holds center stage, watched by a mixed group of admiring people positioned to one side who point to both marvels: the dead Minotaur and Theseus himself (see Ling 1991.138).[3] There are many examples of Achilles making a spectacle of himself on Scyros, usually watched and framed by a col-

Figure 9.1 Achilles on Scyros, Pompeii VI 9 6.

lection of observers and participants, as, for example, in the House of the Dioscuri (fig. 9.1), where there is a stark contrast between the problematically feminized Achilles and the surrounding "real" men and women (see Ling.1991.132–34). Then there is the painting in the House of M. Lucretius Fronto (Pompeii V 4 11, h, north wall), showing the seduction of Venus by Mars, where a group of attendants and Mars himself all focus the viewer's attention onto that most spectacular of art objects, the goddess herself—all but one of the attendants, that is, for one looks almost out of the corner of her eye toward the viewer, as if slyly to say, "Come on, you look too" (Ling 1991, plate XIA). Then there is the fascinating painting in the house Pompeii VI 1 10 (Ling 1991.211) of a painter at work, where the subject is the object (interestingly, it is a *female* artist): she is observed by two women peeping in around the door.[4] In the Middle Ages, the directive function of internal viewers becomes much more explicit with the development of demonstrative figures whose purpose is to mediate the theological message of the work to the external viewer (Gandelman 1990.14–35).

So much for the internal viewers; visual art may act as a prism on the nature of reading generally in that it offers yet another clearly "visible" viewer, external to the picture plane, whose eye is constructed in a certain position with regard to the artwork, and who is therefore, we might say, indirectly visible. In the history of Western art criticism, this construction of the viewer has been associated especially with the Renaissance (particularly Italian) obsession with perspective. I would suggest, however, that this is only an extreme case of something that is also reflected in classical works. Martin Jay gives an brief instructive account of the history of this notion, that he, for convenience, calls "Cartesian perspectivalism": "The basic device was the idea of symmetrical visual pyramids or cones with one of their apexes the receding vanishing or centric point in the painting, the other the eye of the painter or the beholder. The transparent window that was the canvas, in Alberti's famous metaphor, could also be understood as a flat mirror reflecting the geometricalized space radiating out from the viewing eye."[5] The "implied reader" of a text is, perhaps, as simple and as problematical as that.[6]

Part of the theoretical background to the thinking behind this chapter is an attempt to connect the insights of "wild-side" reader-response criticism with insights relating to "the gaze" as developed in the theory (particularly the feminist and psychoanalytical theory) of film and art criticism. Laura Mulvey's 1975 essay, "Visual Pleasure and Narrative Cinema," is, of course, seminal here. Her analysis of the voyeuristic and scopophilic aspects of the male gaze and the resultant female objectification, as constructed by and in classic Hollywood cinema, has had enormous influence and widespread progeny.[7] But the theory of the gaze has not in general (and particularly not at first) been about communication, the dynamics of the production of meaning, and the possibilities for *differences* in "freedom" and "control" between authors, readers, etc., as has the theory of reader response. Some critics are moving in that direction, but, in its essence, psychoanalytical theory is based on a premise of absolutism to which poststructuralist reader-response theory is fundamentally opposed. Among the most developed critiques of the monolithic

view of the male viewer is that of Gaylyn Studlar (1988), who argues for
a closer attention to masochism (in the technical psychoanalytical sense
rather than the popular) in theories of looking, which would deconstruct
the male-female and subject-object oppositions. C. Armstrong (1989)
mentions, rightly I think, a fetishization of Freudian theory that has con-
tributed to a totalizing view of the male gaze.[8] She argues for a reading
(in this case of Brandt's photographs of female nudes in distorted positions) that "elid[es] the positions of male subject-female object" (66) by
suggesting a kind of "identification *within* rather than *against*" for the
photographer and/or viewer and model; thus the oddly emphasized and
framed female body parts become the (male) spectator's own also. (She
does admit that elements of "male-gaze" objectification are persistent
even within this subversive photography.) Many feminist critics seek to
(re?)appropriate the act of looking in more positive and fruitful ways for
women: a worthy project, it seems to me, but a problematical one. E.
Ann Kaplan (1983) believes that we have reached the stage at which it is
meaningful at least to imagine an equitable "mutual gazing." Eighteen
years on, I am not sure that we are any further, but perhaps eighteen
years is not very long.[9]

    The same thing is happening in literary criticism (and see below on
Fetterley and resistance). Helen Elsom, for example, wants to argue that
pornography and romance literature can be "libidinal or intellectual"
(1992.230): in so far as pornography and romance literature expose
women as objects, it is possible to identify *with* that objectification (not
okay) or to identify it (okay: feminist criticism). The choice between the
two, according to Elsom, is in the eye of the beholder. Something of the
argument of this chapter will be that, at some level, such a choice is very
difficult to achieve because identification of something does not undo or
negate the possibility of identification *with* it. Perhaps identification of
objectification can only be achieved at a level that is aware of itself precisely as different from the identification with objectification that still
takes place. Therefore it is not entirely free. We are all caught. Viewing, like everything else, cannot become equitable and creative by our
saying so—nor, perhaps, can it become so *without* our saying so.

    I am looking at meta-issues here. My particular interest is to won-
der what might be the scope for maneuver in critical moves such as those
just described. I am intrigued by the dynamics of Victor Burgin's 1992
reading of the photographer Helmut Newton's *Self-portrait with Wife
June and Model, Paris, 1981* (fig. 9.2), in which Burgin further develops
the voyeuristic/scopophilic theory of looking by arguing that the active

Figure 9.2 *Self-portrait with Wife June and Model, 1981, Paris,* by
Helmut Newton.

male voyeur (the photographer) is also both fetishist and *exhibitionist*. But
why is it that a man as viewed object is (powerfully) exhibitionist? And
yet often if a woman is an exhibitionist she is a spectacle, a sight, an object to be looked at in a way that is much less powerful than the control
that the male exhibitionist seems to wield.[10] It is partly to do with representation—we all know the tendency for men-as-viewed-objects
(whether overtly erotic or not) to be portrayed as *doing something*, and
men who are portrayed not "doing something" to be read as "feminine"
(disempowered, deviant); but it is partly also to do with the learnt patterns of the reading of representation that make us all inclined to read
women's representations as specular and fundamentally oppressive; this
is the sense in which all this is a reader-response issue.

Throughout this essay, I shall distinguish and also fudge three levels of viewing or reading: (1) the addressee or the visible "internal"
viewer; (2) the implied reader or the literal viewpoint, that is, the centric
ray or angle from which a painting is constructed as being seen; and

(3) the metaphorical point of view or interpretation. I take "viewpoint" to be the literal position of the eye observing the text or object and "point of view" to be the interpretation, in a metaphorical sense—but since it is precisely this distinction that I am questioning, I do not use these terms entirely consistently. These are three precise categories that seem to me to be critically useful, but it is crucial to the vision of art that I am offering that these distinctions are also fudged. While we can indeed see in works of literary and visual art a viewer who has a straightforward material presence, that internal viewer is only part of an infinitely receding series of viewers. The eye on the end of the centric ray, whether it is in one position or many, is built into the work of art and, as such, is part of it. Even this viewer (us) whom we imagined to be external becomes a part of the work it views. Likewise the viewer it views (or we view) as internal is and is not within the work. And then there's the act of reading, which creates another level of viewing. And so on and so on into the abyss. This abyss, let it be stressed, is for me not a site of meaningless-ness but a teeming sea of meaning, where the interactions of viewer and viewed are essential to their mutual construction as (both) creators and sites of meaning.

Postmodern critics are fond of talking about fragmentation of the viewpoint. An example would be W. V. Dunning's 1991 article (see also Foucault 1988), which argues that, before postmodernism, there is a uni-vocal viewpoint and point of view in art because there is a univocal sense of the self, and that postmodern painting rejects the single viewpoint (lit-erary and metaphorical), in keeping with the fragmented postmodern sense of "self." Point taken; but what is fascinating in this is that while many critics seek to expose a difference between "old monoviews" and "postmodern fragmentation," the locus for the moment of fragmenta-tion—for it is often seen in historical terms—depends on the viewpoint of the critic. I mean that a critic of twentieth-century painting (or liter-ature or whatever) may be much more ready to assign simple univocal-ity of viewpoint to a Renaissance painting or an ancient poem than is the student of those more distant artworks. Is fragmentation in the eye of the beholder? I think so, and, moreover, it is possible to look at a viewpoint, an act of looking, as both univocal and fragmented, if you also fragment the critic as reader.

There is one level of reading that is monovisual in the sense that we look at certain works of art from a particular angle, but it is still possible to fragment that monoview by other readings—and perhaps by the very act of reading that monoview critically. To take the case of that literal angle: there are certain paintings that are designed for a particular position, and therefore designed to be seen from a certain angle by real viewers on the ground. In this case, a clearly "visible" external viewer is constructed with a monoviewpoint.[11] There are also paintings that are designed to *look as if* they are being seen from a certain angle, for example from far below, which is, in fact, not where most spectators would actually be standing (see Henderson 1996.268). So, in this case, the viewer and the act of reading have been fragmented. Indeed some parts of the picture plane might work on different angles than others,[12] as in much postmodern painting.[13] A famous (and premodern) example of the use of several pictures planes within the same painting is the strange smudge on Holbein's *The Ambassadors*. A representation of a human skull, it cuts a threatening slash across the straightforward prosperity of the two ambassadors. As Claude Gandelman says (1990.52): "It is commonly accepted by art historians that the picture was to be hung beside a door so that a spectator who was about to cross the threshold might direct his glance slantwise across the canvas, thereby perceiving the skull." On the one hand, then, there must be more than one viewer taking more than one viewpoint, but, on the other hand, even that one might be able to take a monoview, one that incorporates or consists of the fragmented literal viewpoint. It is here that one might break down the distinction between external and internal viewer, which is nevertheless necessary to the act of interpretation. Oppositions are useful but always already undermined: that undermining is part of their usefulness rather than destructive. As suggested above, an awareness that multiple points of view exist in and of the same painting can help shed light on the mutual dependence of viewers and viewed. Jacques Lacan's 1977 analysis of the Holbein makes the skull into a site of interaction between subject and object: by it, "as subjects, we are literally called into the picture, and represented here as caught." This interaction between seeing subject and seen object is especially pertinent to the ancient situation, where it is in the power of the eye to desire and to harm, to fascinate and to invoke fascination, and so on.[14]

It is the argument of this essay that resisting reading is very problematical. This notion of "resistance" refers in particular to a book entitled *The Resisting Reader* (Fetterley 1978), whose author argues for a feminist reading practice that consists of exposing what she calls the authorial reading, but refusing it, seeing things differently. The project strikes me as both positively provocative and seriously flawed, for it risks simply replacing one monoview with another, and, moreover, it does not give sufficient credit to the multiplicity of perspectives in the act of reading. It could be, I suggest, that there are some readings that, at some level, we cannot unread, even though we may seek, as a political act, to reject them, to try to deny their power over us. Here we run into difficulties, however, because the "fragmented readings" presented at the beginning of this paper are not contradictory interpretations vying for authoritative acceptance by a monovisual reader, rather they are multiple and interdependent elements in the act of reading. Nevertheless, there is an element in critical strategy that no one avoids in practice, which is to offer conflicting readings as real alternatives. One of the "different levels of reading" is someone else's point of view. I do not mean to imply that it is never meaningful to say "that reading is wrong, unhelpful, unpersuasive," since we all say these things and feel that there is a point in doing so. Rather, there are some responses to works of literature and art (and indeed other cultural artifacts and institutions) that are *necessary* because they are part of the way we have been constructed as readers by those cultural forces. Part of my aim is to counter the notion that the deconstruction of hierarchies dissolves them into nonexistence. No critic, I suggest, has that power. It is the fragmentation of the viewer that allows, or rather necessitates, the having and eating of this particular cake.

So to the question of what this chapter is about. I shall be offering some readings of the Portland Vase, for example, and of Lucian's *Essay on Portraiture*. Through these readings, I seek to consider some theoretical questions: can you have a fragmented multiple viewpoint in ancient art (or art criticism)?[15] Is it possible to resist—to unread—the monovision in art and literature? Once a reading is fragmented, which it necessarily is, can you resist the readings that have been broken off (to continue the metaphor)? Parts of my argument involve the genderedness of the spectator and of reading, which I seek to use as an example of something that has a more general application than the by now established point that reading as a woman is different. Several of my examples relate to the erotics of the text and the reading of erotic art, since it is with erotic content and erotic metaphors (metaphors, that is, for the reading of content that need not be overtly erotic) that such issues of gendered power and resistance are especially visible, but I hope that this might be a particular case with a more general application: there are some readings that are *or can be read* as directed by the internal viewer. At one important level, they *cannot* be resisted—although, at another, the fragmentation of the viewer (1) allows you to expose and, to some extent, disempower them, and (2) suggests that analysis of the internal viewer

who points you in this direction is an act of interpretation, not an absolute given.

   According to the metaphor of the erotics of the text, a text seduces
us, enticing us to try and penetrate its meaning.[16] There is a story, popular in antiquity, about an ardent admirer of Praxiteles' Aphrodite of
Cnidos (the most beautiful statue in the world, according to Pliny *Naturalis Historia* 36.20). It was related by Pliny and Lucian, among others,
that the Cnidian Aphrodite inspired such love in a worshipper that he
contrived to be locked in when the shrine was closed for the night. Alone
with the statue, he raped it, but (in some versions) from behind, since
he feared to face the goddess.[17] This story of sex with the statue, in addition to being a telling indication of ancient attitudes toward cult images,[18] clearly connects with the myth of Pygmalion, whose statue comes
to life before intercourse takes place, at least in the version of Ovid. I
shall not consider Pygmalion in any detail here, but just note that the
iconography of the Cnidian Aphrodite and the myth of Pygmalion's
statue tell very much the same story about women (and about art).[19] It
is a story that is normative for images of women: the overall shape and
pose of the statue, particularly the position of the hands, has a vast progeny in representations of erotic women. In the Sir Edward Burne-Jones
series on Pygmalion and the Image, the statue bears quite a close resemblance to the Aphrodite, particularly in the second painting, *The
Hand Refrains* (whose hand?). Pygmalion, as the active perceiver as well
as the creator of his great work, stands metaphorically for the perceiver
of any erotic art, as does the Cnidian rapist. Is it possible to resist the
reading of the relationship between the looker and the looked at that is
implied by the anecdote about the Aphrodite of Cnidos? The story provides a fine example of the multiplicity of viewers, for it displays and literalizes the merging and interaction of the work of art and the perceiver,
while also implying other readers: the men to whom the story is told
within the narrative (in Ps.-Lucian's version, for example), the reader of
the narrative, and so on, who are likewise implicated in that interaction.

   But is it necessary to read art in this masculinist, penetrative manner? I think so, at least at some level and at least in some cases. This is
not to imply that penetration is the only available metaphor for reading
or that voyeurism the only dynamic for looking; rather it is to suggest
that it is not possible to resist them in certain particular examples. Such
a conclusion might raise difficult issues in the politics of art: Amy Richlin (1992c) confronts similar problems in her reading of rape narratives
in Ovid, and wonders what we should do with a canon in which such vi-

olence against women (and pleasure in it) plays so great a role. She quotes Susanne Kappeler (1986.221): "Art will have to go." This indeed might be the logical conclusion, for perhaps the only possible response to the oppressive violence of looking is not to look at all. All looking, whether directly representational or not, becomes tainted. Could it be that what needs changing is not so much art (literary or visual) but the structures involved in the construction of the act of viewing art? I don't think that can be quite right, because there certainly are variations in the degree of oppressiveness in works of art—and we must not let art or artists off the hook by concentrating responsibility on the viewer. Perhaps we might say that, in our society as it has been constructed, the gaze is "male, possessive, objectifying, aggressive" (at least potentially) and that all representation has tainted elements in its formulation and/or the responses to it, *but* it can still be beautiful and worthwhile (cf. Richlin 1992c.178). Simultaneous multiple levels of reading—taking it more than one way *at once*—might be the answer. Otherwise there is no way of representing or expressing anything: "Art will have to go."

The Pygmalion story is a powerful metaphor for the reading of erotic art: even the resisting reader cannot—and should not—make it vanish. In their stress on the possibility of viewing the statue from front and back, and approaching it through front and back doors, the narratives of the Cnidian story already image the dichotomized and gendered desire to penetrate, where "penetrativism" becomes the play of the gaze (to see more, see again, see differently).[20] The story enacts the interactions of the optic and the haptic (particularly at issue where works of art are displayed): look, don't touch; look *as* touch.[21] Looking here becomes a symptom and a sublimation of desire, for the ancient notion that love enters through the eyes comes into its own when the love goddess can be sexually approached through sight.[22]

The Cnidian Aphrodite is posed in a manner that has become normative in the iconography of women. Her hand is placed above or in the region of the pudenda, ostensibly covering what it, in practice, also displays (Osborne 1994.82). So powerful is this image that it occurs even in places where the ostensible point of the hand—modest covering—is irrelevant, for example, where the statue is clothed. Onto that hand are focused the ambivalent expectations of the male creators of and audiences for erotic women. It is modestly concealing the pudenda, as often the other hand does the breasts—and yet, at the same time, it suggestively points to that which it poses as hiding. Often the hand is holding up drapery, which might almost be taken as a metaphor for the function of the hand itself in the pure version.[23] The viewer's eye is inevitably drawn to that place; even if one "looks" in order to expose the objectification of the "looking," one cannot undo that looking, and one may even reinforce it. The hand becomes a motif in the iconography of women. There was a fashion, which became particularly prevalent in later antiquity, of depicting subjects in the guise of some deity or mythological character. In one example from the third century c.e. now in the Vatican Museo Gregoriano Profano, a lady is represented as Omphale, with all the trappings of Hercules. As such, the statue's sexuality risks confusing the conventional spheres of the genders, for not only does Omphale wear the regalia of the most masculine of heroes, but her story also relates the "demasculization" of the great hero by a woman, who thereby achieves pseudomasculine power. And where has she got her hand? Covering and pointing to the pudenda, in the manner of the Cnidian Aphrodite. In posing her in this way, the sculptor has redeemed her sexuality and restored the expected relationship between the genders. The club and the lion skin no longer function as disturbing phallic symbols, but rather expose by opposition the woman's firm place in the iconography of erotic women.[24] As Clement of Alexandria said (*Protrepticus* 4.50), all statues of naked women are of Aphrodite.

In the painting of the Annunciation by the Master of the Barberini Panels, the fully clothed Virgin has her hand in precisely the position of the Aphrodite, covering the pudenda. The other, as is often the case, both covers and points to the breasts. Norman Bryson says the hands tell us that the painting represents Reflection (1983.101–02), but I think they must also refer to the normative iconography of women.[25] There is nothing very surprising in erotic implications being associated with the Virgin since erotic imagery surrounding her is prevalent in both the literature and art of the Middle Ages and Renaissance. There may, however, be a question to be raised here about authorial intention: even if the master was not conscious of the reading that says that the Cnidian Aphrodite and hundreds like her hold their hands in that way in order both to conceal and to display, nevertheless it is impossible not to associate the Virgin here with that tradition. Whether or not the association was conscious on his part, it may be fruitful for reading. The position of the hands could be subversive, but it is more likely that the eroticism surrounding the Virgin seeks to transform the power and fertility of pagan art in order to express the life-giving power of the Virgin's womb.[26]

Forced viewing of the kind engendered by the Cnidian story can arise from a painting on an Attic oinochoe, now in the Museum of Fine

Arts, Boston, of a sleeping nymph about to be surprised (as the modern caption says) by two satyrs. The sleeping female falling victim to predatory males is a popular story pattern in art and literature, with lots of variations.[27] In this case, our reader's-eye view is given little room for maneuver, for we are made to join with the satyrs' approach even while we voyeuristically observe it. The overall shape of the iconography here makes the two satyrs into internal viewers, looking at the woman, whose ability to look back is seriously impaired. They, like us, are mobile, while she is static; they are sentient and she is not; they are active, she is passive. It is not only women who are observed in works of art, of course, nor only men who are viewers, but (1) for the case I am making here, the issue of gender is simply illustrative, not crucial, and (2) that gendered arrangement is very common.[28]

A similar iconographic pattern is presented on the Portland Vase (figs. 9.3 and 9.4). This magnificent piece of Roman glassware is generally agreed to be Augustan[29] and shows two parallel scenes, separated by masks under the handles. Like the Aphrodite of Cnidos, this is a work designed in the round: it does not have a clear front and back. I shall follow Kenneth Painter and David B. Whitehouse's designation of the sides.[30] Side I shows a seated woman cradling in her lap a snake or *draco* and stretching out her arm to hold that of an approaching young man. Above her is a winged Cupid, complete with bow and arrows, while, on her left, she is flanked by a thoughtful looking bearded man. There is a tree in the center background and another behind the bearded man, spilling over onto the other side. On side II, a reclining woman, who is believed by some commentators to be asleep, has her hand flung over her head and holds a downward-pointing torch. She is flanked by two seated but upright observers: on her left, a young man, on her right, a woman whom all observers see as a goddess. Behind the central woman is, again, a tree. All three figures rest on blocks, while both sides also show architecture, which on side II may include fallen blocks.

Iconographic detection games, so popular among classical art historians, have often been played with the figures, so much so that Painter and Whitehouse are moved to tabulate thirty-three different interpretations in their appendix. To mention but a few: the narrative has been associated with the Trojan myth, Theseus and Ariadne, Bacchus and Ariadne, the ancestry of Augustus, and, by earlier scholars, that of Alexander Severus. A popular interpretation places the scene somewhere in the story of Peleus and Thetis.[31] According to Bernard Ashmole (1967), on side I we see (from left to right) Peleus, Thetis, and Poseidon (as a dis-

Figure 9.3 Portland Vase, side I.

Figure 9.4 Portland Vase, side II.

appointed lover, hence not carrying his trident), while, in the sleeping scene, the central figure is Helen, watched by Achilles and Aphrodite in Elysium. Both sides are held to offer messages of life after death and apotheosis. D. E. L. Haynes (1968) sees the vase differently: again starting on side I, Peleus is indeed the first character, but he has just got up from resting at a shrine of Aphrodite (Ashmole thought he had just entered the realm of the gods), and is being encouraged on his quest for his beloved by the other two characters on that side, two marine deities probably Tethys and Oceanus. On the sleeping side (II) is an exhausted Thetis, passively but unconsciously awaiting and perhaps dreaming of the approaching Peleus, and watched over by Aphrodite and Hermes (or just possibly Ares). Erika Simon's 1957 reading is representative of those that connect the vase with contemporary events; she sees the animal in the woman's lap as the snake in which form, according to Julian family myth, Apollo engendered Augustus (Suetonius *Augustus* 94.4). The central woman on both sides is Augustus's mother Atia, the young man is Apollo, while the other observers are Chronos and Venus Genetrix. Recently, the "Trojan myth" reading has been given added nuance by S. J. Harrison (1992), who makes the young man on side II Paris (rather than

Achilles) observing the recumbent (perhaps sleeping) Helen under the gaze of Aphrodite. He argues that the original purpose of the vase was as a wedding gift.[32] Painter and Whitehouse's own interpretation is that the vase is a propaganda piece for Augustus, but one that was designed for a select circle, and that the woman with snake is indeed Atia with Apollo, but the young man whose arm she holds is Augustus himself, with Chronos looking on to authenticate the new Golden Age that Augustus inaugurates. They read the other side as depicting Hecuba's dream about the birth of Paris, with the young man as Paris himself and the other observer as Aphrodite. The whole then tells the story of the birth of Rome from the ashes of Troy.

I find it quite easy to enter into and enjoy but also to resist these readings. It would be possible to construct many other narratives for the vase, especially if we are not bound by the need to "identify the myth." It is perhaps worth noting that the penchant for "identifying the myth" (supplying the story about which the vase itself is not explicit) is an example of the voyeuristic mode of reading or viewing, but that the iconography also has strong scopophilic elements, since it represents an arrested erotic moment that fetishizes the very act of looking. But the two modes are not mutually exclusive. We can (and critics do) read either side first: I personally am inclined to read side I as a sequel that confirms the latent eroticism of side II (remembering that my designations—from Painter and Whitehouse 1991.33—are only a convenience), but equally the advancing Eros on side I could be moving the narrative forward to the more static side II. Since he is looking in the direction opposite his movement, Eros's position points to the fluidity of the narrative's direction. The medium is crucial to the iconography here, for circles are infinite and narrative on a vase can go round and round for ever.[33] One story the vase tells us is the circularity of eros, mapped onto the cycles of life and death in the passage of the generations. Such a story would be appropriate both to the vase's original ancient function as a wedding gift (if such it was), and to its last, among grave goods.[34] The artist, I suggest, invites us to write our own narrative, for he has been singularly sparing in straightforward identification of the characters. Only one is kitted out with attributes: the flying Eros above the awake woman is winged and holds both torch and bow, so this artist knew how to use identificatory icons. Many of the identifications suggested involve characters who have very obvious signifiers (winged sandals for Hermes, for example), but they have not brought them onto this vase. There are some other suggestions from the iconography: the creature in the awake woman's lap (which could even be part of her) looks oceanic to most people and so places her in a marine setting; the bearded man is very Poseidonesque, even without his trident. But the whole, apart from Eros, is understated: we can only be sure that we are viewing an erotic scene.[35] Admittedly, Painter and Whitehouse's version has the young men who are generally seen as lovers approaching and observing not beloveds but mothers. I find this hard to square with the eroticism of side II in particular (the connection between the sleeping woman and the marble statue in the Vatican Museum of Ariadne asleep, with her right arm draped languidly over her head, is hard to avoid).[36] Alternatively, if we follow Painter and Whitehouse's reading, there is a latent and potentially disturbing, but not entirely unsurprising, eroticism in these scenes of mothers and sons. But to me, now, the "meaning" of the vase cannot be other than the sum of its interpretations.

Once we have written our own story for the figures on the vase, however, we might still ask what the iconography does for us as viewers. I suggest that the viewer is enticed to join the lookers in viewing the centrally placed woman. Somehow they manage to view the woman as art object, and erotic art object at that, even though they themselves are part of a work of art. This is the unresistible reading of the Portland Vase. At one level, you resist the centric ray when you look at the lookers rather than at the object of their gaze, but, at another level, you cannot because you are looking at them *as* lookers, following their line of sight to the true work of art between them. Of course, a vase is different from a painting, while the representations we see without going to the British Museum (pictures in books) cheat by creating a flat picture plane. To what extent are we looking at a flat surface? When we look at a given side of the vase, we have a certain play with the third dimension in the presence of the tree that, placed as it is behind the central figure, gives a hint at depth. Conversely (!), the bend of the vase surface plays against this hint of depth, causing instead the woman to project into the foreground, so to speak, quite literally.[37] If you look at this vase from the monoviewpoint, the woman stands out and the lookers stand back behind her—just as you are standing back in front of her. Due to the convex surface of the vase, its internal viewers are not on the same plane with the woman, but stand physically behind her. In this respect, they are similar to the external viewers standing physically in front of her. I suspect that even if you stand so that one of the lookers is directly in front of you, your decentered gaze emphasizes the true center of the painting by its very awareness of being askew. It is another act of looking, but one that cannot remove the centrality of the forward view, and the erotic and artistic implications of it. You can't unread the reading of the woman as art object. This, I suggest, applies also to literature, for the internal spectators on the Portland Vase might act as a metaphor for the implied reader of erotic discourse. "We," as readers, are not as objective as we might like to think.

For the purposes of a certain type of feminist critique that is, to some extent, active in the subtext of this paper, it would be convenient to see a simple pattern of male-viewer/female-viewed that always works, or near enough. Although it is clear that this is indeed a very common structure, it is becoming more generally recognized that issues of gender are rather more complicated, and that when we try to construct neat oppositions and hierarchies about gender (among other things) they are always already deconstructed (that does not mean they are destroyed).[38] For students of the ancient world, the position of goddesses is one that can challenge simple notions about gender, for, as has long been recognized, goddesses confuse the "proper" dynamics of power by playing roles that are both masculine and feminine—in the case of Venus, ultra feminine.[39] Hence the goddess on the Portland Vase, although female, plays an active role in looking at the sleeping woman and constructing her as an erotic art object. That the goddess says "Aphrodite" to most viewers enhances her power to confuse the ultra feminine with "masculine" power. Likewise, images of men where the pleasure suggested is primarily scopophilic and that offer passive roles for the Roman male to try on serve both to confuse the straightforward hierarchies implied in the more common "voyeuristic" viewing strategies and also (I suggest) to reinforce them. Narcissus, playing "both" roles at once, is, of course, the paradigm for this duality.

One image that fits nicely into the scheme of powerless, looked-at women, powerful "looking" men, and still more powerful goddesses is the well-known Pompeian wall painting depicting the sacrifice of Iphigenia, now in the National Museum in Naples (fig. 9.5).[40] Iphigenia is carried to her death by two attendants, while the sacrificing priest and the girl's unhappy father look on (or fail to). Above, two divine beings bring the hind who will replace Iphigenia as victim. Iphigenia is the center of both story and painting; she is eroticized by the simple association of virgin sacrifice with sex and also by the strong marriage imagery that surrounds the story. She is the object of this work of art. Yet no one will look at her. All the men of the painting, spectators to events though they are, are looking in different directions, neither at the girl nor out of

Figure 9.5 Sacrifice of Iphigenia, Pompeii VI 8 3.

the picture plane. Agamemnon, to hammer the point home, has his face covered by drapery and by his hand and is turned away from the scene of sacrifice. All this expresses the denial of spectatorship in those who nevertheless remain "spectators"—they dare not look. Only the external spectator dares to look at the taboo, unspeakable object of art, yet even his or her gaze is constantly drawn away by that of the internal viewers. Away and back, for this is a refusal to look that actually enhances looking. Iphigenia's parted clothes visually echo the averted gaze of the male participants, turned aside in both directions. All this aversion serves to focus the external viewer's gaze on the central figure.[41] The Portland Vase, too, has attracted the story of Iphigenia to the list of its interpretations (Smart 1984). The figures on side II would represent Achilles, Iphigenia, and, unusually, Artemis. If this reading is followed, then "Iphigenia" avoids not only the viewer but also "Achilles"—almost hides from him with her upturned arm—in a pose appropriate both to maidenly modesty and to fear of sacrifice. "Achilles" gazes directly but with his back turned; "Artemis" gazes ambiguously, for although she directs the external viewer's gaze toward the reclining figure, it is not clear whether she herself is looking at her, at "Achilles," or nowhere. The Iphigenia story is a traditional scenario of aversion, where we are told not to look at what is being represented: don't look at proper women and/or human sacrifice. Euripides, in *Iphigenia at Aulis*, uses the conventions about what can and cannot be shown on stage to stop us from looking at the sacrifice, but, in case this is not enough to avoid the pollution of seeing human sacrifice, he whisks the girl away and has a hind substituted for her as victim. But all his efforts to screen us from his taboo subject fail, for the play ends on a note that can only be falsely happy, falsely propitious; we are left looking at—or consciously averting our gaze from—the obscenity of that which should not be seen.

With this notion of the necessary but self-destructive action of the gaze, we might compare Jaš Elsner's 1996b treatment of Narcissus as "a myth of the fallibilities of the gaze and of the subject as viewer," in that the viewer loses his identity in the act of viewing that he cannot avoid. Elsner offers a powerful and subtle reading of the Narcissus myth as a metaphor for the seductive effects of art, the problems of naturalism, and the risked loss of subjectivity involved in the act of reading and viewing. At one level, Narcissus and other stories of the vulnerability of beautiful men (Actaeon, Endymion, and, particularly, Hermaphroditus) may reflect conscious or unconscious insecurities in the Roman male sense of self,[42] while, at the same time, reinforcing the power of the phallus and its connection with male viewing. They may offer the pleasure of identifying with passive positions, while, at the same time, serving to reinforce phallic control (by whomever it is wielded) by opposition. But what if we are looking at a woman? Françoise Frontisi-Ducroux (1996.85), discussing erotic art in which the external gaze is closely aligned with that of an internal viewer, argues that the male lover retains mastery of the gaze in a heteroerotic situation, but is more willing or forced to lose it in a homoerotic situation. However much the power of the phallus may include expression of the power of the male over the male or, equally, may express male anxieties or pleasures in passive or "weakened" identifications, nonetheless it seems hard to escape from a reading of woman as "other" in a way that male images, even when "problematized," are not.

An example of such a "problematized" male image is the Death of Pentheus in the House of the Vettii (Pompeii VI 15 1, triclinium n, east wall; see Ling 1991, plate XIB), in which "powerful" dressed (or semidressed) women (Bacchants, of course) surround the agonized, naked, central Pentheus.[43] One holds his arm, another his head, "as if" about to tear him apart, while another is about to throw a rock at his head. His open gesture (one arm and one leg outstretched, head turned up and away) exposes further his weakness and helplessness, foreshadowing his imminent dissolution. The plate next to it in Ling 1991 (XIC), depicts the Sack of Troy from the House of the Menander (Pompeii I 10 4, *ala* 4, left wall), and is exactly opposite in gendered terms, with white-bodied, seminaked women being dragged by soldiers from the divine statues to which they cling hopelessly. Pentheus's weakness and potential loss of self say "inversion" in bold letters, as does Euripides' famous version of the same story.[44] We could say that the Death of Pentheus offers a masochistic pleasure, while the pleasure in the Sack of Troy is sadistic, but, in doing so, we would be repeating and reinforcing precisely the male supremacy in identification that such a reading seeks to expose. Perhaps, however, if we are concerned with considering Roman viewing pleasures that would be the right thing to do. And perhaps we, too, are caught.[45]

The iconographic arrangement of the Portland Vase and similar works, which directs the gaze of the external viewer onto a (usually female) art object, is frequently paralleled in literature as well as visual art and reflects quite closely the situation of Roman elegy.[46] There is a certain relationship between the positions of the nymph and satyrs on the Attic oinochoe, the characters on the Portland Vase, and Propertius 1.3—that paradigm for the elegiac mistress as art object (see Sharrock 1991). There the lover comes to his mistress late, drunk, and wanting sex but fearing to wake her up until the moon does it for him and she accuses him of neglecting her. As is well known, the most direct link with visual art in Propertius 1.3 is with the Vatican Ariadne, but the iconographic pattern forms part of a much wider nexus, one that blurs the distinction between internal and external viewers. Indeed the Vatican Ariadne is an important link in the story of viewers that this paper tells, for there the "external" spectator has to play the role taken by the internal spectators in other versions of the iconographic pattern. The "sleeping" woman on the Portland Vase reminds many people of the sleeping Ariadne, so by looking at her we take on the role of Bacchus.

I should like now to connect this schema with an unlikely parallel: Lucian's *Essay on Portraiture* and his *Apology*. The connection need not be one of conscious imitation, although it could well be, since Lucian's constant aim is to display his classical learning; rather the treatment and consequent construction of woman as viewed and men as viewers produced by these two works of verbal art resemble each other closely in terms of literary genre and in their approach to the representation of women. Both are indicators and instigators of the conception of erotic (and other) women in antiquity. In the *Essay*, we may see an image of the sleeping Cynthia, while the *Apology*, in some measure, reflects the tirade of the woken Cynthia.

In this diptych of dialogues, we see Lucian at his most cultured and courtly, for they were written when Lucian was connected, to some degree, with the court of Lucius Verus at Antioch in 163–64 c.e. (Jones 1986.75–76), and they celebrate Verus's mistress Pantheia, who was probably a professional courtesan from Smyrna. The *Essay* is a dialogue between two characters, Lycinus (who stands for Lucian himself)[47] and Polystratus, which begins with Lycinus describing in ecstatic terms the sight he has just had of a beautiful woman passing by with her retinue. Drawing on elements from many famous works of art, he fuses together a composite picture of the woman, from which, remarkably, his interlocutor is able to recognize the object in question as a countrywoman of his. Polystratus then takes over the eulogy by praising her many spiritual charms. The two descriptions are a verbal portrait of the lady, which Polystratus is charged to take to her as a panegyric. In the *Apology*, he returns with her reply, which modestly disclaims such praise and denies Lycinus the right to use it. Lycinus then makes his defense, for this has become a pseudo-court case, which Polystratus is again to relate to the lady. We do not hear of her reaction, so Lycinus has had the last word. This may not be the most obvious example of erotic discourse, but, under the polite veneer, we cannot avoid an eroticism similar to that which was to flourish in the polite society of the Middle Ages and that we call courtly love.[48] Such celebration of a woman's body cannot avoid the erotic, and indeed, in this case, it is quite clearly—if elliptically—signaled at the opening of the dialogue when Lycinus describes himself as turned to stone at the sight. Now this is partly the stupefaction that is the appropriate response to divinity, but it could also be a symbol for male sexual arousal. That we should take it as such in this instance is, I think, shown by Polystratus's remark that it is normally young boys who have that effect on Lycinus. This is the Pygmalion story inverted: the viewer is turned to stone, only to turn the lady into a statue—or is it the statues into a lady? Like Pygmalion, Lycinus and Polystratus create a woman, body and mind.

The dialogue is a rhetorical game between men, a game about the genre of description, specifically in its panegyric manifestation. Despite Lycinus's claim for a distinction between panegyric and flattery with regard to truth (itself, of course, part of the flattery), the nature of panegyric as a genre demands that the topoi depersonalize the object, and therefore panegyric questions the notion of straightforward accuracy. Perhaps one could take it further: character is constructed in perception, as is beauty, for panegyric makes explicit the rendering of life's particulars via literary generalities. A woman has teeth like "a lovely necklace of gleaming pearls" (9) because that is a topos of beauty. The interlocutors' game is literary criticism in the form of an object lesson on the nature and technique of panegyric, and so, of necessity, it universalizes and depersonalizes its object. The primary objective of panegyrical celebration is to display the skill of the panegyrist, while the ostensible "object" of the encomium is, in truth, no more than a tool in the display of that art. As in Propertius 1.3, we have an unreal woman, a piece in the game, given pseudoreality when she "comes to life." Then suddenly in the *Apology*, the near-explicit unreality of the *Essay* seems overturned, and everything is natural and realistic. But note one point: the lady's speech is reported, not given in person. The reality she achieves here, I suggest, is just as much a stereotype as that in the panegyric and so is part of the fiction (within fiction). Like Cynthia's tirade, it is still "his story." Lycinus and Polystratus are, of course, also characters in a work of art and can therefore never have a complete and simplistic reality, and yet they seem to acquire and maintain a realism—an impression of reality—to which the lady could never aspire. She is a work of art in a way that they are not. In this, we might perhaps compare the men with the two satyrs and Pantheia with the sleeping nymph or, better, all of them with the characters on the Portland Vase. The interlocutors may be part of the work of art, but they partake in it as written-in readers, while the lady is there as an art object.[49]

The most famous element in the *Essay* is the way in which the woman's portrait is constructed from various bits of great works of art, literary as well as visual. The Cnidian Aphrodite is there of course; indeed, unsurprisingly, the description begins with her, while many other statues and paintings contribute, as does Homer, the "best of painters." Before the start of his set-piece panegyric, however, Lycinus/Lucian proceeds by asking Polystratus questions: whether he has seen a certain work, whether he has been to a certain famous place, which work by Pheidias (for example) he would praise most highly (the right answer is the Lemnian Athena), and so on, all of which serve to draw his interlocutor (and through him the reader) into a common perspective concerning cultured values. In this practice of culling the best bits from each work of art in order to produce Lycinus's own, there is a hint of the story pattern that produced the anecdote about Zeuxis, that when he sought a model for his Helen he took the best bits of five maidens, as no one woman could be supremely beautiful (Pliny *Nat. Hist.* 35.64). The boundaries between real women and artistic representations of women have become seriously fudged at this stage. Let us look for a moment at what sort of reality the woman has. At first, she has a country, Smyrna, but no name. Eventually Polystratus half-supplies a name: it is "the same as Abradatas's wife." Of course he is being polite in not actually speaking her name, but it does conveniently allow for depersonalization. More-over, this apparent touch of realism provides another opportunity for the artful display of learning, for the reference is to the heroine of Xenophon's *Cyropaideia* (Jones 1986.76). The name is Panthea, "All-goddess," or Pantheia "All-divine," just as Lycinus has been describing. This is not to say that we are meant to perceive the lady as a total fiction. My point is, rather, that "we," as cultured second-century gentlemen like Lycinus and Polystratus, do imagine that we are talking about a real person, but our way of visualizing her is as an art object, a composite of the arts of mankind.[50] Woman conceived as art object is made into art object.

In the *Apology*, the lady is made to comment quite explicitly about the glaring colors of the "set panegyric," as if she were allowed to give expression to her sense of the universalizing, depersonalizing nature of this type of praise. But, ironically, even that modesty with which she makes her disclaimer is forced to add to her representation as a perfect work of art. Lycinus replies that he will by no means detract from his portrait, but rather will add this further grace. Lycinus's ultimate defense of his excessive praise, particularly the comparisons with goddesses and/or works of art, is to remind the lady that this is panegyric, in which the use of illustrations has powerful aesthetic value, and she will just have to submit and provide herself for the topoi of the genre. The main point of "her" objection is worth noting: it is wrong, even sacrilegious, to com-pare her with goddesses. Comparison with goddesses and with particu-lar artistic representations of goddesses gets mixed up. Lycinus himself uses this confusion by disclaiming any impiety since it was the works of art, not the goddesses, with which he compared her. But it is, I think, still a telling comment on the ancient attitude toward the female—women, goddesses, statues—that the confusion is so pervasive throughout the diptych. It is in contexts such as these that the anecdote about the Cni-dian Aphrodite and her admirer and rapist becomes not a bizarre story of one man's folly in regards to artistic and religious sensibility but a nor-mative pattern that differs from ordinary attitudes only in degree. Women, goddesses, and statues are all the same thing.

This has been a discussion largely of active male viewers and passive female objects. Even where the pattern is shifted or destabilized, as, for example, in the active roles of goddesses or in the fetishized male body (Narcissus providing the paradigm case), it seems to me that the dominant mode of reading is enhanced by the awareness that these cases involve such a paradigm shift. (Being common does not, after all, make something normative.) In the case of Lucian's *Essay*, the male viewers are themselves also on display and are exposed as exhibitionists. But it is they themselves who display themselves, a rhetorical sleight of hand enhanced by the overt identification of one of them with the author. The pleasure of the reader in watching this display is perhaps narcissistic, since the invitation to identify and so to reinforce one's status is very strong: identification leaves little room for the reader to resist the role of "cultured second-century gentleman." It almost seems to me as if there is no way of presenting women (and the same point could be made of other "Other" groups) that is not at least partly repressive, for if images reflect the stereotypes, then they are contributing to their continued prevalence, while if they disrupt the stereotypes, they may simply reinforce the "rules of gender" by the fact that they are so obviously in opposition to a norm. Whatever they do, they are inclined to "display" women; however "displayed" men may be, they somehow retain control. In the depiction of the triumphant Theseus in the House of Gavius Rufus, mentioned at the start of this essay, although the hero is clearly the central focus of the painting, displayed by the various internal viewers for all to see and not shown in an active position, it is crucial for the force of the picture that he is Theseus *triumphant*. What he is doing is destroying the Minotaur and rescuing the children of Athens, as shown by the child on the side opposite the crowd taking his hand in a gesture of supplication. Theseus may be displayed, but it is as an active hero who maintains, indeed reinforces, his sense of control.

Women are to be seen. Mary Ann Caws, in her essay on surrealist images of women (called, incidentally, "Ladies Shot and Painted"), quotes John Berger on the "woman, who is also looking, [and] is made to 'treat herself first and foremost as a sight.'"[51] They are discussing a picture of a naked woman with a mirror over her middle part, which the viewer therefore sees reversed and out of synch. The woman is also looking in the mirror and so avoiding the gaze of the viewer. Is it the case, then, that all verbal and visual representations of women are necessarily oppressive? As Caws asks (1986.269): "Is there some way of looking that is not the look of an intruder, some interpretation from which we would

exempt ourselves as consumers?" A negative response to that question
might be held to be the logical conclusion of the arguments proposed
in this chapter. Perhaps this is something we just have to live with.[52]
Proposition: you cannot avoid viewing the women in Lucian and on the
Portland Vase as art objects of a different order from the lookers, usually
men, who view them. This is a reactionary statement, for it returns authority to the text.

The debate in reader-response circles is often said to center on
whether the text or the reader has authority in the production of meaning.[53] Part of the difficulty, perhaps, lies in the metaphor of authority—
as has been noted before, the assigning of authority is a patriarchal act—
a metaphor that is generally taken to be prescriptive rather than
descriptive. I mean that the discussion is not really about what *ought* to
happen, which side of the dichotomy reader versus text *ought* to be privileged, but a less judgmental description of what actually does happen,
whether readers in fact make meaning or whether texts in fact do so. One
needs to ask not just where authority for meaning lies but for what purposes? If a reading cannot be avoided, then that sounds like a claim for
univocality. There would be three possibilities: (1) all readers must see
this reading and their doing so is a guarantee of its rightness; or (2) every
reader must really think this way, but does not realize it; or (3) once a
reader has seen this reading it cannot be ignored. I am not sure that anyone holds any of these views consistently and in practice. Perhaps an example would help. Discussing Vermeer's painting *The Artist in His Studio*, Norman Bryson (1983.114) says that the turned back of the painter
excludes the spectator's presence. It seems to me, however, that it rather
subsumes the spectator into the artist's viewpoint: looking at the model
who is the true work of art. It is hard to resist this viewpoint, following
the gaze of the artist-cum-internal viewer, however one might want to
interpret that viewpoint. But Bryson appears to have resisted it, or not
to have thought of it in that way. To answer my three possibilities: (1) my
reading is wrong because Bryson does not mention or see it; (2) he does
see the woman as art object, but he has so far internalized such visions of
women that he is not aware of it as a "reading"; or (3) he would not be
able to resist it once he saw it. None of these is very convincing. There
may be a middle way, though it will not offer the easy, balanced solution
that that phrase usually implies. Such a way goes like this: at the opening of this paper I made precise distinctions between three types of
viewer, distinctions that I introduced in order to deconstruct, but can you
unread that reading? Deconstruction does not unread the hierarchical

oppositions it takes apart. Fragmentation in the reader allows you to see the spectator of *The Artist in His Studio* both as excluded and as subsumed into the artist, but *not* to ignore the tension. This is an illustration of the act of reading: these two incompatible readings are both operative on different levels. In this case, as so often, gender may provide a locus for interpretation, for the *Artist* has many parallels to but also significant differences from the Pompeian wall painting of a paintress at work that was mentioned at the beginning. Both paintings include an artist, artistic materials, a model, an internal painting, and a strong element of voyeurism—in the Vermeer, this voyeurism is suggested by the curtain on the viewer's left, which has obviously just been drawn aside to allow the viewer to look in; in the Pompeian painting, it is channeled through the two women peeping round the door to watch the events of the painting. In the Vermeer, the artist is a man, a man who retains all the creative power of his status as artist, while also denying his visibility by his turned back and dark clothing. Little of the internal painting is visible; the center of the artist's and our gaze is the female model, the art object, whose own gaze is properly downcast. In the Pompeian painting by contrast, the internal picture (the Priapus) is an observer, while the artist herself is positioned and constructed also as a work of art, a sight, an object of beauty. Vermeer's artist's arm is at work on his canvas; the arm of the Pompeian artist is drawn back (filling the brush with paint) with the intention and result of exposing and enhancing the folds of her clothing and the desirability of her body.[54]

Those who are interested in infinite regress in the field of viewing art are fond of the image of the mirror. One of the ways in which the relationship between work of art and viewer is described is as "me looking at art / art looking at me," which becomes me looking at (looking at [looking at (looking at)]) and so on, ad infinitum. Looking at looking is like being between opposing mirrors where the image bounces back and forth to infinity. Likewise each viewer sees another viewer in front of him. There the analogy breaks down, however, for the value in such fragmentation is that it can be a framework for difference, for the multiplicity of readings that must be our response to any work of art.

Notes

I am grateful to John Henderson, Jaš Elsner, and Francis Frascina for reading and very helpfully criticizing a draft of this chapter, and to Richard Wallace for many conversations on the way. In the final stages, David Fredrick made many constructive suggestions.

1. My argument is obviously much indebted to various exponents of reader-response criticism. For a general introduction to this topic, see Suleiman and Crosman 1980, Tompkin 1980, Freund 1987. The best work by a classical scholar relating to reception theory is Martindale 1993. For me, one of the most interesting insights exposed by reader-response criticism is the multiplicity of levels involved in the act of reading. Some critics (traditional ones like Booth and, perhaps, Iser) make more or less precise distinctions between implied readers internal to the text and real or external readers (however many further divisions they may make within each category).

2. Already my examples deconstruct their differences, for drama is as much a visual art as a textual one. From the viewer's perspective, the internal audience of drama is more like the internal viewer in art than it is like the internal audience of a narrative poem.

3. The gendered arrangement here is discussed further toward the end of this essay.

4. The artist is painting what appears to be a herm-like Priapus, who seems to look back at her, further playing with the interactions of viewers internal and external to the painting (or rather "paintings," the one in Pompeii VI 1 10 and that within it). At her feet, a rather knowing-looking child holds up some free-standing painting (perhaps an exemplar? but it does not look much like the Priapic figure). Richard Wallace made the intriguing suggestion to me that the paintress might be Venus and the child Cupid. See also J. R. Clarke 1993, esp. 278–79, 282, and 293, where he discusses a bowl fragment (now in the Museum of Fine Arts in Boston) on which decorative sculpted herms gaze at lovemaking couples, and seem "ready . . . to leap out of their decorative roles and join the lovers." Also Myerowitz 1992 and Frontisi-Ducroux 1996.90: a lamp acts to emphasize the role of the internal spectator as deictic voyeur. See also Michel 1980 for a wide-ranging study of the internal viewer in ancient, particularly Pompeian, art.

5. See Jay 1988.6–7. As Jay notes, the eye on the end of the centric ray was assumed to be singular and static. This does not mesh with the way scientists would now describe vision (which is much more dynamic and apparently almost chaotic). For the totalizing effect of the "centric ray" account of vision in art, see Bryson 1983, particularly 94, Henderson 1996.250. Jay concludes with a timely reminder that all the various "scopic regimes" (ways of visualizing the process of vision) are patterns we construct in order to shed light on the process, not competing theories only one of which corresponds to some absolute reality.

6. I am referring in particular to Iser 1974. The term "implied reader," which is, I think, his coinage, is used by Iser (mostly, and in practice) of a reader who is assumed or projected by the author (or the text) and who is, on the whole, fairly monovisual. Deconstructive readings of this reader have added considerable nuance to it, but not out of all recognition.

7. Mulvey's "two aspects" in the gaze—voyeurism and scopophilia—involve an opposition between an active, sadistic voyeurism that, in Mulvey's analysis,

implies a demand for a narrative and a sense of control, and, on the other hand, a passive, masochistic scopophilia that denies and so compensates for (potential) loss and that is concentrated timelessly on the act of looking. The opposition is not, however, a simple dichotomy but rath\er a distinction of viewpoint that encompasses interrelated elements. Many visual and verbal images elicit readings or viewings that are both scopophilic and voyeuristic, possibly even at the same time. It seems to me that, whatever their interesting differences, both aspects are (at least potentially) liable to objectify the recipient and to construct the viewer in a position of power, even if one aspect does so more directly than the other. For a lucid analysis of Mulvey's theories and their relationship to ancient looking, see Fredrick 1995, with bibliography in his notes 12 and 13.

8. Almost no psychoanalytical theory is free of this tendency, even (ironically) when it draws attention to it.

9. Doane 1987 also argues against the totalizing reading of the gaze as male, while agreeing (as all critics do) that in many genres the gaze is constructed as male. Snow 1989 draws attention to the risk that elements in the act of viewing that are not adequately accounted for by the male gaze theory may be occluded by the very power of that theory. See also Penley 1989, who is interested in the possibilities of viewers taking up positions of identification on more than one layer at once. (At least, so it seems to me. It is possible that I am imposing on her the notion that these multiple positions can be taken *simultaneously*.) Mulvey, in a 1992 chapter, states (or hopes) that "feminist theory and criticism and, indeed, feminist art make use of this fragmentation, avoiding the blinkered vision of a single anthropomorphic perspective" (70–71). See also Stehle 1990, who argues for the existence (or the appropriative reading) of a nonpossessive gaze in Sappho.

10. On objectification, see, for example, Burgin 1992.232–36, Armstrong 1989.69, Elsner 1996b, Frontisi-Ducroux 1996.89. Frontisi-Ducroux is interesting also on the way in which the same representational feature (she is talking of frontality) acts differently for the different genders.

11. There is a story about Kandinsky, that he could not recognize a haystack in Monet's *Haystack* (except by the catalogue), and it was suggested that this was because the picture was hung upside down. The truth of this anecdote is less important than the existence of such a story. See Caws 1989.145 and Marin 1988.

12. See, for example, Masaccio's *Trinity*, on which Bryson 1983.109.

13. See Dunning 1993.133: "One of the two primary characteristics of the flatbed picture plane [he refers to Steinberg 1972] is the post-modern tendency to fragment the painted image by structuring multiple perspectives around pluralist viewpoints." See also Arnheim 1982.

14. See Barton 1993.91ff. and Frontisi-Ducroux 1996.

15. In late antiquity, Procopius certainly seemed to have a sense of something that could be called fragmentation of the viewpoint, to judge from his description of the church of Hagia Sophia in Constantinople, where he suggests that the wealth of detail causes the viewpoint to fragment—and this is a good

thing. See Roberts 1989.74–75. For the general late antique tendency to "fragment" the classical literary and artistic material, see Malamud 1993, esp. 157.

16. See, for example, Barthes 1975, Chambers 1984, Gubar 1982.

17. The story is told at Lucian *Essay in Portraiture* (*Imagines*) 4, Pliny *Nat. Hist.* 7.127, Valerius Maximus 8.11.4. In the version told by Ps.-Lucian (*Amores* 15–16), it is speculated that the rapist approached the statue from behind because he was using it "as a boy" (17). See Elsner 1991.156–57 and Goldhill 1995.103–04.

18. See Osborne 1994.84: "The viewer of the sculpture is put in the fantasy position of being able to see Aphrodite naked with impunity. Praxiteles represents the unrepresentable." On ancient attitudes to cult statues as both works of art and divine presences, see Gordon 1979 and Freedberg 1989.74–77.

19. See Sharrock 1991 and Elsner and Sharrock 1991. The motif of Pygmalion as a metaphor for writers, readers, and critics has been most forcibly used by J. Hillis Miller 1990.

20. See Osborne 1994.84, where he discusses the way the statue's position "in the round" necessitates the spectator's engagement (of desire) in the possible narratives of response to the statue.

21. I am particularly grateful to some perceptive comments by John Henderson here.

22. On the connection between love and sight in antiquity, see A. Walker 1992.

23. See Frontisi-Ducroux 1996.90 (and her reference to Pinney 1990), who shows how the drapery acts as "an iconic metaphor for *Aidos*, Modesty, which, far from being in conflict with Eros, assists it right up to the final act." On the Cnidian Aphrodite generally, see Havelock 1995, esp. chap. 4, on works inspired by Praxiteles' statue, Spivey 1996.177–86, Stewart 1997, esp. 97–107, 222: "what the Knidia's instinctive gesture of modesty . . . belied in practice."

24. On the instabilities of gender involved in this iconographic game, see also Kampen 1996b. In the Hercules and Omphale in the triclinium in the House of M. Lucretius (Pompeii IX 3 5; see Havelock 1971, plate XII), even the cross-dressing and the fact that Omphale gazes at Hercules seem to reinforce his masculine power by opposition. Havelock says: "The queen wears Herakles' standard uniform, the lion's skin, over her head and shoulders and rests her soft hand on his club." Can we avoid having it both ways?

25. Bryson says of this painting that four of the five stages of the Annunciation story have been suppressed—Disquiet, Inquiry, Submission, Merit—and only Reflection has been displayed. This perhaps underestimates the role of the reader. Painting may claim to freeze narrative time, but, in the act of suggesting narrative, it cannot maintain the suppression of other narrative elements.

26. Piling up examples of this pose would serve little purpose. Since this discussion centers on looking, however, we might just note one where the gaze is crucial. A painting by Avigdor Arikha entitled *Pudicity* (1986) shows a naked seated woman with one hand partially covering her pubic hair. At the titular level

of the painting, she is clearly concealing her pudenda, yet the position of the hand, particularly the almost pointing fingers, and the power of tradition necessarily make her concealment also a disclosure. The other hand has obviously just moved from across her breasts (in the ancient manner) to in front of her face, which is turned slightly away and partially covered by the hand, her eyes closed or downcast. The elbow, however, remains covering/pointing to the breast, so the painter has it both ways. The anxious refusal of the image to meet the looker's gaze emphasizes the act of viewing.

27. There is, for example, the story related by Ovid at *Fasti* 6.319–46, of Priapus's failed rape of the sleeping Vesta. The embarrassed god finds it necessary to claim he thought she was a nymph and, therefore, fair game. So common is the motif that Ovid is moved to warn women that they should not get drunk and fall asleep at a party, lest they suffer some sexual indignity (*Ars Amatoria* 3.761–68). See Richlin 1992c. In a number of works of Picasso, including one entitled *Satyr and Sleeping Woman*, the motif of sleepwatching is programmatic for the activity of artist, viewer, and artist as viewer in the production of meaning. See Steiner 1988.131–33 and Frontisi-Ducroux 1996.83, 86–87, and 91–92.

28. Its near relative, where a beloved mortal male is watched by a goddess, is among the most common of images where adult males are looked at, especially in a totalizing way. There, of course, the goddess is playing a properly male role. A visual example of such role reversal can be seen in the eponymous painting in the House of the Wounded Adonis (Pompeii VI 7 18, *viridarium*, north wall), where the young man reclines against his divine lover in a very Venus-like pose. Interestingly, the lines of sight in this painting are not quite straightforward. Venus is undoubtedly looking at her beloved, but her gaze is a little unfocused. Adonis, undoubtedly the object, has large, up-turned eyes—presumably because he is dying, but with the additional effect that he turns those eyes toward the most desirable object of sight, Venus herself. Even in the midst of his objectification, as *dying* beloved, Adonis retains some power of sight. See Carratelli 1993.428–29.

29. See Painter and Whitehouse 1991. They end with the claim that "the Portland Vase can only have belonged to the emperor Augustus himself."

30. That is, the designations they give on p. 33. I can only assume that there is a misprint in the designations given on the photograph on p. 35.

31. This reading goes back at least to Winckelmann 1776.861.

32. See also Hind 1979, who sees the vase as an essay in the assimilation of Greek myth to Roman myth and Roman history, interpreting side I as an illustration of Virgil *Aeneid* 4 and side II, more conventionally, as depicting Peleus, Thetis, and Poseidon/Zeus. Smart 1984 will be discussed further below. The long-running debate has continued most recently in the form of two notes in *JHS* 115 (1995) by Haynes and Hind. See also *J. Glass. Stud.* 32 (1990), a volume devoted to the Portland vase, and Skalsky 1992.

33. The circularity of narrative in mural friezes around a room is analyzed by Henderson 1996.

34. See Harden et al. 1968.49 for the story, which seems to originate in the seventeenth century, that the vase was found in a sarcophagus on the Appian Way in 1582. This story may or may not be true.

35. See Fredrick 1995 for the importance of releasing the erotic potential of mythological painting.

36. Ariadne was an enormously popular subject in Pompeian art: see Fredrick 1995.271–72. For the Vatican Ariadne, see the LIMC entry, number 118.

37. The technical production of the vase contributes here, for the pictures were created by carving the white glass in low relief against the blue glass. For the technical aspects of the vase's production, see Harden 1983.

38. An excellent analysis of the problematics of gender with regard to Roman elegy is offered by Wyke 1995. See also Sharrock 1995.

39. For the goddess playing a male role in erotic matters, see Dover 1978.172.

40. Pompeii VI 8 3 (House of the Tragic Poet). See Ling 1991.134–35, where he mentions that Agamemnon's covered face is an allusion to the "famous masterpiece by the early fourth-century painter Timanthes." On this painting and the powers of sight, see also Frontisi-Ducroux 1996.84.

41. I thank the anonymous reader for this suggestion.

42. See Barton 1993, Skinner 1993, Sharrock 1995.

43. The flowing material behind and between his legs might hint at a weakened and floppy phallus.

44. But even in losing himself, he paradoxically emphasizes his individuality by comparison with the Bacchants.

45. For one thing, I would suggest that very few people would say that for a woman looking the identifications of sadism and masochism are simply reversed.

46. Such also is the pattern of the *ecphrasis* in Theocritus's first *Idyll*, where a cup is described as depicting a beautiful woman flanked by two suitors.

47. Lucian's name is derived from the Latin "Lucius." He normally Hellenizes it to "Lycinos." See Jones 1986.8. I have partially re-Latinized it.

48. C. P. Jones 1986.77. For Lucian's later influence generally, see Robinson 1979.

49. For objectification as a feature of erotic viewing, see Elsner 1996b.

50. For a similar "scattering" of the female body in erotic discourse, this time that of Petrarch, see Vickers 1982.

51. Caws 1986.272. The position of a woman in art as a self-conscious "sight" has been much discussed. See Berger 1972 and, differently, Nead 1992. Elsner 1996b exposes the power of Narcissus as an image of this state of being observed: "He looks at himself as one who is being looked at."

52. See also Devereaux 1990 and Nochlin 1991.35–37, which includes treatment of the Velázquez *Rokeby Venus*, whom we see from behind, her face reflected in the mirror in which she gazes at herself, but does not return our gaze. (Nochlin

is actually more interested in the politically motivated slashing of this painting.) Nochlin's essay, like Fetterley's book to which, in some ways, it is similar, represents both an important project and an oversimplification. The response to Nochlin by L. Jordanova, in Bryson et al. 1994, offers a highly nuanced approach to a subject that Nochlin, for political reasons, prefers to see in starker terms. See also Snow 1989. For the roles played by mirrors in the rhetoric of gender in antiquity, see Wyke 1994b, and more generally for the mirror in the construction of women vis-à-vis (!) looking, see La Belle 1988.

53. I am much intrigued, although not entirely convinced, by the 1990 essay by Riffaterre, which argues for a reader-response critical method that nevertheless has the text demand certain precise responses. This might be authorial intention by another name, but I don't think so.

54. Frontisi-Ducroux 1996.85 reads the turned back of an erotic pursuer on a Greek vase as "provok[ing] the onlooker (voyeur), the Athenian drinker of images, into slipping into the skin of the seducer, to succumb with him to the call of beauty, and to enter into the game as active subject."

Bibliography

Abu-Lughod, L. 1986. *Veiled Sentiments: Honor and Poetry in a Bedouin Society.* Berkeley.

Achard, G. 1981. *Pratique rhétorique et idéologie politique dans les discours de Cicéron.* Mnemosyne Supplementum 68. Leiden.

Adams, J. N. 1982. *The Latin Sexual Vocabulary.* Baltimore.

Adkin, N. 1983. "The Teaching of the Fathers Concerning Footwear and Gait," *Latomus* 42.885–86.

Ahl, F. M. 1976. *Lucan: An Introduction.* Ithaca.

———. 1986. *Seneca: Trojan Women.* Ithaca.

Alcoff, L. 1988. "Cultural Feminism versus Post-Structuralism: The Identity Crisis in Feminist Theory," *Signs* 13.405–36.

Anderson, G. 1986. *Philostratus: Biography and Belles Lettres in the Third Century A.D.* London.

———. 1993. *The Second Sophistic: A Cultural Phenomenon in the Roman Empire.* London.

Anderson, W. S. 1966. "Horace *Carm.* 1.14: What Kind of Ship?" *CP* 41.84–98.

André, J. 1981. *Traité de physiognomonie: Anonyme latin.* Paris.

Andreae, B., and B. Conticello. 1974. *Le sculture di Sperlonga.* Antike Plastik 14. Berlin.

Armstrong, C. 1989. "The Reflexive and the Possessive View: Thoughts on Kertesz, Brandt, and the Photographic Nude," *Representations* 25.57–70.

Arnheim, R. 1982. *The Power of the Center: A Study of Composition in the Visual Arts.* Berkeley.

Ashby, T. 1906. "The Classical Topography of the Roman Campagna II," *PBSR* 3.1–212.

Ashmole, B. 1967. "A New Interpretation of the Portland Vase," *JHS* 87.1–17.

Asmis, E. 1984. *Epicurus' Scientific Method.* Ithaca.

———. 1989. "Seneca's *On the Happy Life* and Stoic Individualism," *Apeiron* 22.219–55.

Atkinson, J. M. 1984. *Our Masters' Voices: The Language and Body Language of Politics.* London.

Axer, J. 1989. "Tribunal-Stage-Arena: Modelling of the Communication Situation in M. Tullius Cicero's Judicial Speeches," *Rhetorica* 7.299–311.

Bailey, C. 1926. *Titi Lucreti Cari De Rerum Natura,* 3 vols. Oxford.

Bann, S. 1989. *The True Vine: On Visual Representation and the Western Tradition.* Cambridge.

Bargellini, P. 1991. "Le Terme Centrali di Pompei," in *Les Thermes Romains*. Collection de l'École française de Rome 142.115–28.

Barthes, R. 1975. *The Pleasure of the Text*, trans. R. Miller. London.

Bartmann, E. 1991. "Sculptural Collecting and Display in the Private Realm," in Gazda 1991.71–88.

Bartoli, P. S. 1790. "Memorie di varie escavazioni fatte in Roma," in *Miscellanea filologica critica e antiquaria*. Rome. 1.222–73.

Barton, C. 1993. *The Sorrows of the Ancient Romans: The Gladiator and the Monster*. Princeton.

———. 2001. *Roman Honor: The Fire in the Bones*. Berkeley.

Bartsch, S. 1989. *Decoding the Ancient Novel: The Reader and the Role of Description in Heliodorus and Achilles Tatius*. Princeton.

———. 1994. *Actors in the Audience: Theatricality and Doublespeak from Nero to Hadrian*. Cambridge.

———. 1997. *Ideology in Cold Blood: A Reading of Lucan's Civil War*. Cambridge, Mass.

Bateson, G. 1972. *Steps to an Ecology of Mind*. New York.

Baudry, J.-L. 1974–75. "Ideological Effects of the Basic Cinematographic Apparatus," *Film Quarterly* 28.2.39–47.

———. 1976. "The Apparatus," *Camera Obscura* 1.104–26.

Baxandall, M. 1988. *Painting and Experience in Fifteenth-Century Italy*, second ed. Oxford.

Beall, S. M. 1993. "Word-Painting in the *Imagines* of the Elder Philostratus," *Hermes* 121.350–63.

Beardsworth, A., and T. Keil. 1997. *Sociology on the Menu: An Invitation to the Study of Food and Society*. London.

Beare, W. 1955. *The Roman Stage: A Short History of Latin Drama in the Time of the Republic*. London.

Becatti, G. 1961. *Scavi di Ostia*, vol. 4: *Mosaici e pavimenti marmorei*. Rome.

Bek, L. 1980. *Towards Paradise on Earth: Modern Space Conception in Architecture: A Creation of Renaissance Humanism*. Analecta Romana Instituti Danici, supplement 9. Rome.

———. 1983. "*Questiones Convivales*: The Idea of the Triclinium and the Staging of Convivial Ceremony from Rome to Byzantium," *ARID* 12.81–107.

Bell, A. 1997. "Cicero and the Spectacle of Power," *JRS* 87.1–22.

Bell, D., and G. Valentine, eds. 1995. *Mapping Desire: Geographies of Sexualities*. London.

———. 1997. *Consuming Geographies: We Are Where We Eat*. London.

Benedict, R. 1946. *The Chrysanthemum and the Sword*. New York.

Bennett, J. 1987. *The Hunger Machine: The Politics of Food*. Montreal.

Berger, J. 1972. *Ways of Seeing*. London.

Berger, P. L., and T. Luckmann. 1967. *The Social Construction of Reality*. London.

Bergmann, B. 1991. "Painted Perspectives of a Villa Visit: Landscape as Status and Metaphor," in Gazda 1991.49–70.

———. 1994. "The Roman House as Memory Theater: The House of the Tragic Poet in Pompeii," *Art Bulletin* 76.225–56.

———. 1996. "The Pregnant Moment: Tragic Wives in the Roman Interior," in Kampen 1996c.199–218.

Bergstrom, J. 1979. "Enunciation and Sexual Difference," *Camera Obscura* 3–4.32–69.

Bieber, M. 1939. *The History of the Greek and Roman Theater.* Princeton.

Blänsdorf, J. 1982. "Die Komödienintrige als Spiel im Spiel," *A&A* 28.131–54.

Blok, A. 1981. "Rams and Billy-Goats: A Key to the Mediterranean Code of Honour," *Man* 16.427–40.

Blok, J. 1987. "Sexual Asymmetry: A Historiographical Essay," in *Sexual Asymmetry: Studies in Ancient Society,* ed. J. Blok and P. Mason. Amsterdam. 1–57.

Boeder, M. 1996. *Visa Est Vox: Sprache und Bild in der spätantiken Literatur.* Frankfurt.

Bompaire, J. 1958. *Lucien écrivain: Imitation et création.* Paris.

Bonfante, L. 1989. "Nudity as a Costume in Classical Art," *AJA* 93.543–70.

Booth, A. 1991. "The Age for Reclining and Its Attendant Perils," in W. J. Slater 1991.105–20.

Bordo, S. 1993. *Unbearable Weight: Feminism, Western Culture, and the Body.* Berkeley.

Boswell, J. 1980. *Christianity, Social Tolerance, and Homosexuality: Gay People in Western Europe from the Beginning of the Christian Era to the Fourteenth Century.* Chicago.

———. 1989. "Concepts, Experience, and Sexuality," *Differences* 1.67–87.

Botsford, G. 1909. *The Roman Assemblies from Their Origin to the End of the Republic.* New York.

Bourdieu, P. 1977. *Outline of a Theory of Practice,* trans. R. Nice. Cambridge.

———. 1979. "The Sense of Honor," in *Algeria 1960,* ed. P. Bourdieu, trans. R. Nice. Cambridge. 95–131.

———. 1984. *Distinction: A Social Critique of the Judgement of Taste,* trans. R. Nice. Cambridge, Mass.

———. 1990. *The Logic of Practice,* trans. R. Nice. Stanford.

———. 1991. "The Economy of Linguistic Exchanges," in *Language and Symbolic Power,* ed. J. B. Thompson, trans. G. Raymond and M. Adamson. Cambridge, Mass. 37–89.

Bowen-Ward, R. 1992. "Women in Roman Baths," *Harvard Theological Review* 85.125–47.

Bowersock, B. 1969. *Greek Sophists in the Roman Empire.* Oxford.

Bowie, E. 1970. "The Greeks and Their Past in the Second Sophistic," *P & P* 46.3–41, reprinted in *Studies in Ancient Society,* ed. M. I. Finley. London 1974.166–209.

Boyle, A. J., ed. 1988. *The Imperial Muse: Ramus Essays on Roman Literature of the Empire, To Juvenal through Ovid*. Berwick, Australia.

———. 1997. *Tragic Seneca: An Essay in the Theatrical Tradition*. London.

Bradley, K. 1991. *Discovering the Roman Family: Studies in Roman Social History*. Oxford.

Bragantini, I. 1997. "VII 12, 18–20 Lupanare," in *Pompeii: Pitture e mosaici* 7.528.

Braidotti, R. 1994. *Nomadic Subjects: Embodiment and Sexual Difference in Contemporary Feminist Theory*. New York.

Braudel, F. 1981. *The Structures of Everyday Life: Civilization and Capitalism, Fifteenth–Eighteenth Century*, vol. 1. New York.

Bremmer, J. 1992. "Walking, Standing, and Sitting in Ancient Greek Culture," in *A Cultural History of Gesture*, ed. J. Bremmer and H. Roodenburg. Ithaca. 15–35.

Brennan, T. 1996. "Epicurus on Sex, Marriage, and Children," *CP* 91.346–52.

Brilliant, R. 1963. *Gesture and Rank in Roman Art*. New Haven.

———. 1984. *Visual Narratives: Storytelling in Etruscan and Roman Art*. Ithaca.

Brokaw, C. A. 1942. "A New Approach to Roman Pictorial Relief," *Marsyas* 2.17–42.

Bronfen, E. 1992. *Over Her Dead Body: Death, Femininity, and the Aesthetic*. Manchester.

Brown, F., E. Richardson, and L. Richardson, Jr. 1993. *Cosa III: The Buildings of the Forum*. Memoirs of the American Academy in Rome 37. University Park, Pa.

Brown, P. 1992. *Power and Persuasion in Late Antiquity: Towards a Christian Empire*. Madison.

Brown, R. 1987. *Lucretius on Love and Sex: A Commentary on* De Rerum Natura *IV, 1030–1287*. Leiden.

Brown, S. 1992. "Death as Decoration: Scenes from the Arena on Roman Domestic Mosaics," in Richlin 1992b.180–211.

———. 1993. "Feminist Research in Archaeology: What Does It Mean? Why Is It Taking So Long?" in Rabinowitz and Richlin 1993.238–71.

———. 1997. "'Ways of Seeing' Women in Antiquity: An Introduction to Feminism in Classical Archaeology and Ancient Art History," in Koloski-Ostrow and Lyons 1997.12–42.

Bryant, J. 1996. *Moral Codes and Social Structure in Ancient Greece: A Sociology of Greek Ethics from Homer to the Epicureans and Stoics*. Albany.

Bryson, N. 1983. *Vision and Painting: The Logic of the Gaze*. London.

———. 1988. *Calligram: Essays in New Art History from France*. Cambridge.

———. 1994. "Philostratus and the Imaginary Museum," in *Art and Text in Ancient Greek Culture*, ed. S. Goldhill and R. Osborne. Cambridge. 255–83.

Bryson, N., M. A. Holly, and K. Moxey, eds. 1994. *Visual Culture: Images and Interpretations*. Hanover, N.H.

Burgin, V. 1992. "Perverse Space," in Colomina 1992.219–40.

———. 1996. *In/Different Spaces: Place and Memory in Visual Culture.* Berkeley.

Butcher, S. H. 1951. *Aristotle's Theory of Poetry and Fine Art,* 4th ed. New York.

Butler, J. 1993. *Bodies That Matter: On the Discursive Limits of "Sex."* New York.

Calder, W. M., III. 1970. "Originality in Seneca's *Troades,*" *CP* 65.75–82.

Caldwell, R. 1989. *The Origin of the Gods: A Study of Greek Theogonic Myth.* Oxford.

Cantarella, E. 1996. *Passato prossimo: Donne romane da Tacita a Sulpicia.* Milan.

Carratelli, G. P., ed. 1993. *Pompei: Pitture e mosaici.* Enciclopedia dell'arte antica classica e orientale, vol. 4. Rome.

Carson, A. 1990. "Putting Her in Her Place: Woman, Dirt, and Desire," in Halperin, Winkler, and Zeitlin 1990b.135–69.

Caws, M. A. 1986. "Ladies Shot and Painted: Female Embodiment in Surrealist Art," in *The Female Body in Western Culture: Contemporary Perspectives,* ed. S. R. Suleiman. Cambridge, Mass. 262–87.

———. 1989. *The Art of Interference: Stressed Readings in Verbal and Visual Texts.* Cambridge.

Cèbe, J.-P. 1987. *Varron: Satires Ménippées,* vol. 8. Collection de L'École française de Rome 9. Rome.

Chambers, R. 1984. *Story and Situation: Narrative Seduction and the Power of Fiction.* Manchester.

Clarke, J. R. 1990. "Notes on the Coordination of Wall, Floor, and Ceiling Decoration in the Houses of Roman Italy, 100 B.C.E.–235 C.E.," in *IL 60: Essays Honoring Irving Lavin on His Sixtieth Birthday,* ed. M. A. Lavin. New York. 1–29.

———. 1991a. *The Houses of Roman Italy, 100 B.C.–A.D. 250: Ritual, Space, and Decoration.* Berkeley.

———. 1991b. "The Decor of the House of Jupiter and Ganymede at Ostia Antica: A Private Residence Turned Gay Hotel?" in Gazda 1991.89–104.

———. 1993. "The Warren Cup and the Contexts for Representations of Male-to-Male Lovemaking in Augustan and Early Julio-Claudian Art," *Art Bulletin* 75.275–94.

———. 1996. "Hypersexual Black Men in Augustan Baths: Ideal Somatotypes and Apotropaic Magic," in Kampen 1996c.184–98.

———. 1998. *Looking at Lovemaking: Constructions of Sexuality in Roman Art, 100 B.C.–A.D. 250.* Berkeley.

Clarke, M. L. 1953. *Rhetoric at Rome.* Glasgow.

Clay, D. 1998. *Paradosis and Survival: Three Chapters in the Epicurean Philosophy.* Ann Arbor.

Clover, Carol J. 1992. *Men, Women, and Chainsaws: Gender in the Modern Horror Film.* Princeton.

Coarelli, F. 1971–72. "Il complesso pompeiano del Campo Marzio e la sua decorazione scultorea," *Atti della Pontificia Accademia romana di archeologia.* Rome. 99–122.

————. 1992. *Il foro Romano*, 2 vols., 2nd ed. Rome.

Coleman, K. M. 1990. "Fatal Charades: Roman Executions Staged as Mythological Enactments," *JRS* 80.44–73.

————. 1993. "Launching into History: Aquatic Displays in the Early Empire," *JRS* 83.48–74.

————. 1999. "Mythological Figures as Spokespersons in Statius' *Silvae*," in *Im Spiegel des Mythos: Bilderwelt and Lebenswelt*, ed. F. De Angelis, S. Muth, and T. Hölscher. Wiesbaden. 67–80.

Colomina, B., ed. 1992. *Sexuality and Space*. Princeton.

Conan, M. 1987. "The Imagines of Philostratus," *Word and Image* 3.162–71.

Corbeill, Anthony. 1996. *Controlling Laughter: Political Humor in the Late Roman Republic*. Princeton.

————. 1997. "Dining Deviants in Roman Political Invective," in Hallett and Skinner 1997.99–129.

————. 2001. "Education in the Roman Republic: Creating Traditions," in *Education in Greek and Roman Antiquity*, ed. Y. L. Too. Leiden. 261–87.

Cousin, J. 1935. *Études sur Quintilien*. Paris.

Crary, J. 1993. *The Techniques of the Observer*. Cambridge, Mass.

Creed, B. 1993. *The Monstrous-Feminine: Film, Feminism, Psychoanalysis*. London.

D'Arms, J. H. 1990. "The Roman *Convivium* and the Idea of Equality," in *Sympotica: A Symposium on the Symposium*, ed. O. Murray. Oxford. 308–20.

————. 1991. "Slaves at Roman Convivia," in W. J. Slater 1991.171–83.

Darwin, C. 1965 [1872]. *The Expression of the Emotions in Man and Animals*. Chicago.

David, J.-M. 1979. "Promotion civique et droit à la parole: L. Licinius Crassus, les accusateurs et les rhéteurs latins," *MEFRA* 91.135–81.

————. 1980. "*Eloquentia popularis* et conduites symboliques des orateurs de la fin de la République: Problèmes d'efficacité," *QS* 12.171–211.

————. 1983a. "Les orateurs des municipes à Rome: Intégration, réticences et snobismes," in *Les bourgeoisies municipales italiennes aux IIe et Ier siècles av. J. C.* Paris. 309–23.

————. 1983b. "L'action oratoire de C. Gracchus: L'image d'un modèle," in *Demokratia et Aristokratia*, ed. C. Nicolet. Paris. 103–16.

————. 1992. *Le patronat judiciaire au dernier siècle de la République romaine*. Rome.

Dawson, C. 1944. *Romano-Campanian Mythological Landscape Painting*. Yale Classical Studies 9. New Haven.

Deichmann, F. W. 1946. "Die Lage der constantinischen Basilika der heiligen Agnes an der Via Nomentana," *RAC* 22.213–34.

DeJong, I., and J. P. Sullivan, eds. 1994. *Modern Critical Theory and Classical Literature*. Leiden.

Demand, N. 1994. *Birth, Death, and Motherhood in Classical Greece*. Baltimore.

Detienne, M. 1965. "En Grèce archaïque: Géométrie, politique et société," *Annales* 20.425–41.

————. 1977. *The Gardens of Adonis*, trans. J. Lloyd. Atlantic Highlands, N.J.

————. 1979. *Dionysos Slain*, trans. M. and L. Muellner. Baltimore.

Devereaux, M. 1990. "Oppressive Texts, Resisting Readers and the Gendered Spectator: The New Aesthetics," *JAAC* 48.337–47.

Dickie, M. W., and K. M. D. Dunbabin. 1983. "*Invidia rumpantur pectora*: The Iconography of Phthonos/Invidia in Graeco-Roman Art," *JbAC* 26.7–37.

Dixon, S. 1997. "Continuity and Change in Roman Social History: Retrieving 'Family Feeling(s)' from Roman Law and Literature," in Golden and Toohey 1997b.79–90.

Doane, M. A. 1982. "Film and the Masquerade: Theorising the Female Spectator," *Screen* 23.314.74–88.

————. 1987. *The Desire to Desire: The Women's Film of the 1940s*. Bloomington.

————. 1991. *Femme Fatales: Feminism, Film Theory, Psychoanalysis*. New York.

Dodds, E. R. 1951. *The Greeks and the Irrational*. Los Angeles.

Douglas, M. 1972. "Symbolic Orders in the Use of Domestic Space," in *Man, Settlement, and Urbanism*, ed. P. J. Ucko, R. Tringham, and G. W. Dimbleby. London.

Douglass, F. 1845. *Narrative of the Life of Frederick Douglass, An American Slave. Written by Himself*. Boston.

Dover, K. J. 1978. *Greek Homosexuality*. Cambridge, Mass.

duBois, P. 1988. *Sowing the Body: Psychoanalysis and Ancient Representations of Women*. Chicago.

————. 1995. *Sappho Is Burning*. Chicago.

————. 1996. "Archaic Bodies-in-Pieces," in Kampen 1996c.55–64.

Duby, G., and M. Perrot. 1992. "Writing the History of Women," in Pantel 1992a.ix–xxi.

Dunbabin, K. M. D. 1989. "*Baiarum Grata Voluptas*: Pleasures and Dangers of the Baths," *PBSR* 57.6–49.

————. 1991. "Triclinium and Stibadium," in W. J. Slater 1991.121–48.

————. 1996. "Convivial Spaces: Dining and Entertainment in the Roman Villa," *JRA* 9.66–80.

Duncan, N. 1996. *BodySpace: Destabilizing Geographies of Gender and Sexuality*. London.

Dunning, W. V. 1991. "The Concept of Self and Post-Modern Painting: Constructing a Post-Cartesian Viewer," *JAAC* 49.331–36.

————. 1993. "Post-Modernism and the Construct of the Divisible Self," *BJA* 33.132–41.

Dupont, F. 1992. *Daily Life in Ancient Rome*, trans. C. Woodall. Oxford.

Dworkin, A. 1987. *Intercourse*. New York.

Dwyer, E. J. 1982. *Pompeian Domestic Sculpture*. Archeologica 28. Rome.

Dyson, S. L. 1993. "From New to New Age Archaeology: Archaeological Theory and Classical Archaeology," *AJA* 97.195–206.

Eagleton, T. 1983. *Literary Theory: An Introduction*. Minneapolis.

———. 1996. *The Illusions of Postmodernism*. London.

Edwards, C. 1993. *The Politics of Immorality in Ancient Rome*. Cambridge.

———. 1994. "Beware of Imitations: Theatre and the Subversion of Imperial Identity," in Elsner and Masters 1994.83–97.

———. 1996. *Writing Rome: Textual Approaches to the City*. Cambridge.

———. 1997. "Unspeakable Professions: Public Performance and Prostitution in Ancient Rome," in Hallett and Skinner 1997.66–95.

Efron, D. 1972. *Gesture, Race, and Culture*. The Hague.

Elsner, J. 1991. "Visual Mimesis and the Myth of the Real: Ovid's Pygmalion as Viewer," *Ramus* 20.154–68.

———. 1995. *Art and the Roman Viewer*. Cambridge.

———. 1996a. *Art and Text in Roman Culture*. Cambridge.

———. 1996b. "Naturalism and the Erotics of the Gaze: Intimations of Narcissus," in Kampen 1996c.247–61.

Elsner, J., and J. Masters, eds. 1994. *Reflections of Nero: Culture, History, and Representation*. Chapel Hill.

Elsner, J., and A. R. Sharrock 1991. "Re-Viewing Pygmalion," *Ramus* 20.149–82.

Elsom, H. 1992. "Challirhoe: Displaying the Phallic Woman," in Richlin 1992b.212–30.

Fantham, E. 1982. *Seneca's Troades: A Literary Introduction with Text, Translation, and Commentary*. Princeton.

Featherstone, M., M. Hepworth, and B. S. Turner, eds. 1991. *The Body: Social Process and Cultural Theory*. London.

Feldman, S. 1962. "Blushing, Fear of Blushing, and Shame," *Journal of the American Psychoanalytic Association* 10.368–85.

Ferguson, M. W., M. Quilligan, and N. J. Vickers, eds. 1986. *Rewriting the Renaissance: The Discourses of Sexual Difference in Early Modern Europe*. Chicago.

Ferrea, L. 1995. "Uno specchio in bronzo con 'symplegma' e con cornice con segni zodiacali," *Bollettino dei Musei Comunali di Roma* 9.133–45.

Fetterley, J. 1978. *The Resisting Reader: A Feminist Approach to American Literature*. Bloomington.

Findlen, P. 1993. "Humanism, Politics, and Pornography in Renaissance Italy," in Hunt 1993b.49–108.

Fitzgerald, W. 1985. "Lucretius' Cure for Love in the *De Rerum Natura*," *CW* 78.73–86.

———. 1995. *Catullan Provocations: Lyric Poetry and the Drama of Position*. Berkeley.

Flaig, E. 1995. "Entscheidung und Konsens. Zu den Feldern der politischen Kommunikation zwischen Aristokratie und Plebs," in Jehne 1995.77–127.

Flitterman-Lewis, S. 1990. *To Desire Differently: Feminism and the French Cinema*. Urbana.

Foss, P. 1995. "Age, Gender, and Status Divisions at Mealtime in the Roman House: A Synopsis of the Literary Evidence." Web document from

"Kitchens and Dining Rooms at Pompeii: The Spatial and Social Relationship of Cooking to Eating in the Roman Household." Ph.D. diss., University of Michigan, 1994.

———. 1997. "Watchful *Lares*: Roman Household Organization and the Rituals of Cooking and Dining," in Laurence and Wallace-Hadrill 1997.196–218.

Foucault, M. 1978. *Introduction. The History of Sexuality*, vol. 1, trans. R. Hurley. New York.

———. 1979. *Discipline and Punish: The Birth of the Prison*, trans. A. Sheridan. New York.

———. 1984. "The Order of Discourse," in *Language and Politics*, ed. M. Shapiro. Oxford. 108–38.

———. 1985. *The Use of Pleasure. The History of Sexuality*, vol. 2, trans. R. Hurley. New York.

———. 1986. *The Care of the Self. The History of Sexuality*, vol. 3, trans. R. Hurley. New York.

———. 1988. "*Las Meniñas*," in Bryson 1988.91–105.

Fowler, B. 1997. *Pierre Bourdieu and Cultural Theory: Critical Investigations*. London.

Foxhall, L. 1998. "Pandora Unbound: A Feminist Critique of Foucault's *History of Sexuality*, in Larmour, Miller, and Platter 1998.122–37.

Fraenkel, E. 1957. *Horace*. Oxford.

Frank, A. W. 1991. "For a Sociology of the Body: An Analytical Review," in Featherstone, Hepworth, and Turner 1991.36–102.

Frappier-Mazur, L. 1993. "Truth and the Obscene Word in Eighteenth-Century French Pornography," in Hunt 1993b.203–21.

Freccero, C. 1990. "Notes of a Post–Sex Wars Theorizer," in *Conflicts in Feminism*, ed. M. Hirsch and E. Fox Keller. New York. 305–25.

Fredrick, D. 1995. "Beyond the Atrium to Ariadne: Erotic Painting and Visual Pleasure in the Roman House," *ClAnt* 14.266–87.

———. 1997. "Reading Broken Skin: Violence in Roman Elegy," in Hallett and Skinner 1997.172–93.

———. 1999. "Haptic Poetics," *Arethusa* 32.49–83.

Freedberg, D. 1989. *The Power of Images: Studies in the History and Theory of Response*. Chicago.

Freund, E. 1987. *The Return of the Reader*. London.

Frontisi-Ducroux, F. 1996. "Eros, Desire, and the Gaze," in Kampen 1996c.81–100.

Galinsky, K. 1996. *Augustan Culture: An Interpretive Introduction*. Princeton.

Gamel, M. K. 1999. "Reading as a Man: Performance and Gender in Roman Elegy," *Helios* 25.79–95.

Gandelman, C. 1990. *Reading Pictures, Viewing Texts*. Bloomington.

Gantz, T. 1993. *Early Greek Myth: A Guide to Literary and Artistic Sources*. Baltimore.

Gardner, J. F. 1986. *Women in Roman Law and Society*. Bloomington.

———. 1993. *Being a Roman Citizen*. New York.

Garland, R. 1995. *The Eye of the Beholder: Deformity and Disability in the Greco-Roman World*. Ithaca.

Garnsey, P. 1988. *Famine and Food Supply in the Greco-Roman World*. Cambridge.

Gazda, E., ed. 1991. *Roman Art in the Private Sphere*. Ann Arbor.

Geffcken, K. 1973. *Comedy in the* Pro Caelio. Mnemosyne Supplementum 30. Leiden.

Gelzer, M. 1968. *Caesar: Politician and Statesman*, trans. P. Needham. Cambridge, Mass.

Gilligan, J. 1997. *Violence: Reflections on a National Epidemic*. New York.

Ginzburg, C. 1980. "Tiziano, Ovidio e i codici della figurazione erotica nel '500," in *Tiziano e Venezia: Atti del Convegno internazionale di studi*. Vicenza. 124–35.

Giuliani, L. 1986. *Bildnis and Botschaft: Hermeneutische Untersuchungen zur Bildniskunst der römischen Republik*. Frankfurt.

———. 1987. "Die seligen Krüppel: Zur Deutung von Mißgestalten in der hellenistischen Kleinkunst," *AA* 701–21.

Gleason, M. 1995. *Making Men: Sophists and Self-Presentation in Ancient Rome*. Princeton.

Gledhill, C. 1994. "Image and Voice: Approaches to Marxist-Feminist Criticism," in *Multiple Voices in Feminist Film Criticism*, ed. D. Carson, L. Dittmar, and J. R. Welsch. Minneapolis. 109–23.

Golden, M., and P. Toohey. 1997a. "General Introduction," in Golden and Toohey 1997b.1–9.

———. eds. 1997b. *Inventing Ancient Culture: Historicism, Periodization, and the Ancient World*. London.

Goldhill, S. D. 1995. *Foucault's Virginity: Ancient Erotic Fiction and the History of Sexuality*. Cambridge.

Gordon, P. 1996. *Epicurus in Lycia: The Second-Century World of Diogenes of Oenoanda*. Ann Arbor.

———. 1997a. "Epicureanism," in *Encyclopedia of Classical Philosophy*, ed. D. Zeyl. Westport, Conn. 208–14.

———. 1997b. "The Lover's Voice in *Heroides* 15: Or, Why Is Sappho a Man?" in Hallett and Skinner 1997.274–91.

———. (forthcoming). "Remembering the Garden: The Trouble with Women in the School of Epicurus," in *Philodemus and His New Testament World*, ed. J. Fitzgerald, G. Holland, and D. Obbink. Leiden.

Gordon, R. L. 1979. "The Real and the Imaginary: Production and Religion in the Graeco-Roman World," *Art History* 2.5–34.

Gosling, J. C. B., and C. C. W. Taylor. 1982. *The Greeks on Pleasure*. Oxford.

Gotoff, H. 1986. "Cicero's Analysis of the Prosecution Speeches in the *Pro Caelio*: An Exercise in Practical Criticism," *CP* 81.122–32.

———. 1993. "Oratory: The Art of Illusion," *HSCP* 95.289–313.

Gowers, E. 1993. *The Loaded Table: Representations of Food in Roman Literature.* Oxford.

———. 1995. "The Anatomy of Rome from Capitol to Cloaca," *JRS* 85.23–32.

Graber, M. 1990. "The Eye of the Beholder: Perceptual Relativity in Lucretius," *Apeiron* 23.91–116.

Graf, F. 1992. "Gestures and Conventions: The Gestures of Roman Actors and Orators," in *A Cultural History of Gesture*, ed. J. Bremmer and H. Roodenburg. Ithaca. 36–58.

Greene, E. 1998. *The Erotics of Domination: Male Desire and the Mistress in Latin Poetry*. Baltimore.

Greenidge, A. 1901. *The Legal Procedure of Cicero's Time*. Oxford.

Gregory, J. 1991. *Euripides and the Instruction of the Athenians*. Ann Arbor.

Gruen, E. 1974. *The Last Generation of the Roman Republic*. Berkeley.

———. 1990. *Studies in Greek Culture and Roman Policy*. Leiden.

———. 1991. "The Exercise of Power in the Roman Republic," in *City-States in Classical and Medieval Italy*, ed. A. Molho, K. Raaflaub, and J. Emlen. Ann Arbor. 251–67.

———. 1996. "The Roman Oligarchy: Image and Perception," in *"Imperium Sine Fine": T. Robert S. Broughton and the Roman Republic*, ed. J. Linderski. Stuttgart. 215–34.

Gualandi-Genito, M. C. 1986. *Le lucerne antiche del Trentino*. Trento.

Gubar, S. 1982. "The Blank Page and Female Creativity," in *Writing and Sexual Difference*, ed. E. Abel. Brighton. 73–93.

Gunderson, E. 1996. "The Ideology of the Arena," *ClAnt* 15.113–51.

Gurval, R. A. 1995. *Actium and Augustus: The Politics and Emotions of Civil War.* Ann Arbor.

Habinek, T. 1997. "The Invention of Sexuality in the World-City of Rome," in Habinek and Schiesaro 1997.23–43.

Habinek, T., and A. Schiesaro, eds. 1997. *The Roman Cultural Revolution*. Cambridge.

Hacking, I. 1986. "Making up People," in *Reconstructing Individualism: Autonomy, Individuality, and the Self in Western Thought*, ed. T. Heller, M. Sosna, and D. Wellbery. Stanford. 222–36.

Hägg, T. 1983. *The Novel in Antiquity*. Oxford.

Hall, D. 1998. "Ancient Roman Prostitutes." Honors Thesis, University of Arkansas.

Hall, E. 1966. *The Hidden Dimension*. Garden City, N.Y.

Hallett, J. P. 1989. "Female Homoeroticism and the Denial of Reality in Latin Literature," *Yale Journal of Criticism* 3.209–27.

———. 1993. "Feminist Theory, Historical Periods, Literary Canons, and the Study of Greco-Roman Antiquity," in Rabinowitz and Richlin 1993.44–72.

Hallett, J. P., and M. B. Skinner, eds. 1997. *Roman Sexualities*. Princeton.

Halperin, D. M. 1990. *One Hundred Years of Homosexuality*. London.

———. 1993. "Is There a History of Sexuality?" in *The Lesbian and Gay Studies Reader*, ed. H. Abelove, M. A. Barale, and D. M. Halperin. London. 416–31.

Halperin, D. M., J. J. Winkler, and F. Zeitlin. 1990a. "Introduction," in Halperin, Winkler, and Zeitlin 1990b.3–20.

———. eds. 1990b. *Before Sexuality: The Construction of Erotic Experience in the Ancient Greek World*. Princeton.

Hanson, J. 1959. *Roman Theater-Temples*. Princeton.

Harden, D. B., 1983. "New Light on the History and Technique of the Portland Vase and Auldjo Cameo Vessels," *J. Glass. Stud.* 25.45–54.

Harden, D. B., et al. 1968. *Masterpieces of Glass*. London.

Hardie, P. 1993. *The Epic Successors of Virgil: A Study in the Dynamics of a Tradition*. Cambridge.

———. 1997. "Questions of Authority: The Invention of Tradition in Ovid's *Metamorphoses*," in Habinek and Schiesaro 1997.182–98.

Harris, W. V. 1989. *Ancient Literacy*. Cambridge, Mass.

Harrison, G. W. M., ed. 2000. *Seneca in Performance*. London.

Harrison, S. J. 1992. "The Portland Vase Revisited," *JHS* 112.150–53.

Havelock, C. M. 1971. *Hellenistic Art*. London.

———. 1995. *The Aphrodite of Knidos and Her Successors: A Historical Review of the Female Nude in Greek Art*. Ann Arbor.

Haynes, D. E. L. 1968. "The Portland Vase Again," *JHS* 88.58–72.

———. 1995. "The Portland Vase: A Reply," *JHS* 115.146–52.

Hecht, J. J. 1956. *The Domestic Servant Class in Eighteenth-Century England*. London.

Helbig, W. 1868. *Wandgemälde der vom Vesuv verschütteten städte Campaniens*. Leipzig.

———. 1899. *Führer durch die öffentlichen Sammlungen klassischer altertümer in Rom*, 2nd ed., vol. 2. Leipzig.

Hellegouarc'h, J. 1972. *Le vocabulaire latin des relations et des partis politiques sous la République*, 2nd ed. Paris.

Henderson, J. 1988. "Lucan / The Word at War," in Boyle 1988.122–64.

———. 1996. "Footnote: Representation in the Villa of the Mysteries," in Elsner 1996a.235–76.

Henry, M. M. 1992. "The Edible Woman: Athenaeus' Concept of the Pornographic," in Richlin 1992b.250–68.

Herter, H. 1958. "Effeminatus," in *Reallexikon für Antike und Christentum*, ed. T. Klauser. Stuttgart. 4.620–50.

Hillard, T. 1992. "On the Stage, Behind the Curtain: Images of Politically Active Women in the Late Republic," in *Stereotypes of Women in Power*, ed. B. Garlick, S. Dixon, and P. Allen. New York. 37–64.

Hind, J. 1979. "Greek and Roman Epic Scenes on the Portland Vase," *JHS* 99.20–25.

———. 1995. "The Portland Vase: New Clues towards Old Solutions," *JHS* 115.153–55.

Hölkeskamp, K. 1995. "*Oratoris maxima scaena*: Reden vor dem Volk in der politischen Kultur der Republik," in Jehne 1995.11–49.

Holly, M. A. 1996. *Past Looking: Historical Imagination and the Rhetoric of the Image.* Ithaca.

Hope, V. 1997. "A Roof over the Dead: Communal Tombs and Family Structure," in Laurence and Wallace-Hadrill 1997.69–90.

Hopkins, K. 1983. *Death and Renewal.* Cambridge.

Horsfall, N. 1971. "*Incedere* and *Incessus*," *Glotta* 49.145–47.

Hubbell, H. 1919–20. "The *Rhetorica* of Philodemus," *Transactions of the Connecticut Academy of Arts and Sciences* 23.243–382.

Humphrey, J. H., ed. 1991. *Literacy in the Roman World.* Ann Arbor.

Hunt, L. 1993a. "Introduction: Obscenity and the Origins of Modernity, 1500–1800," in Hunt 1993b.9–45.

———, ed. 1993b. *The Invention of Pornography: Obscenity and the Origins of Modernity, 1500–1800.* New York.

Irigaray, L. 1978. Interview in *Les femmes, la pornographie et l'érotisme*, eds. M.-F. Hans and G. Lapouge. Paris.

Iser, W. 1974. *The Implied Reader: Patterns of Fiction from Bunyan to Beckett.* Baltimore.

Jacobelli, L. 1991. "Le pitture e gli stucchi delle Terme Suburbane di Pompei," *4. Internationales Kolloquium zur römischen Wandmalerei. Kölner Jahrbuch für vor- und Frühgeschichte* 24.147–52.

———. 1995. *Le pitture erotiche delle Terme suburbane di Pompei.* Rome.

James, L., and R. Webb. 1991. "To Understand Ultimate Things and Enter Secret Places: Ecphrasis and Art in Byzantium," *Art History* 14.1–17.

Jameson, M. H. 1990. "Domestic Space in the Greek City-State," in *Domestic Architecture and the Use of Space*, ed. S. Kent. Cambridge. 92–113.

Janan, M. 1994. *"When the Lamp Is Shattered": Desire and Narrative in Catullus.* Carbondale, Ill.

Jay, M. 1988. "Scopic Regimes of Modernity," in *Vision and Visuality*, ed. H. Foster. Seattle. 3–23.

———. 1993. *Downcast Eyes: The Denigration of Vision in Twentieth-Century French Thought.* Berkeley.

Jebb, R. 1868. "On Mr. Tennyson's Lucretius," *Macmillan's Magazine* 104.97–103.

Jehne, M., ed. 1995. *Demokratie in Rom? Die Rolle des Volkes in der Politik der römischen Republik.* Stuttgart.

Jenkins, R. 1992. *Pierre Bourdieu.* London.

Jenks, Chris. 1995. *Visual Culture.* London.

Jenkyns, R. 1998. *Virgil's Experience.* Oxford.

Johns, C. 1982. *Sex or Symbol: Erotic Images of Greece and Rome.* Austin.

Jones, A. 1994. "Dis/playing the Phallus: Male Artists Perform Their Masculinities," *Art History* 17.546–84.

Jones, C. P. 1986. *Culture and Society in Lucian.* London.

———. 1991. "Dinner Theatre," in W. J. Slater 1991.185–98.

Jongman, W. 1988. *The Economy and Society of Pompeii*. Amsterdam.

Joshel, S. R. 1992a. *Work, Identity, and Legal Status at Rome: A Study of the Occupational Inscriptions*. Norman, Okla.

———. 1992b. "The Body Female and the Body Politic: Livy's Lucretia and Verginia," in Richlin 1992b.112–30.

———. 1997. "Female Desire and the Discourse of Empire: Tacitus's Messalina," in Hallett and Skinner 1997.221–55.

Kambitsis, J. 1972. *L'Antiope d'Euripide*. Athens.

Kampen, N. B. 1979. "Observations on the Ancient Uses of the Spada Reliefs," *AC* 48.583–600.

———. 1981. *Image and Status: Roman Working Women in Ostia*. Berlin.

———. 1994. "Material Girl: Feminist Confrontations with Roman Art," *Arethusa* 27.111–37.

———. 1996a. "Gender Theory in Roman Art," in Kleiner and Matheson 1996.14–25.

———. 1996b. "Omphale and the Instability of Gender," in Kampen 1996c.233–46.

———, ed. 1996c. *Sexuality in Ancient Art*. Cambridge.

Kaplan, E. A. 1983. "Is the Gaze Male?" in *Powers of Desire: The Politics of Sexuality*, ed. A. Snitow, C. Stansell, and S. Thompson. New York. 309–27.

———. 1997. *Looking for the Other: Feminism, Film, and the Imperial Gaze*. New York.

Kappeler, S. 1986. *The Pornography of Representation*. Minneapolis.

Kaster, R. A. 1988. *Guardians of Language: The Grammarian and Society in Late Antiquity*. Berkeley.

———. 1995. *C. Suetonius Tranquillus: De Grammaticis et Rhetoribus*. Oxford.

Keaveney, A. 1983. "Sulla and the Gods," in *Studies in Latin Literature and Roman History, III*, ed. C. Deroux. Collection Latomus 180. Brussels. 44–79.

Kellum, B. 1996. "The Phallus as Signifier: The Forum of Augustus and Rituals of Masculinity," in Kampen 1996c.170–83.

———. 1997. "Concealing/Revealing: Gender and the Play of Meaning in the Monuments of Augustan Rome," in Habinek and Schiesaro 1997.158–81.

———. (forthcoming). *The Play of Meaning*.

Kennedy, D. 1992. *The Arts of Love: Five Studies in the Discourse of Roman Love Elegy*. Cambridge.

Kenney, E. J. 1968. "Doctus Lucretius," *Mnemosyne* 4.366–92.

Keuls, E. C. 1985. *The Reign of the Phallus: Sexual Politics in Ancient Athens*. New York.

Kilmer, Martin. 1983. "Genital Phobia and Depilation," *JHS* 102.104–12.

———. 1993. *Greek Erotica on Attic Red-Figure Vases*. London.

Kleiner, D. E. E., and S. B. Matheson. 1996. *I Claudia: Women in Ancient Rome*. Austin.

Klose, F. 1933. *Die Bedeutung von honos und honestas*. Breslau.

Kluckhohn, C. 1960. "The Moral Order in the Expanding Society," in *The City Invincible*, ed. C. H. Kraeling and R. M. Adams. Chicago. 391–404.

Koch, G. 1993. *Sarkophage der römischen Kaiserzeit*. Darmstadt.

Kockel, V. 1995. "Forum Augustum," *Lexicon Topographicum Urbis Romae*, vol. 2, ed. E. M. Steinby. Rome. 289–95.

Koloski-Ostrow, A. O. 1997. "Violent Stages in Two Pompeian Houses: Imperial Taste, Aristocratic Response, and Messages of Male Control," in Koloski-Ostrow and Lyons 1997.243–66.

Koloski-Ostrow, A. O., and C. L. Lyons, eds. 1997. *Naked Truths: Women, Sexuality, and Gender in Classical Art and Archaeology*. London.

Koortbojian, M. 1995. *Myth, Meaning, and Memory on Roman Sarcophagi*. Berkeley.

———. 1996. "*In Commemorationem Mortuorum*: Text and Image along the 'Street of Tombs,'" in Elsner 1996a.210–33.

Koskela, H. 1997. "Bold Walk and Breakings: Women's Spatial Confidence Versus Fear of Violence," *Gender, Place, and Culture* 4.3.301 and electronic text.

Köstermann, E. 1933. "*Incedere* und *Incessere*," *Glotta* 21.56–62.

Krause, C. 1976. "Zur baulichen Gestalt des republikanischen Comitiums," *MDAI(R)* 83.31–69.

Krautheimer, R. 1937. *Corpus Basilicarum Christianarum Romae: The Early Christian Basilicas of Rome, Fourth–Ninth Centuries*. Vatican City.

Krenkel, W. A. 1980. "Fellatio and Irrumatio," *WZRostock* 29.77–88.

La Belle, J. 1988. *Herself Beheld: The Literature of the Looking Glass*. Ithaca.

Lacan, J. 1977. *The Four Fundamental Concepts of Psychoanalysis*, ed. J.-A. Miller, trans. A. Sheridan. New York.

Laplanche, J., and J.-B. Pontalis. 1968. "Fantasy and the Origins of Sexuality," *International Journal of Psycho-Analysis* 49.1–18.

Laqueur, T. 1990. *Making Sex: Body and Gender from the Greeks to Freud*. Cambridge, Mass.

Larmour, D. H. J., P. A. Miller, and C. Platter, eds. 1998. *Rethinking Sexuality: Foucault and Classical Antiquity*. Princeton.

Laurence, R. 1997. "Space and Text," in Laurence and Wallace-Hadrill 1997.7–14.

Laurence, R., and A. Wallace-Hadrill, eds. 1997. *Domestic Space in the Roman World: Pompeii and Beyond. JRA*, supplementary series 22. Portsmouth, R.I.

de Lauretis, T. 1984. *Alice Doesn't: Feminism, Semiotics, Cinema*. Bloomington.

———. 1987. *Technologies of Gender: Essays in Theory, Film, and Fiction*. Bloomington.

Leach, E. W. 1988. *The Rhetoric of Space*. Princeton.

Lefebvre, H. 1991. *The Production of Space*. Oxford.

Lehmann, K. 1941. "The *Imagines* of the Elder Philostratus," *Art Bulletin* 23.17–42.

Lehmann, S. 1989. "Die Reliefs im Palazzo Spada und ihre Ergänzung," in *An-tikenzeichnungen und Antikenstudium in Renaissance und Frühbarock. Akten des internationalen Symposions 8–10 September 1986 in Coburg*, ed. R. Harprath and H. Wrede. Mainz. 221–63.

Lehmann-Hartleben, K., and E. C. Olsen. 1942. *Dionysiac Sarcophagi in Baltimore*. Baltimore.

Leigh, M. 1995. "Wounding and Popular Rhetoric at Rome," *BICS* 40.195–212.

———. 1997. *Lucan: Spectacle and Engagement*. Oxford.

Levi, D. 1941. "The Evil Eye and the Lucky Hunchback," in *Antioch-on-the-Orontes*, vol. 3, ed. R. Stillwell. Princeton. 220–32.

Levi, P. 1961. *Survival in Auschwitz*. New York.

Lindberg, D. C. 1976. *Theories of Vision from Al-Kindi to Kepler*. Chicago.

Lindsay, W. 1900. *The* Captivi *of Plautus*. London.

Ling, R. 1991. *Roman Painting*. Cambridge.

Lissarague, F. 1990. "The Sexual Life of Satyrs," in Halperin, Winkler, and Zeitlin 1990b.53–81.

———. 1992. "Figures of Women," in Pantel 1992a.139–229.

Lochin, C. 1994. "Pegasos," *Lexicon Iconographicum Mythologiae Classicae* 7.1.214–30.

Long, A. A. 1986. *Hellenistic Philosophy: Stoics, Epicureans, Skeptics*. Berkeley.

Loraux, N. 1987. *Tragic Ways of Killing a Woman*, trans. A. Forster. Cambridge.

MacMullen, R. 1966. *Enemies of the Roman Order: Treason, Unrest, and Alienation in the Empire*. Cambridge, Mass.

Maier-Eichhorn, U. 1989. *Die Gestikulation in Quintilians Rhetorik*. Frankfurt.

Malamud, M. 1993. "Vandalizing Epic," *Ramus* 22.155–73.

Manfredini, A. 1985. "Qui commutant cum feminis vestem," *RIDA* 32.257–71.

Marcadé, J. 1961. *Roma Amor: Essai sur les représentations érotiques dans l'art étrusque et romain*. Geneva.

———. 1962. *Eros Kalos: Essay on Erotic Elements in Greek Art*. Geneva.

Marin, L. 1988. "Towards a Theory of Reading in the Visual Arts: Poussin's *The Arcadian Shepherds*," in Bryson 1988.63–90.

Marsh, T. 1992. "Epilogue: The (Other) Maiden's Tale," in Richlin 1992b.269–84.

Martindale, C. A. 1993. *Redeeming the Text: Latin Poetry and the Hermeneutics of Reception*. Cambridge.

Massey, D. 1994. *Space, Place, and Gender*. Minneapolis.

———. 1996. "Masculinity, Dualisms, and High Technology," in Duncan 1996.109–26.

Massey, D., and L. McDowell. 1994. "A Woman's Place?" in Massey 1994.91–211.

Masters, J. 1992. *Poetry and Civil War in Lucan's* Bellum Civile. Cambridge.

———. 1994. "Deceiving the Reader: The Political Mission of Lucan *Bellum Civile* 7," in Elsner and Masters 1994.151–77.

Mattei, S. 1994. *Luciano di Samosata: Descrizioni di opera d'arte.* Nuova Universale Einaudi 217. Turin.

Mayne, J. 1995. "Paradoxes of Spectatorship," in *Viewing Positions: Ways of Seeing Film,* ed. L. Williams. New Brunswick, N.J. 155–83.

McDonald, W. 1943. *The Political Meeting Places of the Greeks.* Baltimore.

Meier, C. 1965. "Populares," *RE* suppl. 10.549–615.

Merchant, C. 1983. *The Death of Nature: Women, Ecology, and the Scientific Revolution.* San Francisco.

Meskell, L. 1997. "The Ancient Body's Trajectory through Time: The Irresistible Body and the Seduction of Archaeology," in Montserrat 1997.139–61.

Metz, C. 1982. *The Imaginary Signifier: Psychoanalysis and Cinema,* trans. C. Britton, A. Williams, B. Brewster, and A. Guzzetti. Bloomington.

Michel, D. 1980. "Bemerkungen über Zuschauerfiguren in pompejanischen sogenannten Tafelbildern," in *La regione sotterrata dal Vesuvio.* Naples. 537–98.

Miles, G. 1995. *Livy: Reconstructing Early Rome.* Ithaca.

Millar, F. 1984. "The Political Character of the Classical Roman Republic, 200–151 B.C.," *JRS* 74.1–19.

———. 1986. "Politics, Persuasion, and the People before the Social War (150–90 B.C.)," *JRS* 76.1–11.

———. 1995. "Popular Politics at Rome in the Late Republic," in *Leaders and Masses in the Roman World: Studies in Honor of Zvi Yavetz,* ed. I. Malkin and Z. W. Rubinsohn. Leiden. 91–114.

———. 1998. *The Crowd in Rome in the Late Republic.* Ann Arbor.

Miller, J. H. 1990. *Versions of Pygmalion.* Cambridge, Mass.

Miller, P. A. 1998. "Catullan Consciousness, the 'Care of the Self,' and the Force of the Negative in History," in Larmour, Miller, and Platter 1998.171–203.

Mirabella, M. B. 1995. "Mute Rhetorics: Women, the Gaze, and Dance in Renaissance England," *Genre* 28.413–44.

Modleski, T. 1988. *The Women Who Knew Too Much: Hitchcock and Feminist Theory.* New York.

Montserrat, D., ed. 1997. *Changing Bodies, Changing Meanings: Studies on the Human Body in Antiquity.* London.

Morales, H. 1996. "The Torturer's Apprentice: Parrhasius and the Limits of Art," in Elsner 1996a.182–209.

Morisaki, S., and W. B. Gudykunst. 1994. "Face in Japan and the United States," in *The Challenge of Facework,* ed. S. Ting-Toomey. Albany. 47–93.

Mossman, J. 1995. *Wild Justice: A Study of Euripides' Hecuba.* Oxford.

Müller, F. G. J. M. 1994. *The So-Called Peleus and Thetis Sarcophagus in the Villa Albani.* Iconological Studies in Roman Art I. Amsterdam.

Mulvey, L. 1975. "Visual Pleasure and Narrative Cinema," *Screen* 16.6–18.

———. 1981. "Afterthoughts on 'Visual Pleasure and Narrative Cinema' Inspired by *Duel in the Sun,*" *Framework* 15.12–15.

———. 1989. *Visual and Other Pleasures.* Bloomington.

————. 1992. "Pandora: Topographies of the Mask and Curiosity," in Colomina 1992.53–71.

Myerowitz, M. 1992. "The Domestication of Desire: Ovid's *Parva Tabella* and the Theater of Love," in Richlin 1992b.131–57.

Narducci, E. 1997. *Cicerone e l'eloquenza romana: Retorica e progetto culturale.* Rome.

Nast, H. J., and A. Kobayashi. 1996. "Re-Corporealizing Vision," in Duncan 1996.75–93.

Nead, L. 1992. *The Female Nude: Art, Obscenity, and Sexuality.* London.

Neudecker, R. 1988. *Die Skulpturenausstattung römischer Villen in Italien.* Mainz.

Nicolet, C. 1980. *The World of the Citizen in Republican Rome*, trans. P. S. Falla. Berkeley.

Nietzsche, F. 1984. *Human, All Too Human*, trans. M. Faber. Lincoln, Neb.

————. 1990. *Beyond Good and Evil*, trans. R. J. Hollingdale. London.

Nochlin, L. 1991. "Women, Art, and Power," in *Visual Theory*, ed. N. Bryson, M. A. Holly, and K. Moxey. Oxford. 13–46.

North, J. 1990. "Democratic Politics in Republican Rome," *P & P* 126.3–21.

Nussbaum, M. 1986. "Therapeutic Arguments: Epicurus and Aristotle," in *The Norms of Nature: Studies in Hellenistic Ethics*, ed. M. Schofield and G. Striker. Cambridge. 31–74.

————. 1989. "Beyond Obsession and Disgust: Lucretius' Genealogy of Love," *Apeiron* 22.1–9.

————. 1990. "'By Words Not Arms': Lucretius on Gentleness in an Unsafe World," *Apeiron* 23.41–90.

————. 1994. *The Therapy of Desire: Theory and Practice in Hellenistic Ethics.* Princeton.

————. 1996. "Therapeutic Arguments and Structures of Desire," in *Feminism and Ancient Philosophy*, ed. J. Ward. New York. 195–216.

Obbink, D. 1989. "The Atheism of Epicurus," *GRBS* 30.187–223.

Oliensis, E. 1997. "The Erotics of *Amicitia*: Readings in Tibullus, Propertius, and Horace," in Hallett and Skinner 1997.151–71.

Orlin, E. M. 1997. *Temples, Religion, and Politics in the Roman Republic.* Leiden.

Ormand, K. 1994. "Lucan's *Vix Auctor Fidelis*," *ClAnt* 13.38–55.

Osborne, R. 1994. "Looking on—Greek Style: Does the Sculpted Girl Speak to Women Too?" in *Classical Greece: Ancient Histories and Modern Archaeologies*, ed. I. Morris. Cambridge. 81–96.

Oudart, J.-P. 1977–78. "Cinema and Suture," *Screen* 18.35–47.

Packer, J. E. 1997. "Report from Rome: The Imperial Fora, a Retrospective," *AJA* 101.307–31.

Painter, K., and Whitehouse, D. B. 1991. "The Portland Vase," in *Roman Glass: Two Centuries of Art and Invention*, ed. M. Newby and K. Painter. London. 33–43.

Pantel, P. Schmitt. 1992a. *A History of Women in the West*. Vol. 1: *From Ancient Goddesses to Christian Saints*. Cambridge, Mass.

———. 1992b. "Women and Ancient History Today," in Pantel 1992a.464–72.

Papadopoulos, J. K. 1994. "Pasiphae," *Lexicon Iconographicum Mythologiae Classicae* 7.1.193–200.

Pardo, M. 1993. "Artifice as Seduction in Titian," in *Sexuality and Gender in Early Modern Europe*, ed. J. G. Turner. Cambridge. 55–89.

Parker, H. 1992. "Love's Body Anatomized: The Ancient Erotic Handbooks and the Rhetoric of Sexuality," in Richlin 1992b.90–107.

———. 1997. "The Teratogenic Grid," in Hallett and Skinner 1997.47–65.

Pavolini, C. 1983. *Ostia: Guida archeologica Laterza 8*.

Pearson, M. P., and C. Richards. 1994. "Ordering the World: Perceptions of Architecture, Space, and Time," in *Architecture and Order: Approaches to Social Space*, ed. M. P. Pearson and C. Richards. London. 1–37.

Penley, C. 1989. *The Future of an Illusion: Film, Feminism, and Psychoanalysis*. Minneapolis.

Penwill, R. 1994. "Image, Ideology, and Action in Cicero and Lucretius," *Ramus* 23.68–91.

Perelli, L. 1982. *Il movimento popolare nell' ultimo secolo della repubblica*. Turin.

Petersen, L. H. 1997. "Divided Consciousness and Female Companionship: Reconstructing Female Subjectivity on Greek Vases," *Arethusa* 30.35–74.

Pina Polo, F. 1995. "Procedures and Functions of Civil and Military *Contiones* in Rome," *Klio* 77.203–16.

———. 1996. *"Contra Arma Verbis": Der Redner vor dem Volk in der späten römischen Republik*, trans. E. Liess. Stuttgart.

Pinney, G. F. 1990. "Figures of Speech: The Picture of Aidos," *Metis* 5.185–204.

Pitchford, N. 1997. "Reading Feminism's Pornography Conflict: Implications for Postmodernist Reading Strategies," *Genders* 25.3–38.

Pollini, J. 1996. "The 'Dart Aphrodite': A New Replica of the 'Arles Aphrodite Type,' the Cult Image of Venus Victrix in Pompey's Theater at Rome, and Venusian Ideology and Politics in the Late Republic–Early Principate," *Latomus* 55.757–85.

Pollock, G. 1988. *Vision and Difference: Femininity, Feminism, and the Histories of Art*. London.

Pomeroy, S. B. 1975. *Goddesses, Whores, Wives, and Slaves: Women in Classical Antiquity*. New York.

Pöschl, V. 1975. "Zur Einbeziehung anwesender Personen und sichtbarer Objekte in Ciceros Reden," in *Ciceroniana: Hommages à Kazimierz Kumaniecki*, ed. K. Kumaniecki, A. Michel, and R. Verdière. Leiden. 206–26.

Poster, M. 1989. *Critical Theory and Poststructuralism: In Search of a Context*. Ithaca.

Purcell, N. 1995. "Forum Romanum (the Republican Period)," in *Lexicon Topographicum Urbis Romae*, ed. E. M. Steinby. Rome. 325–36.

Purinton, J. 1993. "Epicurus on the Telos," *Phronesis* 38.281–320.

Quint, D. 1992. *Epic and Empire*. Princeton.

Rabinowitz, N. S. 1992. "Tragedy and the Politics of Containment," in Richlin 1992b.36–52.

———. 1993a. "Introduction," in Rabinowitz and Richlin 1993.1–20.

———. 1993b. *Anxiety Veiled: Euripides and the Traffic in Women*. Ithaca.

———. 1998. "Slaves with Slaves: Women and Class in Euripidean Tragedy," in *Women and Slaves in Greco-Roman Culture: Differential Equations*, ed. S. R. Joshel and S. Murnaghan. London. 56–68.

Rabinowitz, N. S., and A. Richlin, eds. 1993. *Feminist Theory and the Classics*. New York.

Ramage, E. 1961. "Cicero on Extra-Roman Speech," *TAPA* 92.481–94.

Rawson, B. 1991. "Adult-Child Relationships in Roman Society," in *Marriage, Divorce, and Children in Ancient Rome*, ed. B. Rawson. Oxford. 7–30.

Rawson, E. 1985. *Intellectual Life in the Late Roman Republic*. Baltimore.

———. 1987. "*Discrimina Ordinum*: The *Lex Julia Theatralis*," *PBSR* 55.83–114.

Reardon, B. P., ed. 1989. *Collected Ancient Greek Novels*. Berkeley.

Redfield, R. 1968 [1953]. *The Primitive World and Its Transformations*. Harmondsworth.

Rendell, J., B. Penner, and I. Borden. 2000. *Gender, Space, Architecture: An Interdisciplinary Introduction*. London.

Rhodes, P. J. 1981. *A Commentary on the Aristotelian* Athenaion Politeia. Oxford.

Richardson, L., Jr. 1987. "A Note on the Architecture of the Theatrum Pompei in Rome," *AJA* 91.123–26.

———. 1992. *A New Topographical Dictionary of Ancient Rome*. Baltimore.

Richlin, A. 1981. "The Meaning of *Irrumare* in Catullus and Martial," *CP* 76.40–46.

———. 1991. "Zeus and Metis: Foucault, Feminism, Classics," *Helios* 18.160–80.

———. 1992a. *The Garden of Priapus: Sexuality and Aggression in Roman Humor*. Oxford.

———, ed. 1992b. *Pornography and Representation in Greece and Rome*. Oxford.

———. 1992c. "Reading Ovid's Rapes," in Richlin 1992b.158–79.

———. 1992d. "Introduction," in Richlin 1992a.xiii-xxxiii.

———. 1993a. "Not Before Homosexuality," *Journal of the History of Sexuality* 3.4.523–73.

———. 1993b. "The Ethnographer's Dilemma," in Rabinowitz and Richlin 1993.272–303.

———. 1995. "Making Up a Woman: The Face of Roman Gender," in *Off With Her Head! The Denial of Women's Identity in Myth, Religion, and Culture*, ed. H. Eilberg-Schwartz and W. Doniger. Berkeley. 185–213.

———. 1996. "The Roman Forum as Gendered Space," abstract, Annual Meeting of the American Philological Association, Session 8, Section 70, New York.

————. 1997a. "Towards a History of Body History," in Golden and Toohey 1997b.16–35.

————. 1997b. "Gender and Rhetoric: Producing Manhood in the Schools," in *Roman Eloquence: Rhetoric in Society and Literature*, ed. W. Dominik. New York. 90–110.

————. 1997c. "Carrying Water in a Sieve: Class and the Body in Roman Women's Religion," in *Women and Goddess Traditions in Antiquity and Today*, ed. K. L. King. Minneapolis. 330–74.

————. 1999. "Cicero's Head," in *Constructions of the Classical Body*, ed. J. I. Porter. Ann Arbor. 190–211.

Ricks, C. B. 1987. *The Poems of Tennyson*, 2nd ed., 3 vols. London.

Riezler, K. 1942–43. "Comment on the Social Psychology of Shame," *American Journal of Sociology* 48.457–65.

Riffaterre, M. 1990. "Compulsory Reader Response: The Intertextual Drive," in *Intertextuality: Theories and Practices*, ed. M. Worton and J. Still. Manchester. 56–75.

Riggsby, A. 1997. "'Public' and 'Private' in Roman Culture: The Case of the Cubiculum," *JRA* 10.36–56.

Rimé, B., and L. Schiaratura. 1991. "Gesture and Speech," in *Fundamentals of Nonverbal Behavior*, ed. R. Feldman and B. Rimé. Cambridge. 239–81.

Rives, J. 1994. "Venus Genetrix Outside Rome," *Phoenix* 48.294–306.

Roberts, M. 1989. *The Jeweled Style: Poetry and Poetics in Late Antiquity*. Ithaca.

Robin, D. 1993. "Film Theory and the Gendered Voice in Seneca," in Rabinowitz and Richlin 1993.102–21.

Robinson, C. 1979. *Lucian and His Influence in Europe*. London.

Rosenmeyer, T. G. 1993. "Seneca's *Oedipus* and Performance: The Manto Scene," in *Theater and Society in the Classical World*, ed. R. Scodel. Ann Arbor. 235–44.

Rubiés, J.-P. 1994. "Nero in Tacitus and Nero in Tacitism: The Historian's Craft," in Elsner and Masters 1994.29–47.

Rudd, N. 1994. *The Classical Tradition in Operation*. Toronto.

Rutz, W. 1960. "Amor Mortis bei Lucan," *Hermes* 88.462–75.

Salvan, J. 1962. *To Be and Not To Be: An Analysis of Jean-Paul Sartre's Ontology*. Detroit.

Sampaolo, V. 1986. "Pitture," in *Le collezioni del Museo Nazionale di Napoli: I mosaici, le pitture, gli argenti, le terrecotte invetriate, i vetri, i cristalli, gli avori*, ed. M. R. Borriello. Rome. 1.172–73.

Sanders, D. 1990. "Behavioral Conventions and Archaeology: Methods for the Analysis of Ancient Architecture," in *Domestic Architecture and the Use of Space*, ed. S. Kent. Cambridge. 43–72.

Saylor, C. 1990. "*Lux Extrema*: Lucan, *Pharsalia* 4.402–81," *TAPA* 120.291–300.

Scagliarini, D. C. 1974–76. "Spazio e decorazione nella pittura pompeiana," *Palladio* 23–25.3–44.

Scarry, E. 1985. *The Body in Pain*. Oxford.

Schefold, K. 1952. *Pompejanische Malerei: Sinn und Ideengeschichte*. Basel.

Scheler, M. 1957. "Der 'Ort' des Schamgefühls und die Existenzweise des Menschen," in *Gesammelte Werke*. Bern. 10.67–154.

Schilling, R. 1954. *La religion romaine de Venús depuis les origins jusqu'au temps d'Auguste*. Paris.

Schreiber, T. 1894. *Die hellenistischen reliefbilder*. Leipzig.

Scott, J. 1986. "Gender: A Useful Category of Historical Analysis," *American Historical Review* 91.1053–75.

———. 1993. "The Evidence of Experience," in *The Lesbian and Gay Studies Reader*, ed. H. Abelove, M. A. Barale, and D. M. Halperin. London. 397–415.

Seager, R. 1972. "Cicero and the Word *Popularis*," *CQ* 66.328–38.

Sedley, D. 1998. *Lucretius and the Transformation of Greek Wisdom*. Cambridge.

Segal, C. 1984. "Senecan Baroque: The Death of Hippolytus in Seneca, Ovid, and Euripides," *TAPA* 114.311–25.

———. 1993. *Euripides and the Poetics of Sorrow: Art, Gender, and Commemoration in Alcestis, Hippolytus, and Hecuba*. Durham.

———. 1994. "Philomela's Web and the Pleasures of the Text," in *Modern Critical Theory and Classical Literature*, ed. I. J. F. DeJong and J. P. Sullivan. Leiden. 258–80.

Shapiro, H. A. 1992. "Eros in Love: Pederasty and Pornography in Greece," in Richlin 1992b.53–72.

Sharrock, A. R. 1991. "Womanufacture," *JRS* 81.36–49.

———. 1995. "The Drooping Rose: Elegiac Failure in *Amores* 3.7," *Ramus* 24.152–80.

Sichtermann, H. 1992. *Die Mythologischen Sarkophage*. Die Antiken Sarkophagreliefs Berlin. 12.2.

Sider, D. 1997. *The Epigrams of Philodemus: Introduction, Text, and Commentary*. Oxford.

Sieveking, J. 1925. "Das römische Relief," in *Festschrift Paul Arndt*. Munich. 14–34.

Silverman, K. 1980. "Masochism and Subjectivity," *Framework* 12.2–9.

———. 1988a. "Masochism and Male Subjectivity," *Camera Obscura* 17.30–67.

———. 1988b. *The Acoustic Mirror: The Female Voice in Psychoanalysis and Cinema*. Bloomington.

———. 1994. "Fassbinder and Lacan: A Reconsideration of Gaze, Look, and Image," in Bryson, Holly, and Moxey 1994.272–301.

Simon, E. 1957. *Die Portlandvase*. Mainz.

Sjöqvist, E. 1951. "Pnyx and Comitium," in *Studies Presented to David M. Robinson*, ed. G. Mylonas. St. Louis. 1.400–11.

Skalsky, R. L. 1992. "Visual Trope and the Portland Vase Frieze: A New Reading and Exegesis," *Arion* (3rd series) 2.42–71.

Skinner, M. B. 1979. "Parasites and Strange Bedfellows: A Study in Catullus' Political Imagery," *Ramus* 8.137–52.

———. 1993. *"Ego Mulier*: The Construction of Male Sexuality in Catullus," *Helios* 20.107–130.

———. 1996. "Zeus and Leda: The Sexuality Wars in Contemporary Classical Scholarship," *Thamyrus* 3.103–23.

———. 1997. "Introduction: *Quod Multo Fit Aliter in Graecia* . . . ," in Hallett and Skinner 1997.3–25.

Slater, N. W. 1998. "Passion and Petrifaction: The Gaze in Apuleius," *CP* 93.18–48.

Slater, W. J. 1991. *Dining in a Classical Context*. Ann Arbor.

Smart, J. D. 1984. "The Portland Vase Again," *JHS* 104.186.

Smith, W. R. 1914 [1889]. *Lectures on the Religion of the Semites*. London.

Snow, E. 1989. "Theorizing the Male Gaze: Some Problems," *Representations* 25.1.30–41.

Solomon-Godeau, A. 1997. *Male Trouble: A Crisis in Representation*. New York.

Sordi, M. 1978. "La tradizione storiografica su Tiberio Sempronio Gracco e la propaganda contemporanea," *MGR* 6.299–330.

Spiegel, J., and Machotka, P. 1974. *Messages of the Body*. New York.

Spivak, G. C. 1976. "Translator's Preface," in J. Derrida, *Of Grammatology*. Baltimore. ix–xc.

Spivey, N. 1996. *Understanding Greek Sculpture: Ancient Meanings, Modern Readings*. London.

Stallybrass, P. 1986. "Patriarchal Territories: The Body Enclosed," in *Rewriting the Renaissance: The Discourses of Sexual Difference in Early Modern Europe*, ed. M. W. Ferguson, M. Quilligan, and N. J. Vickers. Chicago. 123–42.

Stambaugh, J. E. 1978. "The Functions of Roman Temples," *ANRW* 2.16.1.554–608.

———. 1988. *The Ancient Roman City*. Baltimore.

Starr, R. J. 1991. "Reading Aloud: *Lectores* and Roman Reading," *CJ* 86.4.337–43.

Stehle, E. 1990. "Sappho's Gaze: Fantasies of a Goddess and a Young Man," *Differences* 2.1.86–125.

Stein, E., ed. 1990. *Forms of Desire: Sexual Orientation and the Social Constructionist Controversy*. New York.

Steinberg, L. 1972. *Other Criteria: Confrontations with Twentieth-Century Art*. Oxford.

Steiner, W. 1988. *Pictures of Romance: Form against Context in Painting and Literature*. Chicago.

Stewart, A. 1990. *Greek Sculpture: An Exploration*. New Haven.

———. 1997. *Art, Desire, and the Body in Ancient Greece*. Cambridge.

Stone, S. 1994. "The Toga: From National to Ceremonial Costume," in *The World of Roman Costume*, ed. J. L. Sebesta and L. Bonfante. Madison. 13–45.

Stuart-Jones, H., ed. 1912. *The Sculptures of the Museo Capitolino*. Oxford.

Studlar, G. 1988. *In the Realm of Pleasure: Von Sternberg, Dietrich, and the Masochistic Aesthetic*. Urbana.

Suleiman, S. R., and I. Crosman, eds. 1980. *The Reader in the Text: Essays on Audience and Interpretation*. Princeton.

Sullivan, J. P., and P. Whigham, eds. 1987. *Epigrams of Martial Englished by Divers Hands*. Berkeley.

Summers, D. 1987. *The Judgement of Sense: Renaissance Naturalism and the Rise of Aesthetics*. Cambridge.

Sutton, D. F. 1986. *Seneca on the Stage*. Leiden.

Sutton, R. F., Jr. 1992. "Pornography and Persuasion on Attic Pottery," in Richlin 1992b.3–35.

Swain, S. 1996. *Hellenism and Empire: Language, Classicism, and Power in the Greek World A.D. 50–250*. Oxford.

Swift, J. 1973. *The Writings of Jonathan Swift*, ed. R. A. Greenberg and W. B. Piper. New York.

Talbert, R. A. 1984. *The Senate of Imperial Rome*. Princeton.

Tarrant, R. J. 1985. *Seneca's* Thyestes. Atlanta.

Taylor, L. R. 1949. *Party Politics in the Age of Caesar*. Berkeley.

———. 1966. *Roman Voting Assemblies*. Ann Arbor.

Tennyson, A. 1868. "Lucretius," *MacMillan's Magazine* 104.

Thommen, L. 1995. "Les lieux de la plèbe et de ses tribuns dans la Rome républicaine," *Klio* 77.358–70.

Thompson, L., and R. T. Bruère. 1970. "The Vergilian Background of Lucan's Fourth Book," *CP* 65.152–72.

Thompson, M. L. 1961. "The Monumental and Literary Evidence for Programmatic Painting in Antiquity," *Marsyas* 9.36–77.

Tobin, R. 1995. "The Pose of the Doryphoros," in *Polykleitos, the Doryphoros, and Tradition*, ed. W. Moon. Madison. 52–64.

Tompkin, J. P., ed. 1980. *Reader Response Criticism: From Formalism to Post-Structuralism*. Baltimore.

Torelli, M. 1992. *Typology and Structure of Roman Historical Reliefs*. Ann Arbor.

Toynbee, J. M. C. 1934. *The Hadrianic School*. Cambridge.

Treggiari, S. 1969. *Roman Freedmen during the Late Republic*. Oxford.

Turner, J. G. 1993. "Preface and Acknowledgements," in *Sexuality and Gender in Early Modern Europe*, ed. J. G. Turner. Cambridge. xv–xvii.

Turner, P. 1976. *Tennyson*. London.

Valentine, G. 1997. "'My Son's A Bit Dizzy,' 'My Wife's A Bit Soft': Gender, Children, and Cultures of Parenting," *Gender, Place, and Culture* 4.1.37 and electronic text.

Valentini, R., and G. Zucchetti, eds. 1940. *Codice topografico della città di Roma*. Vol. 1: *Il catalogo delle quattordici regioni di Roma*. Rome.

Valenziano, C. 1988. "E sotto la cenere l'eros . . . ," *Il Venerdì di Repubblica* 2.31.145.

Varone, A. 1994. *Erotica pompeiana: Iscrizioni d'amore sui muri di Pompei*. Rome.

Vasaly, A. 1993. *Representations: Images of the World in Ciceronian Oratory*. Berkeley.

Vermeule, C. C. 1981. *Greek and Roman Sculpture in America*. London.

Vermeule, C. C., and M. B. Comstock. 1988. *Sculpture in Stone and Bronze: Additions to the Collections of Greek, Etruscan, and Roman Art, 1971–1988, in the Museum of Fine Arts, Boston*. Boston.

Vernant, J.-P. 1980. *Myth and Society in Ancient Greece*, trans. J. Lloyd. Atlantic Highlands, N.J.

Veyne, P. 1978. "La famille et l'amour sous le haut-empire romain," *Annales* 33.35–63.

———. 1987. "The Roman Empire," in *A History of Private Life*. Vol. 1: *From Pagan Rome to Byzantium*, ed. P. Veyne, trans. A. Goldhammer. Cambridge, Mass. 5–234.

Vickers, N. J. 1982. "Diana Described: Scattered Woman and Scattered Rhyme," in *Writing and Sexual Difference*, ed. E. Abel. Brighton. 95–109.

Vidal-Naquet, P. 1986. *The Black Hunter: Forms of Thought and Forms of Society in the Greek World*, trans. A. Szegedy-Maszak. Baltimore.

Wace, A. J. B. 1910. "The Reliefs in the Palazzo Spada," *PBSR* 5.167–200.

Wagenvoort, H. 1947. *Roman Dynamism: Studies in Ancient Roman Thought, Language, and Custom*. Oxford.

———. 1956. "*Fas sit vidisse*," in *Studies in Roman Literature, Culture, and Religion*, ed. H. Wagenvoort. London. 184–92.

Walker, A. 1992. "*Eros* and the Eye in the *Love-Letters* of Philostratus," *PCPS* 38.132–48.

Walker, B. 1969. Review of Zwierlein 1966, *CP* 64.183–87.

Walker, S. 1983. "Women and Housing in Classical Greece: The Archaeological Evidence," in *Images of Women in Antiquity*, ed. A. Cameron and A. Kuhrt. Detroit. 81–91.

Wallace-Hadrill, A. 1994. *Houses and Society in Pompeii and Herculaneum*. Princeton.

———. 1995. "Public Honour and Private Shame: The Urban Texture of Pompeii," in *Urban Society in Roman Italy*, ed. T. J. Cornell and K. Lomas. London. 39–62.

———. 1996. "Engendering the Roman House," in Kleiner and Matheson 1996.104–14.

Walters, J. 1997. "Invading the Roman Body: Manliness and Impenetrability in Roman Thought," in Hallett and Skinner 1997.29–43.

Webb, R. 1992. "The Transmission of the Eikones of Philostratus and the Development of Ecphrasis from Late Antiquity to the Renaissance." Ph.D. thesis, Warburg Institute, London.

Wickhoff, H. 1900. *Roman Art*, trans. E. Strong. London.

Wiedemann, T. 1992. *Emperors and Gladiators*. London.

Wikan, U. 1984. "Shame and Honour: A Contestable Pair," *Man* 19.635–52.

Williams, C. A. 1992. "Homosexuality and the Roman Man: A Study in the Cultural Construction of Sexuality." Ph.D. diss., Yale University.

———. 1999. *Roman Homosexuality: Ideologies of Masculinity in Classical Antiquity*. Oxford.

Williams, L., ed. 1995. *Viewing Positions: Ways of Seeing Film*. New Brunswick, N.J.

Wilson, E. 1991. *The Sphinx in the City: Urban Life, the Control of Disorder, and Women*. Berkeley.

Wilson, M. 1983. "The Tragic Mode of Seneca's *Troades*," in *Seneca Tragicus: Ramus Essays on Senecan Drama*, ed. A. J. Boyle. Berwick, Australia. 27–60.

Wilson, P. 1988. *The Domestication of the Human Species*. New Haven.

Winckelmann, J. J. 1776. *Geschichte der Kunst des Altertums*, vol. 2. Vienna.

Winkes, R. 1973. "Physiognomonia: Probleme der Charakterinterpretation römischer Porträts," *ANRW* 1 1.4.899–926.

Winkler, J. J. 1990. *The Constraints of Desire: The Anthropology of Sex and Gender in Ancient Greece*. London.

Wiseman, T. P. 1985. *Catullus and His World*. Cambridge.

Wurmser, L. 1981. *The Mask of Shame*. Baltimore.

Wyke, M. 1989. "Mistress and Metaphor in Augustan Elegy," *Helios* 16.25–47.

———. 1994a. "Taking the Woman's Part: Engendering Roman Love Elegy," *Ramus* 23.110–28.

———. 1994b. "Woman in the Mirror: The Rhetoric of Adornment in the Roman World," in *Women in Ancient Societies: An Illusion of the Night*, ed. L. J. Archer, S. Fischler, and M. Wyke. Basingstroke. 134–51.

———. 1995. "Taking the Woman's Part: Engendering Roman Elegy," in *Roman Literature and Ideology: Ramus Essays for J. P. Sullivan*, ed. A. J. Boyle. Bendigo, Australia. 110–28.

Zanker, P. 1966. "Loggia der Spada Reliefs," in *Führer durch die öffentlichen Sammlungen klassischer Altertümer in Rom*, ed. W. Helbig, 4th ed., vol. 2. Tübingen.

———. 1988. *The Power of Images in the Age of Augustus*, trans. A. Shapiro. Ann Arbor.

Zeitlin, F. I. 1985. "Playing the Other: Theater, Theatricality, and the Feminine in Greek Drama," *Representations* 11.63–94.

———. 1990. "The Poetics of Eros: Nature, Art, and Imitation in Longus' *Daphnis and Chloe*," in Halperin, Winkler, and Zeitlin 1990a.417–64.

Zita, J. N. 1998. *Body Talk: Philosophical Reflections on Sex and Gender*. New York.

Zizek, S. 1994. *The Metastases of Enjoyment*. London.

Zweig, B. 1992. "The Mute Nude Female Characters in Aristophanes' Plays," in Richlin 1992b.73–89.

Zwierlein, O. 1966. *Die Rezitationsdramen Senecas*. Meisenheim.

Index

Credits

Figs. 4.1–4.6: Drawings by Zahra Newby.

Figs. 4.7–4.14: Photos Alinari; used by permission.

Figs. 5.2–5.8, 5.10–5.11, 5.13: Photos Michael Larvey.

Figs. 5.9, 5.12: Drawings by John R. Clarke.

Fig. 8.1: Photo Fototeca Unione 10189, American Academy in Rome.

Fig. 8.2: From Andrew Wallace-Hadrill, *Houses and Society in Pompeii and Herculaneum*. Copyright © 1994 by Princeton University Press. Reprinted by permission of Princeton University Press.

Fig. 8.3: Photo Deutsches Archaeologisches Institut Rom 76.1274.

Fig. 8.4: Photo Erich Lessing / Art Resource, N.Y.

Figs. 9.1, 9.5: Alinari / Art Resource, N.Y.

Fig. 9.2: Photo Helmut Newton.

Figs. 9.3–9.4: Photos © The British Museum.